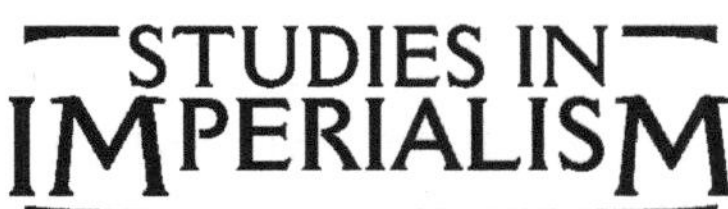

STUDIES IN IMPERIALISM

General editors: Andrew S. Thompson and Alan Lester
Founding editor: John M. MacKenzie

When the 'Studies in Imperialism' series was founded by Professor John M. MacKenzie more than thirty years ago, emphasis was laid upon the conviction that 'imperialism as a cultural phenomenon had as significant an effect on the dominant as on the subordinate societies'. With well over a hundred titles now published, this remains the prime concern of the series. Cross-disciplinary work has indeed appeared covering the full spectrum of cultural phenomena, as well as examining aspects of gender and sex, frontiers and law, science and the environment, language and literature, migration and patriotic societies, and much else. Moreover, the series has always wished to present comparative work on European and American imperialism, and particularly welcomes the submission of books in these areas. The fascination with imperialism, in all its aspects, shows no sign of abating, and this series will continue to lead the way in encouraging the widest possible range of studies in the field. 'Studies in Imperialism' is fully organic in its development, always seeking to be at the cutting edge, responding to the latest interests of scholars and the needs of this ever-expanding area of scholarship.

Photographic subjects

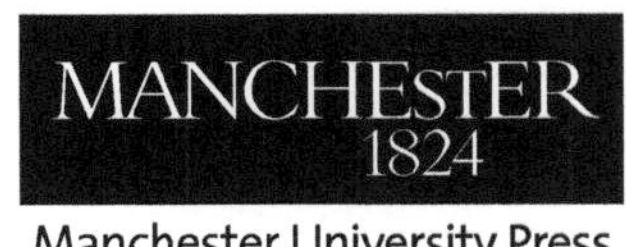

Manchester University Press

Photographic subjects

MONARCHY AND VISUAL CULTURE IN COLONIAL INDONESIA

Susie Protschky

MANCHESTER UNIVERSITY PRESS

Published by Manchester University Press
Oxford Road, Mancheter M13 9PL
www.manchesteruniversitypress.co.uk

British Library Cataloguing-in-Publication Data
A catalogue record for this book is available from the British Library

ISBN 978 1 5261 2437 1 hardback
ISBN 978 1 5261 5699 0 paperback

First published 2019

The publisher has no responsibility for the persistence or accuracy of URLs for any external or third-party internet websites referred to in this book, and does not guarantee that any content on such websites is, or will remain, accurate or appropriate.

Typeset by
Toppan Best-Set Premedia Ltd

CONTENTS

FIGURES

Every effort has been made to obtain permission to reproduce copyright material, and the publisher will be pleased to be informed of any errors and omissions for correction in future editions.

ACKNOWLEDGEMENTS

This book is the outcome of many opportunities and collaborations. It was substantially funded by an Australian Research Council Post-doctoral Fellowship (ARC APD) that commenced in 2010 and finished in 2015. My first thanks go to Professor Susan Broomhall and Associate Professor Jacqueline van Gent for involving me in their Discovery Project, 'Gender, Power and Identity in the Early Modern Nassau Family' (DP1092615). Funding was supplemented by Arts Faculty and SOPHIS (School of Philosophical, Historical and International Studies) grants from Monash University, for which I am grateful.

I have been very fortunate to work with some wonderful archivists and curators, who have been extremely generous in sharing their extensive knowledge of their photograph collections, and who have mirrored my enthusiasm during what is always the most exciting part of any research project: the archives stage. I am indebted to my friend Liesbeth Ouwehand not only for her expertise on the KITLV Collections at the Universiteitsbibliotheek in Leiden, but also for her excellent eye for photographs with interesting stories, and for many years of hospitality and humour. Many thanks to Mieke Jansen at the Koninklijk Huisarchief in The Hague for sharing her deep knowledge of and affection for the extraordinary collections there. She has been very generous in showing me the collections at the KHA, and answering many follow-up emails over several years about individual items. I also thank René Kok and Harco Gijsbers at NIOD in Amsterdam for providing access to the photograph collections from the Dutch military actions in Indonesia (1945–50) that I discuss in the final chapter of this book. Thanks to these curators' institutions, as well as the Nationaal Archief (The Hague), Spaarnestad, the Tropenmuseum (Amsterdam) and the Royal Library (The Hague), for giving permission to reproduce the photographs selected in this book.

During the writing of *Photographic subjects* I have burned through a number of research groups made up of colleagues who will never want to read anything about Queen Wilhelmina ever again. For their forbearance, and also frequent good advice, I especially thank Bain Attwood, Al Thomson, Megan Cassidy-Welch, Seamus O'Hanlon, Kat Ellinghaus, Ernest Koh, Adam Clulow, Julie Kalman, Michael Hau, Carolyn James, Noah Shenker and David Garrioch. I wish to acknowledge that selected parts of Chapters 3, 4 and 5 were previously published in (respectively) *Indonesia and the Malay World* (2012), the *Journal of*

Colonialism and Colonial History (2012) and *BMGN/Low Countries Historical Review* (2015). And I would like to thank Emma Nicholls, Timo de Jong and Joanna Lee for research assistance, particularly Joanna for the final stages of this book's production. I am also grateful to the anonymous reviewers of the book proposal and final manuscript for their incisive suggestions.

It has been a delight to keep crossing intellectual paths on monarchy and imperialism with Matt Fitzpatrick, Robert Aldrich and Cindy McCreery, who have since 2013 been steering new work on monarchy and empire. It has been a privilege to be involved in Robert and Cindy's three conferences at Sydney University on this topic – 'Crowns and Colonies' (2014), 'Royals on Tour' (2015) and 'Monarchies, Decolonisation and Royal Legacies in the Asia-Pacific' (2017) – and to be included in two of the edited volumes they have produced, also published by Manchester University Press.

A big thanks to Ruth Morgan, Claire Spivakovsky and Charlotte Greenhalgh for their support as mentors and peers, friends, colleagues and feminists. Special thanks to my dear friend Amelia Liu, who gave me her house to write in when things got tricky with commuting and childcare and work. I am grateful for our very many 'runches' (run-plus-lunch), which were essential for talking over all kinds of work–life intersections; and I am so inspired by her own professional achievements and her personal calm, dignity and warmth. These are the women without whose support and example I may not have got this book out into the world.

To my cherished family, Tyrone and Henry, I say thank you for making me laugh, and for all your love and support. Thanks Tyrone for coming on the journeys with me that this book required.

I wish my dad was still here to read this book. I know my mother and my sister, Gaby and Tanja, do too. To them I say, *leve de koninginnen.*

ABBREVIATIONS

BPM	*Bataafsche Petroleum Maatschappij* (Batavian Petroleum Company)
KHA	*Koninklijk Huisarchief* (Royal Collections), The Hague
KIT	*Koninklijk Instituut voor de Tropen* (Royal Tropical Institute), Amsterdam
KITLV	*Koninklijk Instituut voor Taal-, Land- en Volkenkunde* (Royal Institute for South-east Asian and Caribbean Studies), Leiden
KNIL	*Koninklijk Nederlandsch-Indisch Leger* (Royal Netherlands-Indies Army)
NL-HaNA	*Nationaal Archief* (National Archives), The Hague
NNGPM	*Nederlandsche Nieuw Guinee Petroleum Maatschappij* (Netherlands New Guinea Petroleum Company)
VOC	*Verenigde Oostindische Compagnie* (Dutch East India Company)

The Netherlands East Indies, c. 1942

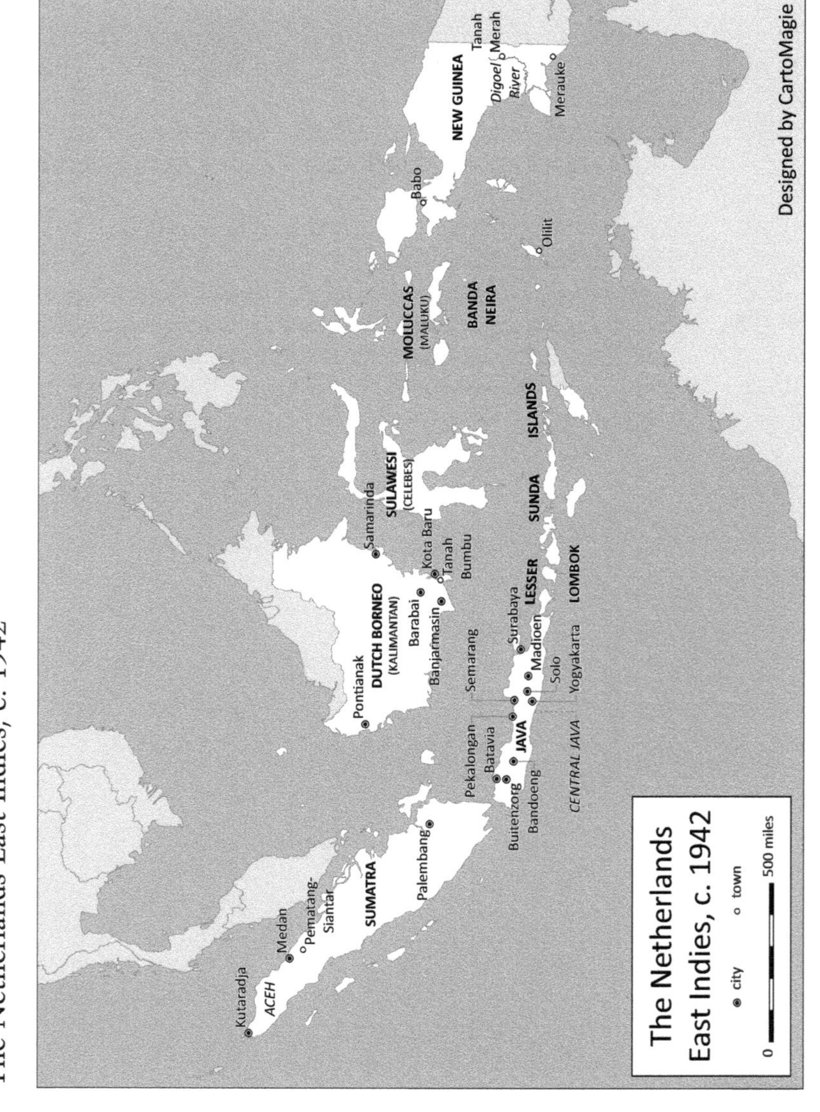

Monarchy and empire in the age of mass photography: the Dutch colonial world during Queen Wilhelmina's reign, 1898–1948

Between 31 August and 6 September 1923, Queen Wilhelmina of the Netherlands marked her silver jubilee, the 25th anniversary of her inauguration. The week-long festivities united disparate populations across the globe, not just in the Netherlands but throughout its empire, which included Suriname and the West Indies in the Atlantic realm, and the East Indies in South-east Asia. The milestone also resonated across the Indian Ocean in places that had not been part of the Dutch colonial world for over a century, including Cape Town in southern Africa, an important former port of call for *Vereenigde Oostindische Compagnie* (United East India Company) ships on their way to the East Indies.[1] Throughout Wilhelmina's reign, from 1898 to 1948, the Dutch monarchy could therefore claim links to a global community of subjects that rivalled those of other European empires.

Among the many gifts Wilhelmina received from her subjects in the Netherlands and its colonies on this occasion was a photograph album from the King of Surakarta in the East Indies.[2] Pakubuwono X's title was *susuhunan*, Javanese for 'Axis of the Cosmos'. In reality, his kingdom was little more than a palace and its surrounds in the city of Solo, Central Java, where he was one among several royals, all of whom had been subjugated to Dutch rule at the end of the Java War in 1830. It was for this reason that the King of Surakarta was obliged to celebrate the regnal milestones of a Dutch queen – in his own *kraton* (palace), no less, and in concert with a commoner, the Resident, a Dutch civil servant with whom the *susuhunan* ceremonially shared his throne on official occasions.

Looking through the pages of the album, Queen Wilhelmina would have had an opportunity to see this for herself. A photograph of Pakubuwono X, the Dutch official J. J. van Helsdingen and their respective wives all enthroned on the *bale buko sri* came after a full-length portrait of the *susuhunan* and a photograph of the pavilion in

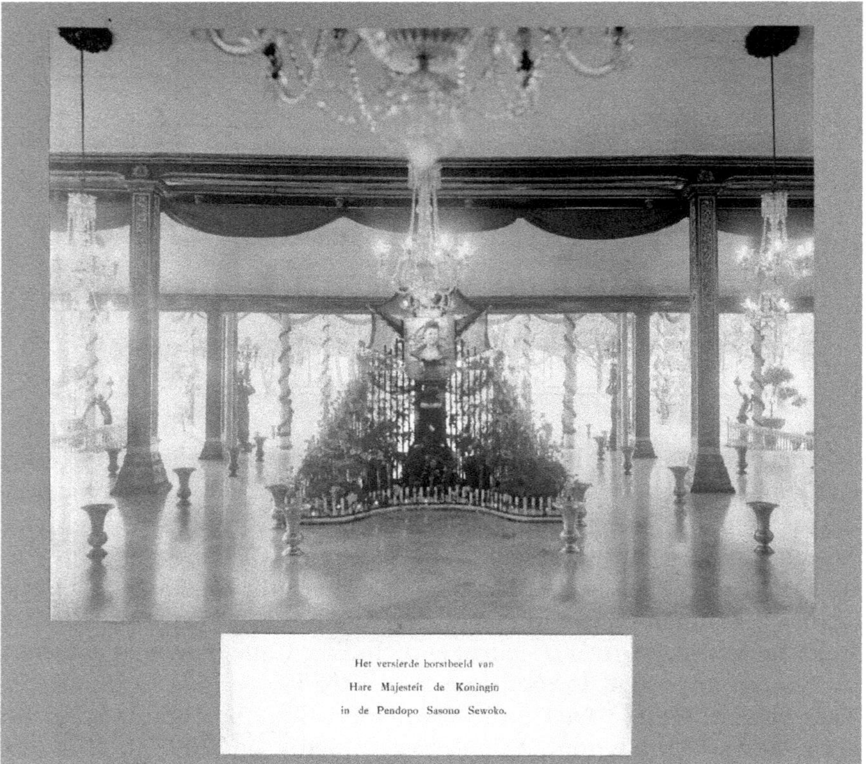

1.1 Album of Pakubuwono X, 'The decorated bust of Her Majesty the Queen in the Pendopo Sasono Sewoko', Surakarta (Central Java), 1923

the *kraton* where the ritual procession held in Wilhelmina's honour culminated. Following those photographs, the Dutch queen would suddenly have been confronted with an image of herself – or rather, a mounted bust, decorated with leaves and flowers and suffused in the glow of a chandelier's electric light (figure 1.1). An effigy was required for the king and official to look at because Queen Wilhelmina was not a guest of honour at the palace – not in 1923, and not ever, anywhere in the Dutch empire, even in the East Indies, at that time the largest, oldest and most lucrative of the Netherlands' colonies to remain after centuries of overseas expansion.

The natural light streaming in from between the pillars and emanating from the chandelier, which served both as crown and nimbus, symbolically bestowed regal and divine attributes on Wilhelmina. Despite her being a pious Christian, the queen might have been uncomfortable with the sacral implications of the nimbus, for heads of the House of

Orange had never ruled by divine right. The light effect was also meaningful in Javanese visual culture where, as Benedict Anderson has shown, the halo could be interpreted as the *tèja* (radiance) 'traditionally associated with the public visage of the ruler', a physical emanation of their divine radiance (*wahyu*).[3] Anthropologist Karen Strassler has identified the same effect in photographs of revered Indonesians in contemporary Javanese visual culture.[4] In Pakubuwono X's photograph, the halo belongs not to a male, Muslim Javanese but to a foreign monarch, a Christian and a woman, all of which makes it an unusual image in the history of Javanese photography.

This image eloquently captures how photography, a visual medium with global reach in the early twentieth century, drew upon Javanese visual practices in dialogue with European conventions. In this photograph we also encounter the major theme of this book: how the relations of a European, female king with her subjects were mediated through photography across a transnational realm that included overseas colonies. Pakubuwono X's photograph album is but one of many examples discussed throughout this book of how both elite and ordinary subjects of the Dutch queen in the East Indies, Indonesians as well as Europeans, used photographs to make subtle political communications with Wilhelmina and each other. These encounters included diplomatic exchanges, appeals to a powerful institution for recognition and negotiations of subjecthood. Pakubuwono X's photograph is also one among countless examples of visual associations made in colonial photography between electricity and Queen Wilhelmina's 'enlightened' rule. I argue in this book that looking at a Dutch monarch through the lenses of cameras in the East Indies sheds new light on Indonesian histories, Dutch histories and their entanglement with each other.

Monarchy and empire

Why *this* queen, Wilhelmina, in particular? Her reign spanned the zenith and fall of Dutch rule in Indonesia. Her half-century as queen, from 1898 to 1948, remains the longest reign of any Dutch monarch to date. Her mother, Queen Emma, was regent in the 1890s, but it was Wilhelmina who became the first sovereign female king to lead the House of Orange. The origins of this dynasty stretched to William the Silent (1533–84), the first Prince of Orange, and coincided with the advent of Dutch overseas expansion under the aegis of the East and West India Companies. Wilhelmina had fewer constitutional powers in her colonies or at home than her nineteenth-century forebears, Kings Willem I, II and III,[5] yet she became the last monarch to preside over the modern Dutch empire in its most complete form, when it comprised

Suriname in South America, the six Caribbean islands of the Netherlands West Indies (Sint Maarten, Sint Eustatius, Saba, Aruba, Bonaire and Curaçao) and the archipelago then known as the East Indies, now Indonesia. It was during Wilhelmina's reign that Dutch sovereignty in this archipelago expanded to the borders that her heir, Juliana, inherited in 1948, and then ceded to the Republic of Indonesia the following year.

Queen Wilhelmina was the figure who loomed large, if symbolically, in the colonial politics of her time. She was monarch when the first parties in favour of East Indies self-rule were founded: Budi Utomo in 1908, the Indische Partij and Sarekat Islam in 1912, and the Nationalist Party in 1927. She was queen when the first communist uprisings erupted in Java and Sumatra in 1926, only to be repressed by the colonial government. She was still on the throne, but exiled in London, when Japanese forces invaded the archipelago in 1942. She was back at the helm when they capitulated in 1945 and Soekarno and Hatta declared Indonesian independence. When the Indonesian National Revolution proceeded to defend this proclamation, Wilhelmina was revered by the Dutch and colonial forces who fought to retain the 'Indies'.

She was a recurring motif in the polemics of renowned Indonesians who lived in the twentieth century. Her regnal milestones marked time in the memoir of an Indonesian elected to the Council of the Indies (*Volksraad*), Achmad Djajadiningrat (1877–1943), who served on this advisory body to the governor-general in the early 1930s.[6] She was affected by the writings of Sutan Sjahrir (1909–66), Indonesia's first prime minister in the revolutionary government, who had been forced to celebrate her birthday when he was imprisoned on Banda in the mid-1930s.[7] She was encountered and fetishised – in the form of a mass-produced portrait, no less – by Minke, the fictional protagonist of Indonesia's most famous novelist, Pramoedya Ananta Toer.[8] And yet she is rarely remembered, except anecdotally, in histories of Indonesia.

Soon after Wilhelmina was inaugurated as queen in 1898, *koninginnedag* (Queen's Day) emerged in the East Indies as an important annual event for celebrating the colony as a Dutch possession and uniting it with other parts of the Dutch colonial world.[9] The rites of passage of leading members of the House of Orange had been celebrated sporadically here since the East India Company had become the primary agent of Dutch power in Asia.[10] However, Wilhelmina was the first monarch whose public birthday and inauguration celebrations became a regular fixture, aimed at unifying Dutch subjects under a common figurehead.[11] These practices commenced in the 1880s, in Wilhelmina's youth, as the fortunes of the House of Orange appeared to be in decline, and in the context of widening political and religious rifts in Dutch society.

Wilhelmina was born into a late nineteenth-century Netherlands where mass political participation manifested as 'pillarisation' (*verzuiling*), with different political and confessional groups nurturing their own institutions to cultivate strong communal identities. From the 1870s liberals and conservatives were united in anxiety over the apparent lack of will towards national unity in the Netherlands.[12] For many, the monarchy seemed a politically neutral solution. *Princesjedag* (Princess's Day) was the initiative of municipal elites who cast the young Wilhelmina as a remedy for the tensions of the day, a common focus of loyalty for Dutch people of all faiths and creeds. Celebrations for her were henceforth organised locally and with mass participation.[13]

The festival was embraced by a monarchy facing a crisis of legitimacy. Wilhelmina's father, King Willem III (or 'King Gorilla', as he was unkindly termed by his detractors), was an unpopular monarch who had the additional misfortune of outliving all three of his (legitimate) male heirs.[14] Wilhelmina's mother, Emma, is generally credited with having grasped that the survival of the Dutch monarchy rested on nurturing its popular appeal. After Willem's death in 1890, it was Emma who organised a five-year tour of the Netherlands with her young daughter. It commenced in 1891 under the motto '*Wij zijn er nog!*' ('We are still here').[15] Emma's efforts to restore public faith in the Dutch monarchy resonated with a wider movement, initiated in Utrecht in 1885 but quickly spreading elsewhere, to celebrate the princess's birthday on 31 August.[16]

From its very inception during the 1880s, then, the week-long festival that came to mark Wilhelmina's birthday emerged as an occasion for the orchestration of unity among the Dutch monarchy's subjects. In the Netherlands' colonies, the potential for displaying the centripetal power of the monarchy was all the greater for the diversity of subjects that could be convened, nowhere more so perhaps than in the East Indies, with its thousands of islands and numerous ethnic, religious and language groups.

Only three book-length works have addressed the entanglement of Wilhelmina's reign with the last decades of Dutch rule in Indonesia. Rita Wassing-Visser used the Dutch Royal Collections to begin cataloguing the bonds forged by gifts between Indonesians and the House of Orange over some 350 years of Dutch colonialism.[17] Her book focused mainly on royal gifts from Indonesia, but it was the first work to demonstrate the extensive traffic of material exchanges for diplomatic purposes between the monarchs of the Netherlands and the East Indies. In 2002 the unpublished Masters dissertation of Pieter Eckhardt became the first historical study to examine what he termed the Dutch monarchy's 'symbolic significance' in Indonesia, from the end of the First World War to just before the Japanese occupation (1918–40).[18] Using Indies and Dutch newspapers and the memoirs of colonial officials, Eckhardt established how Wilhelmina was invoked and addressed by political actors during the last two decades of Dutch rule. He argued that the monarchy functioned chiefly as a symbol of political unity and colonial continuity in the East Indies, and upheld the privileges of the Dutch elite. Finally, a recent book by Geert Oostindie conducted a fresh survey of the House of Orange and the Netherlands' colonies.[19] Responding to the assertion by an eminent biographer of Wilhelmina that 'the whole population, white and brown' threw themselves into celebrations for the Dutch monarchy in her colonies, Oostindie sought to evaluate the bases for *'oranjegevoel'* ('Orange-sentiment').[20] He concluded that, while the House of Orange is deeply imbricated in the Netherlands' colonial history, and royal celebrations became mass, orchestrated spectacles across the Dutch empire during Wilhelmina's reign, ultimately she appealed mainly to Western-educated elites, especially Dutch-born colonists and Indigenous royals such as Pakubuwono X, who preferred her only to the humiliating alternative of consorting with commoner officials.[21]

Oostindie's book skirted close to but ultimately did not address a major lacuna in recent studies of monarchy and empire that has prompted the writing of this book: namely, that we can only know what colonial authorities *intended* for the consumption of colonial populations at royal celebrations. Yet official sources such as news reports and festival programmes cannot reveal whether and for what purposes audiences in the colonies took a foreign, European monarch to heart. A focus on spectacles and their prescriptive meanings has, up until very recently, driven the historiography of European monarchs and their empires, largely as a result of David Cannadine's influential book *Ornamentalism* (2001).[22] Cannadine was concerned to refute the premise of Edward Said's germinal works, *Orientalism* (1979) and *Culture and Imperialism* (1993). These had argued that colonial rule in the Middle East and North Africa was built on British and French notions of their fundamental racial difference from and superiority to Indigenous subjects.[23] Cannadine countered that the British ruled their empire by analogy, finding 'voluntary collaborators' – including among racial 'Others' – by supporting or constructing class hierarchies in their colonies.[24] In white settler contexts, British authorities bestowed royal honours where such titles did not previously exist. In India, most famously, they integrated Indigenous castes and dynasties into a global hierarchy of royals with the British monarchy at its apex. Cannadine was concerned to reconstruct how the British 'saw' their empire, and thus gave due attention to how imperial authority was portrayed as spectacle through visual and material culture. In concentrating on representation, however, he provided little evidence as to how this ornamental structure was 'seen', or thoughtfully received and creatively responded to, by people in the colonies.[25]

Very recently, historians of empire have begun to research these important audiences whose views Cannadine was unable to account for. A number of books have examined European monarchies from colonial perspectives to explain how Indigenous people engaged with colonial authorities. Charles Reed's 2016 monograph on British royal tours to India, New Zealand and South Africa showed that encounters with British royals were important for Indigenous people, as opportunities to contest their social status and articulate rights and claims for belonging.[26] Further, through their participation at royal festivals, imperial subjects 'provincialised the British Isles, centring the colonies in their political and cultural constructions of empire, Britishness, citizenship, and loyalty'.[27] Local print cultures were essential to promoting these responses, especially in the absence of physical meetings between monarchs, Indigenous royals and colonial commoners.[28]

Two further essay collections also published in 2016, one edited by Robert Aldrich and Cindy McCreery, the other by Sarah Carter and Maria Nugent, have each confirmed and extended Reed's observations for the 'British world'. Nugent and Carter examined how Indigenous people in settler colonies included Queen Victoria 'in their lives and struggles' by 'incorporating her into their intellectual thought, political rhetoric, and narrative traditions'.[29] Victoria was thus a shared figure, claimed by settlers and Indigenous people alike, and 'embroidered into far-reaching debates and discourses on such crucial matters as rights and responsibilities, community and belonging, citizenship and non-citizenship, race and difference, and authority, sovereignty, and destiny'.[30] Aldrich and McCreery set a wider scope for their collection based on the observation that, well into the twentieth century, 'crowns and colonies' were often paired together. By contrast, republican governments *and* princedoms without empires formed a distinct minority in Asia, Africa and Oceania, not to mention Europe.[31] The modern British empire was thus by no means unique, and there was a whole world of monarchies and empires that needed to be integrated into studies of imperialism. Aldrich and McCreery followed up with a second essay collection in 2018, focusing on royal tours in the Dutch, German, French, Mughal, Japanese, Portuguese, Belgian and Italian empires, and importantly, on Indigenous royal visits to European courts.[32] Together, these collections have fundamentally reoriented the study of monarchy and empire to demonstrate the global and, simultaneously, highly localised importance of both institutions to social life, culture and politics in the modern world.

Photographic subjects is, in part, the outcome of my involvement in some of these projects, as well as forays into other locales to historicise the encounters between Wilhelmina and her colonial subjects throughout the 'Dutch world', principally the East Indies, the Netherlands and southern Africa.[33] This book also builds on the shorter studies of Dutch scholars who have investigated, first, the dynamics of encounters between a female king and her European and colonial subjects, and second, the importance of visual and material cultures in enabling these encounters. It is, most importantly, the result of extensive archival research in colonial and royal collections that hold photographs and other primary sources generated not just by Europeans but also of and by Indonesians.

I often use the term 'female king' rather than 'queen' in this book, both as a literal translation of the Dutch *koningin* and to foreground how gender inflects kingship as a political institution in historical context.[34] To this day, female heads of state remain a rarity, and before the Second World War they were even more unusual. Hereditary queens were the exception to this global order, and yet Wilhelmina's cousin, Queen Victoria (r. 1837–1901), remains almost the only monarch whose gender is seriously incorporated into histories of modern empire. Dutch scholars Maria Grever, Berteke Waldijk and Susan Legêne are the only historians to have examined how Wilhelmina was invoked as a specifically female king by her subjects, particularly women, in the Netherlands and its colonies.[35] Legêne has additionally been instrumental to critically integrating the role of visual, material and museum cultures into understandings of Dutch colonialism in transnational context during Wilhelmina's reign.[36] Her discussion of a 1938 colonial exhibition at the Tropenmuseum in Amsterdam – at which a photograph was taken showing Wilhelmina's empty throne occupying a central, symbolic location – was a stimulus to my formulation of this book.[37] It got me thinking about the creative opportunities that an *absent* queen provided for subjects who were strewn across an empire and reflecting on their subject relations to Dutch authority. Particularly, it got me thinking about photographic subjects.

Photography and empire

Why photography, and not some other medium that fostered a more 'globalised' world in the early twentieth century? After all, a century ago Wilhelmina was able to avoid touring her colonies while still reaching her subjects there by a variety of means, all of them the result of technological innovations that we now take almost for granted. Her voice, her image, the work of her hands, even a sight of her in the flesh were all accessible to people far from her palaces in the Netherlands by virtue of radio and film, mass print cultures, and expanding transport methods and networks.[38]

Contrary to Anglophone scholarship, George V was not the first European monarch to address his subjects by radio; it was Queen Wilhelmina, in a broadcast on 31 May 1927.[39] The people of Suriname and the West Indies first heard Wilhelmina's voice over the wireless the next day, and it was the turn of her East Indies subjects on 2 June. Wilhelmina's annual *koninginnedag* and Christmas broadcasts were heard in the Indies throughout the 1930s.[40] She addressed 'her people' in the colonies via radio when her husband, Prince Hendrik, died in 1934, and at her fortieth jubilee in 1938.[41] The wonders of synchronic experience that radio enabled were most spectacularly demonstrated during the wedding festivities for the Crown Princess Juliana. Her engagement was announced on radio in late 1936. On 28 December, the Paleis Noordeinde in The Hague, together with the Astana Mangkunegaran of Prince Mangkunegoro VII of Surakarta, co-hosted a remarkable celebration. A daughter of the prince, Gusti Raden Ajeng Siti Nurul Kusumowardhani, performed her part in a *serimpi* dance – which usually requires four women – before Princess Juliana at Noordeinde. The music, played by a gamelan orchestra, was broadcast live from the Mangkunegaran, where the other three dancers simultaneously performed their parts. So impressed was Juliana with this feat that she had it repeated at the gala ball after the wedding itself, on 7 January 1937. The marriage ceremony was also broadcast on radio.[42] Wilhelmina's Radio Oranje broadcasts, which she also used in 1942 to lament the Japanese occupation of the Indies, are largely responsible for her post-war reputation as arguably the best-loved Dutch monarch in history.[43]

Wilhelmina's subjects in the colonies could also see her and the royal family on the big screen. Indeed, the major milestones of her reign were captured on film.[44] Moving pictures had come to the East Indies in 1900. The first film shown in the capital, Batavia, included images of Wilhelmina and Hendrik in The Hague. Europeans in the audience were allegedly offended when 'native' viewers, who sat in a separate area of the cinema, chattered among themselves and looked away when the obligatory picture of the queen was shown before a screening.[45]

If they had the means and the inclination, people in the colonies who wished to see Wilhelmina from the streets in Amsterdam or The Hague could also travel to the Netherlands with increasing ease during her lifetime. Travel by steamship was faster than ever before. In 1900 the *Rotterdamsche-Lloyd* departed for Batavia every week, and the journey took just over three weeks.[46] The first flight from Amsterdam to Batavia departed in 1924. In 1932 the flight took nine days; in 1940, 55 hours. In 1938 fresh orchids from the East Indies were delivered by plane to Wilhelmina at the Olympic Stadium in Amsterdam for her fortieth regnal jubilee. It was an example of how aeroplanes were used less for people than for transporting mail, but nonetheless it was the beginning of mass air travel. Ulbe Bosma has estimated that in any given year in the 1930s, there were up to 30,000 East Indies people in the Netherlands.[47] Scholars of the Dutch world have demonstrated the cosmopolitan, transnational identities and social networks that elites who travelled the 'colonial migration circuit' between the Netherlands and its colonies were able to cultivate in this period.[48]

But it was the advent of mass photography, which coincided roughly with the beginning of Wilhelmina's reign, that enabled a wide variety of people throughout the Dutch empire to participate in and commemorate royal celebrations in ways that neither radio nor film permitted. Not until Queen Emma's regency in the 1890s were photographs of royal occasions widely published; before then, they were rare.[49] At the turn of the century, when Wilhelmina's reign commenced, it was mainly studio photographers who had the equipment and expertise to produce images of royal festivals. There had been a robust studio industry on Java since the 1860s, one that expanded rapidly throughout the archipelago in subsequent decades.[50] Skilled photographers were in high demand during this period, not just for taking portraits but for a more diverse range of tasks. Isidore van Kinsbergen (1821–1905), for example, had photographed Javanese antiquities and worked as a theatre designer before he was commissioned, in 1874, to work on a presentation album for King Willem III's silver jubilee.[51] The album contained views of Javanese urban and rural landscapes, as well as portraits of 'native types' and unnamed Javanese and Balinese elites. It was sent to Wilhelmina's father as a gift from the 'schoolchildren of the Netherlands Indies', ostensibly to provide him with a visual education about the distant lands and peoples whom he governed as part of a greater Kingdom of the Netherlands. Similarly, in 1890, when Wilhelmina turned ten, the 'children of Surabaya' sent her a boxed set of photographs mounted on large plates to mark the occasion. This time, along with views of the city, the album also contained photographs of how locals celebrated the princess's birthday, so that Wilhelmina could see for herself, if only in still pictures, how her Indies subjects honoured their future queen.[52]

Throughout her life, the most common format in which Wilhelmina herself was seen by her subjects was through photography. By 1880, the year Wilhelmina was born, significant advances in photographic and print technologies were already under way that would lead, in the next two decades, to a greatly increased circulation of images, books and news media in the East Indies as well as in Europe. From the 1890s onwards, portraits of the princess were sold to the public at affordable prices in postcard, cabinet photo and *carte-de-visite* format.[53] By the time of her inauguration as an 18-year-old, Wilhelmina was already the most photographed Dutch monarch to have ever lived. All her subsequent rites of passage – her marriage in 1901, the birth of her only living heir in 1909, her silver jubilee in 1923, her fortieth jubilee in 1938, and her golden jubilee and abdication in 1948 – received exhaustive coverage, both in official and vernacular sources, to an extent that none of her predecessors had ever experienced.[54] It was common practice for children living in the large cities of Java to receive portraits of Wilhelmina as prizes or tokens at the *kinderfeest* (children's festival) that invariably formed part of the programme of royal celebrations.[55] Mass-produced photographs of the queen brought her colonial subjects into festivities as spectators and consumers who responded to poster advertisements of the queen exhorting people to attend royal celebrations, or who purchased postcards of the royal family, illustrated *gedenkboeken* (commemorative books) and special newspaper issues.[56] Most importantly, as I will argue in this book, with the rise of amateur photography in the early twentieth century, the camera actively involved people in the colonies in royal celebrations as makers of and subjects in images.

The family photograph album emerged in the late nineteenth century as a visual and material medium for commemorating the constitution of the bourgeois family. Albums in this period were collections of formal portraits commissioned from studio photographers, whose craft was a specialised skill unfamiliar to most of their clients, and whose creations offered a novel opportunity, formerly restricted to Europe's nobility, for middle-class families to compile archives of their own 'dynasties'.[57] By the early twentieth century, in Asia as well as in Europe, advances in camera, film and processing technologies had made photography progressively demystified and inexpensive, such that a growing number of enthusiasts could afford to pursue an amateur interest in the practice and assemble their own family albums.[58] In archival collections from the former East Indies, the proliferation of such albums from the 1920s onwards attests to the popularity of amateur photography among the colony's well-to-do. The families of Europeans and Indo-Europeans of the professional classes, of wealthy, often Western-educated Javanese, and of Chinese merchants and businessmen are all represented in early twentieth-century collections.[59]

During Wilhelmina's tenure, then, the proliferation of photographic illustrations in the print media, the development of hand-held cameras and roll film, and the broader shift of photography from the hands of expert studio photographers into the realm of laypeople, enabled groups and individuals from a broad range of backgrounds to engage with, produce and manipulate images of the queen and royal celebrations in the colonies and the metropole – popular interventions that film and radio did not at that time permit.

In this social and technological context, photographic images of the queen emerged as the most ubiquitous proxy for her absent self in the colonies. Her physical remove from the East Indies ought not, then, to be seen as a deficiency (relative to, for example, the personal tours of royals throughout the British empire) – a silence in the colonial record of the Dutch monarchy and its empire. Rather, by virtue of presiding over the advent of mass photography, the absent Queen Wilhelmina stimulated a rich variety of creative photographic encounters with her colonial subjects, in the ordinary and vernacular as well as the elite and official realms, in ways that extend our understanding of how photographic subjects were made in imperial settings.

Monarchy, photography and the Netherlands East Indies

Queen Wilhelmina was by no means alone in never personally touring her colonies. Queen Victoria also preferred to stay at home. Nevertheless, royal tours were increasingly common in these queens' lifetimes: the Belgian Prince (later King) Albert travelled to Congo in 1909; the Italian King Vittorio Emanuele III visited Somalia in 1934 and Libya in 1938; no fewer than eleven British royals toured Ceylon, from the 1860s to 1947.[60] In this context, Queen Wilhelmina was under pressure from lobbyists in the East Indies to undertake a royal tour herself. She twice rejected petitions, one in 1909 and another in 1919, led by no less than the governor-general, J. P. van Limburg Stirum.[61] The executive committee steering this petition comprised senior figures from the Java Bank, the Batavian Petroleum Company and the Royal Shipping Company; the chief administrator of a major tea estate; and a Sundanese scholar-official (the only Indonesian on the panel) specialised in Islamic law.[62] Also listed, in calligraphic script, were the names of more or less the entire multi-ethnic Indies establishment. The Indigenous aristocracy and government officials were represented by the sultans of the Outer Provinces and the regents of Java and Madura. The residents and other high Dutch officials of the *Binnenlandsch Bestuur* (Interior Administration) covered the European arm of the civil service. The captains, majors and lieutenants of various Chinese communities were also signatories. The president of the Deli Planters' Society on Sumatra put his name to the petition, as did the commanders of the colonial army. Priests, directors of hospitals and orphanages, editors of major European newspapers and the presidents of various political parties represented pillars of the East Indies community.

These men were responsible for an elaborate illuminated address (*oorkonde*) to the queen, a large paper scroll illustrated with colour pencil drawings of Javanese antiquities and a likeness of Jan Peterszoon Coen (1587–1629), the Indies' first governor-general and founder of the capital, Batavia, three centuries earlier. Coen's portrait was encircled by a medallion bearing an abridged version of his famous refrain, 'Despair not, as something great can be accomplished in the Indies' (*dispereert niet, want daer can in Indië wat groots verricht woorden*), a phrase first penned in a letter to the directors of the East India Company in 1618. These words were often repeated in triumphalist works by supporters of Dutch colonialism in the Indies well into the twentieth century.[63] Finally, accompanying the hundreds of names put to the *oorkonde* was the outcome of 'The Queen to the Indies' campaign: a petition that purportedly gathered one and a quarter million signatures from across the Indonesian archipelago.[64]

I say 'purportedly' because, while the 1919 *oorkonde* is today held in the Royal Collections (*Koninklijk Huisarchief*) at the Paleis Noordeinde in The Hague, the petition bearing the million-plus signatures is not. It was allegedly 'mislaid' at the palace – a symptom but probably not the cause of the campaign's failure.[65] Many reasons were offered as to why Wilhelmina could not greet her subjects in the East Indies. Some were political and constitutional: the queen was unable to take a 'sabbatical' from her reign, particularly as her heir was not yet old enough to act as regent in her absence (Juliana was only ten). At a time when the Netherlands was embroiled in a border dispute with Belgium, these concerns were especially pertinent.[66] In addition, as Pieter Eckhardt has shown, letters between Van Limburg Stirum and the Minister for the Colonies, A. C. D. de Graeff (a future governor-general himself), reveal concerns in The Hague about the precise scope of Wilhelmina's authority in the Indies.[67] Numerous non-Dutch royals had been received by Indies dignitaries, but some observers doubted whether appropriate company and facilities could be offered to the queen. Finally, there were apprehensions about her health and safety; whether she could withstand the climate of the tropics, the kinds of diseases that were endemic in the Indies and the political turmoil of recent times.[68] When push came to shove, then, monarchists in the Netherlands doubted whether it was feasible for Queen Wilhelmina to reign anywhere else but from afar.

Significantly, journalists and political elites in both the Indies and the Netherlands expressed concern that a personal visit from the queen would underwhelm her Asian subjects, who were deemed accustomed to a pomp and splendour from their rulers that was simply not *de rigueur* at the Dutch court. In 1919 the Java newspaper *De Locomotief* held that if Wilhelmina was not prepared to appear as an eastern empress – 'Baginda Maharadja Wilhimina', as she was usually referred to in Malay – then locals would be disappointed.[69] A letter from De Graeff to Van Limburg Stirum similarly queried the prudence of an in-person visit from the queen:

> because H.M., with respect to the Indies people, should lose her *halo* if She were to present herself ... as an ordinary person of flesh and blood, the Queen must remain before the native unveiled in a *nimbus* of sublime mystery or mysterious sublimity.[70] [my emphasis]

As we can see in the photograph from Pakubuwono X's album gift (figure 1.1), a divine glow about the Queen of the Netherlands could be more readily manufactured by other means: with electric lights, an effigy and a camera. Indeed, this book reveals the many modes in which Indies people creatively engaged with the absent queen through photography, both as a stand-in for the physical monarch in colonial rituals, and as a practice for articulating nuanced social and political relations within a transnational, colonial context.

Chapter 2 of this book departs from precisely this point, examining closely what it meant to behold the queen in her absence, through images used at royal celebrations. Scholars have noted, in passing, that portraits of Wilhelmina were ubiquitous at public and official venues throughout the East Indies.[71] This chapter uses photographs taken at public rituals for the Dutch monarchy to bring portraits of Wilhelmina out from the backdrops they are assumed to have occupied. In attending to the materiality of these portraits – their status as objects as well as images – the chapter demonstrates how images of the queen actively constituted social relations in different registers, depending on the context in which she was invoked.[72] Certainly, state portraits, often in painted form, hung behind Dutch authorities at official occasions, but a diverse array of effigies made of composite paintings or photographs were used in pageants at provincial celebrations where the participation of local communities was central to festivities. Adaptations to the form and function of her portrait were thus tailored by Wilhelmina's audience, and according to their particular needs and conventions. Photographic sources made by spectators enable the reconstruction of these interactions between colonial authorities, representations of the monarch and live audiences, and in the process show how the monarchy was made in the colonies by many hands and multiple gazes. Visual reworkings of her image in the East Indies also express one of

Wilhelmina's fundamental visual functions in the Dutch empire, as explored throughout this book: to represent the Dutch colonial regime's ability to accommodate difference, diversity and the discontiguity of people and territories across the Dutch colonial world. Indeed, analysing how the queen was localised through visual practices at royal celebrations throughout the East Indies provides new historical evidence of monarchy's broader imperial functions: as an institution that bestowed subjecthood upon peoples with differing political rights in modes that nation-states, with their claims for demographic homogeneity and territorial unity, struggled to replicate.

In Chapter 3, the analysis of photographs taken at royal celebrations in the East Indies during Wilhelmina's reign reminds us how local and even family loyalties often ran deeper than national identities in the age of empire.[73] This chapter shows that the rise of mass photography, particularly amateur forms such as 'family' photography, shaped the development of a popular, imperial monarchy in the Dutch colonial world. It demonstrates how snapshot photography, and practices of exchanging photographs of royal celebrations in the East Indies between friends and family across the Dutch world, enhanced imperial networks and articulated membership of a transnational community. This chapter also reveals how the participation of amateur photographers in commemorating royal festivals coincided with, and plausibly influenced, the emergence of the 'ordinary' royalty that has become the hallmark of modern, secular, parliamentary monarchies.[74] For the Dutch world, the consolidation of mass photography in the 1930s was crucial in this regard. Colonial archives show that it was in this period that amateur photography was booming. It was also in the 1930s that Crown Princess Juliana, Wilhelmina's heir, started her own branch of the House of Orange. Female kingship constituted an unusual amalgamation of roles that were more often divided between a king and his female consort. Being capable of both reigning and reproducing a dynasty enhanced the appeal of twentieth-century Dutch queens, who could be both sovereigns and child-bearers. Significantly, Juliana encouraged court photographers to publish 'family' photographs foregrounding her position as wife and mother. This chapters thus identifies the early reproductive years of Wilhelmina's daughter, and the international, colonial context in which Juliana's marriage and child-bearing were publicised, as the origin of the Dutch monarchy's popularisation in what was to become a 'long century' of reigning female kings, beginning with Queen Regent Emma in 1890 and ending with Queen Beatrix in 2013.[75] In the East Indies, amateur photographers collected images of the 'ordinary' Juliana in printed sources such as postcards and newspaper clippings, while taking snapshots of their own participation in local festivals. Chapter 3 therefore reveals the framework of a visual economy in which amateur colonial photographers articulated monarchist loyalties through their consumption as well as production of photographs, in practices that reinforced Dutch monarchs beginning to represent themselves accessibly to their subjects.

Chapter 4 extends the methodology of examining amateur snapshots together with commercial photographs and published commemorative books, this time to investigate how a liberal reformist interpretation of Wilhelmina's reign was embedded in the visual motif of electric illuminations at royal celebrations in both the East Indies and the Netherlands. The queen became synonymous with the Ethical Policy in 1901 when she outlined new terms of reference for colonial rule in her annual address to parliament, the *troonrede* or 'speech from the throne'.[76] Illuminations had long been part of royal celebrations in the Netherlands and the East Indies, but Wilhelmina's reign coincided with the electrification of the colonies, and thus with their modernisation under Dutch rule. This chapter reveals the changing historical circumstances in which photographs of illuminations became imbricated with discourses of the queen's benevolent, 'ethical' reign over her empire. I demonstrate how a visual rhetoric entangled in textual narratives of Wilhelmina's enlightened kingship spread across the Dutch colonial world, with the timing of its emergence contingent on local factors. In the Netherlands, it was not until the 1930s that commemorative books of royal celebrations seized on the spectacle of electrical illuminations, whereas in the East Indies, the motif appears already in the 1920s. Here, the rise of communist, nationalist and other anti-colonial movements prompted a retreat from the Ethical Policy, including its more radical promise of 'Association': the idea of Dutch officials sharing power with Indigenous elites. In this tense political context, Dutch officials focused on the visible outcomes of their less contested acts of governance, such as infrastructure improvements, including electrification programmes. European writers and photographers represented the small areas under Indigenous authority as backward slums, and in the process arrogated the implementation of modernisation for Dutch rule alone. The place of traditional Indigenous elites in these official visual narratives was, literally, in the dark.

This is not to argue that power and modernity was only linked in the photographs of Dutch authorities. On the contrary, Chapter 4 demonstrates how electrification was also meaningful to Indigenous photographers, who commemorated illuminations at royal celebrations for their own purposes *and* as gifts for Queen Wilhelmina. Indeed, photographs sent from the Indies to the queen that showed nocturnal light displays in modern colonial cities intersected with seemingly unrelated offerings, such as group portraits of Indies Chinese associations. I argue that, together, such photographic gifts portrayed a modern Indies to Wilhelmina, representing bids from her subjects for recognition as members of a colonial society where workable alternatives to juridical citizenship existed. Social status and opportunities were entrenched by institutions (including a legal system) that could extend 'European equivalence' to groups and individuals able to demonstrate their civility and modernity.[77] Photographs by Indigenous spectators and participants at royal celebrations thus provide new evidence for the selective cultural and political practices of Indonesia's emerging middle classes, and particularly, the wide range of opportunities they took to style themselves as international 'moderns' rather than nascent nationalists or, indeed, colonial loyalists.[78] Indonesians who photographed electric illuminations at royal celebrations espoused cosmopolitan tastes and interests in ways that resonated with other aspirational city-dwellers across colonial South-east Asia in the 1920s and 1930s.[79]

Chapter 5 looks further at Indigenous perspectives of royal celebrations, this time in the guise of photographic gifts from Central Java's kings and princes to the Dutch monarchy. Wilhelmina and Juliana's abiding absence from the East Indies was reciprocated by the vast majority of Indigenous royals, who numbered in the hundreds in the late colonial period, and who mostly refused to attend her court in the Netherlands.[80] Three royals from Central Java – *susuhunan* Pakubuwono X (whom we have already encountered), Sultan Hamengku Buwono VIII and Prince Pakualam VII – were among the repeat abstainers. Significantly, they also sent Wilhelmina some of the most remarkable photograph albums in the Royal Collections. These instances of 'snapshot diplomacy', as I term them, have all but escaped notice as sources on Dutch–Indonesian relations in the early twentieth century. I show how the absence of Central Java's royals from Wilhelmina's court was, most fundamentally, a refusal to accept an encounter on the Dutch queen's terms. Instead, snapshot diplomacy restored some agency to the modes of these men's self-representation. An analysis of the material qualities of the albums, and elements of dress and comportment in portraits of the kings and prince themselves, shows how Central Java's royals combined assertions of their own power with deferrals to the Dutch monarchy. To position themselves in photographs as hereditary elites with venerable courts gave them access to an international fellowship of royalty that few could share. It was also politic, however, to show themselves as contemporary, cosmopolitan, competent leaders on their own soil. The photograph albums thus provide new historical under-standings of Indonesian royal courts responding to multiple pressures: from the colonial government, a foreign monarchy and mounting challenges to their dwindling powers from emerging Indonesian political parties.

Chapter 6 returns to the spectacle of royal celebrations. It constitutes the first study of folk and ethnic 'types' in photographs from royal celebrations, in the context of the heyday of folklore studies (*volkskunde*) in the Netherlands and ethnography (*volkenkunde*) in the East Indies. In the process, the imperial functions of the Dutch monarchy in the early twentieth century emerge more clearly, as an institution invoked to impose unity across diverse subjects constituting the multi-ethnic, territorially discontiguous Kingdom of the Netherlands. This chapter analyses the gendered dimensions of how Wilhelmina and Juliana were expected to represent their relations with this complex body politic. Once again, photographs both of these women and of royal celebrations held in their honour offer fresh perspectives on the institution of Dutch kingship in colonial context, and on aspects of Indonesian history that are entangled with the House of Orange. As female kings, Wilhelmina and Juliana were expected to look upon their polities in the Netherlands and the East Indies very differently. Both women were photographed wearing the folk costumes of regional Dutch women, who were in turn displayed for them at mass royal celebrations in the Netherlands. The diverse ethnic groups of the Indonesian archipelago were likewise encouraged to participate in royal pageants, in modes that allowed them to be differentiated according to costume, material culture and customs such as dance. Wilhelmina was not, however, expected to embody her colonial subjects. Instead, she received miniature replicas of them in the form of dolls and models, and patronised ethnographic exhibitions in the metropole. The queen's gaze and recognition thus sufficed for her subjects in the East Indies. Underpinning this dynamic of oversight (from the monarch) and spectacle (provided by her subjects) were governing imperatives that were imbricated with ethnographic concerns.[81] The personal photographs taken by Dutch authorities at royal celebrations in the East Indies most clearly demonstrate how an intellectual interest in ethnography could be combined with acts of governance, but recent scholarship on the rise of folk studies in interwar Europe suggests important parallels. The symbolic role of imperial monarchy in this historical context was to integrate diversity within nations and empires. Photographic practices that arose with the popularisation of folk studies and ethnography in the early twentieth century, and that assisted with the visual identification and classification of groups of people, were readily extended to representing harmonious differences at royal celebrations.

Chapter 7 brings us to the end of Dutch colonialism in Indonesia, the close of Wilhelmina's half-century as queen of the Dutch imperium and the contested period of decolonisation that coincided with Juliana's reign. This chapter examines the commemoration of Queen's Day celebrations in the personal photographs of Dutch soldiers who were deployed to Indonesia during the counter-insurgent 'military actions' of 1945–49, a period known in Indonesian histories as the National Revolution. Indonesia was one of the first countries in South-east Asia to achieve independence from a European colonial power, and it did so through a violent, protracted civil and anti-colonial war. This conflict has been the recent subject of scholarship that revises the nature and extent of the atrocities committed on both the Dutch and Indonesian sides of the conflict.[82] While the uses of photography in the war have begun to enter these historical debates,[83] this chapter is the first study to use Dutch authorities' photographs to examine continuity and change at the end of empire in Indonesia.

Chapter 7 reveals that, after the disruption of the Japanese occupation, Dutch soldiers readily revived traditions for commemorating Wilhelmina as part of their attempted reconquest of Indonesia. Colonial photographic practices were also extended to Juliana's brief period of reign as queen of Dutch New Guinea in the 1950s. In both settings, Dutch authorities recorded their role in royal celebrations by making 'family' albums, observed the use of images of the queen as objects in ritual, and photographed local participation in celebrations to portray *rust en orde* (peace and order) and unity in diversity under Dutch rule. In wartime, these rituals had new meaning. Indeed, I argue that heavily militarised Queen's Day parades were strategic displays of conventional fighting power and a material part of counter-insurgency strategies that celebrated the (re-)claiming of Dutch territorial sovereignty. Further, Dutch soldiers actively revived the association of their monarchy with benevolent colonial rule during the conflict. Amateur and propaganda photography were recruited to the battle for civilian hearts and minds, as soldiers captured royal festivals' transformation into occasions for food distribution and tending to civilian populations shattered first by the Japanese occupation and then by civil and colonial war. In portraying the monarchy as (still) benevolent, and their own soldiering as a humanitarian effort, Dutch combatants invoked the monarchy as a legitimising agent of Dutch sovereignty in Indonesia, even as the empire in the 'East' disintegrated.

Notes

1 Although the Cape Colony was formally ceded to the British in 1814, Dutch settlers and their descendants there and throughout southern Africa demonstrated their continuing affection for the House of Orange by joining many of the major celebrations

held for Wilhelmina during her reign: S. Protschky, 'Orangists in a red empire: salutations from a Dutch queen's supporters in a British South Africa', in R. Aldrich and C. McCreery (eds), *Crowns and Colonies: Monarchies and Empires* (Manchester: Manchester University Press, 2016), pp. 97–118.

2 Royal Collections, The Netherlands (henceforth KHA), FA/0772.

3 B. Anderson, *Language and Power: Exploring Political Cultures in Indonesia* (Ithaca, NY: Cornell University Press, 1990), p. 31.

4 K. Strassler, *Refracted Visions: Popular Photography and National Modernity in Java* (Durham, NC: Duke University Press, 2010), pp. 283–4.

5 These kings reigned 1815–40, 1840–49 and 1849–90, respectively. J. Koch, *Koning Willem I 1772–1843* (Amsterdam: Boom, 2013); J. van Zanten, *Koning Willem II 1792–1849* (Amsterdam: Boom, 2013); D. van der Meulen, *Koning Willem III 1817–1890* (Amsterdam: Boom, 2013).

6 Most poignantly, his account of an audience with Wilhelmina at her court in 1929 is full of regret at the Sundanese protocols he was not permitted to observe in her presence: A. Djajadiningrat, *Herinneringen van Pangeran Aria Achmad Djajadiningrat* (Amsterdam and Batavia: G. Kolff & Co., 1936), p. 19.

7 The text in question was Sutan Sjahrir, *Indonesische overpeinzingen* (Amsterdam: De Bezige Bij, 1945). Cees Fasseur shows that Wilhelmina wrote to Juliana about this collection in 1946: C. Fasseur, *Wilhelmina; Krijgshaftig in een vormeloze jas* (Amsterdam: Balans, 2001), pp. 521–2.

8 P. A. Toer, *This Earth of Mankind*, trans. M. Lane (Ringwood, Vic.: Penguin, 1982), pp. 4, 6. First published as *Bumi Manusia* (Jakarta: Hasta Mitra, 1980). Minke's infatuation with the image of Wilhelmina is also mentioned by Strassler, *Refracted Visions*, pp. xiv–v.

9 J. van Osta, *Het theater van de staat; Oranje, Windsor en de moderne monarchie* (Amsterdam: Wereldbibliotheek, 1998), pp. 105, 137, 233, 235; P. Eckhardt, '"Wij zullen handhaven!" Oranje feesten in Indië (1918–1940)', *Indische Letteren; Feesten in Indië*, 21.1 (2006): 31–44.

10 A. Zuiderweg, 'Vuurwerk, illuminaties en wijnspuitende fonteinen; VOC-feestvreugde in Batavia', *Indische Letteren; Feesten in Indië*, 21.1 (2006): 81–94. In the VOC period, celebrations were for the Princes of Orange. The House of Oranje-Nassau became a monarchy in 1813.

11 H. te Velde, *Gemeenschapszin en plichtsbesef; Liberalisme en nationalisme in Nederland, 1870–1918* (The Hague: SDU, 1992), pp. 123, 132; G. van Schoonhoven, '"Houd Oranje boven in de troep eronder": De geschiedenis van de nationale feestdag Koninginnedag', in R. Meijer and H. J. Schoo (eds), *De monarchie; Staatsrecht, volksgunst en het huis van Oranje* (Amsterdam: Prometheus, 2002), pp. 137–68, at pp. 139–47; G. Oostindie, *De parels en de kroon; Het koningshuis en de koloniën* (Amsterdam: De Bezige Bij, 2006), pp. 75, 78; J. van Osta, 'The emperor's new clothes: the reappearance of the performing monarchy in Europe, c. 1870–1914', in H. te Velde (ed.), *Mystifying the Monarch: Studies on Discourse, Power, and History* (Amsterdam: Amsterdam University Press, 2006), pp. 181–92, at p. 187.

12 S. Stuurman, *Wacht op onze daden; Het liberalisme en de vernieuwing van de Nederlandse staat* (Amsterdam: Bert Bakker, 1992); Te Velde, *Gemeenschapszin en plichtsbesef*.

13 Van Osta, 'The emperor's new clothes', p. 187; Van Osta, *Het theater van de Staat*, pp. 91, 116, 126–8, 137; Te Velde, *Gemeenschapszin en plichtsbesef*, pp. 122–3, 130.

14 Te Velde, *Gemeenschapszin en plichtsbesef*, pp. 16, 121–2, 130–4, 140–1, 268–70; P. Drooglever, 'De monarchie in Indië', *Ex Tempore*, 17 (1998): 221–36, at p. 123.

15 Van Osta, *Het theater van de Staat*, p. 87.

16 Most scholars contend that socialists were the only significant group to oppose the monarchy: Te Velde, *Gemeenschapszin en plichtsbesef*, pp. 123, 130–3; Van Osta, *Het theatre van de Staat*, pp. 115–17, 125–7, 135. One holds that there were also socialists in favour of the monarchy: N. Wilterdink, 'The monarchy contested: anti-monarchism in the Netherlands', *The Netherlands' Journal of Social Sciences*, 26.2 (1990): 3–16, at p. 8.

17 R. Wassing-Visser, *Koninklijke geschenken uit Indonesië; Historische banden met het huis Oranje-Nassau (1600–1938)* (Den Haag/Zwolle: Stichting Historische Verzamelingen van het Huis Oranje-Nassau/Waanders, 1995). There is also an English translation: R. Wassing-Visser, *Royal Gifts from Indonesia: Historical Bonds with the House of Orange-Nassau (1600–1938)* (The Hague/Zwolle: House of Orange-Nassau Historic Collections Trust/Waanders, 1995).

18 P. Eckhardt, 'Wij zullen handhaven! De symbolische betekenis van de Nederlandse monarchie in Nederlands-Indië 1918–1940', MA dissertation, University of Amsterdam, 2002.

19 Oostindie, *De parels en de kroon*.

20 The biographer was Cees Fasseur: Oostindie, *De parels en de kroon*, p. 95.

21 Oostindie, *De parels en de kroon*, pp. 88, 91, 92, 95, 138.

22 D. Cannadine, *Ornamentalism: How the British Saw Their Empire* (London: Allen Lane, 2001). Oostindie did not cite this work of Cannadine's, so he did not engage with this problem directly.

23 E. W. Said, *Orientalism: Western Conceptions of the Orient* (New York: Pantheon, 1978); E. W. Said, *Culture and Imperialism* (London: Random House, 1993).

24 Cannadine, *Ornamentalism*, p. 124.

25 Cannadine, *Ornamentalism*, p. 111: 'By these interconnected pageants and mutually reinforcing ceremonials, the British Empire put itself on display, and represented itself to itself, more frequently, more splendidly, more ostentatiously and more globally than any other realm.' Cannadine did not address the Dutch empire in his brief overview of other European monarchies and their empires (p. 71). Oddly, given the scopic concerns of the book, Cannadine also paid no attention to photography.

26 C. V. Reed, *Royal Tourists, Colonial Subjects and the Making of a British World, 1860–1911* (Manchester: Manchester University Press, 2016), p. xxvi.

27 Reed, *Royal Tourists*, pp. xix–xx; see also pp. 80, 125.

28 Reed, *Royal Tourists*, p. 82.

29 M. Nugent and S. Carter, 'Introduction: Indigenous histories, settler colonies and Queen Victoria', in M. Nugent and S. Carter (eds), *Mistress of Everything: Queen Victoria in Indigenous Worlds* (Manchester: Manchester University Press, 2016), pp. 1–24, at p. 1.

30 Carter and Nugent, 'Introduction', p. 5.

31 R. Aldrich and C. McCreery, 'European sovereigns and their empires "beyond the seas"', in R. Aldrich and C. McCreery (eds), *Crowns and Colonies: European Monarchies and Overseas Empires* (Manchester: Manchester University Press, 2016), pp. 1–26, at p. 6.

32 R. Aldrich and C. McCreery, 'Empire tours: royal travel between colonies and metropoles', in R. Aldrich and C. McCreery (eds), *Royals on Tour: Politics, Pageantry and Colonialism* (Manchester: Manchester University Press, 2018), pp. 1–22.

33 For my publications in this field, see the Bibliography.

34 Following W. Monter, *The Rise of Female Kings in Europe, 1300–1800* (New Haven, CT: Yale University Press, 2012).

35 M. Grever, 'Vorstin voor heel het vaderland? Orangisme en feminisme in het laatste kwaart van de negentiende eeuw', *De Negentiende Eeuw*, 23.1 (1999): 76–88; M. Grever, 'Koningin Wilhelmina en het feminisme of de ogenschijnlijke onverenig-baarheid van karakters', *Tijdschrift voor Genderstudies*, 2.3 (1999): 4–19; M. Grever, 'Colonial queens: imperialism, gender and the body politic during the reign of Victoria and Wilhelmina', *Dutch Crossing: A Journal of Low Countries Studies*, 26.1 (2002): 99–114; M. Grever and B. Waaldijk (eds), *Transforming the Public Sphere: The Dutch National Exhibition of Women's Labor in 1898* (Durham, NC: Duke University Press, 2004); M. Grever and B. Waaldijk, 'Women's labor at display: feminist claims to Dutch citizenship and colonial politics around 1901', *Journal of Women's History*, 15.4 (2004): 11–18; M. Grever, 'Staging modern monarchs: royalty at the World Exhibitions of 1851 and 1867', in H. te Velde (ed.), *Mystifying the Monarch: Studies on Discourse, Power, and History* (Amsterdam: Amsterdam University Press, 2006), pp. 161–79; S. Legêne and B. Waaldijk, 'Mission interrupted: gender, history and the

colonial canon', in S. Stuurman and M. Grever (eds), *Beyond the Canon: History for the Twenty-First Century* (Basingstoke: Palgrave Macmillan, 2007), pp. 188–204. See also Protschky, 'Orangists in a red empire'. Historians of the early modern House of Orange have comprehensively integrated gender into their analysis of this dynasty's ruling strategies: S. Broomhall and J. van Gent, *Dynastic Colonialism: Gender, Materiality and the Early Modern House of Orange-Nassau* (London: Routledge, 2016); S. Broomhall and J. van Gent, *Gender, Power and Identity in the Early Modern House of Orange-Nassau* (London: Routledge, 2016).

36 S. Legêne, 'Enlightenment, empathy, retreat: the cultural heritage of the *Ethische Politiek*', in P. ter Keurs (ed.), *Colonial Collections Revisited* (Leiden: CNWS Publications, 2007), pp. 220–45; S. Legêne, 'Flatirons and the folds of history: on archives, cultural heritage and colonial legacies', in S. W. Wieringa (ed.), *Traveling Heritages: New Perspective on Collecting, Preserving and Sharing Women's History* (Amsterdam: Aksant, 2008), pp. 47–64; S. Legêne, 'Dwinegeri: multiculturalism and the colonial past (or: the culture borders of being Dutch)', in B. Kaplan, M. Carlson and L. Cruz (eds), *Boundaries and their Meanings in the History of the Netherlands* (Leiden: Brill, 2009), pp. 223–42; S. Legêne, *Spiegelreflex; Culturele sporen van de koloniale ervaring* (Amsterdam: Bert Bakker, 2010).

37 Legêne, 'Dwinegeri', p. 240.

38 By the work of her hands, I refer to Wilhelmina's painting career. An exhibition of her works travelled the Dutch colonies in 1933, including the East Indies: E. van Heuven-van Nes, '"Een aandachtige bezichting ten volle waard": De tentoonstelling van het werk van koningin Wilhelmina', in M.E. Spliethoff, E. van Heuven-van Nes, M. Jansen and P. Rem, *Koningin Wilhelmina; Schilderijen en tekeningen* (Zwolle: Waanders and Stichting Paleis Het Loo, 2006), pp. 37–56, at pp. 43–5.

39 J. Schaap, *Het recht om te waarschuwen; Over de Radio Oranje-toespraken van koningin Wilhelmina* (Amsterdam: Anthos, 2007), pp. 79, 81.

40 Eckhardt, 'Wij zullen handhaven!', pp. 46–8. On radio and also film in the East Indies, see V. Kuitenbrouwer, 'Songs of an imperial underdog: imperialism and popular culture in the Netherlands, 1870–1960', in J. M. MacKenzie (ed.), *European Empires and the People: Popular Responses to Imperialism in France, Britain, the Netherlands, Belgium, Germany and Italy* (Manchester: Manchester University Press, 2011), pp. 90–123, at pp. 112–13.

41 P. de Zeeuw (ed.), *Vorstin en Volk; Woorden van H.M. Koningin Wilhelmina* (Baarn: Hollandia, 1945), pp. 65, 89.

42 Wassing-Visser, *Koninklijke geschenken uit Indonesië*, pp. 219–20; H. Beunders, 'Regina vivat! Regie vivat? In de publicitaire monarchy is de liefde tussen volk en vorst als het leven zelf', in R. Meijer and H. J. Schoo (eds), *De monarchie; Staatsrecht, volksgunst en het huis van Oranje* (Amsterdam: Prometheus, 2002), pp. 101–36, at p. 112.

43 Fasseur, *Wilhelmina; Krijgshaftig in een vormeloze jas*, pp. 336, 486–8; Schaap, *Het recht om te waarschuwen*, p. 25; B. van der Boom, 'Orangisme en de bezetting', in H. te Velde and D. Haks (eds), *Oranje onder; Populair Orangisme van Willem van Oranje tot nu* (Amsterdam: Prometheus/Bert Bakker, 2014), pp. 221–42, at pp. 221–3, 232–3; De Zeeuw (ed.), *Vorstin en volk*, pp. 142–3, 155–6.

44 Van Osta, *Het theater van de Staat*, pp. 100–1; Schaap, *Het recht om te waarschuwen*, p. 45.

45 R. Mrázek, *Engineers of Happy Land: Technology and Nationalism in a Colony* (Princeton, NJ: Princeton University Press, 2002), pp. 110–11. On film in the Indies, see also J. G. Taylor, 'Ethical policies in moving pictures: the films of J. C. Lamster', in S. Protschky (ed.), *Photography, Modernity and the Governed in Late-Colonial Indonesia* (Amsterdam: Amsterdam University Press, 2015), pp. 41–70.

46 U. Bosma, *Indiëgangers; Verhalen van Nederlanders die naar Indië trokken* (Amsterdam: Bert Bakker, 2010), pp. 112–13, 192.

47 Bosma, *Indiëgangers*, pp. 215, 217.

48 On 'cultural citizenship' in the Dutch colonial world, see M. Bloembergen and R. Raben, 'Wegen naar het nieuwe Indië, 1890–1950', in M. Bloembergen and R. Raben

(eds), *Het koloniale beschavingsoffensief; Wegen naar het niewe Indië, 1890–1950* (Leiden: KITLV Press, 2009), pp. 7–24; C. Drieënhuizen, 'Social careers across imperial spaces: an empire family in the Dutch-British world, 1811–1933', *Journal of Imperial and Commonwealth History*, 44.3 (2016): 397–422; Legène, 'Dwinegeri', pp. 223–42. On the colonial migration circuit, see Bosma, *Indiëgangers*, pp. 26–8, 42–3, 106, 110, 193–4; U. Bosma and R. Raben, *Being 'Dutch' in the Indies: A History of Creolisation and Empire, 1500–1920*, trans. W. Shaffer (Athens, OH: Ohio University Press, 2008), p. 57. On modes of citizenship in the British colonial world, see D. Gorman, *Imperial Citizenship: Empire and the Question of Belonging* (Manchester: Manchester University Press, 2006); Reed, *Royal Tourists*, pp. xviii, xxiv, 5, 125–9.

49 M. Jansen, 'Moeder en dochter in het Koninklijk Huisarchief', *Fotografisch Geheugen*, 79 (2013): 7–9, at p. 7.

50 *Toekang Potret: 100 Years of Photography in the Dutch East Indies 1839–1939*, trans. M. Gibbs (Rotterdam/Leiden: Fragment/Museum voor Volkenkunde, 1989); S. Wachlin, *Woodbury & Page: Photographers Java* (Leiden: KITLV Press, 1994); L. Ouwehand, *Herinneringen in beeld; Fotoalbums uit Nederlands-Indië* (Leiden: KITLV Press, 2009).

51 KHA FA/0719. On Kinsbergen, see G. Theuns-de Boer and S. Assa (with contributions by S. Wachlin), *Isidore van Kinsbergen (1821–1905): Photo Pioneer and Theatre Maker in the Dutch East Indies* (Zaltbommel, Leiden and Amsterdam: Aprilis and KITLV Press, 2005), pp. 276–8.

52 KHA Album FA/1002. The photographer in this instance is unknown.

53 M. Jansen, 'De nationale gedaante', in *Oranje in de nationale streekdrachten* (Apeldoorn: Nationaal Museum, Paleis Het Loo, 2012), pp. 8–17, at pp. 10–11.

54 Van Osta, *Het theater van de staat*, pp. 10, 15; Oostindie, *De parels en de kroon*, p. 52.

55 One of the earliest examples is described on a programme for the 'Nationaal Kinderfest' held in Surabaya in 1890 to celebrate Wilhelmina's tenth birthday. The first prize of the raffle was 'a large pastel portrait' of the princess. Children who attended were given a voucher to redeem for a small portrait: KHA FA/1002.

56 Echkardt, 'Wij zullen handhaven!', p. 25.

57 On the middle-class family archive and its development in the nineteenth century, see A. Baggerman, 'Autobiography and family memory in the nineteenth century', in R. Dekker (ed.), *Egodocuments and History: Autobiographical Writing and its Social Context since the Middle Ages* (Hilversum: Verloren, 2002), pp. 161–74, at p. 163. On family photographs and dynasty, see G. Batchen, *Forget Me Not: Photography and Remembrance* (Amsterdam/New York: Van Gogh Museum/Princeton Architectural Press, 2004), p. 10.

58 R. C. Morris, 'Introduction. Photographies east: the camera and its histories in East and Southeast Asia', in R. C. Morris (ed.), *Photographies East: The Camera and its Histories in East and Southeast Asia* (Durham, NC: Duke University Press, 2009), pp. 1–28, at p. 21; S. Protschky, 'Tea cups, cameras and family life: picturing domesticity in elite European and Javanese family photographs from the Netherlands Indies, c. 1900–1942', *History of Photography*, 36.1 (2012): 44–65.

59 See particularly the Special Collections of the Koninklijk Instituut voor Taal-, Land- en Volkenkunde (henceforth KITLV), Leiden; the photographic collections of the Koninklijk Instituut voor de Tropen, Amsterdam; and also some collections outside the Netherlands, such as the Dutch East Indies collection at the National Gallery of Australia, Canberra.

60 Aldrich and McCreery, 'European sovereigns and their empires "beyond the seas"', pp. 11, 19.

61 The first petition was launched in January 1909 by the *Algemeen Nederlandsch Verbond* (General Dutch Alliance). Since Wilhelmina was about to give birth to Juliana, it was directed at getting her husband, Prince Hendrik, to the Indies: KHA A50 XVI 1b; see also Th. Colenbrander, 'De Koningin naar Indië', *De Gids*, 83 (1919): 162–3, at p. 162. The 1919 petition, launched by the governor-general in the context of rebellions organised by Sarekat Islam, is discussed in Eckhardt, 'Wij zullen

handhaven!', pp. 27–35; and B. de Graaff and E. Locher-Scholten, *J.P. Graaf van Limburg Stirum; Tegendraads landvoogd en diplomaat* (Zwolle: Waanders, 2007), pp. 212–13, 249–50.

62 KHA A50 XVI 23. The executive committee comprised E. A. Zeilinga, president and director of the Java Bank; W. F. van Beuningen, secretary of the *Bataafsche Petroleum Maatschappij* (BPM); K. A. R. Bosscha, chief administrator of the Malabar tea estate; C. van der Linden and Mr W. de Bruyn Kops, respectively, president-director and secretary of the *Koninklijke Paketvaart Maatschappij*; and Raden Dr Hoesein Djajadiningrat (1886–1960) of the famous Serang Regency. Hoesein and his brother, Achmad Djajadingrat (who sat on the Council of the Indies), were Dutch-educated, and Hoesein was a well-known official and scholar of Islam: see G. Pijper, 'Professor Dr. Pangeran Ario Hoesein Djajadiningrat. 8 December 1886–12 November 1960', *Bijdragen tot de Taal-, Land- en Volkenkunde*, 117.4 (1961): 401–9.

63 KHA A50 XVI 23. Indeed, a facsimile of Coen's letter appears in the chapter on 'The Dutch in the East Indies' by J. C. Kielstra in *Gedenkboek van het Algemeen Nederlandsch Verbond* (Dordrecht and Amsterdam: Wereldbibliotheek, 1923), pp. 279–300, at p. 281.

64 The figures are mentioned in the text of the *oorkonde*: KHA A50 XVI 23. At least some of these signatures were obtained under duress. In Medan, for example, police intimidated villagers into signing: De Graaff and Locher-Scholten, *J.P. Graaf van Limburg Stirum*, p. 251.

65 Discussed in Oostindie, *De parels en de kroon*, pp. 105–7.

66 It should be noted that in 1922, the Dutch constitution was amended to allow Wilhelmina to take leave for a period in order to travel abroad: Fasseur, *Wilhelmina; Krijgshaftig in een vormeloze jas*, p. 160.

67 Eckhardt, 'Wij zullen handhaven!', pp. 30–1.

68 S. Kalff, 'Indië en het Oranjehuis', *Het Koloniaal Tijdschrift*, 8 (1919): 1351–71, at pp. 1369–70; Fasseur, *Wilhelmina; Krijgshaftig in een vormeloze jas*, pp. 78–9, 161.

69 Eckhardt, citing *De Locomotief*, in 'Wij zullen handhaven!', pp. 32–3.

70 Cited from letters dated 12 September 1919 in Eckhardt, 'Wij zullen handhaven!', p. 35.

71 Eckhardt, 'Wij zullen handhaven!', pp. 28–9; Oostindie, *De parels en de kroon*, p. 52.

72 E. Edwards and J. Hart, 'Introduction: photographs as objects', in E. Edwards and J. Hart (eds), *Photographs, Objects, Histories: On the Materiality of Images* (London: Routledge, 2004), pp. 1–15, at pp. 1, 4.

73 Bosma, *Indiëgangers*, p. 49; C. Drieënhuizen, 'Objects, nostalgia and the Dutch colonial elite in times of transition, ca. 1900–1970', *Bijdragen tot de Taal-, Land- en Volkenkunde*, 170 (2014): 504–29; Drieënhuizen, 'Social careers across imperial spaces'.

74 M. Billig, *Talking of the Royal Family* (London: Routledge, 1992), p. 203; L. Phillips, 'Media discourse and the Danish monarchy: reconciling egalitarianism and royalism', *Media, Culture & Society*, 21 (1999): 221–45, esp. pp. 225–6.

75 Regarding Emma, it is worth noting that regents did not rule as sovereigns. Instead, they 'exercised formal authority on an interim basis': Monter, *The Rise of Female Kings in Europe*, p. xvi.

76 Only a few sentences of the oration referred to the East Indies, but they included the pillars of what would define the policy: an inquiry into the 'diminished welfare' (*mindere welvaart*) of the Javanese, decentralisation of the colonial administration, and further 'pacification' of north Sumatra in the so-called 'Outer Provinces' (*Buitengewesten*): Queen Wilhelmina, 'Troonrede van 17 September 1901', in *Troonredes, Openingsredes, Inhuldingsredes 1814–1963*, introduced and annotated by E. van Raalte ('s-Gravenhage: Staatsuitgeverij, 1964), pp. 193–4, at p. 194.

77 B. W. Luttikhuis, 'Beyond race: constructions of "Europeanness" in late-colonial legal practice in the Dutch East Indies', *European Review of History*, 20.6 (2013): 539–58. With a different conclusion, focusing more on the importance of race in Indies social hierarchies, see A. L. Stoler, *Carnal Knowledge and Imperial Power*

(Berkeley, CA: University of California Press, 2002). For an overview of the debates about race and other factors intersecting to determine social mobility in the East Indies, see S. Protschky, 'Race, class and gender: debates over the character of social hierarchies in the Netherlands Indies, circa 1600–1942', *Bijdragen tot de Taal-, Land- en Volkenkunde*, 167.4 (2011): 543–56.

78   H. Schulte Nordholt, 'Modernity and middle classes in the Netherlands Indies: cultivating cultural citizenship', in S. Protschky (ed.), *Photography, Modernity and the Governed in Late-Colonial Indonesia* (Amsterdam: Amsterdam University Press, 2015), pp. 223–54; T. Hoogervorst and H. Schulte Nordholt, 'Urban middle classes in colonial Java (1900–1942): images and language', *Bijdragen tot de Taal-, Land- en Volkenkunde*, 173 (2017): 442–74.

79   S. L. Lewis, *Cities in Motion: Urban Life and Cosmopolitanism in Southeast Asia, 1920–1940* (Cambridge: Cambridge University Press, 2016); S. Protschky, 'Modern times in Southeast Asia, 1920s–1970s', in S. Protschky and T. van den Berge (eds), *Modern Times in Southeast Asia, 1920s–1970s* (Leiden: Brill, 2018), pp. 1–14.

80   On some of the Indonesian royals who *did* attend Wilhelmina's court, see S. Protschky, 'Strained encounters: royal Indonesian visits to the Dutch court in the early twentieth century', in R. Aldrich and C. McCreery (eds), *Royals on Tour: Politics, Pageantry and Colonialism* (Manchester: Manchester University Press, 2018), pp. 233–49.

81   As also noted by Legène, *Spiegelreflex*, p. 96.

82   B. Luttikhuis and D. Moses (eds), *Colonial Counterinsurgency and Mass Violence: The Dutch Empire in Indonesia* (London: Routledge, 2014); G. Oostindie, in cooperation with I. Hoogenboom and J. Verwey, *Soldaat in Indonesië 1945–1950; Getuigenis van een oorlog aan de verkeerde kant van de geschiedenis* (Amsterdam: Prometheus, 2015); R. Limpach, *De brandende kampongs van Generaal Spoor* (Amsterdam: Boom, 2016).

83   L. Zweers, *De gecensureerde oorlog; Militairen versus media in Nederlands-Indië 1945–1949* (Zutphen: Walburg Pers, 2013); R. Kok, E. Somers and L. Zweers, *Koloniale oorlog 1945–1949; Van Indië naar Indonesië* (Amsterdam: Carrera, 2015); S. Protschky, 'Soldiers as humanitarians: photographing war in Indonesia (1945–49)', in J. Lydon (ed.), *Visualising Human Rights* (Perth: UWA Publishing, 2018), pp. 39–62.

CHAPTER TWO

Behold the queen: portraits of the monarch in colonial ritual

In 1923 Queen Wilhelmina's brother-in-law, Adolf Friedrich von Mecklenburg (1873–1969), toured the Moluccas and Dutch New Guinea. It was the year of Wilhelmina's silver jubilee, and for the twenty-fifth year since her coronation, she was not touring her empire. In her absence, '*Hertog* (Duke) Adolf', as he became known on his travels, accrued celebrity status in the Netherlands Indies.[1] That he was German nobility and only related to the queen by her marriage to Hendrik made no difference.[2] He was the closest thing to a member of the House of Orange on Indies soil since Wilhelmina's 'seafarer' uncle, Prince Hendrik, had made the journey in the 1830s. Thus, when the duke left Batavia for the eastern provinces of the Indies on 13 October he was 'seen off by the highest in the land, officials and private citizens'.[3]

Hertog Adolf was accompanied by an old chum, R. A. van Sandick, Resident of the Moluccas, and by Max Büttner van der Jagt, who took a vacation from his post as Resident of Kedu, Central Java, to join the tour. Van der Jagt (1873–1960) was an ardent monarchist, a man opposed to liberal colonial reforms and, later, a member of the ultra-conservative Fatherland Club (*Vaderlandsche Club*), founded in the Indies in 1929. He and the duke were on an official reconnaissance mission informing a petition to the colonial government for a new, multinationally funded trade and plantation concession in New Guinea. As an erstwhile governor of Togo, a protectorate in German West Africa, Hertog Adolf was considered well qualified to comment on colonial matters. Indeed, in the account of their 'Moluccan tour' that Van der Jagt published in 1935, he portrayed the queen's brother-in-law as an intrepid figure, a 'sportsman, former Africa-*trekker* and renowned lion hunter'.[4] Their joint recommendations to the colonial government – to import and contract under penal sanctions a labour force of 'coolies' (indentured labourers) to New Guinea – were consistent with Dutch precedent in other parts of the archipelago, notably the east coast of Sumatra, as well as German colonies in Africa. Plans to develop the concession were approved, but were first delayed and ultimately abandoned as the global depression of the early 1930s engulfed the Indies.[5]

In Van der Jagt's book, the failure of the mission is somewhat buried at the end of a narrative that focuses instead on the optimism of the tour, which coincided with the jubilee celebrations for Wilhelmina. One of the highlights occurred on 16 September, when Hertog Adolf, Van der Jagt and Sandick arrived in Olilit, a small Christian village in the Tanimbar Islands, today Timor Laut in the Indonesian province of Maluku. A fortnight after the celebrations for Wilhelmina had officially ended, locals here re-enacted the ceremony for the duke as a flesh-and-blood royal guest of honour. Van der Jagt gave a brief description of the local schoolchildren's parade through the village for the occasion:

> The indispensable flute orchestra blasted the *Wilhelmus* [the Dutch national anthem], followed by a procession of youths and girls, decorously dressed ... They carried the portrait of the Queen in front and sang songs and [gave] dialogues for the Duke in Malay originally [composed] for the 25-year jubilee festival for the Queen.[6]

He also took several photographs of the celebration, one of which illustrated his book. It showed local men and boys bearing a standard in the queen's honour.[7] An unpublished photograph of the children holding a framed portrait of Wilhelmina survives among Van der Jagt's government papers in The Hague (figure 2.1). The portrait shown in the photograph probably hung on a classroom wall in ordinary circumstances, but on this occasion it was removed, taken outside and paraded through the village like an effigy, then displayed to the visiting Dutch officials and the queen's brother-in-law at the culmination of the pageant.

Hertog Adolf's royal presence at this ceremony in 1923 was historically anomalous for the period of Wilhelmina's reign. By contrast, the written and visual account of the Dutch official, Van der Jagt, is entirely typical. The photographs from Queen's Day (*koninginnedag*) festivals in the Indies are vital sources for showing how portraits of Wilhelmina became important elements in public rituals to compensate for her abiding absence from her own celebrations. Certainly, there are parallels between the Dutch queen's and other European monarchs' *symbolic* presence in their colonies through, for example, figural representations such as monuments and statues, likenesses on coins and postage stamps, and state portraits in schools and government offices.[8] Regardless, Wilhelmina's constant, corporeal absence is unassailable. It is precisely for this reason that her image was so laden with ritual significance, not just as a flat picture in the backdrop but as an object with the status of an effigy, with rites to enable.

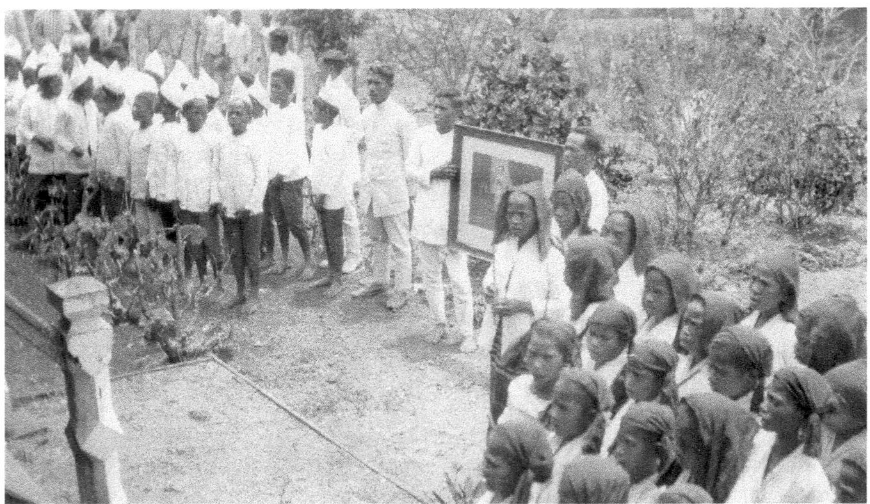

2.1 M. B. van der Jagt, re-enactment of *koninginnedag* celebrations for
Duke Adolf Friedrich von Mecklenburg, Olilit (Tanimbar Islands),
26 September 1923

The absence of the queen from her colonies has driven historians of the Dutch monarchy to doubt Wilhelmina's influence there, and to query the impact of royal festivals on Indigenous observers.[9] In the British empire, even with its history of more numerous royal tours, the monarch was only rarely honoured in person.[10] Yet scholars of royal festivals have been resolute on the efficacy of spectacle and performance in the 'invention of traditions' to legitimise British monarchs and their representatives before their colonial subjects, and to cement allegiances with Indigenous aristocrats.[11] What is missing from this scholarship on both the British and Dutch empires is a treatment of how ritual involving images of European monarchs in their colonies evolved in their physical absence, and how the rise of mass photography in the first half of the twentieth century enabled such practices.

To answer these questions, I attend to the materiality of portraits of Wilhelmina, as recorded in photographs taken at royal celebrations. Such an approach privileges the *content* of photographs, aims to retrieve what participants at royal celebrations *did* with the portraits of Wilhelmina pictured in them, and examines the forms of encounter between images and people that occurred at royal festivals. In this chapter, the social uses of the photographic sources themselves are not the principal aim of enquiry – except to acknowledge, following Geoffrey Batchen, that a photograph of a portrait has an inherently commemorative function, to honour the person (doubly) pictured.[12] To that end, photographs of images of Wilhelmina are themselves components of the ritual they served to commemorate.

Governors-general and state portraits of the queen

Like their counterparts in the British empire, the men appointed as governors-general of the Netherlands East Indies often had a class-based affinity with the Dutch crown.[13] Of the ten men who served during Wilhelmina's reign, half were aristocrats themselves, mostly *jonkheeren* (noblemen) and one *graaf* (count).[14] Governors-general were answerable to the Dutch parliament through the Minister for the Colonies in The Hague. But in the Indies, much like the viceroys of British crown colonies, they were the queen's deputy (*onderkoning*: literally, 'underking') and the highest authorities in the land.[15] There was something of the royal aura that accrued to this position, even in the age of parliamentary (or 'constitutional') monarchy. As the last pre-war governor-general of the Indies, the impressively-named A. W. L. Tjarda van Starkenborgh Stachouwer put it: 'The Minister for the Colonies stood across from the parliament and in fact had to defend what he had not ordained, which he could not always do. He was no *chef* [boss] of the GG, that was the "king".'[16]

While Wilhelmina never toured the East Indies herself, her viceroys frequently did so in her name. When they arrived in major towns, governors-general were met with similar public ceremonial as was employed for Queen's Day, as we shall see in later chapters. Triumphal arches (*erepoorten*) were erected at the entrance to city quarters, there were public processions, and images of Wilhelmina were paraded about.[17] In 1920, when Governor-General Johan Paul van Limburg Stirum (served 1916–21) visited Pontianak in Dutch Borneo, photographs of his tour were presented in an album to the Resident, K. A. James, by Sultan Mohammad Shafiuddin II (1866–1924).[18] Two photographs in the album show painted portraits of Wilhelmina adorning arches at the entrances to villages in the district. The paintings were flanked by banners in Malay and Dutch that addressed Van Limburg Stirum as the queen's 'representative'.[19] Passing beneath these arches mounted with images of Wilhelmina, the governor-general may well have perceived more acutely than usual that he was the queen's 'underking'.

Celebrations for the Dutch monarchy were great occasions for governors-general. Both official palaces on Java – one on the Koningsplein at Rijswijk in Batavia, the other at the hill station in Buitenzorg to the south of the capital – held life-sized, painted state portraits of the queen on permanent display. The portrait at Buitenzorg hung in the 'pillar gallery', a spacious room with a polished marble floor, white columns and a domed ceiling hung with crystal chandeliers. It showed Wilhelmina frontally facing the viewer in her crown and coronation robes. While the painting's provenance and current whereabouts are unknown, its erstwhile existence is well documented.[20] In 1921, for example, Governor-General Van Limburg Stirum allowed the fashionable photographer Thilly Weissenborn, of Lux Fotostudio, to photograph the interiors of the palace, including the Wilhelmina portrait in the pillar gallery.[21] Several fine photographs exist of the state portrait of Wilhelmina at Buitenzorg Palace during the term of Van Starkenborgh Stachouwer (served 1936–42). One shows the viceroy, *susuhunan* Pakubuwono X of Surakarta and their daughters seated before the painting at Wilhelmina's fortieth jubilee celebrations (figure 2.2).

Another portrait of Wilhelmina hung in the palace at Rijswijk in Batavia. Its provenance is better known than that of its Buitenzorg counterpart. It was painted in 1900 by Pieter de Josselin de Jong (1861–1906), who won medals at world exhibitions in the late nineteenth century and was in King Willem III's favour. His portrait shows the queen seated on her throne in three-quarter profile.[22] Photographs were made throughout the 1920s, 1930s and early 1940s showing governors-general making speeches and receiving distinguished guests as they stood before the portrait at royal celebrations.[23] A photograph from Governor-General Van Starkenborgh's reign is among the most spectacular. It shows a gala dinner on Queen's Day in the late 1930s. The De Jong portrait of Wilhelmina hangs at the head of the table, behind the viceroy, and a room full of men in dinner suits stand to raise a toast to her (figure 2.3). Many of them turn their heads towards the portrait rather than the governor-general.

These likenesses of the queen at the governor-general's palaces were permanently fixed and larger than life, a symbol of the endurance of the monarchy, while her representative, the *onderkoning*, came and went every five years. On a day-to-day basis, the paintings may well have receded into the background and become part of the palace furniture. But on public, official occasions, especially as commemorated in photographs at royal celebrations, portraits of the queen became focal points of proceedings that symbolically reinforced the authority of her chief representative.

The power and legitimacy that such portraits lent the office of governor-general was perhaps most evident where colonial sovereignty was challenged by Indonesian resistance. In 1903, one year before he was elevated to the rank of governor-general himself, Lieutenant-General J. B. van Heutsz presided over the surrender of the last Sultan of Aceh, Muhammad Daud Sjah II (1864–1939) at Kuta Raja. It was the formal

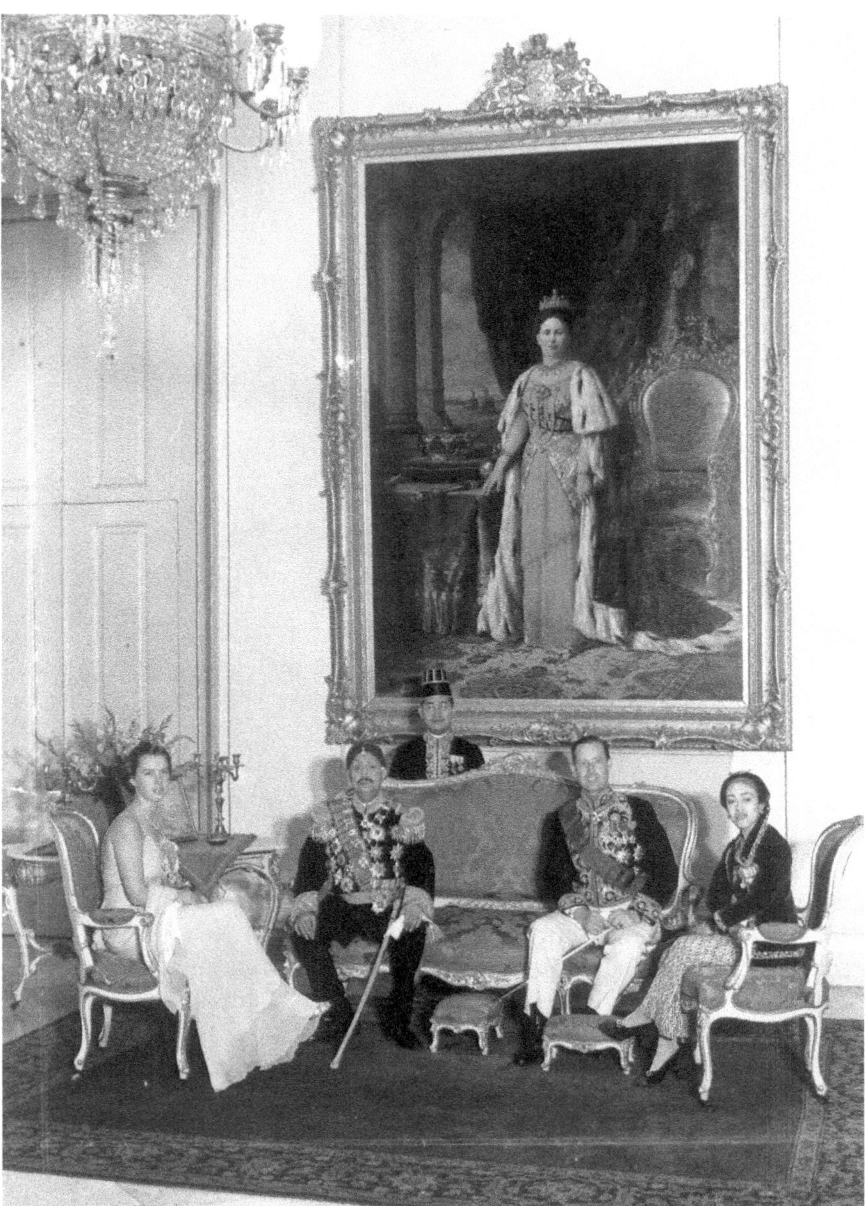

2.2 Unknown photographer, portrait of Queen Wilhelmina at Buitenzorg Palace (Java), behind (seated): Governor-General A. W. L. Tjarda van Starkenborgh Stachouwer, *susuhunan* Pakubuwono X and their daughters, c. 1938

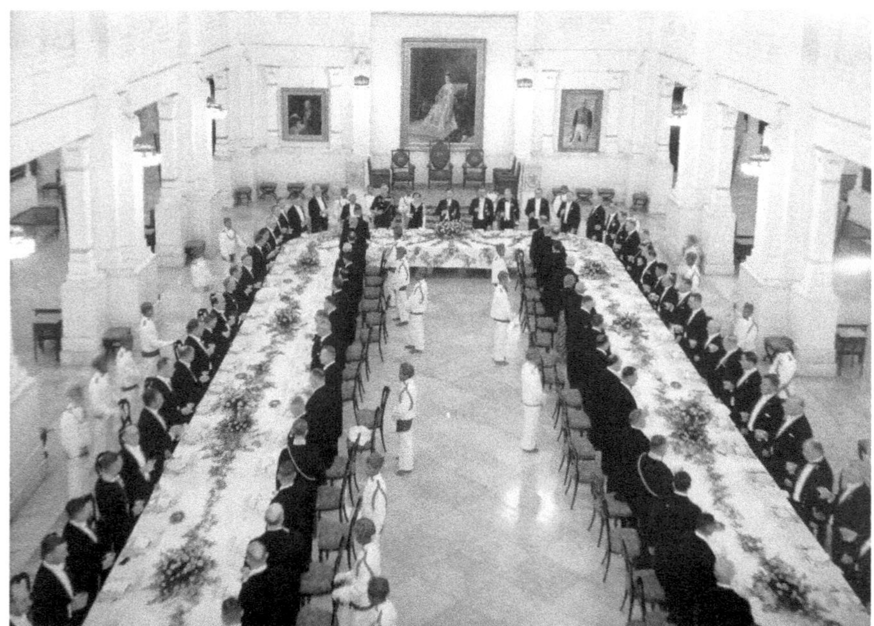

2.3   Unknown photographer, state portrait of Wilhelmina by Pieter de Josselink de Jong (1900) at Rijswijk Palace, Batavia (Java), 31 August, c. 1936–40

conclusion to the long and bitter war of Dutch conquest over Aceh that had begun in 1873. A state portrait of the young queen stood behind Van Heutsz and his men at the subjection ceremony, where the sultan was compelled to read out, in Malay, a pledge of loyalty to 'the representative of Her Majesty the Queen' (figure 2.4).[24] The photographer present, C. B. Nieuwenhuis (1863–1922), made sure to include the portrait in all the images he took of the occasion. The photograph was evidently much copied.[25] One of Nieuwenhuis's works was reproduced in the major commemorative book published in the Indies for Wilhelmina's silver jubilee in 1923.[26] The queen was a great admirer of Van Heutsz, whom she feted at length in her 1959 memoir, and it is likely that she was gratified at her symbolic attendance at his career-making moment.[27]

Wilhelmina was also pictorially present in July 1946, when the last viceroy of the Indies, Governor-General Hubertus van Mook (served 1942–48), presided over the Malino Conference in Makassar.[28] The Indonesian National Revolution was under way, a long-drawn-out conflict that followed from the Dutch refusal to accept Indonesia's

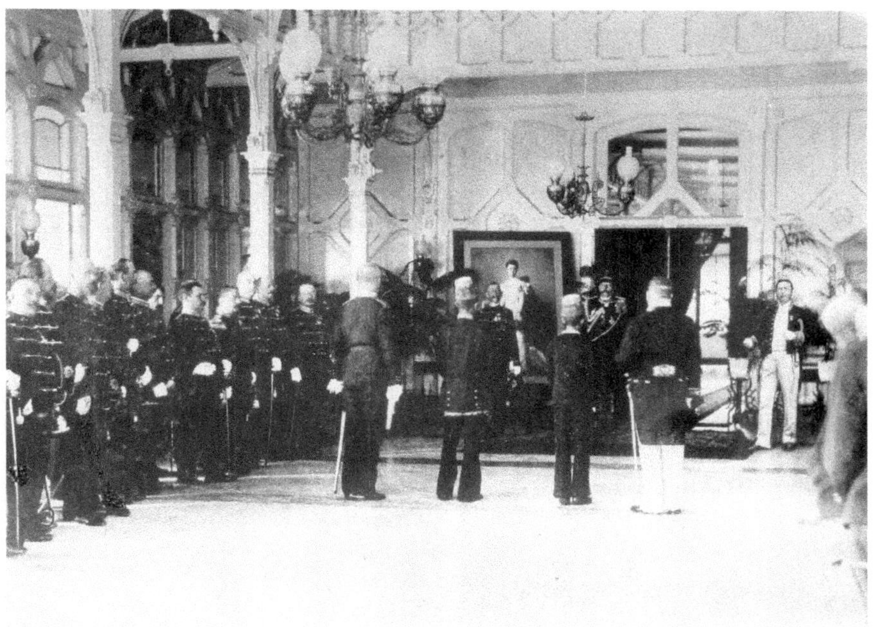

2.4 C. B. Nieuwenhuis, surrender of the Sultan of Aceh, Muhammad Daud Sjah II at Kutaradja (Aceh), 1903

declaration of independence in August 1945. At Malino, Van Mook first proposed the notion of a federation of East Indonesian states with strong links to the Netherlands. He addressed the delegates with a modestly sized, framed portrait of Wilhelmina mounted on a wall behind him (figure 2.5). Times had certainly changed. Wilhelmina's portrait had aged between these two colonial wars which book-ended her reign, the earlier for Aceh, and the later for the whole archipelago. Van Mook stood not in the palaces of his forbears, in what Republicans had renamed Jakarta (Batavia) and Bogor (Buitenzorg), but at a governor's residence on Sulawesi, where Dutch authority was momentarily secure. He delivered his speech in the standard attire of the male office worker – trousers, shirt and tie; no brocaded jacket, and with only two European attendants, no retinue of Javanese servants. It was not at that time assured that the East Indies colonies would cede from the Kingdom of the Netherlands. Yet at Malino and at other key moments throughout his career,[29] the portrait of the queen hovering behind Van Mook conferred the same status on him as his more lavishly appointed predecessors. He remained her *onderkoning*, even as her empire contracted.

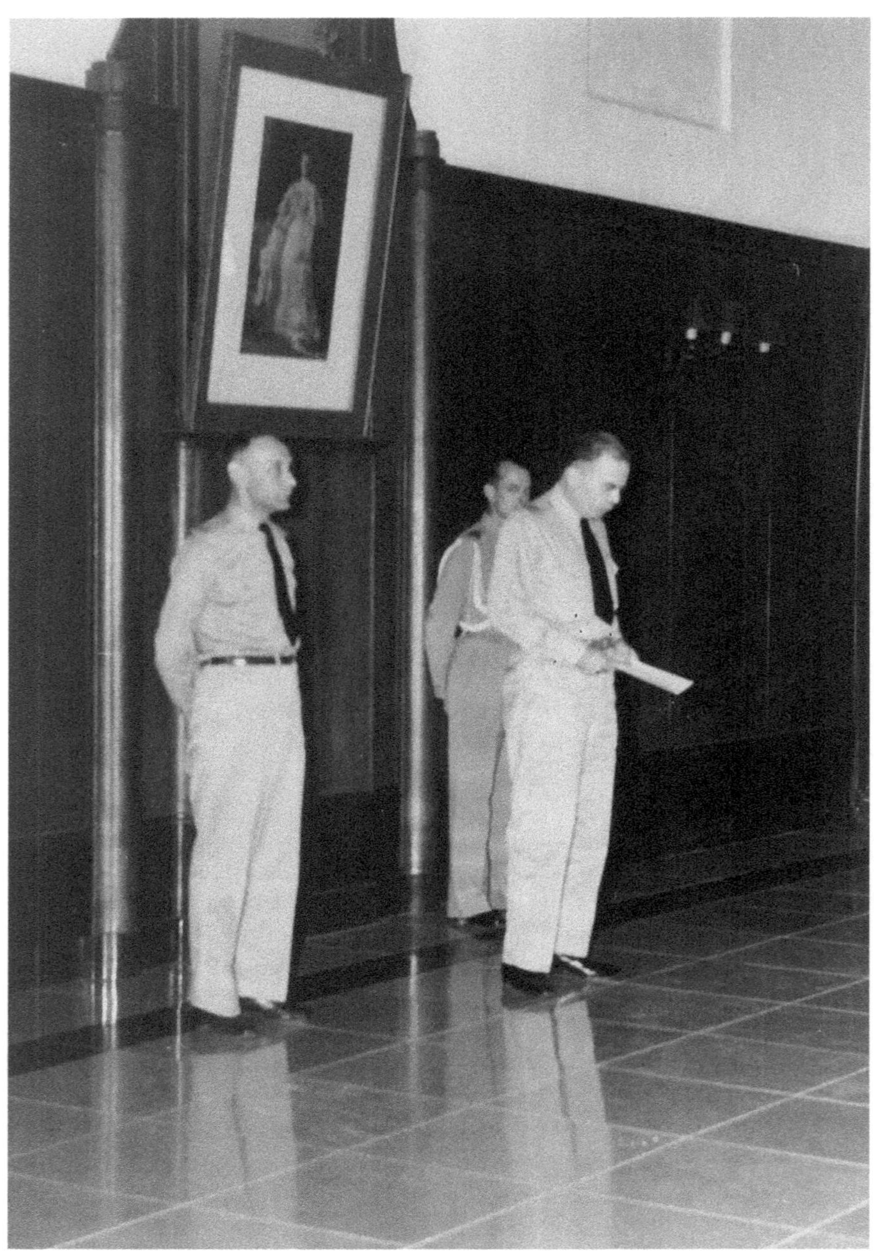

2.5 Unknown photographer, Governor-General Hubertus van Mook at the Malino Conference, Makassar, July 1946

Dutch officials, Javanese royals and portraits of the queen

When agents of the Dutch East Indies Company were first establishing their coastal networks in Asia during the early seventeenth century, they were marginal to the Indigenous worlds that they sought to insert themselves into and profit from. The sultanates of Central Java, which are discussed throughout this book, were based in mountainous, fertile interiors where the powers of monarchs had historically been derived from the labour they could tax or command to work rice fields and maintain infrastructure. At first contact with the Dutch these kingdoms were already Islamic. However, the rulers' divine authority continued to draw upon the sacred mountains that circled their lands. These landscapes were steeped in animistic and Hindu-Buddhist cosmologies, as attested by the great temple complexes of Prambanan and Borobudur, built by the Sanjaya and Sailendra dynasties, respectively, in the ninth century CE. The chronicles (*babad*) composed at Central Javanese courts combine the mythologies and histories of these dynasties, including their descent from the gods, conversion to Islam and encounters with the Dutch. Their textiles, manuscripts, literature and dramatic arts exemplify the syncretic religious and cultural traditions that the royal houses of Central Java share with other South-east Asian courts. Their encounters with Europe, and particularly with Dutch colonists, are evident in the assimilation of Western costume into rulers' formal dress, the adoption of photography in their courts, and the rich record of gift and letter exchanges between European and Indigenous royal houses.[30]

During Wilhelmina's reign, Indigenous princes, sultans and rajas throughout the Indonesian archipelago still numbered in their hundreds, but all were formally subject to Dutch authority. A patchwork of political relations between these rulers and the colonial state had been cobbled together over centuries of Dutch expansion, changing alliances, processes of negotiation and wars of subjugation. In the Princely States (*vorstenlanden*) of Central Java, the kings and princes of Surakarta (the Pakubuwono and Mangkunegoro) and Yogyakarta (Sultan Hamengkubuwono and the Pakualam) were permitted to keep their courts and many of their ceremonial privileges. Yet between 1757 and 1830 they had progressively lost their real power. The Dutch proscribed access to the major sources of these rulers' revenue in the hinterland (*mancanegoro*) around their palaces, banned them from raising their own militias and conducting diplomacy, forbade them from independently naming their successors, and largely restricted these royals to the *kraton* (palace compound).[31] The rulers' rights and responsibilities were renegotiated with Dutch officials at every succession.

At the time of Wilhelmina's inauguration, most other Indigenous royals were subjected to Dutch rule through a standard treaty (*korte verklaring* or 'short declaration'),[32] and were directly answerable to the governor-general. Many of the territories of the so-called *zelf-bestuurders* ('self-governors') were in the 'Outer Provinces' (*Buitengewesten*), a term referring to all the islands that were part of the Netherlands Indies but beyond Java. Indeed, the Indonesian archipelago had for centuries been organised by Dutch authorities into a hierarchy of administrative units. Larger islands generally constituted an entire province, which was subdivided into residencies and districts, each headed by Dutch officials working in concert with Indigenous counterparts drawn from local aristocratic families.[33] The progressive co-optation of minor royals into Dutch structures of governance, culminating in their salaried employment as bureaucrats in the late nineteenth century, has been charted for the *bupati* (regent) families of Java by Heather Sutherland.[34] During Wilhelmina's reign, the close doubling of European and Indigenous hierarchies was most evident on Java and Madura. By contrast, in the Outer Provinces the administrative structure was flatter. That is, lower-ranking European officials often had larger jurisdictions, fewer superiors to report to and more Indigenous administrators to consult than their counterparts on Java.[35] Throughout the Indies, European officials always monopolised the executive levels of government, even after the decentralisation reforms of 1905, when Indigenous officials could be elected rather than appointed to some government bodies such as regional or local councils.[36]

The Princely States of Central Java had exceptional status within the Netherlands Indies. These were 'indirectly' ruled by the colonial administration, and although legally subject to Dutch authority, officials contended here with Indigenous kings and princes who reported only to the governor-general and were formally sovereigns of their own domain. The photographic encounters between Central Java's royals and the Dutch monarchy are the subject of Chapter 5. In the archival collections of Dutch colonial officials, photographs of portraits of the queen at royal celebrations are surprisingly rare. Even the governor of Yogyakarta, P. R. W. van Gesseler Verschuir (served 1928–33), neither photographed nor mentioned the use of the queen's portrait in any ceremonies at his residence or the sultan's palace. The omission was unusual for him, given that he was highly decorated with royal orders and meticulously kept programmes, seating plans, speeches, press clippings and photographs from the *koninginnedag* festivities he presided over.[37] In an album of photographs made at Studio Zindler in Yogyakarta, which was presented to Governor Wouter Abbenhuis as he left his post in September 1940, a photograph shows his predecessor, Johannes

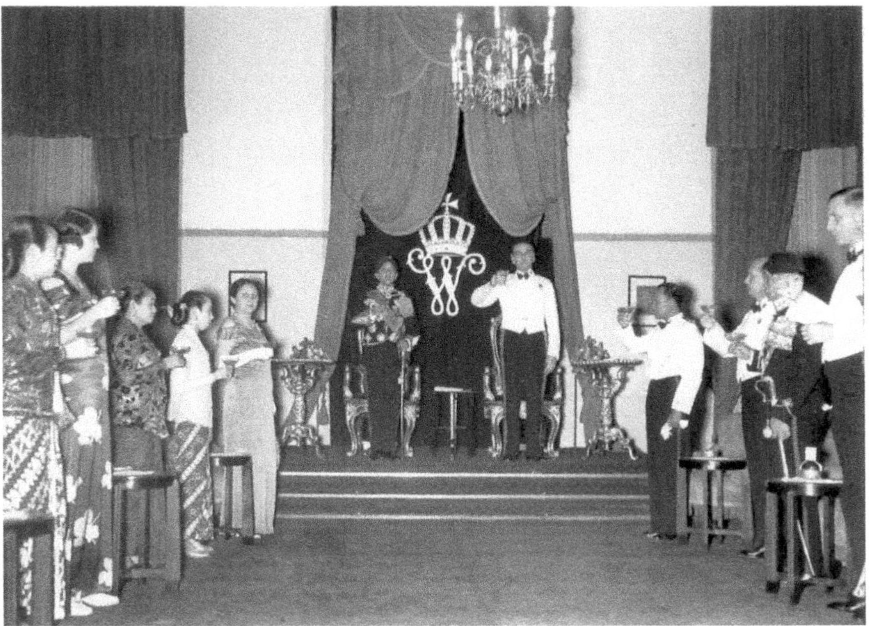

2.6 Unknown photographer, Sultan Hamengku Buwono VIII and Governor Bijleveld raise a toast to Wilhelmina on her fortieth jubilee, Yogyakarta (Java), 1938

Bijleveld (served 1934–39), with Sultan Hamengku Buwono VIII on a dais. The two raise a toast to Wilhelmina's forty years on the throne (figure 2.6). Where a portrait of the queen could easily have been – indeed, would almost certainly have hung in many other circumstances – a large crowned 'W' instead forms the backdrop. The visual focus in photographs of public festivals for the Dutch monarchy in the Princely States was thus on the *partnership* between the Dutch official and his royal Javanese counterpart. This relationship was officially constituted in father–son terms between Dutch governor and Javanese king, respectively, but it also had strangely marital connotations. The Dutch official and the Javanese royal standing side-by-side with linked arms as though in a wedding photograph, as John Monfries perceptively notes, in fact became the iconic photographic image of colonial rule in the Indies (figure 2.7).[38] Photographs in the collections of colonial officials struck a delicate balance, striving to ceremonially uphold the dignity of Javanese rulers while integrating themselves – the agents of the Javanese aristocracy's political, economic and military demise – into the picture.[39]

The fraught relationship between the Dutch resident (who became a 'governor' in 1928) and the kings and princes of Central Java had its

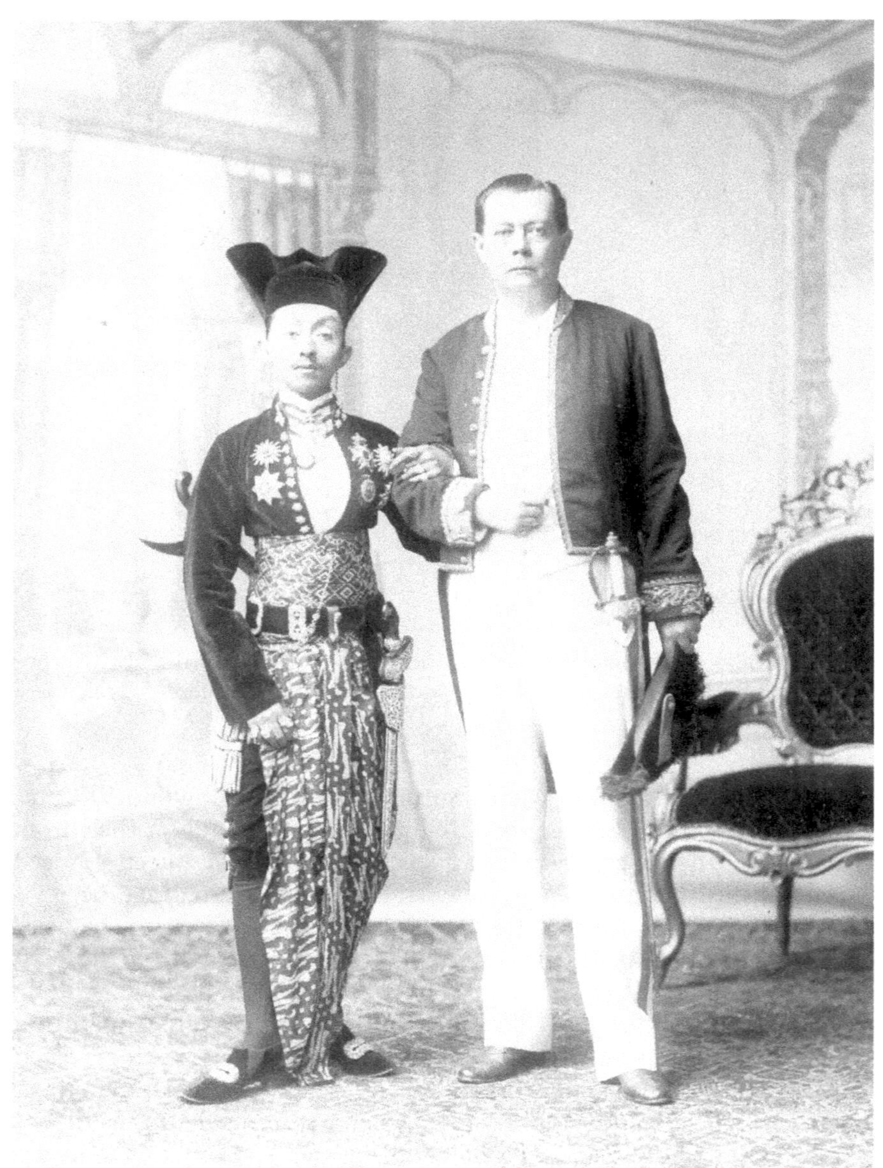

2.7 Studio Charls & Co., Resident Willem de Vogel with a young
Pakubuwono X, Semarang (Java), 1897

origins in the mid-eighteenth century, when the state of Mataram – once the major power on Java – was conquered by the Dutch East India Company and divided into two kingdoms, Surakarta and Yogyakarta. These realms were further subdivided to incorporate two tiny princedoms, the Mangkunegaran in Surakarta in 1757, and the Pakualaman in Yogyakarta in 1813. In the mid-1820s Prince Dipenogoro, a pretender to the sultanate of Yogyakarta – now a hero of nationalist Indonesian history – led a revolt against Dutch rule. Diponegoro was arrested by the Dutch in 1829, and by 1830 the rebellion was quashed. The powers of the four Princely States were progressively constrained during the reassertion of Dutch control. The courts' outer territories (*mancanegoro*) were confiscated in exchange for monetary compensation, making the rulers of Central Java financially dependent on the Dutch government. Technically, they were now also vassals to the Dutch monarch. It was the colonial administration that approved the succession of kings and princes, and conducted their foreign policy.[40] In the words of the eminent Australian Javanist, Stuart Robson:

> the Sultan 'ruled' only by the grace of the colonial government; each generation had to swear allegiance to the Dutch throne, and at each change the noose was twisted even tighter. The Sultan was only a 'Highness', whereas the Dutch Queen was a 'Royal Highness' and the Governor was a 'father' of the Sultan … a humiliation in his own home that would never be forgotten.[41]

To maintain the peace, the colonial administration encouraged the pomp and customary authority of the princely courts. Indeed, the historic origins, religious significance and ethnographic detail of *kraton* (palace) ceremonies spawned a thriving scholarship among Dutch and elite Javanese observers who wrote for specialist journals during the early twentieth century.[42] It may well be, therefore, that the absence of prominent portraits of the queen at royal celebrations in the photographic collections of Dutch officials from Central Java is due to a combination of factors: the rise of Javanism in elite circles, on the one hand, and a diplomatic aversion to directly referencing the compromised sovereignty of the Princely States.[43]

Dutch officials, public festivals and portraits of the queen

The earliest visual evidence we have of how portraits of Queen Wilhelmina were used outside elite, official gatherings – that is, at *public* celebrations in the Indies – comes from the work of studio photographers who made luxury albums to mark the occasion in the year that she was inaugurated. In 1898 two major studios in the port city of Surabaya, East Java, sent souvenir albums as coronation gifts for Wilhelmina. Each album was bound in velvet, inscribed with gold lettering, and showed the city's celebrations for the new queen. One was by the Armenian photographer Ohannes Kurkdjian (1851–1903), who opened his Surabaya studio two years after arriving in Java in 1886. His atelier became famous for its lavish corporate albums.[44] Wilhelmina must have been impressed with his efforts, for she rewarded him with a royal warrant in 1900, which bestowed the coveted right to use the title of 'court photographer'.[45] The other album was from the renowned studio of Herman Salzwedel (c. 1855–after 1904), who co-founded his first atelier with the polymath Isidore van Kinsbergen in Batavia in 1878 before going solo in Surabaya the following year. Salzwedel sold this studio and went to China in 1894, then returned to the Indies, where the studio was thereafter run by other photographers under his name.[46]

Studio photographs from early in Wilhelmina's reign show that particular registers of use for audiences of different ethnicities and genders dictated how Wilhelmina was visually represented for her people, even in the same festival in the same city. The Salzwedel and Kurkdjian albums both contained photographs of sculpted busts of the queen mounted in wagons at street pageants in Surabaya (figure 2.8). The bust was a three-dimensional effigy. Each album also showed painted portraits of Wilhelmina on public display, for example, in the Arab quarter of the city. Kurkdjian's photograph shows the men and boys (and a camel) of the Hadrami Arab community, which numbered 3,000 people in 1905, gathered in front of a triumphal arch at the entrance to the district (figure 2.9).[47] Some have theatrically drawn their swords. The portrait in the banner that one man carries appears to have been based on a number of likenesses of Wilhelmina that were in circulation in the late 1890s. These commonly had the queen in *décolleté* (with bare neck and shoulders), the standard dress for European women at gala occasions.[48] Perhaps in deference to Arab Muslim notions of female modesty, Wilhelmina appears in the banner portrait dressed in a chin-high collar, which was typical afternoon dress of the period, not the stuff of state portraits and very different from the effigy used in the street parade.[49] The variance in styles of representation that we see in these two likenesses of Wilhelmina very likely reflect the autonomy given to different communities and their committees in designing how they would contribute to public festivities for the queen in Surabaya. In the Outer Provinces, lower administrative officials from the Dutch civil service were responsible for coordinating and co-starring in celebrations for the Dutch monarchy. Here, as the photographs taken by Van der Jagt in Maluku reveal,[50] the queen's portrait was paraded in public

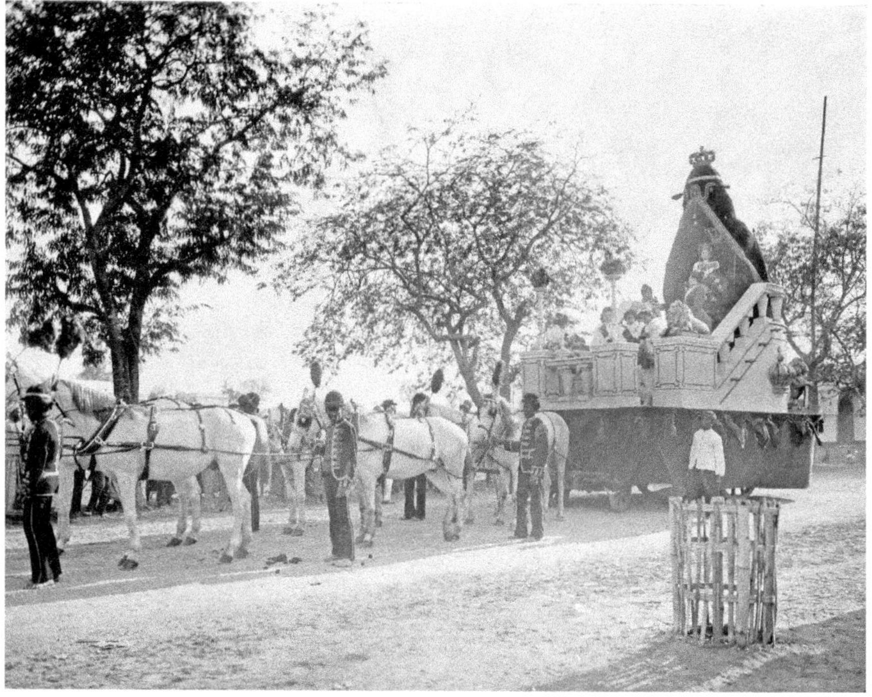

2.8   Studio Herman Salzwedel, bust of Wilhelmina in an allegorical
procession for the inauguration celebrations, Surabaya (Java),
31 August–6 September 1898

for crowds to see, or for groups of important people to have their
photographs taken with.

As hand-held cameras proliferated in the 1920s, studios lost their
monopoly on photography, and amateur sources from a wider range of
people reveal how public festivals proceeded. Dutch officials were among
the producers of many such photographs, which survive in private
collections and in government archives. A particularly rich record exists
in the photographs of Gerard Louwrens Tichelman (1893–1962), who
worked for the *Binnenlandsch Bestuur* (Interior Administration), the
Dutch colonial civil service. He served in Maluku (1916–22), Dutch
Borneo (1923–29) and finally Sumatra (1931–37) before relocating to
Amsterdam and joining the Colonial Institute as a conservator and
archivist for their ethnographic collections. Tichelman made twelve
photograph albums for personal use spanning the Indies part of his
career.[51] Beginning in 1920, four of the albums document his participation
in *koninginnedag* celebrations.[52] Around this time, Tichelman began

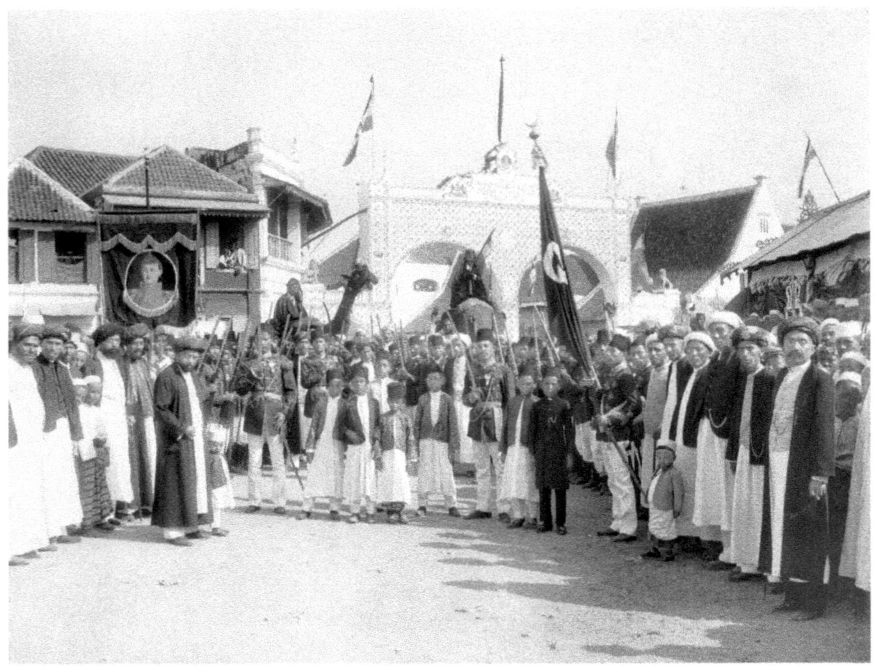

2.9 Onnes Kurkdjian, celebrations in the Arab quarter for the inauguration of Queen Wilhelmina, Surabaya (Java), 31 August–6 September 1898

to note the annual Queen's Day week in his reports to superiors.[53] In the mid-1920s, while stationed in Borneo, he began to collect festival memorabilia such as programmes of events.[54] Tichelman's growing attentiveness to *koninginnedag* follows the wider trend of mounting interest among Dutch authorities in the Indies after the silver jubilee year of 1923, a milestone in Wilhelmina's reign. Colonial officials throughout the Indies took a more orchestrated approach to the festival from this time onwards.

Tichelman's professional stake in the festival increased as he advanced in his own career. From 1923 to 1926 he was posted at Kota Baru on the South-east Coast Residency of Borneo. He served here as *gezaghebber* – literally, 'holder of authority', the entry-level post of Dutch officials in the *Binnenlandsch Bestuur*. This rank was invented for the Outer Provinces, where rapid Dutch expansion in the early twentieth century put the civil service under pressure. To meet demand for officials at the lowest possible cost, the junior ranks of government were inflated. In Borneo, for example, Tichelman reported directly to the Resident rather than to an Assistant Resident.[55] It was here that he first began

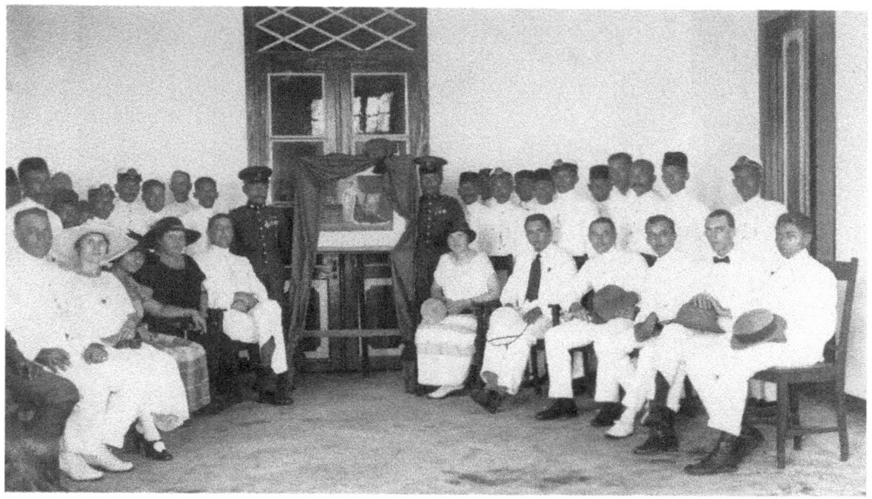

2.10 Collection G. L. Tichelman, officials commemorate *koninginnedag* at Kota Baru (Dutch Borneo), 1924

to regularly take photographs of *koninginnedag* celebrations. These images show how portraits of the queen were used in provincial celebrations. Officials paid their respects to images of the queen, engaged with her portrait in a performance as though it were an effigy, and imbibed some of the queen's authority in the process.

At celebrations in Kota Baru, Borneo, in 1924, Tichelman photographed a painting of uncertain origin, possibly a composite copy of two known portraits of the queen, inside the residency building where government business was conducted.[56] The portrait was propped on an easel, with a curtain parted over it as though a precious object was being unveiled (figure 2.10). On either side, Indigenous officials stood guard as though protecting the portrait. They were surrounded by local and European officials, the former standing in the background and the latter seated in the foreground with their wives. Together, the party forms a guard of honour around the portrait of the queen – a quite different composition to the posture that governors-general adopted, posing with fixed paintings of the queen behind them as though beneficiaries of her enduring support. In the Outer Provinces, officials incorporated the portrait of Wilhelmina more materially into their midst, taking advantage of its portability to bring them together and make a focal point for their commemoration of the occasion.

The following year, in 1925, photographs in Tichelman's personal album show that the official party left the building with this same

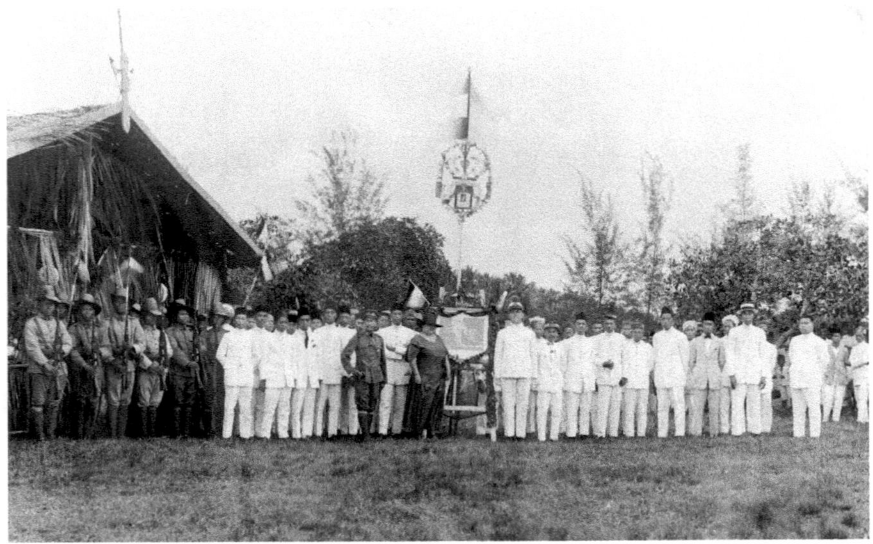

2.11 Collection G. L. Tichelman, officials pose with a portrait of Queen Wilhelmina on *koninginnedag* at Kota Baru (Dutch Borneo), 1925

portrait of the queen. A larger company was photographed outside, where they potentially drew a crowd of spectators who could watch the performance of the photograph being made (figure 2.11). Being outdoors also allowed more to be done to the portrait. Here, its protective curtain was removed and the object was decorated with woven palm fronds, a couple of Dutch flags and a small crown. Mounted on a pole above was another, smaller portrait (possibly a photograph, although it is too small to identify), framed in a garlanded crown and more Dutch flags. Armed guards cluster to the left of the white-clad, mostly Indigenous officials massed on either side of the portrait. Two dark figures to the left stand out: another guard and Tichelman's wife. The tall European official standing to attention on the opposite side is Tichelman himself. He and his wife are the only two Europeans in the photograph, and the closest to the portrait of the queen. Tichelman's official role and ethnic solidarity with Wilhelmina permit this proximity.

In May 1926 Tichelman was promoted to *controleur* and transferred to the Residency of South and East Borneo, where he was based in the town of Barabai. His district had a large population of 100,000 people, where Europeans comprised a tiny minority, just 30 people.[57] Barabai was where Tichelman assumed direct responsibility for choreographing the celebrations and took the largest number of photographs of

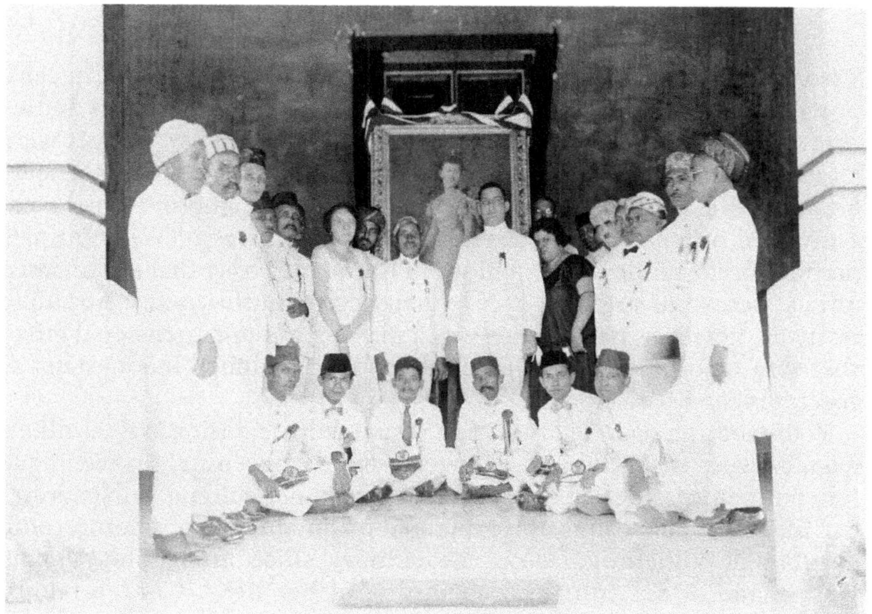

2.12 Collection G. L. Tichelman, officials pose with a portrait of Queen Wilhelmina on *koninginnedag* at Barabai (Dutch Borneo), 1926

koninginnedag. He had been promoted and was also president of the district festival committee.[58] So concerned with the success of the celebrations under his command was Tichelman that he used his own photographs to illustrate a report to the resident on the 1928 celebrations.[59] His photographs from this period reveal the town to have been in possession of a large reproduction of a state portrait by the painter David Bles (1821–99), mounted in an ornate gilded frame. It was an odd choice for a copy. The original painting dates from 1897, and therefore shows a very young Wilhelmina as a princess, before she was even inaugurated.[60] The portrait appears to have hung in the council building of Barabai, where Tichelman presided over meetings with Indigenous officials.[61] Apart from its use here, the painting was also brought out for group portraits at Queen's Day celebrations. It seems not to have been regarded as quite so portable as the painting used at Kota Baru. In Tichelman's albums it is photographed three times under the eaves of the Assistant Residency, where he lived and had his office.[62] Indonesian and Dutch officials cluster around the portrait in these photographs (the resident, De Haan, is pictured beside Tichelman's wife), but Tichelman is once again in direct proximity (figure 2.12).

The queen's portrait in colonial festivals

Two striking features emerge in photographs that show how the queen's portrait was used at royal celebrations in the Netherlands Indies throughout her reign. One is that painted versions of her portrait were clearly preferred, both at gala and public occasions, even after photography became an everyday medium. The second is that photographs reveal a division of labour between 'high' and public uses of Wilhelmina's portrait. In the former context, it was a flat, static object that ornamented official occasions presided over by her viceroy in the Indies. At public festivals, however, her portrait was a moving, three-dimensional effigy that was incorporated into proceedings that included Indonesians as spectators and participants.

A distinction operated in Indies' visual culture during Wilhelmina's reign between the medium used to represent the queen and the technique for commemorating the encounters between her colonial subjects and her likeness. This cannot be explained by an absence of photographic portraits of Wilhelmina. Quite the contrary, since official photographs were made of her from the beginning of her life.[63] Contemporary photographic images of Wilhelmina circulated in the Indies in the form of postcards, in commemorative books and, beginning in the mid-1920s, in newspapers. It could be that a higher status was still accorded painted likenesses – for official purposes, at least – in the Indies.[64] With the notable exception of those that hung in the palaces of the governor-general on Java, few of the paintings in use appear to have been originals. Most were copies, some of them composites, of portraits made in the Netherlands. Ironically, the copies would probably have been made from photographs of paintings.[65] The only state portrait of Wilhelmina ever made by an Indies painter, the famous Bali artist Willem Hofker (1902–81), was likewise based on a photograph of the queen, even though he did have opportunities to see her in person.[66]

C. O. van Kesteren, the curator of an exhibition of Wilhelmina's own paintings in the Indies in 1933, complained in one of his weekly reports to the queen's personal secretary that good likenesses of the monarch were hard to come by.[67] The image of the queen that dominated at royal celebrations in the Indies was almost always 'out of date' and, in the technical sense, unauthorised: a likeness of a likeness, showing a much younger queen than the living version – even, in the case of the Bles copy used in Barabai, an uncrowned Wilhelmina. Well might authorities have been worried, then, that colonial audiences would be disappointed by the difference between reality and image should Wilhelmina make a personal tour of the colony. The absence of the queen from her colonies was therefore not just decreed from the

Netherlands. It was also managed by the uses of her image in the Indies which, in some ways, came to substitute a corporeal version of the queen with a material image that could be adapted for different audiences and, in some cases, used as an effigy.

Conclusion

This examination of the social uses of Wilhelmina's portraits in the Indies is the first time that European royal celebrations in colonial contexts have been subjected to an analysis more typically reserved for studies of non-European monarchies. Photographs taken of, by and for colonial authorities at royal celebrations for the Dutch monarchy during Queen Wilhelmina's reign confirm how colonial officials orchestrated royal spectacles to reinforce *local* authority by visual association with the distant monarch. However, taking an approach that attends more closely to the materiality of images – the ritual uses of the queen's painted image in live celebrations in the Indies, as recorded in photographs – enables sharper insights into the interactions between colonial authorities, representations of the monarch, live audiences and the spectators who viewed the photographic commemoration of the ritual afterwards.

Photographs show that a variety of rituals in fact developed around Wilhelmina's portrait in the Indies. These differed according to the rank of the Dutch official orchestrating or co-starring in events, the status of their Indigenous counterparts, and where in the archipelago the celebration occurred. For the governor-general, at the centre of power on Java, large-scale, permanently fixed, state portraits of the queen, custom-made for use at public audiences in his palaces, reinforced his peerless position in the Indies and the power he derived from being the monarch's *onderkoning*. His interchangeability with the queen was visually reinforced by lower authorities (Indigenous as well as European) when he toured the provinces, where the same street decorations were used for his visits as for *koninginnedag*. In the Princely States of Central Java, the delicate balance between Dutch claims to sovereign power and the appearance of Javanese royal autonomy was visually maintained through occluding the queen's image in favour of showing the partnership between European and Indigenous rulers. The contradictions arising from the early subjugation of the *vorstenlanden* in the history of the modern colonial state, and the concentrated preservation of an Indigenous royalty here, appear to have been resolved by simply not visually referring to the queen where possible. If Javanese kings and princes wished to engage with the queen photographically – and they did, as Chapter 5 demonstrates – they did so privately, through gift offerings that afforded them some agency.

In the Outer Provinces, where colonial officials were removed from the Dutch centre of power, images of the queen were invoked in public spectacles differently again. Here political relations between European and Indigenous authorities varied from district to district, and the Dutch comprised a small demographic minority with jurisdiction over vast, diverse and diffuse Asian populations. A great variety of local traditions were invented for royal celebrations, particularly as regards the ritual use of representations of the queen. In provincial festivals, painted portraits of Wilhelmina ranged from ephemeral decorations mounted on banners in the open air to official portraits that were hung in government buildings in regional capitals. Crucially, all these variants were subject to manipulation: they were hand-made by unknown painters of disparate skills, frequently removed from walls, adorned and accompanied, moved outdoors and carried in processions as an effigy, surrounded by shifting crowds of dignitaries, guarded, saluted, serenaded and, most of all, *photographed*. The materiality of the queen's portraits and the memorial functions of the photographs that were taken of them at colonial rituals were significant components of royal celebrations in the colonies.

These ritual and photographic acts brought the absent monarch among her colonial subjects, and into proximity with those who ruled in her name. The conspicuous inclusion of the queen's portrait in royal celebrations everywhere except the Princely States was key to commemorating the event in photographs for private as well as public consumption, in personal photographs that were made and exchanged by officials, as well as in professional photographs that were destined for wider circulation. Of course, it would have been preferable had the monarch herself been present; and it was not for want of trying on the part of Indies authorities that Dutch royals remained absent from the Netherland's largest and most important overseas possession at the peak of its extent. Of all the technologies that made the Dutch monarchy proximate to its colonial subjects, however, photography was the tool that enabled the most flexible, mutable and creative engagement among and between herself and the people of the Indies.

Notes

1 In 1910 a step-brother of Prince Hendrik, Duke Johann Albrecht of Mecklenburg (1857–1920), also toured the Indies. He visited the Sultan of Yogyakarta, Hamengku Buwono VII, as recorded by the court photographer Cephas: KITLV shelf marks 151243, 27791.
2 I mean 'German' in the post-unification, national sense. The pre-monarchical, dynastic origins of the House of Oranje-Nassau are well established as being mostly 'German': M. E. Hay, 'Russia, Britain and the House of Nassau: the re-establishment of the

Orange dynasty in the Netherlands, March–November 1813', *BMGN/Low Countries Historical Review*, 133.1 (2018): 3–21, at pp. 12–16.

3   M. B. van der Jagt, *Mollukkenreis 10 September–3 November 1923* (Den Haag, 1935), p. 83.
4   Van der Jagt, *Mollukkenreis*, pp. 2, 4.
5   Van der Jagt, *Mollukkenreis*, pp. 81–2, 85.
6   Van der Jagt, *Mollukkenreis*, p. 20.
7   Van der Jagt, *Mollukkenreis*, p. 7.
8   R. Aldrich, *Vestiges of Colonial Empire in France* (New York: Palgrave Macmillan, 2005); D. Cannadine, *Ornamentalism: How the British Saw Their Empire* (London: Allen Lane, 2001), pp. 102–5; G. Oostindie, *De parels en de kroon; Het koningshuis en de koloniën* (Amsterdam: De Bezige Bij, 2006), pp. 48, 52–3, 70, 81, 120; R. Aldrich and C. McCreery, 'European sovereigns and their empires "beyond the seas"', in R. Aldrich and C. McCreery (eds), *Crowns and Colonies: European Monarchies and Overseas Empires* (Manchester: Manchester University Press, 2016), pp. 1–26, at p. 17.
9   Oostindie, *De parels en de kroon*, pp. 58, 70, 73, 88, 92–5, 100.
10   Aldrich and McCreery, 'European sovereigns and their empires', pp. 11, 18, 19.
11   S. Willcock, 'Composing the spectacle: colonial portraiture and the coronation durbars of British India, 1877–1911', *Art History*, 40.1 (2017): 132–55; Cannadine, *Ornamentalism*; D. Cannadine, 'The context, performance and meaning of ritual: the British monarchy and the "invention of tradition", ca. 1820–1977', in E. Hobsbawm and T. Ranger (eds), *The Invention of Tradition* (Cambridge: Cambridge University Press, 1983), pp. 101–64; B. S. Cohn, 'Representing authority in Victorian India', in E. Hobsbawm and T. Ranger (eds), *The Invention of Tradition* (Cambridge: Cambridge University Press, 1983), pp. 165–209.
12   G. Batchen, *Forget Me Not: Photography and Remembrance* (Amsterdam/New York: Van Gogh Museum/Princeton Architectural Press, 2004), p. 10.
13   On the noble origins of many governors-general in the British empire, see Cannadine, *Ornamentalism*, pp. 94, 114–15.
14   Dutch governors-general of the East Indies during Wilhelmina's reign who were *jonkheren* were Carel Herman Aart van der Wijck (served 1893–99), Andries Cornelis de Jonge (served 1926–31), Bonifacius Cornelis de Jonge (served 1931–36) and Tjarda van Starkenborgh Stachouwer (served 1936–42). Johan Paul van Limburg Stirum (served 1916–21) was a count.
15   Oostindie, *De parels en de kroon*, p. 48.
16   Van Starkenborgh further held that 'The GG had his own responsibility and stood in his turn opposite the Council of the Indies [*Volksraad*], although this was not entirely comparable with the parliament': quoted in M. Ravesloot, 'Jonkheer A.W.L. Tjarda van Starkenborgh Stachouwer 1888–1978; Landvoogt in tijden van crisis', MA dissertation, Universiteit Utrecht, 2010, p. 46.
17   The public decorations recorded by G. L. Tichelman in Borneo, whose photographs are discussed below, for the tour of Governor-General A. C. D de Graeff to Borneo in 1928 are a good example: Nl-HaNA, Tichelman 2.21.097.01, inv. nr. 19: *dagboek*, Barabai (1928). See also an album compiled by youths in the Surabaya chapter of the nationalist organisation *Jong Java* in the early 1920s. It shows the adaptation of public decorations for the visit of Governor-General Dirk Fock: KITLV Album 914, shelf marks 45755, 45758–60, 45764.
18   The photographer is unknown, but it must have been someone in the employ of the sultan: KITLV Album 44.
19   See KITLV Album 44, shelf mark 12392, which shows a bust portrait of Wilhelmina of unknown origin, and shelf mark 12389, a full-length portrait that is closely based on an oil painting by Thérèse Schwartze (1851–1918), made of Wilhelmina for her inauguration in 1898, now held at the Paleis Het Loo. The album also has one photograph that shows a portrait of Van Limburg Stirum on an arch: shelf mark 12393.
20   It could well be that it was made by an Indies painter and was lost permanently some time between the Japanese occupation of the Indies (1942–45) and the Indonesian

revolution (1945–49). After the transfer of sovereignty in December 1949, many paintings were removed from the former governor-general's palaces on Java, and it could be that some were lost, stolen or destroyed.

21 KITLV shelf mark 60023406; see also KIT inv. nr. TM-60039462.

22 Netherlands Institute for Art History, https://rkd.nl/en/explore/portraits/record?quer y=wilhelmina+de+josselin+de+jong&start=2 (last accessed 14 November 2017). The painting now hangs at the Paleis Het Loo in the Netherlands.

23 See, for example, photographs showing Van Limburg Stirum addressing an audience c. 1920, KITLV shelf mark 27482; A. C. D. de Graeff addressing the President of the Council of the Indies on Queen's Day in 1929, KIT TM-10001641; and Tjarda van Starkenborgh Stachouwer at a public audience in front of the portrait on Queen's Day in 1940, KITLV shelf mark 32860.

24 A. Stolwijk, *Atjeh; Het verhaal van de bloedigste strijd uit de Nederlandse koloniale geschiedenis* (Amsterdam: Prometheus, 2016), pp. 197–8.

25 See copies in KITLV Album 99, shelf mark 82864, and Album 744, shelf mark 90378. Nieuwenhuis also made group portraits of all present with the Wilhelmina portrait in the background, see Tropenmusem TM-10001949, TM-10001513. The photograph in figure 2.4 has recently been discussed in the context of a longer history of images of Indonesian leaders captured by the Dutch in colonial military campaigns in P. Bijl, *Emerging Memory: Photographs of Colonial Atrocity in Dutch Cultural Remembrance* (Amsterdam: Amsterdam University Press, 2015), pp. 54–60.

26 L. F. van Gent, W. A. Penard and D. A. Pinkes (eds), *Gedenkboek voor Nederlandsch-Indië ter gelegenheid van het regeeringsjubileum van HM de Koningin* (Batavia: G. Kolff & Co., 1923), plate 9. Aceh was in fact never entirely subdued by the Dutch. Some 4,000 troops remained stationed there until the Japanese occupation commenced in 1942, and after the Japanese capitulation in 1945 it was the only province that Dutch authorities did not attempt to reclaim: A. Reid, *An Indonesian Frontier: Acehnese and Other Histories of Sumatra* (Singapore: Singapore University Press, 2005), pp. 339–40; M. C. Ricklefs, *A History of Modern Indonesia since c. 1200* (Stanford, CA: Stanford University Press, 4th edn, 2008), p. 189.

27 Queen Wilhelmina, *Eenzaam maar niet alleen* (Amsterdam: Uitgeverij W. ten Have, 1959), pp. 112–13.

28 T. van den Berge, *H.J. van Mook; een vrij en gelukkig Indonesië* (Bussum: Thoth, 2014), pp. 225–6.

29 Portraits of Wilhelmina also hung in Van Mook's presence in the meeting room of the Council of the Indies (see the photograph, taken in 1930, in Van den Berge, *H.J. van Mook*, p. 103), and in the meeting room at Camp Columbia, Brisbane (Australia), where the Dutch administration was based in 1945 (ibid., p. 196). Van Mook also got his chance to stand beneath the De Josselink de Jong portrait at Rijswijk Palace in March 1947 (ibid., p. 239), when he signed the document that withdrew from the key terms of the Linggadjati Agreement recognising Republican rule over Java, Sumatra and Madura. The agreement was formally cancelled when the Dutch commenced the First Police Action (20 July–4 August 1947) a few weeks later.

30 J. G. Taylor, *Indonesia: Peoples and Histories* (New Haven, CT: Yale University Press, 2003); J. Bennett (ed.), *Crescent Moon: Islamic Art and Civilisation in Southeast Asia* (Adelaide/Canberra: Art Gallery of South Australia/National Gallery of Australia, 2006).

31 V. J. H. Houben, *Kraton and Kumpeni: Surakarta and Yogyakarta, 1830–1870* (Leiden: KITLV Press, 1994), pp. 4, 7, 64, 77–8, 93, 138, 351, 354.

32 Ricklefs, *A History of Modern Indonesia*, p. 178; Oostindie, *De parels en de kroon*, p. 48; R. Cribb, 'Introduction: the late colonial state in Indonesia', in R. Cribb (ed.), *The Late Colonial State in Indonesia: Political and Economic Foundations of the Netherlands Indies 1880–1942* (Leiden: KITLV Press, 1994), pp. 1–10, at p. 5. The courts of Central Java were among the very few kingdoms – 16 out of 282 in the late 1930s – where individual, 'long' political and economic contracts were drawn up every time a new king was crowned: B. D. Kurniadi, 'Yogyakarta in decentralised Indonesia: integrating traditional institution in democratic transitions', *Jurnal Ilmu*

Sosial dan Ilmu Politik, 13.2 (2009): 190–20 at p. 192; J. Monfries, *A Prince in a Republic: The Life of Sultan Hamengku Buwono IX of Yogyakarta* (Singapore: ISEAS Publishing, 2015), p. 69.

33   The system whereby territories were ruled by Indigenous leaders in 'partnership' with Dutch counterparts, in a hierarchy of couples, has often been conceived as 'dualistic' because it consisted in native and European arms of government: C. Fasseur and D. H. A. Kolff, 'Some remarks on the development of colonial bureaucracies in India and Indonesia', *Itinerario*, 10.1 (1986): 31–56, at p. 35.

34   H. Sutherland, 'Notes on Java's regent families: Part I', *Indonesia*, 16 (October 1973), 112–47; H. Sutherland, 'Notes on Java's regent families: Part II', *Indonesia*, 17 (April 1974): 1–42; H. Sutherland, *The Making of a Bureaucratic Elite: The Colonial Transformation of the Javanese* Priyayi (Kuala Lumpur and Hong Kong: Heinemann Educational Books (Asia), 1979).

35   H. W. van den Doel, 'Military rule in the Netherlands Indies', in R. Cribb (ed.), *The Late Colonial State in Indonesia: Political and Economic Foundations of the Netherlands Indies 1880–1942* (Leiden: KITLV Press, 1994), pp. 57–78, at pp. 69–71.

36   F. van Anrooij, *De koloniale staat 1854–1942; Gids voor het archief van het ministerie van Koloniën De Indische archipel* (Den Haag: Nationaal Archief, 2009), pp. 17–18, 21–4.

37   NL-HaNA, Gesseler Verschuir, van, 2.21.069, inv. nr. 39; KITLV Album 1292.

38   Monfries, *A Prince in a Republic*, p. 71.

39   J. Pemberton, *On the Subject of 'Java'* (Ithaca, NY: Cornell University Press, 1994), pp. 90–1.

40   Houben, *Kraton and Kumpeni*, pp. 4, 7, 64, 77–8, 93, 138, 351, 354.

41   S. Robson, 'Introduction', in S. Robson (ed.), *The Kraton: Selected Essays on the Javanese Courts* (Leiden: KITLV Press, 2003), pp. ix–xxvi, at p. xix.

42   As Robson notes, the founding of the Java Institute in 1921 and the publications of its periodical *Djåwå*, which flourished up to 1941, encouraged systematic reflection on court traditions in the Princely States: Robson, 'Introduction', p. ix.

43   Exceptions seem to have been made for events that celebrated Juliana while she was crown princess, and therefore no direct competition for Javanese kings. Pakubuwono X attended the dinner for the wedding of Juliana and Bernhard in 1937, which was held at the palace of the governor of Solo, M. J. J. Treur. The *susuhunan* made a gift of a photograph album showing the dinner proceedings to Juliana. It shows a painted wedding portrait of the couple propped on an easel behind the main dining table. Three separate photographs show the *susuhunan*, the governor and their spouses directly in front of the painting: KHA FA/0777A.

44   R. Jongmans and J. van Dijk, 'Photographs from the Netherlands East Indies: changing perspectives, different views', in J. van Dijk et al., *Photographs of the Netherlands East Indies at the Tropenmuseum* (Amsterdam: KIT Tropenmusem, 2012), pp. 15–38, at p. 27.

45   Correspondence with Mieke Jansen, curator of Photographic Collections, Royal Family Archive, The Hague, 18 February 2014. Kurkdjian appears never to have traded on the title he earned.

46   S. Protschky, 'Herman Salzwedel, antiquity and the camera', in G. Newton (ed.), *Garden of the East: Photography in Indonesia 1850s–1940s* (Canberra: National Gallery of Australia, 2014), pp. 68–70, at p. 69.

47   H. W. Dick, *Surabaya, City of Work: A Socioeconomic History, 1900–2000* (Athens, OH: Ohio University Centre for International Studies, 2002), p. 42.

48   I. Montijn, *Hoog geboren; 250 jaar adelijk leven in Nederland* (Amsterdam/Antwerp: Uitgeverij Contact, 2012), pp. 225–6.

49   E. van Braam and E. Elzinga, *Wilhelmina; Koninklijk gekleed 1880–1962* (Zwolle: Waanders Uitgevers, 1998).

50   There are other examples in the archive, such as from Ambon in 1925 (KITLV Album 577, shelf mark 51921), the Lesser Sunda islands c. 1920 (KITLV Album 444, shelf mark 85848) and New Guinea in the early 1950s (KITLV Album 1094, no shelf mark).

51 KITLV Albums 180–90.
52 KITLV Albums 185–9.
53 NL-HaNA, Tichelman 2.21.097.01, inv. nr. 3: *dagboek*, Amahei (1920); and inv. nr. 9: *dagboek*, Tanah Boemboe (1924).
54 In 1926 and 1927 Tichelman kept copies of *koninginnedag* programmes for the first time. They were printed in Malay and were clearly intended to be distributed to the public: KITLV Special Collections, Collectie Tichelman, H814(35).
55 Van den Doel, 'Military rule in the Netherlands Indies', pp. 69–70.
56 Two photographic state portraits of the queen, made by different court photographers in 1912 (one by P. Clausing, the other by Guy de Coral & Co.), appear to be the basis for this painting. Thanks to Mieke Jansen, curator of Photographic Collections at the Royal Archive in The Hague, for advising on this identification.
57 These figures are from the time Tichelman left in 1928: NL-HaNA, Tichelman 2.21.097.01, inv. nr. 21: *Memorie van Overgave*, Barabai (1926–29), p. 57.
58 NL-HaNA, Tichelman 2.21.097.01, inv. nr. 18: *dagboek*, Barabai (1927); and inv. nr. 20: *dagboek*, Barabai (1929).
59 NL-HaNA, Tichelman 2.21.097.01, inv. nr. 19.
60 See Rijksbureau Kunsthistorische Documentatie, https://rkd.nl/nl/explore/images/164609 (last accessed 20 November 2017).
61 KITLV Album 188, unnumbered photographs on the same page as shelf mark 83651.
62 KITLV Album 189, shelf marks 83745, 83746, both taken in 1926, and Album 187, shelf mark 83589, taken in 1927.
63 M. Jansen, 'Koningin Wilhelmina en de fotografie', in M. E. Spliethoff, E. van Heuven-van Nes, M. Jansen and P. Rem, *Koningin Wilhelmina; Schilderijen en tekeningen* (Zwolle: Waanders and Stichting Paleis Het Loo, 2006), pp. 57–68, at p. 58.
64 All the state portraits of governors-general of the Indies were also made by painters: David van Duuren, 'Governors-general and civilians', in M. Scalliet, K. van Brakel, D. van Duuren and J. ten Kate, *Pictures from the Tropics: Paintings by Western Artists during the Dutch Colonial Period in Indonesia* (Amsterdam: KIT Publishers, 1999), pp. 90–102, at pp. 90–8.
65 Many paintings of Wilhelmina, even in the Netherlands, were made from photographs of her.
66 Wilhelmina did not want to sit for Hofker's portrait – an arduous process for the subject, and one that conferred great prestige on the painter – so she had an unofficial photograph sent to him. He was also allowed to observe the queen and make sketches and colour notes while she visited an exhibition (that is, while she was looking at pictures herself). He was also given access to the dress, jewels and chair she would be painted in. Wilhelmina was reportedly content with the likeness when it was complete. While the portrait was owned by the *Koninklijk Paketvaart Maatschappij* (Royal Shipping Company), and hung at their headquarters on the Koningsplein in Batavia from 1938, it was shipped on loan to Amsterdam for an exhibition in 1939, along with 400 colour reproductions of it. Some of these are all that survive of the painting, which was publicly burned in 1942 when the Japanese invaded the Indies: B. Carpenter, *Willem Hofker 1902–1981: Painter of Bali* (Wijk en Aalburg: Pictures Publishers, 1993), pp. 178, 180.
67 Discussed in P. Eckhardt, 'Wij zullen handhaven! De symbolische betekenis van de Nederlandse monarchie in Nederlands-Indië 1918–1940', MA dissertation, University of Amsterdam, 2002, pp. 59–60.

CHAPTER THREE

Family connections: mass photography, monarchy and the making of colonial subjects

An album, barely the size of a hand, commences with a photograph of dawn breaking in the tropics. In black and white, palm trees are silhouetted against high clouds and a dazzling sunrise. A shard of light glimmers on a river in the foreground. The photograph is captioned, 'Irene born, the Indies awakes' (figure 3.1). On the next page someone has written out, in long-hand, a telephone conversation between two friends:

> Batavia, Princess's Birthday 1939
>
> …
>
> Quarter to ten: Ring!!!!!! 'Hello, Kolff office orders here.'
> 'Oh man, stuff your books. You're speaking with Rick. Felicitations boy, we have a Princess.
> I'm bringing my gear to take a few night photographs, bring that coffin [box camera] of yours too, then you can take a few day[time] pictures.'
> 'Good, then come and get me Rick, and likewise felicitations. Until this afternoon then!'
> And we went for a walk: the night photographs are by Rick Baas, the others are by
>
> Your Freek[1]

This album, now in a Dutch archive, was compiled as a tribute on the birth of Irene, the second daughter of Crown Princess Juliana and Prince Bernhard, on 5 August 1939. Being small, the album was eminently portable, and Freek and Rick, the two Dutch-speaking photographer friends, were able to send it to a third person. The 'Irene album', as I shall call it here, might be conceived as a photographic letter, or alternatively, a book of postcards, showing the impromptu tour of Batavia that Freek and Rick embarked on to mark the birth of a Dutch princess. Their journey offers a glimpse of the colonial capital in the late 1930s. Indonesians on bicycles share the streets with motor cars,

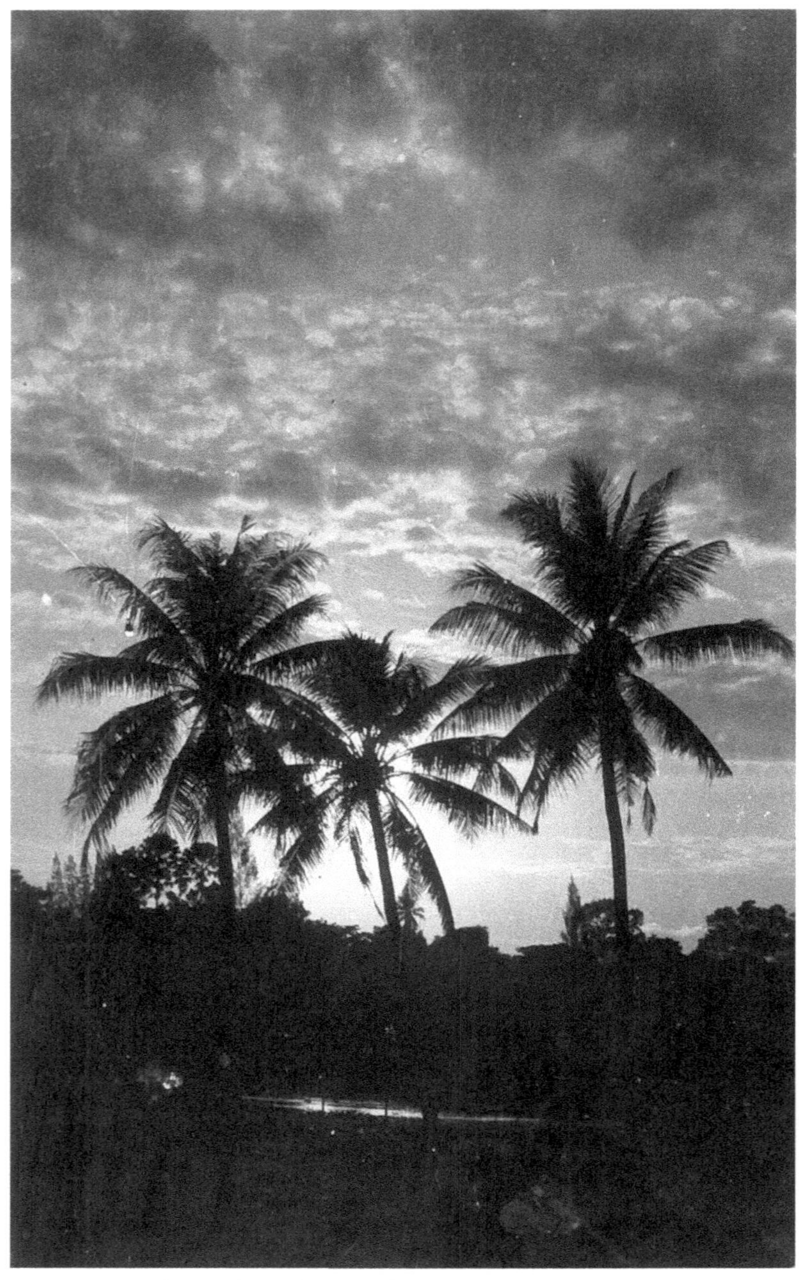

3.1 'Irene born, the Indies awakes', Batavia (Java), 5 August 1939

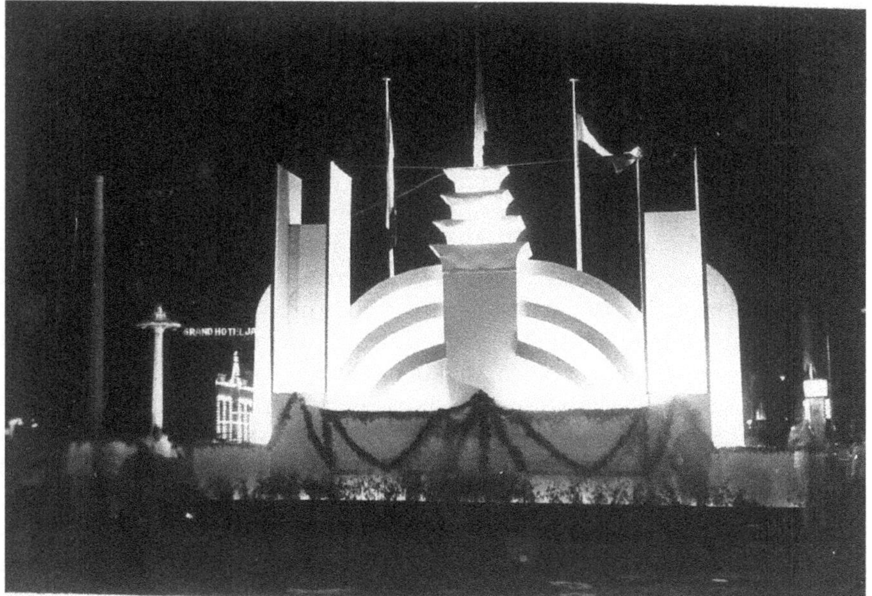

3.2   'Noordwijk bridge. Welcome Irene!' Batavia (Java), 5 August 1939

and buildings are signed with letters in the distinctive art deco style of the period. Night photographs of public spaces festooned with electric lights evoke a festive atmosphere on the Molenvliet, a major canal running through Batavia; at the Pasar Gambir, a famous market; and over the Noordwijk canal (figure 3.2).

The storyline of the Irene album is 'We were here, in Batavia, when a Dutch princess was born.' This narrative was sustained by a pattern of visual motifs shared with many other amateur photographers' works that commemorated royal celebrations throughout the Netherlands Indies in the 1920s and 1930s. These themes included nocturnal illuminations of public buildings, the annual Queen's Day fair at the Pasar Gambir and a procession throughout the main streets of town. Importantly, the Irene album invokes these motifs without recourse to orchestrated spectacles or mass participation. In doing so, it suggests how amateur photography spawned particular kinds of colonial subjects of the queen. Photography enabled networks of people to idiosyncratically signal their investment and participation in public festivals, and to create and maintain communities through the process of making and sharing photographs.

The Irene album and the other amateur collections I examine in this chapter might be said to follow the generic format of 'family albums'. Although the makers and audiences of these collections were not always kin, there are certain analytical benefits to retaining the concept for my purposes here. 'Family photography' invokes a vernacular genre characterised by certain social practices as much as visual conventions, following photographic historians Geoffrey Batchen and Gillian Rose.[2] Amateur photographs of royal celebrations in the Indies, especially those that were placed in family albums, foreground a neglected aspect of globalisation in the twentieth century: the role of family photography in building connections *and* articulating absences within dispersed communities in technologically and culturally novel ways.[3]

This chapter therefore examines how the material and social contexts of family photographs – their embeddedness in objects (albums), texts (captions) and social practices (exchanges between friends and relations) – reveal colonial networks and expressions of communal loyalties, in this case, monarchism. I explain how the making, exchange and collection of photographs of the Dutch monarchy and royal celebrations constituted diverse social relationships, affiliations and aspirations in colonial society.

This chapter also explores the connections between the emergence of family photography as mass photography and the embrace of familial ways of seeing in official royal photography. During Wilhelmina's reign, the rise of the amateur family album as a mode for representing ordinary people's bonds to larger historical events had important consequences for the House of Orange. Using published photographs in commemorative books (*gedenkboeken*) for the monarchy from the Netherlands and the Indies, as well as private collections of photographs in newspapers and postcards, I trace a convergence between elite and non-elite, European and colonial modes of photographically representing family that enabled the popular consumption of the Dutch monarchy. It was Juliana's representation as a wife and mother from the 1930s onwards, rather than photographs of her as a monarch *per se*, that defined this development. The present-day status of European monarchies such as the Dutch royal family as a popular – perhaps even popu*list* – institution therefore has its origins in the early twentieth century, when 'family photography' emerged as a mode of connecting royals with their subjects at 'home', in the colonies as well as the metropole.

Royal celebrations in colonial family albums

During Wilhelmina's reign, the annual *koninginnedag* (Queen's Day) festivities went from 29 August to 6 September, and were celebrated in the Netherlands and its colonies, the East Indies, West Indies, Suriname, as well as places where Dutch imperial claims were located in a more distant past, such as South Africa.[4] Photographs taken by ordinary spectators and participants at royal celebrations became a standard feature of East Indies family albums from about 1923, the year of Queen Wilhelmina's silver jubilee, until the end of Dutch colonial rule in Indonesia (excepting the significant interlude of the Japanese occupation from 1942 to 1945). Celebrations for the Dutch monarchy in these decades were family occasions when the camera was routinely brought out. The common theme of photographs was to show 'what we did on the day' to celebrate. Such photographs record, through a lens shaped by class and ethnicity, the participation of a wide range of Indies people in an annual, ritualised, historicised event that was performed throughout the Indies.

Amateurs' photograph albums offer a rich yet for the most part overlooked source for historians of the Dutch colonial world in the early twentieth century, despite the fact that they represent among the few ego documents left to posterity by large numbers of people from diverse social and cultural backgrounds.[5] To date, such sources have been of interest mainly to art historians, museum specialists and sociologists.[6] With the advent of studio photography in the 1850s, the 'bourgeois archive tradition' that had begun to emerge in the late eighteenth century took on a new character.[7] Families who wanted photographs of themselves in the nineteenth century had to hire professionals for the task, the expense of which excluded all but the well-to-do. Around 1900, with the invention of the portable box camera and roll film, photography became technically accessible to amateurs with more modest means. By the 1920s people on relatively modest incomes in the Indies could afford cameras and assemble albums of their own photographs, as attested to by the thousands of personal albums in archival collections today.[8] An Amateur Photographers Association was formed in Weltevreden, a suburb of Batavia, in 1923.[9] Amateur family photography proliferated in the next decades and, importantly, a wider variety of people from different class and ethnic backgrounds began to use cameras and patronise cheaper studios in these decades. As Karen Strassler's work demonstrates, affordable studios run by Chinese and Japanese photographers served an expanding Asian clientele keen to have their portraits taken.[10]

The work of amateur photographers in the Indies shows that royal festivals in the 1920s and 1930s drew on European carnival traditions, and specifically Dutch customs for celebrating the House of Orange, but with a distinctly local character that involved multi-ethnic Indonesian practices. At home, family members posed for the camera wearing fancy dress, drank toasts to the occasion, feasted and celebrated together. Outside, the main streets of towns large and small were decorated with triumphal arches, the Dutch tricolour, palm fronds woven together to read 'Long live Wilhelmina' and strings of gas or electric lights illuminating the night. Roads were packed with crowds watching local community processions: fraternities of Chinese and Arabs, classes of Indigenous schoolchildren, business associations and special societies. Throngs gathered at the local *alun-alun* (main square) or, in the case of Batavia, the Pasar Gambir, which was appropriated for the week's celebrations. Here, European officials give speeches in Dutch and Malay, gamelan orchestras and theatre troupes performed, bands played in dance pavilions, crowds sang Dutch folk tunes and anthems, and cinemas showed motion pictures of the royal family's celebrations in the Netherlands. *Umbul-umbul*, upright streamers with drooping ends that were stuck into the ground as street decorations, were also on display in cities such as Yogyakarta during Garebeg Mulud, the celebration for the birthday of the prophet Muhammad.[11] Vendors sold Indies street food at *warung* (outdoor stalls), while larger restaurants served beer and European food for the well-to-do. For children especially, and significantly also for 'natives', games and sports competitions were held and prizes given to the winners.

When festivities spilled on to the streets, the portable cameras of the early twentieth century came into their own. With the aid of roll film and rapid shutter speeds, photographers blurred the distinction between spectators and participants. Indeed, amateur photography at royal festivals in the Indies shows not only how such occasions were *orchestrated* by European authorities in the colonies, as I discussed in Chapter 2, and as has been David Cannadine's focus for the British empire,[12] but also, and very importantly, how these festivals were received and responded to by bystanders and participants.

The personal album of a Dutch engineer named E. P. L. de Hoog (figure 3.3), who was posted to New Guinea in the late 1930s, exemplifies many of these features. De Hoog was a member of the exploration team employed by the *Nederlandsche Nieuw Guinee Petroleum Maatschappij* (Netherlands New Guinea Petroleum Company, NNGPM) to establish drilling stations in densely forested and sparsely populated parts of the island.[13] He was also a keen amateur photographer. De Hoog's albums show the period from 1928, when he was stationed in Langkat (Sumatra) as a master driller (*boormeester*), to 1949, when he was in Curaçao in the Dutch West Indies. In the intervening years De Hoog worked in Borneo, New Guinea and Java, and travelled frequently to Europe.[14]

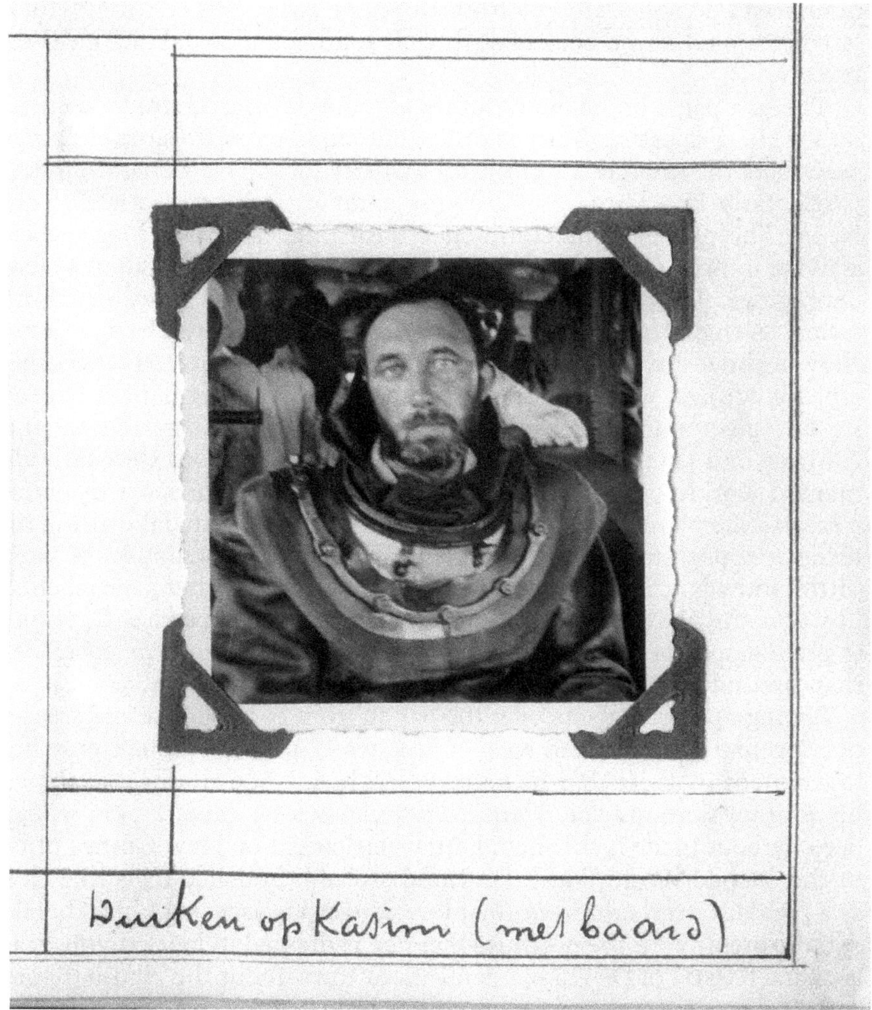

3.3   E. P. L. de Hoog, 1938

The album of De Hoog's time in New Guinea (October 1937–March 1939) is unique among his collections.[15] Like the Irene album, De Hoog's New Guinea album merges a textual genre, the letter, with visual and material modes, the scrapbook and the photo album. His captions throughout frequently address his mother, who was in some other part of the Netherlands Indies, most likely Java.[16] The multi-media format of De Hoog's New Guinea album is in fact common to many family and personal albums from the early twentieth century, which is what makes these objects such rich sources for social and cultural history.[17]

The first pages of the New Guinea album relay the economic context for De Hoog's posting. They include contemporary newspaper clippings describing the importance of the oil industry for the Netherlands Indies, particularly in a climate of growing competition for resources from Japan. The photographs commence with images of De Hoog's team arriving in New Guinea by boat in October 1937, and proceed in a clear chronological pattern, from left to right, like a story board or comic strip.[18] A visual narrative unfolds, often supplemented by captions, showing how the exploration team clears a densely forested landscape, replacing it first with a temporary camp, then with permanent houses for European staff such as De Hoog and communal barracks for the Chinese and Javanese labourers who comprise most of the station's manual workforce.[19] Papuans travelling in canoes transport machine parts for the plant over water. The assembly of the crucial drilling rig receives a page to itself. Captions such as 'the construction of your (little) son' identify De Hoog's own handiwork.[20] Another page labelled 'my domain' shows the realm of his authority and expertise. Captions to photographs of the machinery in the engine rooms inform the reader that 'around 100 men' worked under De Hoog's direction.[21]

Photographs of sunsets over the bay in front of his house and scenes of congenial meals shared with colleagues express De Hoog's growing investment in a site that he helped establish.[22] The album also shows his journeys around the island to places such as Babo, a port whose deep harbour made it the main Dutch settlement on New Guinea prior to the Second World War.[23] De Hoog probably relished trips like this as a pleasant diversion from the more dangerous aspects of his job. His surly expression in the portrait where he is dressed in hefty diving gear is characteristic of De Hoog's demeanour throughout the album (figure 3.3). His reticence as a photographic subject contrasts drolly with the sentimental language – with terms such as *'zoontjelief'* (beloved son) – that he used to address his mother in captions. Affectionate but also taciturn, proud and self-deprecating; a rich picture emerges, in text and image, of a man wanting to show his mother something of his daily struggles and achievements on the frontiers of the Dutch empire.

De Hoog clearly deemed Queen's Day in Babo an event worth reporting on. The four pages devoted to 6 September 1938, Wilhelmina's fortieth regnal jubilee, are among the few that are precisely dated in the album.[24] They commence with a photograph of a gate adorned with Dutch flags and labelled as the 'entrance to the *pasar malam* [night market]', a reference to festival traditions on Java that were clearly transported to

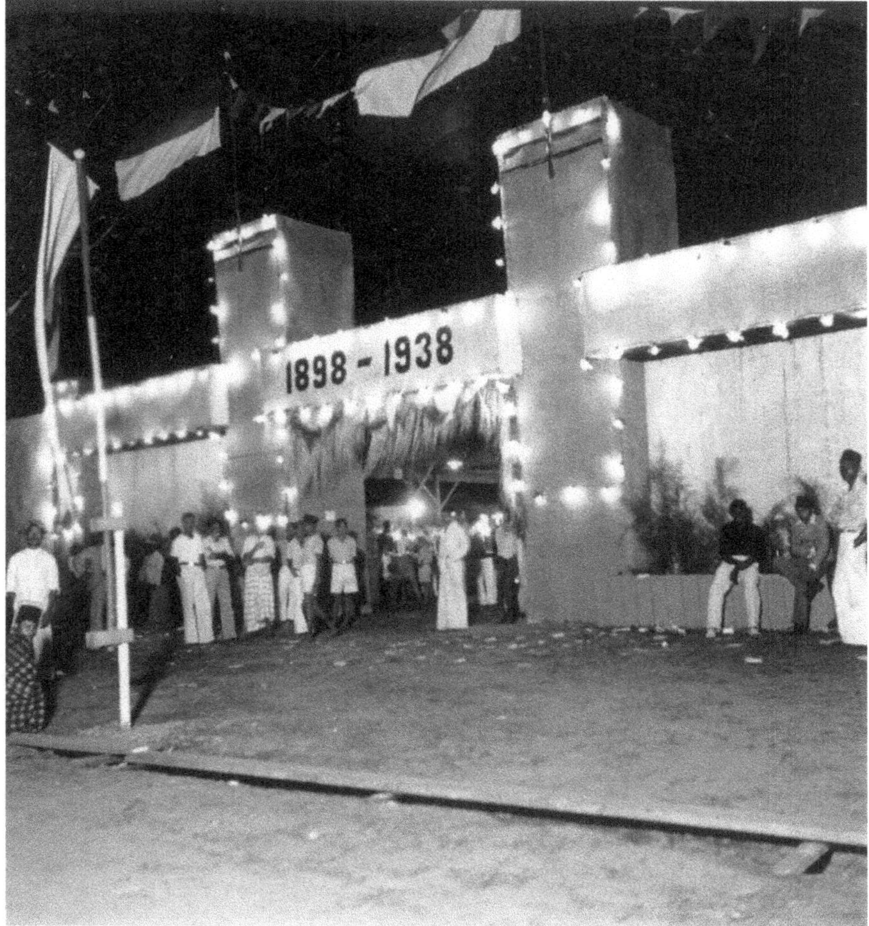

3.4 E. P. L. de Hoog, electric illuminations at the '(festival ground) at night', Babo (New Guinea), 6 September 1938

new territory.[25] The same gate was photographed from the opposite angle, illuminated by electric lights at night (figure 3.4). Other photographs show the involvement of Babo's diverse local population in the festivities. Papuans and the Javanese and Chinese labourers from the drill rig and the town's airfield participate in games and competitions (figure 3.5), eat together in the dining hall, watch dances and theatrical performances, and join the processions (figure 3.6).

It was not exclusively Europeans who engaged with the Dutch monarchy and their own social networks through personal photographs

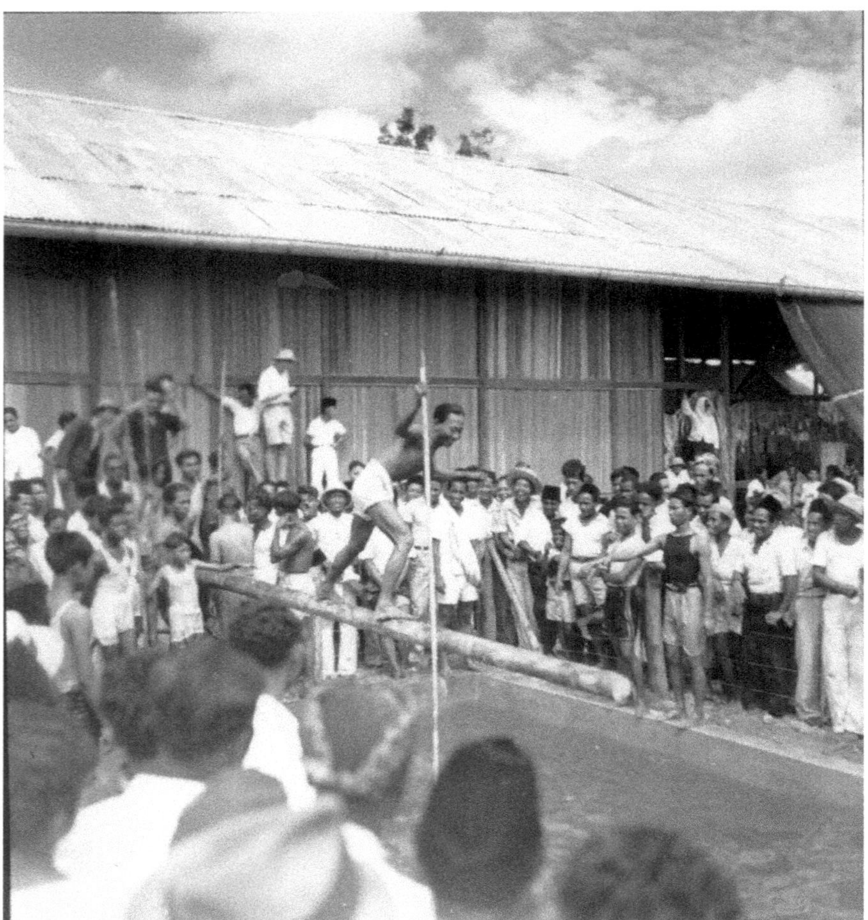

3.5 E. P. L. de Hoog, 'Mast-walking over water', Babo (New Guinea), 6 September 1938

of royal celebrations. Indonesians were also alive to the possibilities for contact in this visual medium on such occasions. In 1923 members of the Surabaya chapter of the Javanese youth group *Jong Java* (Young Java) made an album that featured a series of photographs showing the celebrations for Queen Wilhelmina's silver jubilee. The organisation was founded in 1915, according to the late John Legge, 'to educate its members in their own cultural tradition and to inculcate in them a perception not of an Indonesian nation but at least of a Javanese unity'.[26]

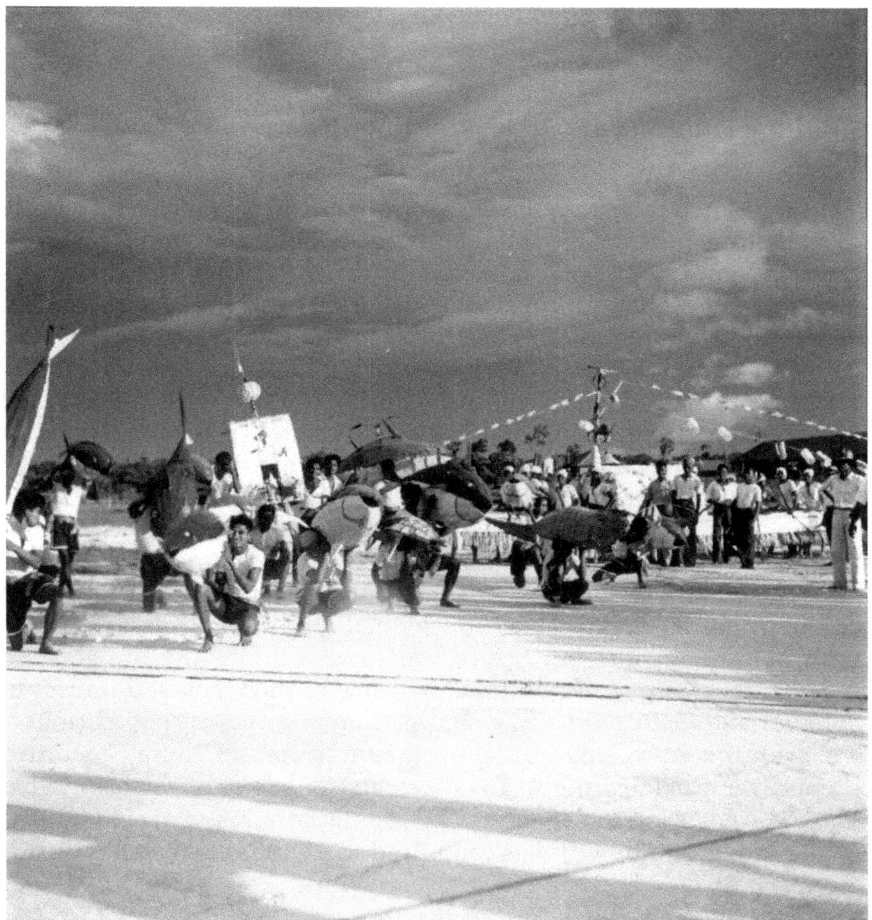

3.6 E. P. L. de Hoog, 'Flight service with aeroplanes in procession',
Babo (New Guinea), 6 September 1938

The album divides its focus between group portraits of teachers and
students of schools for Javanese boys and girls, their excursions to
antiquities such as Prambanan, a major Hindu temple complex, and
photographs of civic decorations in the 'emperor's city' (*keizersstad*)
of Solo during the jubilee festivities, which attracted a visit from the
queen's representative in the Indies, Governor-General Dirk Fock (served
1921–26). The album suggests that one of the colonial regime's key
target audiences for royal spectacles, Indonesian students, was showing

an active interest not just in observing but also in photographing these events.[27]

Making connections: Indies family photographic practices in colonial context

That the Dutch monarchy served as a meaningful focal point for a range of amateur photographers and their networks in the Indies complicates the common understanding of *oranjegevoel* ('Orange sentiment') as a simple expression of political conservatism, colonial nationalism or ethnic solidarity among the Dutch in the Indies and other Dutch colonies.[28] It is, however, in keeping with the flexible meanings ascribed to imperial monarchies in multi-ethnic colonies with no juridical citizenship.[29] I therefore argue for *oranjegevoel* to be understood as a historically specific emotion that was not just personally but also politically and socially significant for the connections, relations and negotiations of power it enabled among those who expressed it under Wilhelmina's reign. In doing so, I aim to nuance Ann Stoler's recent assertion that scholars ought to pay more attention to 'sentiment' as the overlooked 'substance' of 'colonial governing projects'. I agree with her conclusion, but Stoler's method of following the grain of official archives provides limited evidence of the reach and impact of colonial authorities' affective concerns among subject populations.[30] To examine how amateur photographers in the Indies recorded themselves participating in royal celebrations is to investigate what *oranjegevoel* meant to the queen's subjects as an 'emotional community' in the Indies and how it was mobilised to define membership of this group.[31]

From the late nineteenth century onwards, opportunities to travel more frequently between different parts of the Dutch empire, together with improved international communications, forged a cosmopolitan or 'transnational' sense of community in elite colonial circles.[32] A rising number of middle-class Europeans as well as a minority of wealthy, Indigenous Indonesians were able to participate in what Dutch historian Ulbe Bosma has referred to as a 'colonial migration circuit'.[33] A similar situation has been described for other multi-ethnic, multi-religious European empires in this period.[34] The emergence of amateur and mass photography in the early twentieth century enabled the circulation of images across diverse private networks and an international public sphere.[35] Family photographs that signalled *oranjegevoel* provided an opportunity to demonstrate a privileged class identity, one premised on a cosmopolitan notion of colonial 'citizenship' and loyalty to a distant European monarchy.[36]

Caroline Drieënhuizen has demonstrated how material objects from the Indies, such as ethnographic artefacts, antique colonial furniture and artworks, reveal colonial identities and networks among transmigrants who moved between the Netherlands and its colonies.[37] Similarly, I argue that when Indo/European families photographed their participation in royal births, birthdays and marriages, and particularly when they sent these photographs to acquaintances and family members in other parts of the Dutch colonial world, they claimed membership of a globally dispersed network of subjects throughout the Dutch empire. Further, in colonial circles, to cultivate a transnational identity brought monarchists somewhat closer to royalty than their metropolitan counterparts. For even as nationalism strengthened in the first decades of the early twentieth century in popular culture and high politics alike, *internationalism* reigned supreme among Europe's aristocracy, including the House of Orange, as evidenced by their peripatetic lifestyles, multilingual social networks and complex family trees with branches into many countries.[38] The transnational experiences, global historical ties and multi-ethnic kin structures of royalty oddly parallelled those of many ordinary colonial families in the Dutch imperium and, indeed, in colonial cities throughout South-east Asia where mixed-race and expatriate communities flourished.[39]

For E. P. L. de Hoog, dwelling at length on photographs of Queen's Day celebrations in Babo might have reassured his mother that, even though her 'beloved son' was far away in New Guinea, the two were brought together – in spirit and sentiment, if not in space – through ritual celebrations for the Dutch monarchy. For Freek and Rick, photographing their city on the day Princess Irene was born united them in celebration with other people in their social world from whom they were geographically separated. In both examples, the photographic acts of making and sending 'family' snaps spatially stretched domestic spaces beyond the home.[40] These same acts also constituted relationships: between friends and relatives scattered across the Netherlands and its colonies, and between these people and the Dutch monarchy. For people in the East Indies, the emerging visual conventions of family photography shaped and expressed a historically specific mode of *oranjegevoel*, a sentiment of belonging to a dispersed, diverse family of subjects held together, like a web of historical and affective threads, by fidelity to the royal household at its apex. Family photographs of Indies people participating at royal celebrations thus proclaimed 'we are together'.

For Freek and Rick, in *not* showing images of organised festivities or official portraits of the baby princess (which would necessarily have been taken half a world away, in the Netherlands), and instead in photographing a day unfold in Batavia, they chose to privilege

[65]

spontaneity, foreground colonial temporality and spatiality, and celebrate a sense of synchronicity with events in the Netherlands. On certain calendar days, such photographs temporally reunited families separated by space. They also connected Indies family activities with those of a distant monarchy that could only be approached by most Indies people, regardless of their social class, through images. In this regard, family photographs of royal festivals also proclaimed 'We were there'. They show ordinary people making history through participating in Indies events and turning a narrative about elite, Dutch history into a transnational story with colonial actors at its centre.

Family albums therefore illustrate one of the key effects of the advent of mass photography in the early twentieth century: the emergence of the 'camera as historian'[41] and the notion that 'anyone can be a witness of history and that history needs everybody to be its witnesses'.[42] Amateur photographers at royal festivals in the Indies positioned themselves not as spectators of an event located in the metropole, or choreographed by Dutch authorities in the colonies, but as creators of and participants in rituals within a web of connections – personal, public, local and international. These rituals were held in honour of a monarchy undergoing a process of democratisation due, in part, to the very photographic practices that amateur photographers used to record royal milestones in the Indies, where there was no political democracy until the overthrow of Dutch rule.[43]

Ordinary royals: the vernacular shift in photographs of the Dutch royal family

The incorporation of a vernacular style of family photography into the repertoire of more traditional modes of representing royalty, such as painted and photographed state portraits, is an important but thus far neglected component of how the House of Orange managed its public image. During the final decade of Wilhelmina's reign, a period when her heir married and reproduced and thus guaranteed the succession of the dynasty, allowing the release of images to newspapers and publishers that showed the princely family in an informal, intimate light was a vital strategy by which the Dutch monarchy was able to communicate its resemblance to and unity with its subjects around the world. The democratisation of the Dutch monarchy – or perhaps, more accurately, of its photographic representation – has its roots in the advent of mass photography during the early years of Wilhelmina's reign. However, it was not until the queen's heir, Juliana, reached her maturity that the vernacular shift in representations of the House of Orange was complete.

Official photographs of the reproductive phase of Queen Wilhelmina's life emphasised the regal dignity of her family. In 1901 Wilhelmina married Prince Hendrik of Mecklenburg-Schwerin (1876–1934). An *Oranje-Album* commemorating the wedding of Wilhelmina and Hendrik in 1901 was issued to the Dutch public for 50 cents, the cost of a few tram rides, and illustrated with 45 plates, many detailing the couple's family history.[44] The volume contained several official photographs taken of Wilhelmina in her youth: one of her as a little girl with her mother, Queen Regent Emma (both clad in mourning black, the photograph having been taken within a year of Willem III's death), and a formal portrait of the royal family taken the year before Wilhelmina's wedding. Hendrik's family was visually constituted through individual busts of his relatives. Wedding photographs of the royal couple emphasised their remoteness from their subjects through their rich clothing, dignified posture and splendid surroundings.

In 1909 Hendrik and Wilhelmina welcomed the birth of their only surviving child, the Crown Princess Juliana.[45] Family photographs published in the Netherlands and the Indies during Juliana's childhood showed Wilhelmina in a new light, as a doting mother. This persona is best illustrated in a well-known image taken when Juliana was three years old and subsequently reproduced in numerous *gedenkboeken* (commemorative books) for the remainder of her life (figure 3.7).[46] Wilhelmina and Juliana's fine dresses, the queen's jewellery, the opulent satin divan on which she and her daughter perch and the elegant room forming the backdrop of the photograph all continue to stress the wealth and privilege of royalty.

Three decades later the crown princess was grown, married and had started a family of her own. In January 1937 Juliana married Prince Bernhard of Lippe-Biesterfeld (1911–2004), and between 1938 and 1947 the couple had four daughters. Photographs of Juliana's branch of the House of Orange in these years differed markedly from those of the same period in her mother's life. Over the decade that culminated in Juliana's inauguration as queen in 1948, a more informal style of representing the princely family became standard in mass-mediated images of the Dutch monarchy. Rather than depicting the monarchy's remoteness from (most of) their subjects through emphasising their wealth, dignity, responsibility and privilege, the hallmark of the new photographic style was resonant with the visual forms adopted by ordinary people. Like the albums of amateur photographers everywhere, Juliana's genealogy and childhood development were depicted for the public in the format of a family album.

The new style of accessible royalty that Juliana represented in her photographed role as 'ordinary' wife and mother was prompted by two

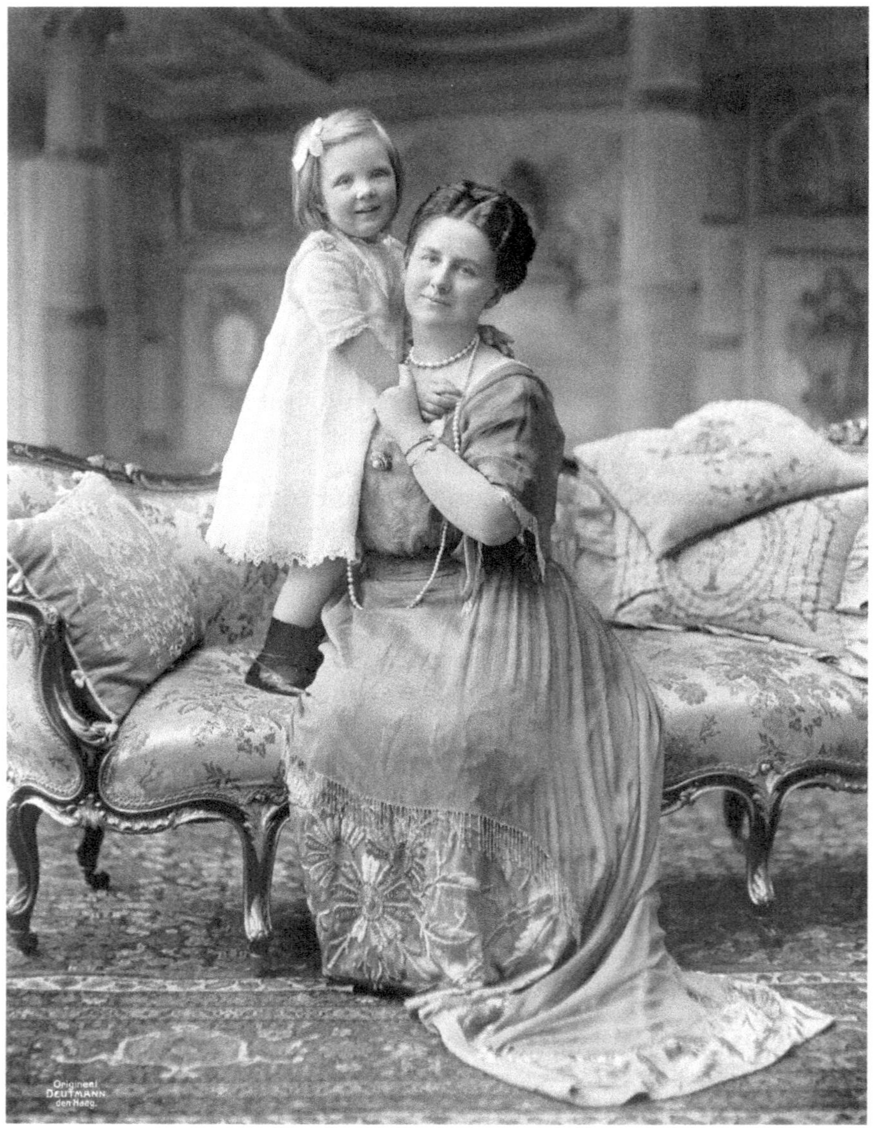

3.7 Herman Deutmann, Queen Wilhelmina and Crown Princess Juliana, 1912

factors: first, an unusual coincidence of important occasions in the House of Orange that kept it much in the public eye from the late 1930s onwards; and second, social and political changes in the Netherlands that forced a democratisation of the public image of the monarchy. Both these transformations occurred in the context of a vernacular revolution in photography that radically altered how middle-class families in the Netherlands and its colonial possessions represented themselves and their histories.[47]

The decade leading up to Juliana's inauguration as queen was a busy one for the royal family. Her marriage to Bernhard in 1937 was swiftly followed by the birth of their first daughter and future Queen of the Netherlands, Beatrix, in 1938. That same year Queen Wilhelmina celebrated her fortieth regnal year. As war descended on Europe in 1939, Juliana's second daughter, Irene, arrived. Margriet, born in 1943, made it three girls for Bernhard and Juliana, and a good news story for supporters of the Dutch monarchy in the Netherlands and the Indies as they endured their respective occupations by German and Japanese forces. The arrival in 1947 of a fourth daughter, Marijke (or Christina, as she was known after 1963), served as a metaphor for Dutch survival and renewal in the post-war era.

A *gedenkboek* published specifically for an Indies audience in 1937 to celebrate the princely couple's engagement and wedding signals the dramatic generational shift in how the Dutch royal family came to be represented during the thirty-six years separating the weddings of Wilhelmina and Juliana. The *Nederlandsch-Indisch herinnerings-album* (*Netherlands Indies Commemoration Album*) was one of the most densely illustrated volumes from the period.[48] Among the hundreds of photographs it contained were three pages of images from the youths of the bride and groom laid out in a border montage surrounding captions arranged in the centre. One page collated photographs of Bernhard as an infant held in the arms of his father, and as a little boy, with his mother, dressed in the obligatory sailor-suit widespread in images of well-off European children in the early twentieth century. Juliana too was shown as a baby, in her pram and in the arms of her mother. One page showed photographs of the crown princess as a little girl on her pony, paddling in a rowing boat on an outing with her parents, and taking part in activities that would have been familiar to ordinary Dutch people (except, of course, those who had grown up in the tropical Indies), such as ice-skating on frozen canals (figure 3.8).

Photographs of Juliana and her kin portrayed a novel image to the public of a royal family united in mutual contentment, in modest dress and surroundings, and engaged in many of the same leisure activities as middle-class Europeans. Certainly, state portraits and official photographs from Juliana and Bernhard's wedding ceremony emphasised formality, pomp and splendour. But from their marriage onwards, and particularly once Juliana began to produce children, the photographs of her family that circulated in the mass media – in newspapers,

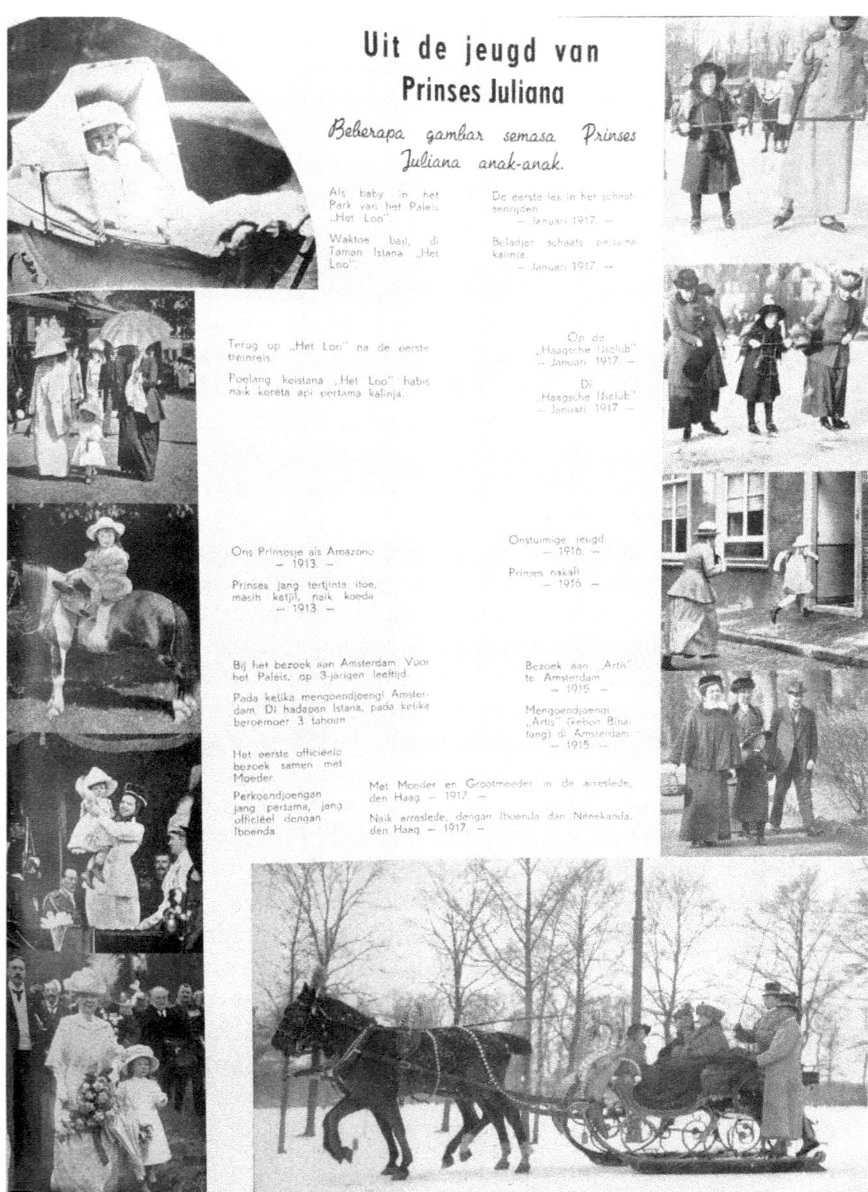

3.8 Page from the book published in the East Indies to commemorate Juliana and Bernhard's wedding

commemorative volumes and on postcards – drew attention away from the Dutch monarchy's wealth and nobility and focused instead on their modesty and ordinariness. Importantly, Juliana had a direct hand in her public image insofar as court photographers were only allowed to publish their portraits with her express permission.[49] The amateur turn in family photography thus appears to have influenced how Juliana chose to have her family depicted by court photographers for public consumption. Some two decades before similar images of the British royal family emerged in the public sphere, photographs of Juliana and her kin in the late 1930s already portrayed the Dutch monarchy as figures of 'popular identification'.[50] Dutch scholar Peter Jan Margry is thus correct in pointing out that it was Juliana who democratised the image of the Dutch monarchy. However, his assertion that this development dates from the first televised broadcast of *koninginnedag* in 1952 needs to be brought back some fifteen years, to Juliana's (married) depiction in photographs.[51]

In 1948, the year Juliana became queen, a remarkable photograph of the princely family was published in one of the numerous *gedenk-boeken* issued in the Netherlands to celebrate the succession (figure 3.9). The photograph was originally taken in 1943 to mark the birth of Margriet, Juliana's third daughter. Five years later it was reproduced in *De gouden kroon* (*The Golden Crown*), in a chapter titled 'Granny and her grandchildren' ('Oma en haar kleinkinderen') on a page of photographs arranged much like a family album. At its centre Juliana holds up her new baby. She and her second-born, Irene, proudly gaze into the camera. Her husband Bernhard and their eldest daughter, Beatrix, smile at an observer to their left. The plainly furnished room is ornamented by only two objects, both of them from the East Indies. One is a wooden *wayang golek* puppet from Java, the other a painting of a Balinese girl by the Indies artist Willem Hofker (1902–81), the only colonial artist to make official portraits of both Wilhelmina and Juliana, in 1937 and 1948 respectively.[52]

The photograph represents defiance in a time of adversity. During the German occupation of the Netherlands (1940–45), queen and crown princess were separated to ensure the safety of the monarchy. Wilhelmina reigned in exile from London, while Juliana and her family stayed in Canada, where Margriet was born. Meanwhile, the Netherlands Indies was occupied by Japanese forces. The portrait of a thriving princely family, united in asylum and buoyed by the arrival of a new member, depicts a dynasty assured. The Indies art objects in the domestic interior suggest a colony endangered but still held in the 'family' of overseas possessions that comprised the Kingdom of the Netherlands.

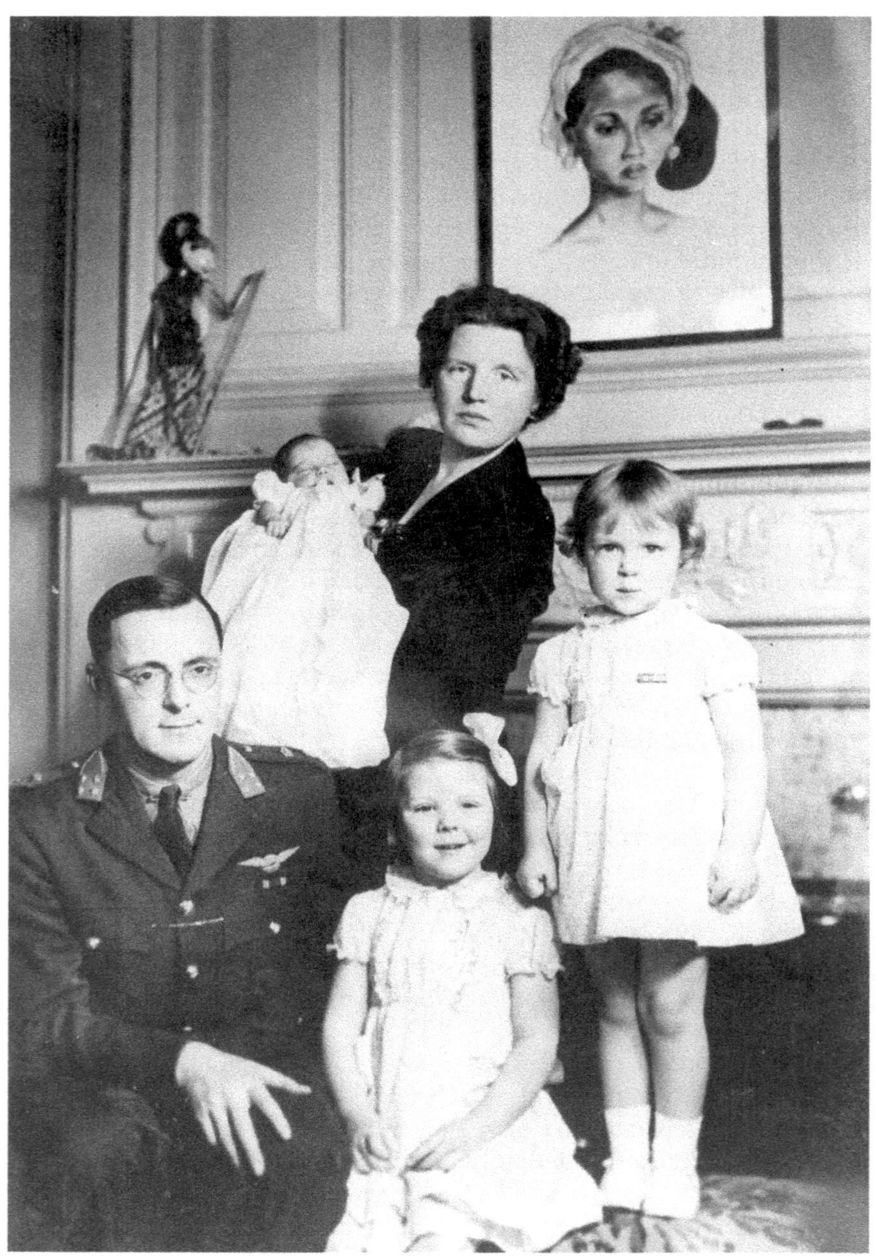

3.9 The princely family in Ottawa (Canada), soon after the birth of
Princess Margriet on 19 January 1943

Reprinted in 1948, when the war in Europe was over but the Dutch battle for sovereignty in the Indonesian archipelago was under way, the caption to the photograph was pregnant with meaning. 'The princely parents know', it held, '… that, in spite of everything, this photo shall come among those who watch over and fight for freedom, for the moment that the princely family can return.'[53] 'Return', in the original context of the photograph's making, referred to Juliana, Bernhard and their children going back to the Netherlands at the war's end. In 1948, in the midst of nationalist revolution and civil war in the Indies, and with its loss as a Dutch possession imminent, 'return' additionally invoked Dutch hopes of colonial subjects being (re-)drawn into the royal fold.

The way the Dutch royal family came to be photographically represented in the 1930s was by no means common to other European monarchies in the same era. Swiss historian Alexis Schwarzenbach's work on photographic cultures surrounding the British, Belgian and Italian monarchies traces a similar shift towards more visually accessible royals, but identifies a different register and reason for this change. Royals in these countries were depicted by court photographers as 'romantic' figures out of fairy tales rather than as people whom ordinary folk might identify with – except that such imagery reflected the rising incidence of royals marrying commoners for love rather than fellow aristocrats for status (here is the democratic connection).[54] In the Dutch context, by contrast, the same political development – the democratisation of monarchy – resulted in a bourgeois vision of the royal family. The Dutch monarchy thus reinforced the (self-)image of the Netherlands as a middle-class country in this period.[55]

The historically novel notion that royals should not be considered *too* far removed from commoners had been gathering momentum in the Netherlands since the late nineteenth century, during Wilhelmina's childhood and especially after she became queen, in the context of social and political changes that led to the universal franchise.[56] Scholars of the Dutch monarchy have frequently noted that the basis for royal legitimacy shifted from heredity to popularity in this period.[57] The enthusiasm that the House of Orange developed for family photography in the early twentieth century revived waning public support for royalty.[58] The family album was co-opted by hereditary elites as a populist visual mode for representing the precepts of blood and lineage upon which aristocracy rested. In doing so, monarchs departed from their traditional, private and privileged reliance upon paint and canvas for depicting their dynasties to embrace a more democratic format.[59] Family snaps of royal children at play, or in the company of modestly dressed parents in their private apartments, emphasised the semblance between royal families and households everywhere, while also fostering middle-class aspirations for the affluent lifestyles that aristocrats manifestly continued to enjoy.

The vernacular trend in royal family photography that emerged in the decade when Juliana married and had her four children signalled a permanent representational shift whose legacy remains visible in present-day images of the Dutch monarchy.[60] Family snaps of Dutch royalty from the 1930s onwards evoked a notion of celebrity that we have since become accustomed to, where people of renown are like and yet not like 'us', the ordinary spectator. The bourgeois, nuclear vision of the Dutch royal family was only seriously suspended on occasions when dynasty and inheritance *must* be at the forefront of royal occasions: at inaugurations, which rest on the principle of lineage and succession. Even so, Indies families could participate in such extraordinary historical events through ordinary, inclusive ways, such as family photography, that allowed them to record their place in these occasions, if only for family posterity.

Amateur archives: official photographs of the monarchy in private Indies collections

The vernacular shift in photographs of the Dutch royal family over the last decade of Wilhelmina's reign illustrates the convergence of elite and popular photographic practices in the early twentieth century, in the Netherlands as well as its colonies. In the East Indies, photographs of Juliana and her family circulating during the 1930s and 1940s certainly resonated with the Dutch monarchy's loyal supporters among Europeans and Indo-Europeans, who often kept newspaper clippings and picture postcards in their family archives. It is perhaps no coincidence that collectors of these images were often keen amateur photographers themselves who practised an 'everyday' form of portraiture and collecting in their own family contexts.[61]

The private papers of some amateur photographers in the Indies who admired Juliana reveal that the 'ordinary monarchy' held appeal in the colonies. Often amateur personal albums kept in custodial institutions are not accompanied by additional documents that detail the lives of their makers, particularly where these were people without particular fame. However, some are embedded in archives of multiple sources that flesh out the lives and interests of the photographers and their families. These need not necessarily have accumulated around people of renown. The Indo-European Foltynski clan is a case in point. Max Foltynksi Jr (1897–1979), born and raised in the Indies, was of Polish-Dutch heritage. As an adult, he worked in various large cities on Java for the *Nederlands-Indische Levensverzekering en Lijfrente Maatschappij* (Netherlands Indies Life Insurance and Annuity Company), a profession that placed him among the respectable, white-collar working classes of the Indies. Max and his Indo-European wife, Petronella Peeters (1897–1978), produced a collection of fourteen photograph albums of their Indies family life spanning the years 1915 to 1928.[62] Among them is an album with photographs commemorating celebrations in Bandung for Wilhelmina's silver jubilee in 1923 (see the photographs discussed in the next chapter). The incorporation of royal milestones into family histories in the Indies is evident in how the Foltynskis photographed their participation in colonial festivals and subsequently displayed those images in their family album.

Photography made the Dutch monarchy's fortunes into an Indies family affair in other ways. Max Foltynski's private papers show that he kept a special supplement printed in the local newspaper, the *Java Bode*, to celebrate the birth of Princess Beatrix in 1938.[63] It was the first time the newspaper had used the rotogravure process, a new printing technology that enabled cheap, high-resolution photographic reproductions. The supplement opened with a full-page portrait of the princely family, followed by two pages of montages that combined official photographs with family snaps: state portraits of Juliana, images from hers and Bernhard's wedding day, and pictures of the couple appearing before crowds of subjects mixed with informal photographs of them with their new baby and various close-ups of Beatrix.

The Foltynskis continued to follow the fortunes of Juliana's kin for at least another decade. Max's private papers show that, in 1946 and 1947, he either personally visited The Hague or was brought a souvenir by a recent customer of Permentier's at Lange Poten 23, a purveyor of postcards of the royal family. The Foltynski collection thus suggests another method, additional to their own photography, by which monarchists and amateur photographers in the Indies cultivated *oranjegevoel*: through purchasing and collecting published photographs of the House of Orange and integrating these into private family archives.

In the Foltynskis' case, their collection of official royal family photographs might also have contributed to their ethnic and cultural identification as a 'Dutch' family in the Indies. Max Foltynski's mother, Elisabeth Mathilda de Vries, was Dutch, but his father was Polish, and since nationality was decided by paternity in the Indies, Max was officially a Pole. In 1936, in the context of a political climate where Dutch nationality became preferable to general 'European' status in the Indies, Max Foltynski had his surname legally changed to Foltynski-De Vries. The following year he was granted Dutch citizenship.[64] Petronella's nationality followed that of her Dutch father (her mother was born in the Indies and very probably Indo-European), and then her husband. She and Max ended their days in The Hague, the final domicile of thousands of 'repatriates' who had been born and raised in the Indies but who considered themselves Dutch.[65]

Photographs of the royal family similarly provided a way for Europeans from the Indies' ruling class to maintain their Dutch roots. The distinguished anthropologist and former governor of Dutch New Guinea Jan van Baal (1909–93) kept newspaper clippings of Juliana and her family among his private papers. From the beginning of his Indies career, which commenced in the mid-1930s, Van Baal was interested in Juliana and how celebrations for her family were orchestrated in the Indies – or, as he phrased it in the title of a 1937 newspaper article, 'on the Netherlands' farthest shores'.[66] Throughout his term as governor of New Guinea (1953–58), Van Baal avidly recorded the conduct of royal celebrations for the Dutch monarchy in his private albums, focusing particularly on local participation (see figure 7.1). In the months immediately following Indonesia's independence in December 1949, however, he was stationed in Medan, Sumatra. There he subscribed to *De Nederlandse Vereniging* (*The Dutch Society*), the monthly periodical of the Society of Netherlanders on the East Coast of Sumatra (*Vereniging van Nederlanders ter Oostkust van Sumatra*), from which he appears to have retained a cutting that celebrated the birthdays of Beatrix, Margriet and Marijke.

The article contained informal portraits of two of the little girls, and of Juliana (now queen) receiving a garland of 'flower kisses' from delegates of the East Coast Residency's *Oranjebond* (Orange Union). Notwithstanding the persistence of a Dutch community in the new Republic of Indonesia, the article reflects the discursive shift in characterisations of the Netherlands' relations with its former colony. It proclaims an accord between two sovereign states working towards 'freedom and welfare'. Yet the tone of the article was also mournful, contrasting how royal birthdays were celebrated in the post-colonial 'now' (as 'commemorations in closed circles') as opposed to the colonial 'then' ('festivals and flags and joy in the entire land').[67]

Van Baal presumably kept the clipping because it was meaningful for him, both as a civil servant who had represented the queen in a Dutch colony and as a Dutchman abroad. Although deeply invested in the Indonesian archipelago, particularly New Guinea, on a professional and intellectual as well as a personal level, one of the ways that he appears to have maintained a sense of himself as a Dutchman was in communing with his fellow expatriates in the Indies/Indonesia over the fortunes of the royal family. Although more powerful and renowned than a great many other Dutchmen who served in the Indies, Van Baal behaved much like lesser-known Europeans there who integrated published photographs of the monarchy into their family archives to express *oranjegevoel* and articulate a sense of belonging to the Dutch community.

Significantly, these examples of *male* amateur photographers – Max Foltynski, Jan van Baal, E. P. L. de Hoog, Freek and Rick – subvert the usual characterisation of family photography as women's work.[68] Moreover, Foltynski and Van Baal's small collections of published photographs of Juliana and her kin reveal that royal families have not always been primarily women's interests, a perception promoted by the prevalence today of features on European monarchies in so-called 'women's magazines'. Dutch historians have often noted that, in her youth, Wilhelmina's appeal to her male subjects, particularly to fighting men in the Netherlands and its colonies, drew on chivalric notions of masculine sacrifice for a virginal noblewoman. Such imagery was evident in representations of the 14-year-old Wilhelmina's role in public com-memorations for veterans of the campaign to subjugate Lombok (eastern Indonesia) in 1894.[69] During the Second World War, Wilhelmina (then widowed and in her fifties) was lauded in exile for her 'martial' courage in defence of the Dutch realm against German occupying forces.[70] As the first female king in Dutch history, one who reigned in a parliamentary democracy that enacted a universal franchise, Wilhelmina also appealed to first-wave feminists in the Netherlands, a cause to which the queen was only reluctantly enlisted and never officially assented.[71] In the intervening decades it was Crown Princess Juliana who appealed to Dutch subjects, men as well as women, as a more accessible figure of feminine royalty: as a wife and mother. For men who identified as Dutch in the Netherlands Indies, an active interest in the rites of passage of 'their' queen, particularly in the decade following Crown Princess Juliana's marriage, appears to have been a socially sanctioned way of expressing communal solidarity and *oranjegevoel*.

Conclusion

Historians of monarchism in the Dutch imperium have tended to focus on the spectacle of royal celebrations without paying much heed to how colonial audiences responded to them. Further, while scholars often use the term *oranjegevoel* to evoke how Dutch authorities sought to encourage nationalism and monarchism in the colonies, their principal aim has been to describe the assumed *outcome* of how the emotion was mobilised, namely, the formation of an imagined global community of Dutch subjects.[72] The *process* by which such a notional community was formed and maintained has not been properly accounted for. This chapter has revealed the important role of family photography in this regard, especially the extent to which amateur photographers in the Indies enlisted *oranjegevoel* to maintain social ties in a colonial world. Vernacular photography demonstrates that *oranjegevoel* can be understood as something more than a sentiment that was implanted by elites into passive colonial subjects through public spectacles. It was a feeling that the Dutch monarchy's subjects in the Indies actively maintained and deployed by inserting themselves, through photographic practices, into the life-cycles of the queen and her family, and into the (Dutch, imperial) historical narratives that were invoked at royal festivals. The examples in this chapter reveal how photographs 'constitute "little narratives", yet at the same time are constituted by and are constitutive of the "grand", or at least "larger", narratives', following Elizabeth Edwards.[73] More specifically, they give new meaning to the historian of photography Deborah Chambers's observation that '[p]icturing ideas of belonging to a nation and place were ways in which the album came to represent symbols of imagined community, notions of continuity and connections to the past'.[74]

In the early twentieth century, during the latter years of Wilhelmina's reign and throughout the early life of Juliana, amateur photography and particularly the personal album made monarchy a family affair. Spectators and participants at royal celebrations placed photographs of these occasions in their family albums, thereby forging connections of allegiance between their own 'dynasties' and that of the distant Dutch monarchy. Historic events became integrated into family occasions through such practices, and public narratives of monarchy and empire were linked with family histories and local affiliations. *Oranjegevoel* was expressed in the Indies through an autobiographical as well a historical lens. Once both photography and the monarchy had become mass-mediated in the early twentieth century, family photographic practices around royal celebrations actively constituted not just a private sphere, but also a transnational public sphere. The photographic culture surrounding the House of Orange in the Indies and the Netherlands thus exemplifies Gillian Rose's observation that the 'collective experience of "feeling"' is one of the key modes in which family photography has intervened to forge public cultures in the twentieth century.[75]

The 'familiarisation' of the monarchy in photography marked the political pre-eminence of different social groups in the Netherlands and its colonies: in the former, the political rise of the lower and middle classes; in the latter, the political dominance of the Indo/European elite. In the Netherlands, the official image of the royal family was democratised by the emergence of a vernacular style of 'family' photography. In Europe, in the age of parliamentary monarchies, the political functions of royalty were increasingly reduced to ceremonial roles. Familial rites of passage – births, birthdays, anniversaries, deaths and marriages – assumed growing symbolic importance for European royals and their subjects in the age of mass politics.

In the Indies, on the other hand, in the absence of political democracy, Juliana's family in particular was evoked by colonial monarchists to maintain elite privileges. Here, the ruling classes used photography to connect with one another *and*, notionally, the epitome of elite, Dutch cosmopolitan society, the House of Orange. Those who celebrated royal occasions that mattered *widely* (among certain groups in the Dutch colonial world), but not *universally* (in the whole Indies population, or in the global world of empires and nations), marked themselves as distinctive. Photographs created and maintained a sense of 'Dutch' identity in families whose constitution and loyalties might have otherwise been spread across local, colonial interests. Indeed, until the mid-1940s there were distinct social advantages, both in the Netherlands and its colonies, to being considered Dutch or familiar with things Dutch in the Indies and *also* knowledgeable on the Indies.[76] Cultivating loyalty within the home to the grandest of Dutch institutions, the House of Orange, articulated family aspirations as much as clan history and patriotic loyalties.

Notes

1 KITLV Album 1258.
2 On family photography as a vernacular genre, see G. Batchen, *Each Wild Idea: Writing, Photography, History* (Cambridge, MA: MIT Press, 2001), pp. 60, 61, 77. On how manipulations to photographs as objects reveal family sentiments and structures, see G. Batchen, *Forget Me Not: Photography and Remembrance* (Amsterdam/New York: Van Gogh Museum/Princeton Architectural Press, 2004). On the social uses of family photographs in the contemporary era, see G. Rose, *Doing Family Photography: The Domestic, the Public and the Politics of Sentiment* (Farnham: Ashgate, 2010), pp. 1, 18, 23, 35, 41, 46, 54, 57.
3 Rose, *Doing Family Photography*, pp. 5, 6, 18, 46, 54.
4 S. Protschky, 'Orangists in a red empire: salutations from a Dutch queen's supporters in a British South Africa', in R. Aldrich and C. McCreery (eds), *Crowns and Colonies: Monarchies and Empires* (Manchester: Manchester University Press, 2016), pp. 97–119.
5 J. Boerdam and W. O. Martinius, 'Family photographs: a sociological approach', *The Netherlands' Journal of Sociology*, 16.2 (1980): 95–120, at p. 95; M. Hirsch, 'Introduction: familial looking', in M. Hirsch (ed.), *The Familial Gaze* (Hanover, NH: University Press of New England, 1999), pp. xi–xxv, at p. xvi.
6 See, for example, the following key works: Batchen, *Forget Me Not*; J. Hirsch, *Family Photographs: Content, Meaning and Effect* (Oxford: Oxford University Press, 1981); M. Hirsch, *Family Frames: Photography, Narratives and Postmemory* (Cambridge, MA: Harvard University Press, 1997); M. Hirsch (ed.), *The Familial Gaze* (Hanover, NH: University Press of New England, 1999); J. Spence and P. Holland (eds), *Family Snaps: The Meanings of Domestic Photography* (London: Virago Press, 1991); M. Langford, *Suspended Conversations: The Afterlife of Memory in Photographic Albums*

(Montreal: McGill-Queen's University Press, 2001); Rose, *Doing Family Photography*.

7   Quoting A. Baggerman, 'Autobiography and family memory in the nineteenth century', in R. Dekker (ed.), *Egodocuments and History: Autobiographical Writing and its Social Context since the Middle Ages* (Hilversum: Verloren, 2002), pp. 161–74, at p. 163. See also Batchen, *Forget Me Not*, p. 10.

8   The KITLV alone, which is the principal archive consulted for the family albums sections of this chapter, has a collection of some 60,000 photographs, including 1,421 personal photograph albums containing 75,000 photos: see the overview given in L. Ouwehand, *Herinneringen in beeld; Fotoalbums uit Nederlands-Indië* (Leiden: KITLV Press, 2009). Major Indies family album collections also exist in the National Museum van Wereldcultuuren collections, especially the Koninklijk Instituut voor de Tropen (KIT, Royal Tropical Institute) in Amsterdam, outlined in J. van Dijk et al., *Photographs of the Netherlands East Indies at the Tropenmuseum* (Amsterdam: KIT Publishers, 2012); and the Dutch East Indies collection at the National Gallery of Australia in Canberra, outlined in S. Protschky, 'Personal albums from early twentieth-century Indonesia', in G. Newton (ed.), *Garden of the East: Photography in Indonesia 1850s–1940s* (Canberra: National Gallery of Australia, 2014), pp. 48–55. On the development of photography in the Netherlands, see F. Bool et al. (eds), *Dutch Eyes: A Critical History of Photography in the Netherlands* (Zwolle: Waanders, 2007), pp. 58, 64, 78, 94–5, 100, 112.

9   K. Strassler, *Refracted Visions: Popular Photography and National Modernity in Java* (Durham, NC: Duke University Press, 2010), p. 39.

10   K. Strassler, 'Cosmopolitan visions: ethnic Chinese and the photographic imagining of Indonesia in the late colonial and early postcolonial periods', *The Journal of Asian Studies*, 67.2 (2008): 395–432; Strassler, *Refracted Visions*, pp. 14, 15, 81, 82; K. Strassler, 'Modelling modernity: ethnic Chinese photography in the Ethical era', in S. Protschky (ed.), *Photography, Modernity and the Governed in Late-Colonial Indonesia* (Amsterdam: Amsterdam University Press, 2015), pp. 195–222.

11   A. J. Resink-Wilkens, 'The Yogya festival calendar', trans. R. Robson-McKillop, first published 1932, in S. Robson (ed.), *The Kraton: Selected Essays on Javanese Courts* (Leiden: KITLV Press, 2003), pp. 83–90, at p. 87.

12   D. Cannadine, *Ornamentalism: How the British Saw Their Empire* (London: Allen Lane, 2001).

13   NNGPM commenced its operations in New Guinea in 1935. It was a joint-stock venture co-owned by Dutch and American companies, and managed by one of its major shareholders, the *Bataafsche Petroleum Maatschappij* (Batavian Petroleum Company), a subsidiary of Royal Dutch Shell. BPM owned 40 per cent of NNGPM. Standard Vacuum Oil Company also owned 40 per cent of the company. The final 20 per cent was owned by Far Pacific Investments Inc.: NNGPM, *Oil Facilities: Nederlandsche Nieuw Guinee Petroleum Maatschappij* (The Hague: Nederlandsche Nieuw Guinee Petroleum Maatschappij, 1957), p. 9.

14   Four of De Hoog's albums are held in the KITLV Special Collections, Leiden University Library. Album 1040 shows his time on Sumatra in 1928. Album 1041 shows the period 1929–37, and covers work and travel in Europe, Cairo, Singapore, Egypt, New Guinea, Sumatra and Borneo. Album 1042, discussed here, is concerned with New Guinea. Album 1043 covers 1939–49, and shows Java, Borneo and Curaçao. The years 1930–36 are unaccounted for in these albums.

15   KITLV Album 1042.

16   There appear to be some photographs of his mother taken in Bandung, Java, in 1939: KITLV Album 1042.

17   Batchen, *Each Wild Idea*, p. 69.

18   It is a more common feature of family albums from the period *not* to adhere strictly to chronological order: M. Langford, 'Speaking the album: an application of the oral-photographic framework', in A. Kuhn and K. E. McAllister (eds), *Locating Memory: Photographic Acts* (New York: Berghahn, 2006), pp. 223–45, at p. 226.

19 The indentured workers appear to have been imported from Java, but some local Papuans were also working on the site.

20 KITLV Album 1042, unnumbered photograph, shelf mark 140568.

21 KITLV Album 1042, shelf mark 2635.

22 KITLV Album 1042, shelf marks 43961, 140525.

23 NNGPM, *Oil Facilities*, p. 12.

24 There are 22 photographs across the four pages.

25 KITLV Album 1042, shelf mark 140550.

26 J. D. Legge, *Sukarno: A Political Biography* (Singapore: Archipelago Press, 2003), p. 68. See also Hoofdbestuur, Studeerenden Vereeniging Jong-Java, *Jong-Java's Jaarboekje* (Weltevreden: Kolff, 1923), pp. 85, 102, 115.

27 On students as key targets of monarchist propaganda in the Indies, see G. Oostindie, *De parels en de kroon: Het koningshuis en de koloniën* (Amsterdam: De Bezige Bij, 2006), pp. 58, 65, 70, figures 16 and 17.

28 See, for example, P. Eckhardt, 'Wil zullen handhaven! De symbolische betekenis van de Nederlandse monarchie in Nederlands-Indië 1918–1940', MA thesis, University of Amsterdam, 2002, pp. 63–5, 94–9; Oostindie, *De parels en de kroon*, pp. 72, 88, 92.

29 C. V. Reed, *Royal Tourists, Colonial Subjects and the Making of a British World, 1860–1911* (Manchester: Manchester University Press, 2016), pp. xxiii–vi, 79, 80, 125–9.

30 A. L. Stoler, *Along the Archival Grain: Epistemic Anxieties and Colonial Common Sense* (Princeton, NJ: Princeton University Press, 2009), p. 60.

31 B. H. Rosenwein coined this phrase and developed it in her monograph, *Emotional Communities in the Early Middle Ages* (Ithaca, NY: Cornell University Press, 2006); see also B. H. Rosenwein, 'Worrying about emotions in history', *American Historical Review*, 107.3 (2002): 821–45, at pp. 836–7, 841–2. For historical understandings of emotion in family contexts, see S. Broomhall, 'Emotions in the household', in S. Broomhall (ed.), *Emotions in the Household, 1200–1900* (Basingstoke: Palgrave Macmillan, 2008), pp. 1–37, at p. 15; N. Eustace et al., 'AHR conversation: the historical study of emotions', *American Historical Review*, 117.5 (2012): 1487–1531, at pp. 1490, 1504, 1506, 1516–17, 1526.

32 Dutch scholars tend to use the term 'transnational' rather than 'cosmopolitan': S. Legêne, *De bagage van Blomhoff en Van Breugel: Japan, Java, Tripoli en Suriname in de negentiende-eeuwse Nederlandse cultuur van het imperialisme* (Amsterdam: KIT Publishing, 1998); S. Legêne, *Spiegelreflex: Culturele sporen van de koloniale ervaring* (Amsterdam: Bert Bakker, 2010), p. 178; U. Bosma, *Indiëgangers: Verhalen van Nederlanders die naar Indië trokken* (Amsterdam: Bert Bakker, 2010), p. 49.

33 Bosma, *Indiëgangers*, pp. 12, 26, 29, 32, 106, 187–93, 214–15, 218, 233. See also U. Bosma and R. Raben, *Being 'Dutch' in the Indies: A History of Creolisation and Empire, 1500–1920*, trans. W. Shaffer (Athens, OH: Ohio University Press, 2008), pp. xix, 57, 74.

34 Reed, *Royal Tourists*; D. Gorman, *Imperial Citizenship: Empire and the Question of Belonging* (Manchester: Manchester University Press, 2006), pp. 9–10, 18, 19, 21.

35 Ouwehand, *Herinneringen in beeld*, pp. 15–16; R. Jongmans and J. van Dijk, 'Photography from the Netherlands East Indies: changing perspectives, different views', in J. van Dijk et al., *Photographs of the Netherlands East Indies at the Tropenmuseum* (Amsterdam: KIT Publishers, 2012), pp. 21, 25.

36 Legêne, *Spiegelreflex*, p. 207; B. Waaldijk and S. Legêne, 'Ethische politiek in Nederland: cultureel burgerschap tussen overheersing, opvoeding an afscheid', in M. Bloembergen and R. Raben (eds), *Het koloniale beschavingsoffensief: Wegen naar het niewe Indië, 1890–1950* (Leiden: KITLV Press, 2009), pp. 187–216, at pp. 188–9. For a cognate notion of citizenship in the British empire, see Gorman, *Imperial Citizenship*, pp. 2, 5, 18, 21.

37 C. Drieënhuizen, 'Objects, nostalgia and the Dutch colonial elite in times of transition, ca. 1900–1970', *Bijdragen tot de Taal-, Land- en Volkenkunde*, 170 (2014): 504–29; C. Drieënhuizen, 'Social careers across imperial spaces: an empire family in the

Dutch-British world, 1811–1933', *Journal of Imperial and Commonwealth History*, 44.3 (2016): 397–422.

38 I. Montijn, *Hoog geboren; 250 jaar adelijk leven in Nederland* (Amsterdam and Antwerp: Uitgeverij Contact, 2012), p. 183.

39 S. L. Lewis, *Cities in Motion: Urban Life and Cosmopolitanism in Southeast Asia, 1920–1940* (Cambridge: Cambridge University Press, 2016).

40 G. Rose, 'Photographs and domestic spacings: a case study', *Transactions of the Institute of British Geographers*, 28.1 (2003): 5–18, at pp. 11, 12.

41 E. Edwards, *The Camera as Historian: Amateur Photographers and Historical Imagination, 1885–1918* (Durham, NC: Duke University Press, 2012).

42 Strassler, *Refracted Visions*, p. 211.

43 Indonesia's first elections were in 1955.

44 L. Stratenus, *Oranje-album, uitgegeven ter gelegenheid van het huwelijk van H.M. Koningin Wilhelmina der Nederlanden en Z.H. Hertog Hendrik van Mecklenburg-Schwerin* (Amsterdam: Boon, 1901), pp. 4, 7, 17, 18, 29–32, and plates section.

45 Wilhelmina had two miscarriages and a stillbirth before Juliana's safe arrival.

46 See, for example, the book that was published at the time of Wilhelmina's silver jubilee in 1923, when Juliana was 14 years old: W. G. de Bas (ed.), *25 jaar geschiedenis van Nederland 1898–1923* (Amsterdam: Dalmeijer's Volksuniversiteit, 1923), p. 40. The photo was still being reproduced in 2004, when Juliana died: see, for example, H. van Bree, *Het aanzien van Juliana* (Utrecht: Het Spectrum, 2004), p. 19. See also M. Jansen, 'Moeder en dochter in het Koninklijk Huisarchief', *Fotografisch Geheugen*, 79 (2013): 7–9, at pp. 8–9.

47 H. Schulte Nordholt, 'Modernity and middle classes in the Netherlands Indies: cultivating cultural citizenship', in S. Protschky (ed.), *Photography, Modernity and the Governed in Late-Colonial Indonesia* (Amsterdam: Amsterdam University Press, 2015), pp. 223–54; T. Hoogervorst and H. Schulte Nordholt, 'Urban middle classes in colonial Java (1900–1942): images and language', *Bijdragen tot de Taal-, Land- en Volkenkunde*, 173 (2017): 442–74.

48 F. A. W. van der Lip, *Nederlandsch-Indisch Herinnerings-Album aan de verloving en het huwelijk van H.K.H. Prinses Juliana [en] Z.K.H. Prins Bernhard* (Bandoeng: Alubu, 1937).

49 Juliana's court photographer during her Canadian exile was Yousuf Karsh (1908–2002). On Juliana's relationship with court photographers, see M. Jansen, 'Uit de praktijk van hoffotograaf Franz Ziegler', in N. Coppes, M. van Heteren and M. Jansen, *Franz Ziegler, Virtuoso Fotograaf (1893–1939)* (Zutphen: Walburg Pers, 2009), pp. 33–50, at pp. 38–9, 46.

50 On images of the British monarchy in the 1950s, see A. Kuhn, 'A meeting of two queens: an exercise in memory work', in M. Hirsch (ed.), *The Familial Gaze* (Hanover, NH: University Press of New England, 1999), pp. 196–207, at p. 203.

51 P. J. Margry, 'Het "oranjegevoel" van koninginnedag; een ritualistische verzoening met de anachronie van de monarchie', in H. te Velde and D. Haks (eds), *Oranje onder; Populair Orangisme van Willem van Oranje tot nu* (Amsterdam: Prometheus/ Bert Bakker, 2014), pp. 243–66, at p. 246.

52 B. Carpenter, *Willem Hofker 1902–1981: Painter of Bali* (Wijk en Aalburg: Pictures Publishers, 1993), pp. 175–83. The Wilhelmina portrait was commissioned by the *Koninklijk Paketvaart Maatschappij* (Royal Shipping Company) to hang in its Batavia headquarters. The Juliana portrait was intended for the same purpose, but was never shipped to Java because of the Indonesian war of independence. Its current whereabouts are unknown.

53 *De gouden kroon; Gedenkboek bij gelegenheid van het gouden regeringsjubileum van H.M. Koningin Wilhelmina* (Haarlem: De Spaarnestad, 1948), p. 185.

54 A. Schwarzenbach, 'Royal photographs: emotions for the people', *Contemporary European History*, 13.3 (2004): 255–80, at pp. 274–5; A. Schwarzenbach, *Königliche Träume: Eine Kultuurgeschichte der Monarchie von 1789 bis 1997* (Munich: Collection Rolf Heyne, 2012).

55 Interestingly, Dutch queens continued to marry fellow aristocrats (with a special penchant for German ones) rather than commoners throughout the twentieth century. Also, the 'pillarisation' (*verzuiling*) of Dutch society in the late nineteenth century into socialist, liberal, conservative and confessional factions, a process that continued into the early twentieth century, undermines the simplistic image of the Netherlands as a self-contented nation of *bourgeoises*: H. te Velde, *Gemeenschapszin en plichtsbesef; Liberalisme en nationalisme in Nederland, 1870–1918* (The Hague: SDU, 1992), pp. 15–16.

56 Te Velde, *Gemeenschapszin en plichtsbesef*; H. te Velde, 'Cannadine, twenty years on: monarchy and political culture in nineteenth-century Britain and the Netherlands', in H. te Velde (ed.), *Mystifying the Monarch: Studies on Discourse, Power, and History* (Amsterdam: Amsterdam University Press, 2006), pp. 193–203, at pp. 202, 203. Peter Rehwinkel notes that it took until Juliana's reign for royal influence in Dutch politics to cease definitively: P. Rehwinkel, 'Royalty is not essential ... zoolang politici hun verantwoordelijkheid nemen', in R. Meijer and H. J. Schoo (eds), *De monarchie; Staatsrecht, volksgunst en het huis van Oranje* (Amsterdam: Prometheus, 2002), pp. 73–100.

57 This shift began during the regency of Emma, after the death of Willem III, who had been very unpopular: Montijn, *Hoog geboren*, pp. 52, 54; Te Velde, *Gemeenschapszin en plichtsbesef*, pp. 121, 122, 268–9; J. van Osta, 'The emperor's new clothes: the reappearance of the performing monarchy in Europe, c. 1870–1914', in H. te Velde (ed.), *Mystifying the Monarch: Studies on Discourse, Power, and History* (Amsterdam: Amsterdam University Press, 2006), pp. 181–92, at pp. 185, 187, 188; J. van Osta, *Het theater van de Staat: Oranje, Windsor en de moderne monarchie* (Amsterdam: Wereldbibliotheek, 1998), pp. 10, 13, 15, 105, 232. The same shift occurred with respect to the British monarchy in the twentieth century: D. Chambers, 'Family as place: family photograph albums and the domestication of public and private space', in J. M. Schwartz and J. R. Ryan (eds), *Picturing Place: Photography and the Geographical Imagination* (London: I.B. Tauris, 2003), pp. 96–114, at p. 98.

58 Jaap van Osta has noted that images of the 'warm domesticity' of royals' lives became crucial to revising the family's popularity in the early twentieth century, but did not analyse the role of photography in this process: Van Osta, *Het theater van de Staat*, p. 145; Van Osta, 'The emperor's new clothes', p. 183.

59 Portrait painting, once the province of elites, became the model for the professional family photograph: Chambers, 'Family as place', p. 98; J. Woodall, 'Introduction', in J. Woodall (ed.), *Portraiture: Facing the Subject* (Manchester: Manchester University Press, 1997), pp. 1–28.

60 The online photographs officially provided by the Royal Collections in The Hague of the present King Willem-Alexander's family – his daughters, the Princess of Orange, Catharina-Amalia, Princesses Alexia and Ariana, his wife Queen Maxima and even his mother, Princess Beatrix (the former queen) – are a case in point: see https://www.koninklijkhuis.nl/foto-en-video/portretfotos/fotosessies (last accessed 28 March 2018). Photographs of all the adults in their childhood and youth are provided, and the young princesses are shown engaged in activities that most Dutch children would be familiar with, such as riding their bikes, taking the train, going to the beach and taking a boat ride on a river.

61 On the importance of the 'everyday' in understanding Indies family photography, and for revising prevalent historical views of Indo-European society as having been strictly subaltern to 'Dutch' society in the Indies, see P. Pattynama, 'Interracial unions and the Ethical Policy: the representation of the everyday in Indo-European family albums', in S. Protschky (ed.), *Photography, Modernity and the Governed in Late-Colonial Indonesia* (Amsterdam: Amsterdam University Press, 2015), pp. 133–62.

62 KITLV Albums 244–57.

63 KITLV DH1210.

64 Max Foltynski's decision was prescient. In 1939 Poland was occupied by Germany, and in the Indies the following year (after the Netherlands was invaded) all German

nationals and those of German-occupied countries (except the Netherlands: wartime logic) were interned: F. Colombijn, with the assistance of M. Barwegen, *Under Construction: The Politics of Urban Space and Housing during the Decolonization of Indonesia, 1930–1960* (Leiden: KITLV Press, 2010), pp. 229–30.

65 For the Foltynski family history, see KITLV DH1210. On The Hague as an expatriate colonial city, see E. Captain et al. (eds), *De Indische zomer in Den Haag: Het cultureel erfgoed van de Indische hoofdstad* (Leiden: KITLV Press, 2005).

66 Quoted in J. Schoorl, 'In memoriam J. van Baal, 25-11-1909–9-8-1993', *Bijdragen tot de Taal-, Land- en Volkenkunde*, 150.1 (1994): 3–12, at p. 4.

67 *De Nederlandse Vereniging*, 1 March 1950, p. 3: National Archives, The Hague: NL_HaNA, Van Baal, 2.21.205.02 inv. nr. 23.

68 Rose, *Doing Family Photography*, pp. 41, 57.

69 M. Grever, 'Colonial queens: imperialism, gender and the body politic during the reign of Victoria and Wilhelmina', *Dutch Crossing: A Journal of Low Countries Studies*, 26.1 (2002): 99–114, at p. 106; M. Bossenbroek, *Holland op zijn breedst: Indië en Zuid-Afrika in de Nederlandse cultuur omstreeks 1900* (Amsterdam: Bert Bakker, 1996), pp. 210–12, 235.

70 Grever, 'Colonial queens', p. 108; C. Fasseur, *Wilhelmina: Krijgshaftig in een vormeloze jas* (Amsterdam: Balans, 2001).

71 The general male franchise was achieved in the Netherlands in 1917, and women gained the vote in 1920. On Wilhelmina's appeal to feminists, see M. Grever, 'Vorstin voor heel het vaderland? Orangisme en feminisme in het laatste kwaart van de negentiende eeuw', *De Negentiende Eeuw*, 23.1 (1999): 76–88, at p. 76; M. Grever, 'Koningin Wilhelmina en het feminisme of de ogenschijnlijke onverenigbaarheid van karakters', *Tijdschrift voor Genderstudies*, 2.3 (1999): 4–19, at pp. 13–15; M. Grever and B. Waaldijk, 'Women's labor at display: feminist claims to Dutch citizenship and colonial politics around 1901', *Journal of Women's History*, 15.4 (2004): 11–18, at p. 12. On Wilhelmina's reluctance to openly endorse a feminist agenda, even if she supported the promotion of women's work and social contributions, see Grever, 'Koningin Wilhelmina en het feminisme', p. 5.

72 Eckhardt, 'Wij zullen handhaven!', pp. 63–5, 94–9; Oostindie, *De parels en de kroon*, p. 72.

73 E. Edwards, *Raw Histories: Photographs, Anthropology and Museums* (Oxford: Berg, 2001), p. 3

74 Chambers, 'Family as place', p. 105.

75 Rose, *Doing Family Photography*, 7. See also Chambers, 'Family as place', pp. 99, 105.

76 This situation changed after 1945, when Indo-Europeans in particular became refugees/repatriates from the Republic of Indonesia: S. Legêne, *Spiegelreflex: Culturele sporen van de koloniale ervaring* (Amsterdam: Bert Bakker, 2010), p. 175; S. Protschky, 'The flavour of history: food, family and subjectivity in two Indo-European women's memoirs', *Journal of the History of the Family*, 14 (2009): 369–85, at pp. 381–2; Drieënhuizen, 'Objects, nostalgia and the Dutch colonial elite'.

CHAPTER FOUR

Modern subjects: lights, camera and ... 'Ethical' rule!

On the last night of the festival week for Queen Wilhelmina's silver jubilee in 1923, Max Foltynski and his wife, Petronella, joined the crowd of spectators who turned out to admire the electric lights that decorated many of the major buildings in Bandung, the large city in West Java where they lived. One of them took a photograph of the illuminated Bandung Residency, the house occupied by the most senior Dutch administrator in the city (figure 4.1). Someone also photographed Bandung's new Technical College, completed only three years before Wilhelmina's jubilee (figure 4.2). Both images were later placed in an album filled with domestic scenes of children's antics and family dinner parties.

Batavia, the capital of the Indies, also had vocational institutions like Bandung College, among them the Wilhelmina and Juliana schools. It was no coincidence that they were named after the Queen of the Netherlands and her daughter. The schools were the indirect outcome of the Ethical Policy, which was heralded by Wilhelmina herself in 1901 during her annual 'speech from the throne' (*troonrede*) to the Dutch parliament, the States-General. Wilhelmina's oration outlined an inquiry into the 'diminished welfare' (*mindere welvaart*) of Java's people and the decentralisation of the colonial administration.[1] Nowhere did Wilhelmina actually use the words 'Ethical Policy'. The phrase was instead coined by a journalist, Pieter Brooschooft (1845–1921), in what became a renowned pamphlet on colonial politics published several months before Wilhelmina's *troonrede*, in July 1901.[2] The Ethical Policy came to entail a much wider set of reforms than Wilhelmina outlined in her speech, encompassing changes to the colony's financial relationship to the Netherlands, and programmes that offered welfare, education, improved economic opportunities and nominal forms of political representation for Indigenous people. Besides her 1901 speech, Wilhelmina accomplished little else to deserve her lasting association with the Ethical Policy.[3] Yet in the decades that followed her *troonrede*, the

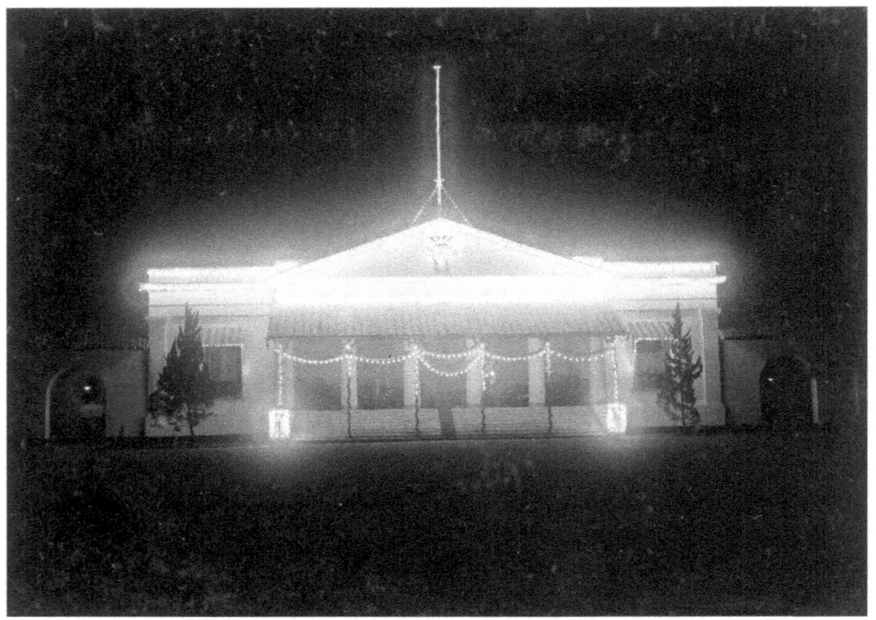

4.1   Collection Max Foltynski, Bandung Residency, 6 September 1923

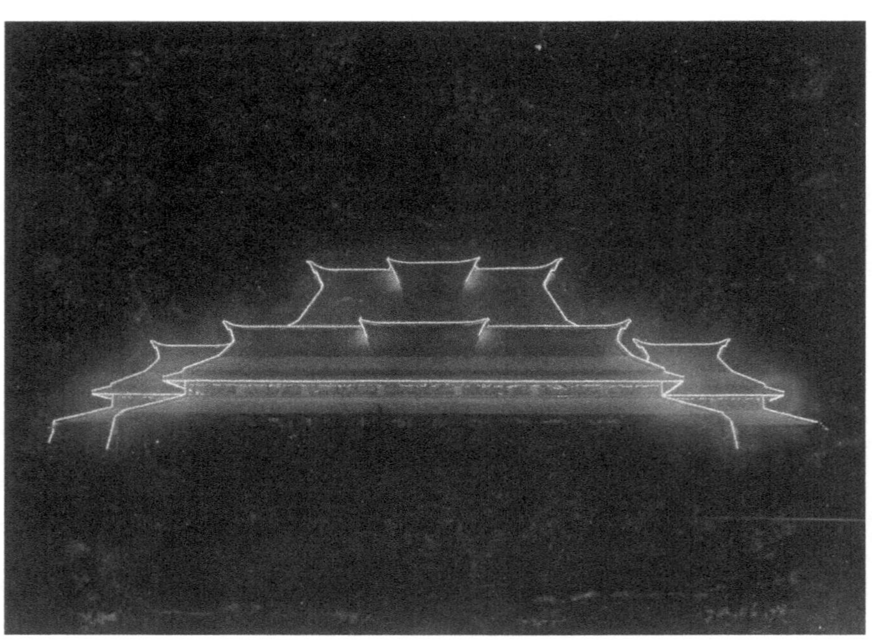

4.2   Collection Max Foltynski, Bandung Technical College,
6 September 1923

Dutch queen became firmly linked to the rhetoric of progressive colonial rule in a wide range of public discourses, both in the Netherlands and its colonies.[4]

While the moral and educational 'uplift' of Indigenous people under colonial tutelage were important components of Ethical thought, the policy's earliest and most enduring focus was on the colony's economic development.[5] The implementation of modernisation projects, often in the form of new infrastructure, offered the advantage of producing tangible outcomes. The photographic depiction of those outcomes is the subject of this chapter, which gives historically specific substance to a pun that works as well in English as it does in Dutch: the association between 'light' (*licht*) and 'enlightenment' (*verlichting*) in late colonial visual culture.

David Cannadine argued that, in the process of uniting British interests with those of Indian aristocrats, Indian symbols of tradition and stasis were co-opted into the iconography of the Raj. In the process, '[t]he splendid anachronism of [the British monarchy's] pageantry at the time of George V's Silver Jubilee and George VI's coronation was deliberately projected as a powerful and reassuring antidote to the high-tech parades and search-light rallies in Mussolini's Italy, Stalin's Red Square and Hitler's Nuremberg'.[6] In the Netherlands East Indies, that tradition was only *one* of the values that monarchy promoted in Asian colonies. Queen Wilhelmina was explicitly connected with modernity in photographs from as early as 1898, and even more strongly during the 1920s, 1930s and 1940s. In the colonies particularly, it was the industrially manufactured glow of electric lights – the very technologies that anti-fascist imperial monarchs purportedly eschewed in Europe – that exemplified enlightened Wilhelmine rule. Photographers participated in an incandescent dialogue, using light-capturing devices to fix an image of radiance generated by machines.

Nineteenth-century monarchs were barred, for technological reasons, from being visually associated with electricity in the same way that Wilhelmina would be. While cameras had been in the Indies since the 1840s, electricity networks were only just beginning to be laid in Java in the early decades of the twentieth century. However, the enthusiasm for images of electric illuminations at royal festivals, among studio as well as family photographers in the Indies, cannot be explained as the consequence of technical advances alone. The other reason for the popularity of electric lights in Indies photographs of celebrations for Wilhelmina was that they provided tangible evidence of the queen's promised modern improvements to the Indies, and thus the principle of Ethical rule, long after its practical abandonment as a policy guideline in colonial circles.

One of the fundamental characteristics of late colonial politics was a growing tension between the official rhetoric of development and the reality of government repression of opposition to Dutch rule in the Indies.[7] The ideology of 'Association' – the uplift of Indigenous elites in preparation for their eventual autonomous rule of the Indies – was already being abandoned at the end of the First World War. The celebration of Wilhelmina's birthday in 1919 – the first festival of its kind since the outbreak of war five years earlier – became an occasion for rallies against communism, both in the Netherlands and the Indies. As I discussed in Chapter 1, the Indies press expressed its concern by agitating for a visit from the queen, arguing that her presence would 'serve to support the waning Ethical Policy'.[8] By the 1920s, however, Dutch authorities in the Indies were increasingly convinced of a mounting radical threat on two fronts: from organised Islam and anti-colonial political parties (nationalists, socialists and communists). A growing number of conservative Europeans in the Indies and anti-colonial groups alike began to view the House of Orange as a symbol of Dutch colonial power, but differed over whether this was desirable. Thus, as Pieter Eckhardt has shown, while most of the celebrations for Wilhelmina's silver jubilee in 1923 went according to official plans, in some places the event presented an opportunity for violent protest. Bombs were detonated in Madiun and Semarang on Java's north coast, injuring several people. In Solo, Central Java, dissenters arranged an alternative to the 'illuminations' organised by authorities by setting fire to European and Javanese officials' homes. Colonial authorities attributed all these attacks either to the Indonesian Communist Party (*Partai Kommunis Indonesia*), or to Sarekat Islam, founded in Surakarta in 1912 to provide a union for local Muslim traders who were opposed to Chinese competition. The organisation's goals and membership broadened in subsequent decades, and it became a significant advocate of self-rule for the Indies. Communist uprisings occurred in Java in 1926 and then Sumatra in 1927. In 1928 the Indies government established its notorious camp for political prisoners, Boven Digoel in New Guinea, to concentrate the growing ranks of its exiled opponents.[9]

It was in this political context of the 1920s – rising hostility to Dutch rule, met by a reactionary shift to the right among colonial authorities – that a visual association between modernity, enlightened colonial rule and the House of Orange began to appear in amateur as well as official photography in the Indies. Through their frequent depiction of electric illuminations at royal celebrations, photographers left the failing political spirit of the Ethical Policy out of the frame to focus instead on its more tangible successes: modern conveniences such as electricity, among other infrastructural improvements. In doing so, well-off family photographers and commercial practitioners – local people who benefited directly from technological progress and whose livelihoods often depended on the maintenance of political stability in the Indies – pioneered a new visual language for celebrating monarchy and empire. They did so more than a decade before official photographers in the Netherlands embraced its benefits as a propaganda tool.

This chapter shows how the emergence of symbolic associations between modernity, enlightened monarchy and Ethical rule in Dutch colonial visual culture was a transnational phenomenon that embraced both the Indies and the Netherlands. However, the *timing* of that emergence was contingent upon local political factors. Photographs of electric illuminations at royal celebrations became popular in Indies visual culture in the early 1920s in response to rising tensions between Dutch and Indo-European conservatives and various radical opposition groups. The historical moment at which electric illuminations emerged in vernacular and official photography was thus unique to political and social developments in the Indies. In the Netherlands, visual connections between light and enlightened rule became salient only in the late 1930s, in response to a sudden cluster of significant events in the royal family, together with the mounting threat of war in Europe.

Illuminations for the House of Orange before the reign of Queen Wilhelmina

In the eighteenth century, when the Dutch East India Company was still the chief agent of Dutch power in Asia, the Netherlands a Republic, and the House of Oranje-Nassau only a princely dynasty, written accounts of celebrations for the House of Orange in Dutch colonies already included descriptions of illuminations. For three days in May 1748, for instance, when Prince Willem IV of Orange was inaugurated as hereditary *stadhouder* (steward) of several Dutch provinces, on the other side of the world in Batavia houses were illuminated and there were fireworks in the gardens and streets beyond the city walls.[10]

In the nineteenth century illuminations in the Netherlands presented unique opportunities for Dutch townspeople and royals to show themselves to each other. When Willem II assumed the throne in 1840, for example, one commemorative book marking his investiture in Amsterdam described the tens of thousands of lanterns decorating the city, and marvelled at the eight hundred gas lamps forming a giant 'W' that crowned a triumphal arch. Another volume, published in 1842, described the progress of Willem II throughout the whole country over a two-year period, a journey punctuated by ceremonial stops in major towns. Each city went to great lengths to beautify its public buildings, grand mansions, canals and main streets for the occasion with nocturnal illuminations, in the form either of lanterns or gas lights.[11] The king and his retinue were expected to inspect and admire these displays. In Leiden, for example, Willem toured the city's illuminations in an open carriage before departing for his next destination through streets lined by an honour guard. In The Hague, Willem carried out his duties on horseback with his wife, Queen Sophie, following behind in the state carriage.[12]

Since none of the nineteenth-century kings (Willem I, II and III) or their twentieth-century female successors set foot in the East Indies while it was part of the Kingdom of the Netherlands, illuminations for the House of Orange in the colonies assumed a function and meaning that differed from those held in the Netherlands. In the colonies, firelight was neither a beacon for attracting monarchs nor a backdrop for their meeting with subjects. Instead, it was a means for Dutch officials in the Indies to dazzle local spectators with the power they wielded in the name of a foreign sovereign. A short chapter appended to the end of the 1842 commemorative volume for Willem II described events in the Netherlands' 'overseas possessions' (*overzeesche bezittingen*).[13] The chapter made special mention of the festivities in Banjarmasin on the south coast of Dutch Borneo (Kalimantan), the site of ongoing conflict between local rulers and colonial forces.[14] When the author of Willem II's commemorative volume informed Dutch readers of 'a magnificent Illumination in the houses [of Banjarmasin], among which those of the Resident and the Chief Ministers especially stood out',[15] he was signalling the long reach of the House of Orange into what were then the most remote and contested corners of the Dutch imperium.

Although photographic processes were brought to the Indies in the early 1840s, written descriptions remained the primary conduit of information about royal celebrations there for much of the nineteenth century. No visual commemorations of illuminations at royal inaugurations were produced in the Indies before Wilhelmina's installation as queen in 1898. The programme of festivities planned to mark the occasion in Batavia outlined innovations in its description of the light displays that were planned throughout the city. While most of the illuminations were generated by firelight and gas lamps, electric lights were to adorn the triumphal arch at the railway station of Batavia's busy commercial harbour, Tanjung Priok, for the governor-general's tour.[16] In performing his sovereign's duties in the Indies on the queen's behalf, the governor-general represented the strengthening association between Dutch authority, monarchy, light and modernity that would characterise official rhetoric for the duration of Wilhelmina's reign. Her inauguration thus symbolised the dawning of a new era, one that combined the gravity of tradition (the continuity of the House of Orange and the custom of celebratory illuminations) with the heady prospect of change (the Netherlands' first female, sovereign monarch, and the use of modern technologies and customs to mark the occasion).[17]

Lighting up the Indies for the queen

In 1898, when Wilhelmina assumed the throne, photographs of electric lights were included in an album gift from the city of Surabaya, East Java.[18] This was no coincidence. 'By 1870', as H. W. Dick observes in his history of the city, Surabaya had 'already become an outpost of industrial Europe'.[19] Its proximity to East Java's sugar-producing hinterland and strategic position at the coastal mouth of the Brantas River situated the city for a commercial boom that began in earnest around the time of Wilhelmina's coronation. By 1900 it was the busiest port and largest metropolis in the entire Netherlands Indies, and one of only three major Indies cities to have an operational electricity network.[20] Indeed, Surabaya was as modern as anywhere in the Netherlands, which had not begun to industrialise on a large scale until the 1890s.[21] Consequently, the city was a magnet for entrepreneurs such as the Armenian photographer Onnes Kurkdjian (1851–1903), who was hired to produce the 1898 presentation album for Wilhelmina, as discussed in the previous chapter.[22] Kurkdjian was not just renowned in Surabaya, where his studio was based, but had also won awards at international competitions in Vienna and Brussels, as the stamps at the bottom of every page in the album proudly advertised. The gift to Wilhelmina included pictures of the European population celebrating at the town's grand café, Grimm and Co., which was decorated for the occasion with electric light bulbs (figure 4.3). Other photographs in the album – of street views clearly showing electricity poles and power lines, for example – revealed the expanding infrastructure throughout the city that enabled such decorations.

In 1901, when Wilhelmina married Prince Hendrik of Mecklenburg-Schwerin, she received another photograph album from the Indies, this time from the Spice-Grower and Trader's Association of Banda Neira.[23] Situated in Maluku among the so-called 'spice islands', Banda Neira had been one of the earliest Dutch East India Company trading posts in Asia and the chief source of nutmeg and mace on the European market in previous centuries. Views of its coastlines, main township and the neighbouring volcano, Gunung Api (Fire Mountain), were frequently invoked by Dutch painters and photographers throughout the nineteenth and early twentieth centuries to historicise Dutch territorial claims to the Indies.[24] Indeed, the dedication at the beginning

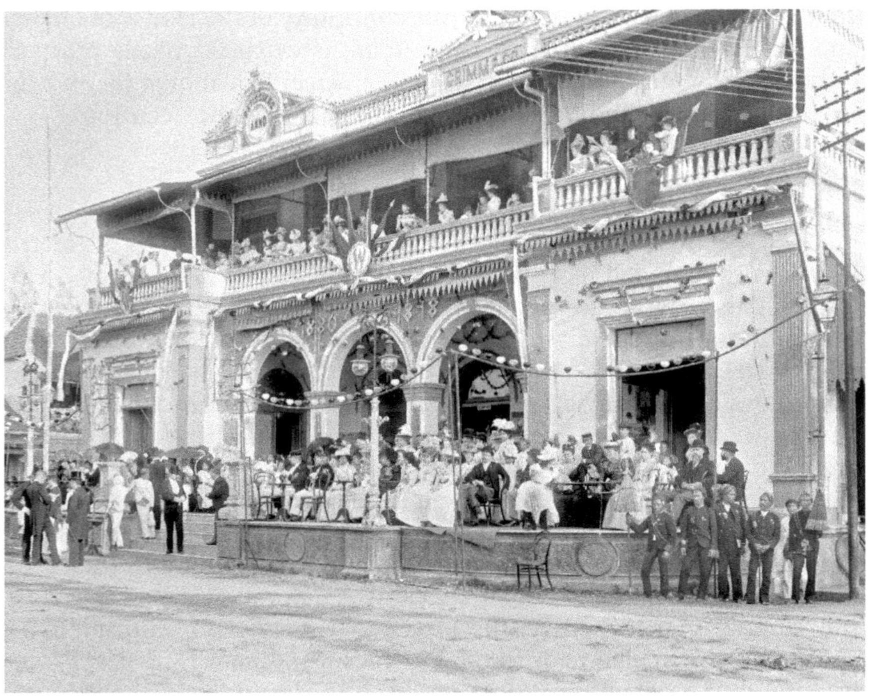

4.3 Onnes Kurkdjian, Europeans awaiting the historical pageant at Grimm & Co., Surabaya (Java), 1898

of the album explicitly mentioned the 300-year history of this 'Hollandsche Kolonie'.[25] In 1901 the residents of the island demonstrated their loyalty to the House of Orange by mounting a colossal 'W' on the forested hillside of Gunung Api (figure 4.4). The caption to the image suggests that this rather unusual monument had first been constructed for Wilhelmina's coronation three years earlier. When illuminated with petroleum gas lights for royal festivals, as it was when the photograph for the 1901 album was taken, the gleaming 'W' was clearly visible to residents of Banda Neira from across the water.

In 1923 an unnamed resident of the city of Pekalongan on Java's north coast sent the queen an album of views of the city during the silver jubilee celebrations (hereafter, 'the Pekalongan album').[26] Whereas earlier albums were often covered in velvet, a fabric that signalled regal luxury in Europe, this one was bound in gold-embroidered *batik*, which was famously associated with Java.[27] The local theme was maintained in the pages of the album, which showed how residential areas of Pekalongan were decorated for the jubilee with Chinese lanterns, a

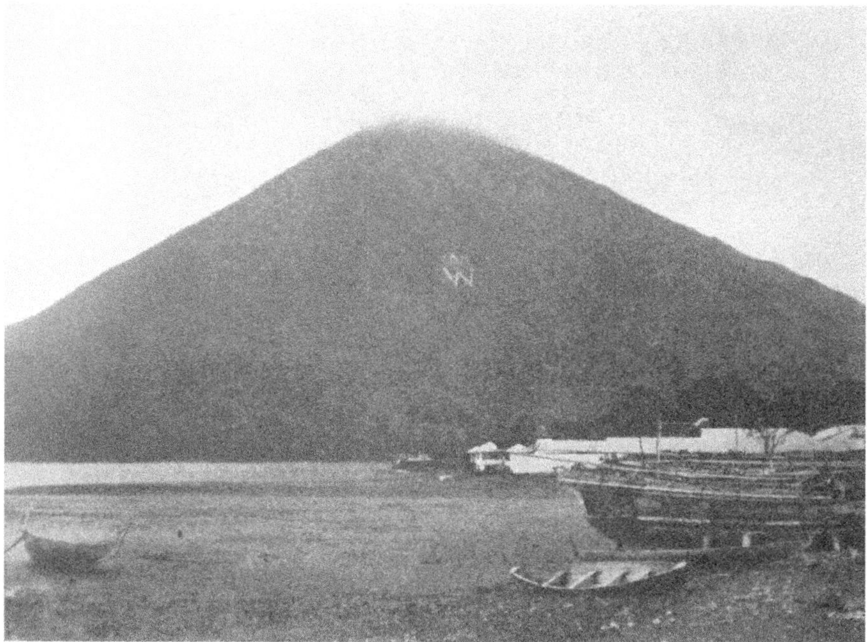

4.4 Unknown photographer, 'Gunung Api with the crowned W illuminated
during the coronation festival and the marriage of HM the Queen',
in *Aan Hare Majesteit Koningin Wilhelmina en Zijne Hoogheid Hertog
Hendrik van Mecklenburg-Schwerin, ter gelegenheid van hoogst derzelver
huwelijk op 7 Februari 1901: Namens Banda's ingezetenen eerbiedig
aangeboden door hun afgevaardigde A.E. Brunier, Directeur van de
Bandasche Perkeniers- en Handels Vereeniging te Banda Neira*
(Banda Neira, 1901)

cheap and easy method of illumination that had been in use for centuries.[28] The long history of Chinese settlement on Java's north coast
was also represented. One photograph showed a Chinese *toko* (shop),
belonging to a certain Liem Swie Lien of Tegal, which was brilliantly
illuminated by electric lights, festooned with the Dutch tricolour and
finished with a sign that read '*Oranje boven*' (Up Oranje).[29] As Karen
Strassler's work on photography in twentieth-century Indonesia reveals,
the Chinese were leaders of Java's photography industry,[30] and it is
possible that the maker of this particular album was of Chinese descent.
If so, then the images from the Pekalongan album suggest that Chinese
photographers were cognisant of and active in shaping visual discourses
of modernisation and Ethical rule in the Indies, perhaps as a means of
asserting their own agency in this process.

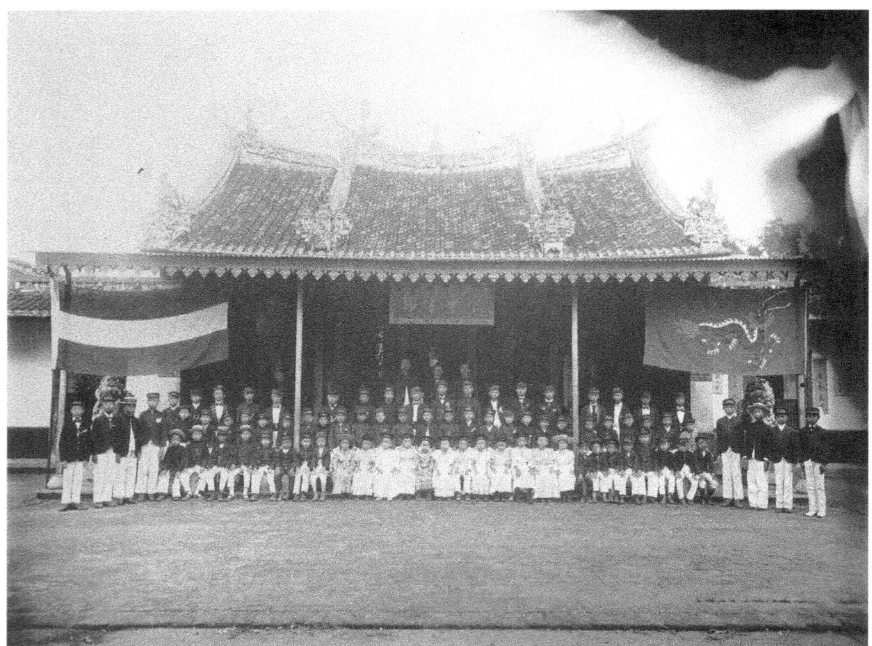

4.5 Unknown photographer, Chinese schoolchildren, *Vereeniging Djawa Hak Boe Tjong Hwee*, Madiun (Java), 1909

Indeed, the collections of the *Koninklijk Huisarchief* (Royal Collections) in The Hague show that Chinese communities on Java sent gifts and letters to Wilhelmina on her birthday throughout her reign. They did so to advance an image of themselves as educated, organised, civilised and loyal 'subjects'.[31] Notable among these is the gift from the General Education Association of Java (*Vereeniging Djawa Hak Boe Tjong Hwee*) for the birth of Juliana in 1909. The gift comprised an album of mounted photographs showing group portraits of the executive members of the organisation, as well as the schools and colleges for Chinese boys and girls throughout Java (figure 4.5).

The association was responsible for overseeing and reforming the schools of the *Tiong Hoa Hwee Koan* (Chinese Association), the first of which was founded on Java in March 1901. The history of the Chinese Association schools coincides with the advent of the Ethical Policy but, as Didi Kwartanada has explained, the movement for Chinese education reform in the Indies took its inspiration from China, Japan and North America rather than from the Netherlands.[32] The motives for education reform among *peranakan* and *totok* (local- and foreign-born Chinese, respectively) included improving the status of Chinese in the

Indies. Resented by both Dutch and Indigenous populations for their concentration in 'pariah' professions such as money lending, tax farming and opium trading, Chinese were legally classified as 'Foreign Orientals' who needed passes to move outside the town quarters where they were permitted to live. The European-equivalent status assigned to Japanese in the Indies in 1899 added insult to these injuries.[33] Among the groups advocating for Chinese communities to reform themselves in the Indies were the *kaoem moeda bangsa Tjina*. Kwartanada interprets this term as 'enlightened Chinese', since the 'youth of the Chinese nation' (following the literal translation) in fact often described themselves in the decades of Wilhelmina's reign as carriers of the 'light' (*terang*) of progress, in contrast to conservatives who remained in the 'age of darkness' (*djaman kegelapan*).[34] The metaphor of light clearly resonated for Chinese in the Indies. It was no coincidence, then, that Wilhelmina was appealed to by education reform groups such as the *Djawa Hak Boe Tjong Hwee*, given her benevolent association with enlightened rule and modernity in the Indies. In this regard, the Chinese of the Indies had much in common with those in South Africa and New Zealand who appealed to British monarchs for recognition of them as loyal subjects in order to challenge the injustices of colonial rule.[35]

The maker of the Pekalongan album similarly included photographs of Chinese schoolchildren in the gift to Wilhelmina.[36] Whoever the maker may have been, his or her work corroborates what is also noticeable in Max Foltynski's photographs of Bandung for the 1923 jubilee: that, notwithstanding the occasional exception, electric illuminations in the Indies appear to have been chiefly reserved for public and government buildings (figure 4.6).[37] All three presentation albums extended in new directions the existing Dutch tradition of holding nocturnal illuminations on royal occasions, by using a modern device (the camera) to record a modern convenience (electricity).

In the late 1930s for the first time a commemorative book was published in the Indies to officially commemorate how the archipelago celebrated the House of Orange.[38] The occasion was the engagement of Crown Princess Juliana to Prince Bernhard in September 1936, followed by their marriage in January 1937. The royal *gedenkboek* issued for the event was only the third work produced in and principally *about* the Indies since 1923,[39] and it was the first Indies volume to consist almost entirely of photographs. Each major city in the Indies was given its own or multiple pages of images, all of them captioned, showing how the population celebrated the event and decorated the town. Only the first few pages of the volume showed the wedding ceremony and celebrations in The Hague and, significantly, none of the photographs from the Netherlands showed any nocturnal illuminations. As we shall

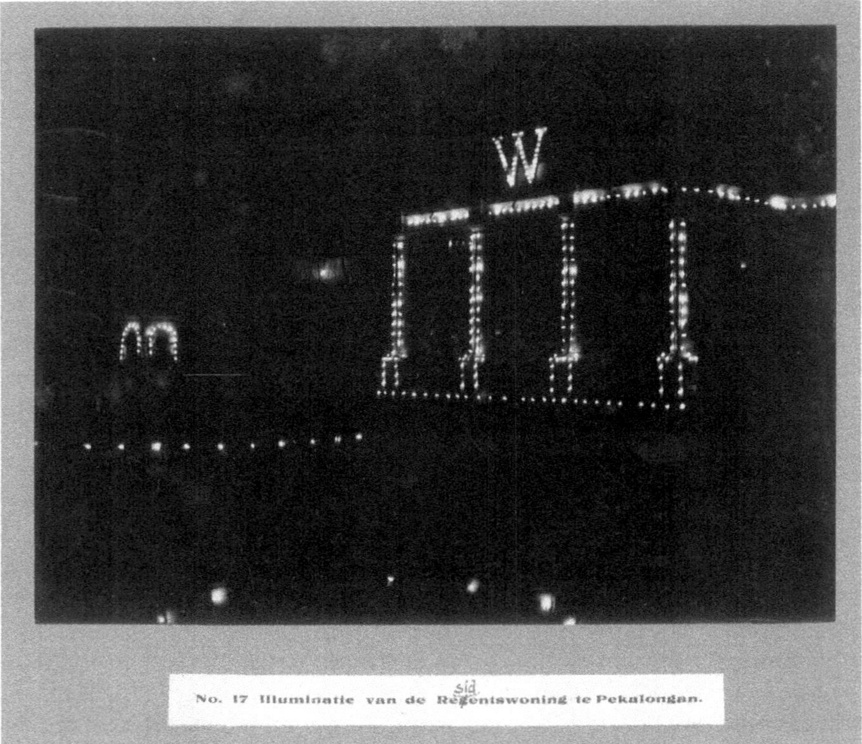

4.6   Unknown photographer, 'Illumination of the Resident's house in Pekalongan', Java, 1923

see shortly, *gedenkboeken* of the same event in the Netherlands amply illustrated the presence of electric lights in Dutch cities. According to the compilers of the Indies *gedenkboek*, however, it was exclusively in the colonies that luminous electric displays heralded the continuation of the Oranje-Nassau dynasty. Page after page of the 1937 book showed electric globes strung across buildings, or strobes that were beamed into public squares, a visual preoccupation with power and light that corroborates research based on textual sources which suggests that electricity was better established and received in the Indies than in the Netherlands during the same period. Indeed, Rudolf Mrázek, in his study of technology and nationalism in the Indies, showed that in 1912 Batavia had a higher concentration of street lamps in its central district than Amsterdam.[40]

Although the 1937 official *gedenkboek* arrived at the visual association between monarchy, enlightened colonial rule and modernity more than a decade later than amateur and studio photographers envisioned it, this volume depicted that connection more comprehensively than any preceding work, in the number and concentration of images it contained, as well as through the fact that the book was commercially published. Furthermore, the book's intended market was not restricted to Europeans: all its text and captions were published in both Dutch and *bahasa Indonesia*, the Malay-based language that had been gaining wider currency as the *lingua franca* of the Indies since the idea of 'Indonesia' was formally framed in 1928.

An astute viewer flipping through the pages of the 1937 *gedenkboek* would have noticed some recurring themes. First, most of the illuminated buildings were located in the cities with the highest concentration of Europeans – on Java and, to a lesser extent, Sumatra.[41] Most of these buildings were in the hands of government and big (European) business, thus highlighting the economic and political power of Dutch authorities. In Buitenzorg, the official seat of the colonial administration, the governor-general's palace was illuminated, and in more remote regions such as Pematang-Siantar in northern Sumatra, it was the house of the Dutch Assistant Resident, the highest local official, that was decorated with electric lights. In Batavia, prominent commercial buildings were illuminated, including the headquarters of King Willem I's *Nederlandsch Handelmaatschappij* (Dutch Trading Company), an institution founded in 1824 to resume some of the commercial functions in the Indies formerly carried out by the Dutch East India Company. The Java Bank, the *Koninklijk Paketvaart Maatschappij* (Royal Shipping Company) and the *Nederlandsch-Indische Levensverzekering- en Lijfrente-Maatschappij* (Netherlands Indies Life Insurance and Annuities Company) were also electrically illuminated. The same was true for the Palace of Justice at Surabaya, the office of the regional military commandant in Kota Raja (capital of the troublesome Aceh province), military clubs in Batavia and Bandung, and police barracks throughout the archipelago. Photographs of these buildings served as a reminder of the Dutch institutions that monopolised authorised violence in the Indies.

The 1937 official *gedenkboek* thus commemorated more than a royal wedding. It bathed the institutions of Dutch colonial authority, acting on behalf of a well-meaning if distant monarchy, in the beneficent light of modernity. To flick quickly through the album generates a bright blur moving across a dim backdrop, one that makes the progress of electrification throughout the Indies appear far more widespread and consistent than it was in reality, and one that obscures – through optimism and radiance rather than gloom and shadow – contemporary uncertainty over what the role of Indigenous elites would be in ushering ordinary Indies people into the light.

Shapes in the dark: the limits of enlightened rule

Among the Indies' *Ethici* (people who ideologically supported the notion of Ethical rule), those 'natives' who comprised the existing local political elite in the late nineteenth century were deemed the best qualified to share power with their Dutch counterparts in the administration. In many cases, especially on Java, these leaders happened to have inherited their positions, and it was their sons who attended the Indies' best schools or Dutch academies abroad in preparation for their future roles.[42] Thus while Dutch as well as Javanese *Ethici* promoted better education for Indies girls, it was high-born Javanese males who were selected to join the Indigenous arm of the civil service.[43]

As in other European colonies in Asia, Indigenous elites in the East Indies were not content with being educated and qualified to serve everywhere that Europeans worked, only to learn that, while they as individuals were competent and capable, the general population whom they represented was not yet ready for 'natives' to make executive political decisions. With few exceptions, even the most progressive Dutch *Ethici* expected Indigenous elites to channel their education and energies into becoming over-qualified 'traditional' rulers whose powers were limited to advisory positions and whose public functions were reduced to ceremonial roles. Photographs of royal celebrations in the Indies eloquently capture some of the contradictions that resulted from this political impasse. On the one hand, they show Dutch propaganda appealing to young, impressionable Javanese audiences; on the other, they suggest how those same spectators may have turned to anti-establishment political alternatives in the absence of inspiring 'traditional' leadership.

Dutch authorities actively recruited schoolchildren throughout the Indies as participants in public royal celebrations to impart the message of enlightened rule under a benevolent monarchy to the next generation of colonial subjects. One study on the reception of the House of Orange in the Indies argues that such orchestrated events probably left the vast majority of non-Europeans unmoved.[44] However, a photograph album made in Surakarta in the 1920s suggests that this thesis may need to be revisited. The album is unusual not just because it provides rare insight into Javanese views of Dutch royal celebrations, but also because its maker(s) and intended audience were almost certainly Javanese youths. Further, the album documents a corporate identity rather than family life. Albums that recorded the activities of Indies companies and organisations were frequently made by working adults for institutional records, as gifts or for commemorative purposes,[45] but they are very rare among youth groups. In this instance, the youths were members of the Surakarta division of *Jong Java* (Young Java). A series of photographs in the album show that the group's activities included nocturnal tours of the city to admire, photograph and commemorate the illuminations that were organised in 1923, first for the visit of the governor-general and then for Wilhelmina's silver jubilee (figure 4.7).[46]

This single album does not furnish comprehensive evidence of Javanese schoolchildren unreservedly taking the Dutch monarchy to heart. It does, however, suggest that one of the colonial regime's key target audiences for royal spectacles was showing an active interest not just in observing but also in recording (through photography) and commemorating (through making an album) these events, in much the same way that middle-class European and Indo-European amateur and studio photographers did. Such a conclusion coheres with other research that draws attention to the formation of middle-class, internationally oriented aspirations among a significant section of the Javanese population in the early twentieth century.[47] To a growing number of upwardly mobile Javanese, the conflation of electricity with enlightenment, modernity and progress was a compelling metaphor. We see it in the evocative title given by Jacques Henry Abendanon to the volume of letters written by the Javanese proto-feminist Raden Ajeng Kartini, *Door duisternis tot licht* (*Through Darkness Towards Light*), which was published after her death, as well as in magazine advertising for Philips light bulbs directed at Indigenous audiences in the 1940s.[48]

Some young Javanese were drawn to Western-style programmes for modernisation in the Indies. Others turned to more radical, nationalist visions for the future, often out of frustration with the community leaders whom Dutch authorities encouraged ordinary Javanese to emulate and obey – namely, local nobility. Aristocrats were expected to maintain and promote the 'traditional' values of Java and to form a buffer between their commoner subjects and the Dutch bureaucracy. The official *gedenkboek* published in 1937 to commemorate Juliana's wedding illustrates this fundamental difference between European and Indigenous rulers. Images of electrically illuminated government buildings abound, but if the *kratons* (palaces) of the kings of Central Java were similarly illuminated, there were few photographs to prove it.[49]

The *kratons*, as it transpires, definitely had access to electricity by the 1930s. In 1915 Victor Zimmerman, an amateur Indologist writing for the periodical *Djåwå*,[50] had expressed approval of this development. Indeed, in the heady days of the Ethical Policy's widespread acceptance

[99]

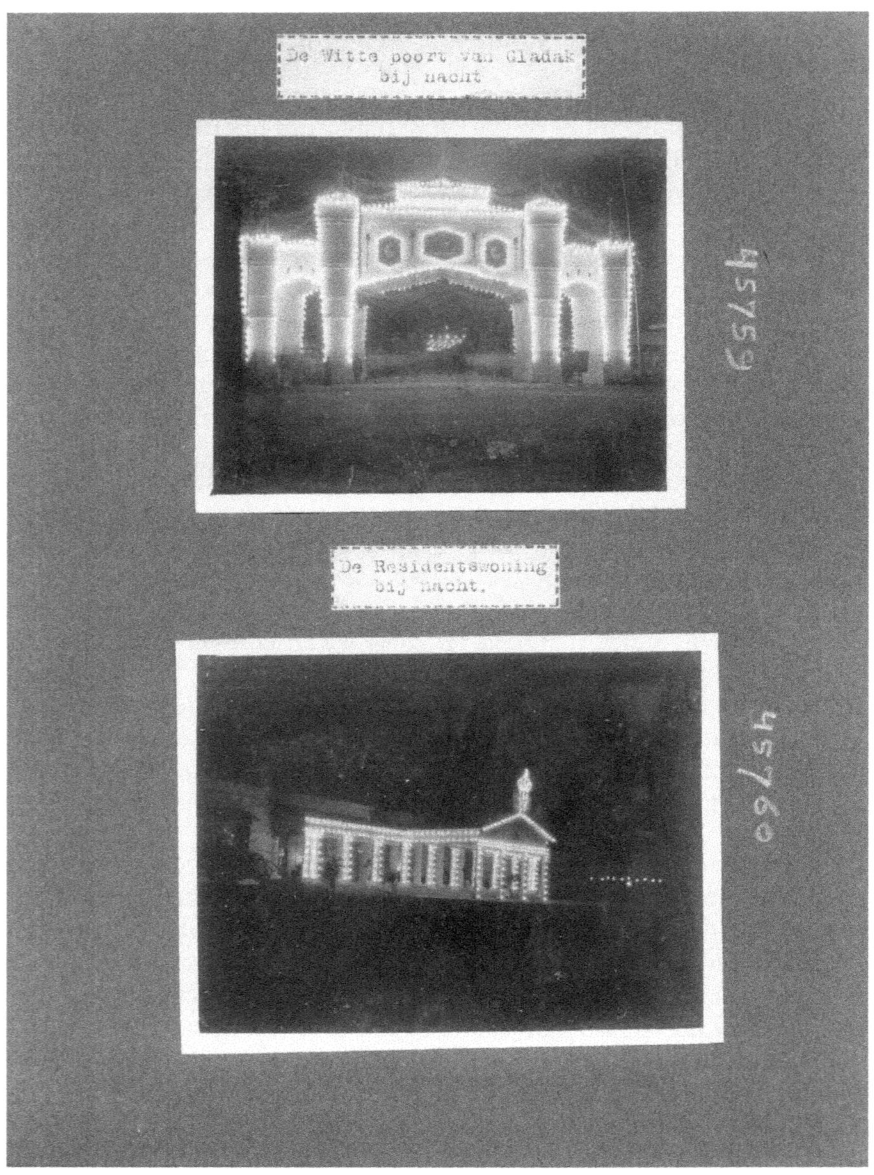

4.7 Unknown photographer, 'Gate at Glodok by night' and 'The Resident's house by night', Java, 1923

among Indies intellectuals, Zimmerman felt that changes to the Surakarta *kraton* had not gone far enough:

> Anyone taking a drive through the Kraton along the main carriage-way will be able to see for himself that courtyards and buildings which really do make a regal impression are interspersed with whole blocks of poverty-stricken slums. Nonetheless, one can incontestably perceive a certain advance on former times, and the more European concepts and ideas find their way into Javanese society, the more will such matters as hygiene be taken into consideration in renovations and in the erection of new buildings, and a logical train of thought will influence the plans being drawn up.[51]

Zimmerman's comments evoke the more patronising, paternalistic forms in which *Ethici* expressed their visions for the future of the Indies. Twenty-five years later, long after the political demise of Ethicism and with the fog of war drifting from Europe towards Asia, more eminent Indies experts expressed doubts over the desirability of a programme that promoted cultural equivalence between Javanese and European elites. Theodor G. T. Pigeaud (1899–1988) was a government scholar living in Yogyakarta between 1932 and 1942 who gained a formidable reputation as an Indologist.[52] In 1940 he published an essay in *Djåwå* that lamented the relentless creep of power lines into the northern square of the sultan's palace:

> [A]t present this beautiful area of spaciousness and calm has been partly spoilt by an extremely ugly overhead powerline, suspended from idiotic silver-coloured poles, which cuts diagonally across the square. It is evidence of precious little taste that these electric wires, which are so ugly and disturbing wherever they are above ground, but nowhere so much as in an unobstructed open space, have not been put underground.[53]

Pigeaud's view that Javanese courtly culture should be quarantined from European-style modernity was corroborated in visual sources. In the Pekalongan album, for instance, the original caption declares the building photographed to be a *regent*'s residence – that is, the house of a high-ranking Javanese official – but the word was crossed out and replaced with *Resident* (the title of a high Dutch official) before the album was sent to Wilhelmina (figure 4.6). The careful correction betrays a conceptual ruling-out of the possibility of non-European leaders being assigned even the symbolic role of championing modernity in the Indies.

There are more examples. In September 1938, two years before Pigeaud's article was published, Queen Wilhelmina celebrated the fortieth anniversary of her reign. The following year, in March 1939, Sultan Hamengku Buwono VIII died and was succeeded by Hamengku Buwono IX. Formal ceremonies marking these occasions were held at

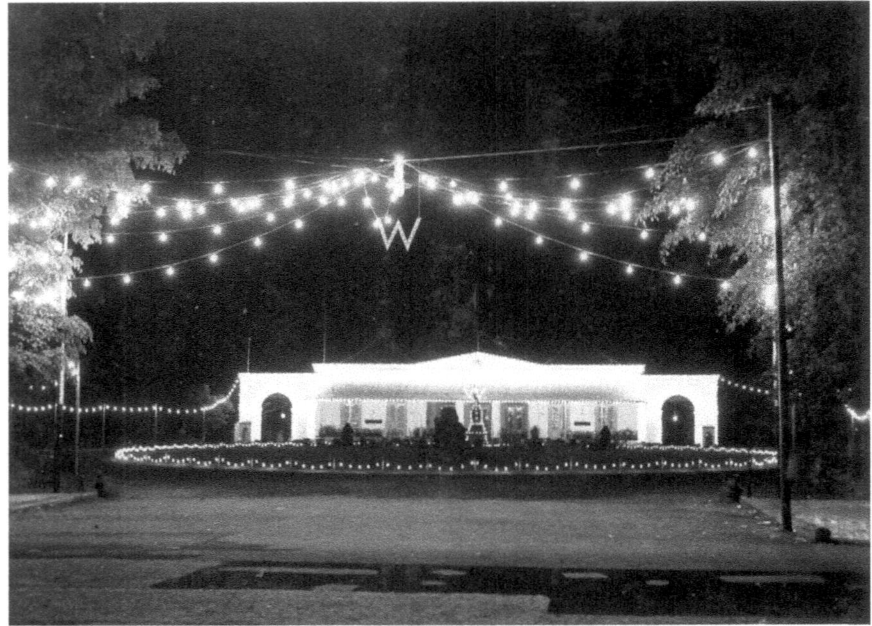

4.8 Collection R. Bijleveld-Visser, governor's house illuminated for the fortieth jubilee of HM Queen Wilhelmina, Yogyakarta (Java), 1938

the Dutch governor's residence as well as the Yogyakarta *kraton*. Johan Wouter Bijleveld (1888–1976), colonel of Yogyakarta's Military Health Service, was present at both events with his camera. A photograph album in the family's collection contains a striking image of the governor's electrically illuminated house and the lights strung across the gate to the sultan's palace to mark Wilhelmina's anniversary (figures 4.8 and 4.9). Images of Hamengku Buwono IX's inauguration, by contrast, focus on the spectacle of daytime processions through the city and the formal ceremony held in the *kraton*.[54] There is not a single photograph of nocturnal illuminations, despite the sultan's capacity to host such displays. Photographs of electric light, it appears, were confined to occasions celebrating the Dutch monarchy. Ceremonies for Javanese kings were to be pictured in daylight or not at all.

Heather Sutherland and John Pemberton have each argued that the royal houses of Central Java were maintained by the Dutch as bulwarks of 'traditional' Javanese courtly life, and as examples to lesser aristocrats of how to use their 'customary' influence to promote obedience to Dutch authority among the local population.[55] Such works have failed to recognise the Dutch regime's preoccupation with Oranje festivals

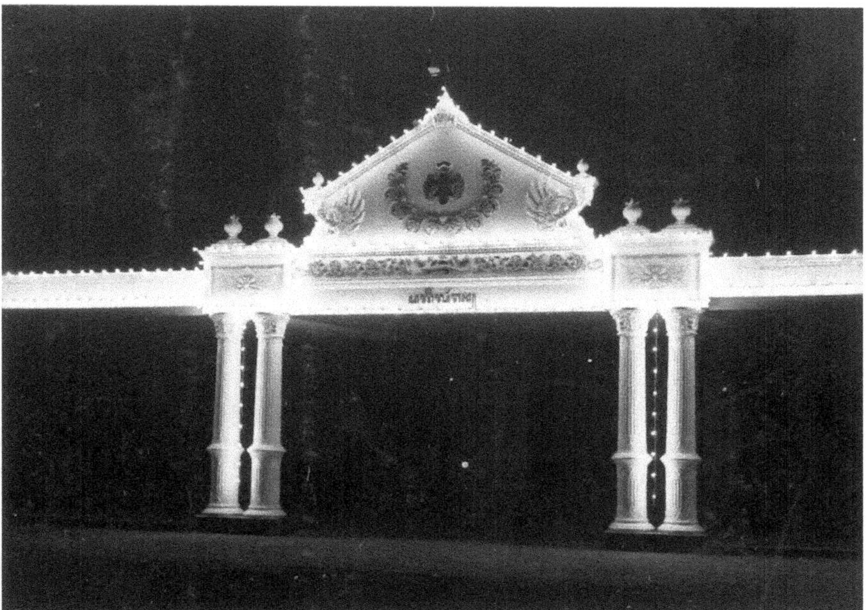

4.9 Collection R. Bijleveld-Visser, the Yogyakarta *kraton* illuminated for the fortieth jubilee of HM Queen Wilhelmina, 1938

in the Indies as the careful cultivation of 'soft' power of the kind demonstrated in Javanese public ritual. They do, however, provide a framework for understanding why the Dutch were concerned about whether the *kratons* of Central Java's kings should be connected to the electricity grid. Dutch authorities were increasingly of the view that it was not the task of 'traditional' Javanese rulers to guide their people into an enlightened future, but to protect them, by conjuring the illusion of continuity, from the dangers of rapid social change exemplified by nationalism, political Islam and communism. Europeans would be the bearers of modernity in the Indies and would determine the doses in which it would be delivered.

The rhetoric of the Ethical Policy frequently suggested that the progress of government modernisation programmes was rapid and uniform. Thus the renowned Indies economist W. M. F. Mansvelt (1891–1945), speaking on the occasion of Wilhelmina's fortieth regnal anniversary in 1938, remarked that the 'accelerated tempo of life' was one of the key features of his time, and claimed that transformations in 'the business world extended equally throughout all parts of Indies society'.[56] Mansvelt's assertions reveal an awareness of the quickening pace of modernisation in the late colonial period, but his characterisation of its even spread was influenced by ideology and wishful thinking, not by empirical observation and practical reality. There were significant differences across the East Indies regarding its exposure to novel technologies, ideologies and forms of social organisation.[57] Despite the triumphalist rhetoric of Dutch authorities, the colonial state had neither the means nor the inclination to modernise the entire archipelago. The overwhelming emphasis on developing Java's infrastructure at the expense of other parts of the Indies is evident not only in the collective name used by the Dutch to describe all the islands beyond Java – *Buitengewesten* or 'Outer Provinces' – but also in the distribution of utilities such as electricity.[58]

A commemorative volume issued for Queen Wilhelmina's silver jubilee in 1923 boasted that the hydroelectric potential of the Netherlands Indies surpassed the combined capacity of advanced industrial nations such as Switzerland and Germany. The fact that less than half a per cent of that potential had been exploited at the time of Wilhelmina's jubilee was deemed not important; an insight, perhaps, into the contemporary presumption of most Dutch authorities that there would be time enough to exploit the Indies' energy resources at the leisure of the colonial regime. The government's limited investment in electrification was mostly directed at the Residencies of Batavia and West Preanger, areas that had some of the highest density of Europeans and the longest histories of European settlement in the Indies. In the Outer Provinces, by contrast, most electrification projects were being carried out as 'particular initiatives', that is, by private contractors.[59]

The haphazard nature of modernisation projects beyond Java is evident in the official reports of civil servants who were posted to the Outer Provinces during the 1920s. The observations of G. L. Tichelman, whom we met in previous chapters, serve to illustrate this. Tichelman's civil service files from the mid- to late 1920s reveal that the progress of electrification in the Outer Provinces was slow, fitful and selective. At the end of his first posting in Dutch Borneo at Tanah Bumbu, in May 1926, the Handover Memorandum (*Memorie van Overgave*) for his successor records how the government was still in the process of collecting funds to finance an electricity network.[60] His next posting to Barabai lasted for three years, until May 1929. Throughout that period, Tichelman's *dagboek* (diary, a register of his official activities that he was obliged to supply to his European superiors) shows that he was regularly preoccupied with the progress of electrification. When he first arrived, construction of a new electricity substation for the town had just commenced. Such was the local excitement when the facility was completed three years later, in June 1929, that a 'festive opening' was held for the occasion.[61] Tichelman's *dagboek* records his enthusiasm not only in detailed written notes, but also in the captioned photographs of the substation that he used to supplement reports to his supervisors (figure 4.10).[62]

Before construction of the substation, Barabai's electricity supply was in the hands of private contractors. Their work, according to Tichelman, occasionally fell 'beneath expectations', resulting in frequent and sustained power shortages.[63] Indeed, photographs from Tichelman's private albums suggest that, as late as 1928, his own office may have been without electricity.[64] There are no photographs of nocturnal illuminations in Tichelman's albums of royal celebrations in Barabai during his term.[65] There is one photograph, however, that shows the power lines connecting the local cinema to the electricity grid. Significantly, the theatre was named after Crown Princess Juliana (figure 4.11).[66] Cinemas were modern innovations in their own right which harnessed light to broadcast moving pictures, and film was recruited to recording Ethical projects under the Dutch.[67] That a camera should be used to make a still image of this technology – physically connected to a fragile but developing electricity grid, and metaphorically linked to the House of Orange – was entirely in keeping with vernacular and official photographic practices closer to the centres of Dutch colonial power. Thus, while elements of the photographs taken by Tichelman in Dutch Borneo differed from images of electric illuminations in Java during the same period, the association in Indies photography between the House of Orange, modernity and enlightened rule was upheld.

Tichelman's written and photographic records reveal that electricity was being established in Barabai in the same pattern that it had followed on Java: for the convenience of a privileged few, mostly Europeans and the urban dwellers among whom they lived. The rest of the region remained immersed in darkness. During the period when Tichelman was posted there, Barabai had a population of more than 98,000 Malays, Dayak, Chinese and other 'Foreign Orientals', as well as some thirty Europeans.[68] Barabai was therefore one of the most densely populated areas of Dutch Borneo. Yet at the time of Tichelman's departure he estimated the uptake of electricity in and around Barabai to be only at 30 per cent of the substation's capacity, and connections to residential areas were still under way. Tichelman's records also show that once electricity was established in Barabai it was the European minority who were its chief beneficiaries. The roads within the main township, Kota Barabai, and its government and council buildings were the first to be connected to the grid.[69]

Images of electrification in Tichelman's private and professional photo albums accompanied other evidence of development in Barabai

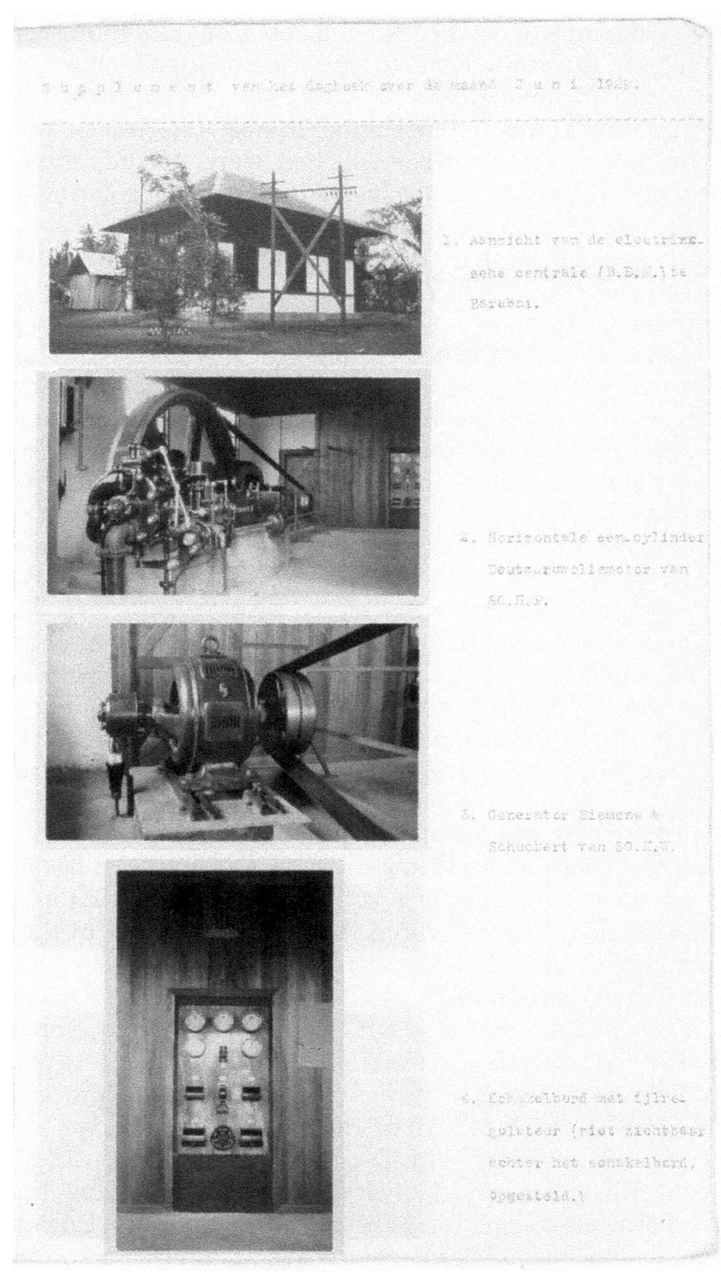

4.10 G. L. Tichelman, photographs from his 1929 government logbook showing the electrical substation at Barabai, Dutch Borneo

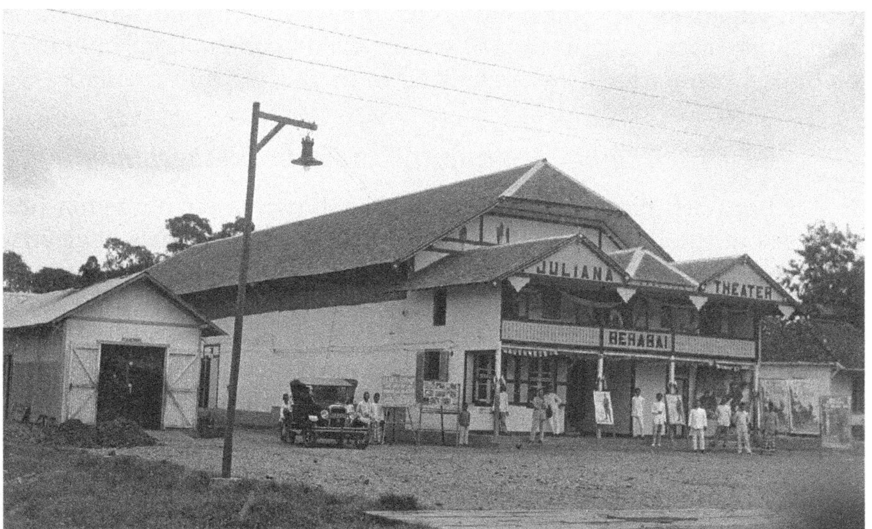

4.11 Collection G. L. Tichelman, the Juliana Theatre in Barabai,
Dutch Borneo

that he carefully documented – petrol pumps (supplied by Royal Dutch
Shell), a hospital, pharmacy and school, as well as new roads, bridges
and irrigation schemes.[70] The flicker of electric lights in Barabai's public
buildings thus signalled the partial fulfilment of the Ethical promise
that Queen Wilhelmina's announcement in parliament had heralded
almost three decades earlier.

Electricity was also lighting the way for the expanding frontiers of
the Dutch colonial state elsewhere. During the 1930s Dutch employees
of multinational corporations were laying claim to what would become
not only the latest territorial addition to the Netherlands Indies, but
also the last province that the Dutch government would cede to the
Republic of Indonesia in 1963, some fourteen years after its independence.
In New Guinea (now Irian Jaya, or West Papua), electricity was at the
vanguard both of commercial expansion and of a renewed Dutch
propaganda campaign to convert yet another native population into
the colonial subjects of a distant monarchy. The New Guinea album
of E. P. L. de Hoog, the Dutch engineer at the Netherlands New Guinea
Petroleum Company whom we encountered in the last chapter, shows
celebrations in the town of Babo for Wilhelmina's fortieth jubilee in
1938. It contains a photograph of an illuminated 'entrance to the *pasar
malam* [night market]' (figure 3.4). The drone of electrical generators,
it seems, defined the geographical frontier of early twentieth-century

Dutch expansion in South-east Asia. They illuminated Eurocentric traditions, interests and ways of seeing, even as the majority of newly colonised populations were relegated to mere shapes in the dark.

Northern lights: illuminations in the Netherlands

It was not until more than a decade after the same phenomenon first emerged in the Indies – in 1936, to be precise – that images of electric illuminations at royal celebrations became the subject of widespread photographic interest in the Netherlands.[71] It began with the same event that had inspired the 1937 *gedenkboek* made in the Indies for Crown Princess Juliana, namely, the announcement of her engagement to Prince Bernhard. Their marriage in 1937, and the birth of Juliana's first child in 1938, the Crown Princess Beatrix, guaranteed the succession. Juliana was to have three more daughters over the next nine years, an abundance of royal issue that had not happened since the reign of King Willem II in the mid-nineteenth century. The latter half of that century was almost ruinous for the House of Orange. Between 1850 and 1884 all three of King Willem III's sons died, together with their mother, Queen Sophie. 'It was as though a dark, disastrous cloud hung over our Royal House', one author of a 1948 commemorative book remarked, before describing the fortuitous birth and survival of Willem's last child, the future queen Wilhelmina, thus: 'But one ray of light remained: a young princess, born in 1880.'[72] To her Dutch subjects, Wilhelmina was from the very beginning a harbinger of light.

The fact that Juliana chose to marry a German prince in 1937 was ironic,[73] given the mounting concern in the Netherlands at that time about the actions of its neighbour across the eastern border. A veiled reference to the threat of war appeared in a book commemorating Wilhelmina's fortieth year as queen in 1938, once again invoking the association with light that seemed to follow her everywhere: 'The future throws its shadow', the author reflected, 'but also its light – let it come!'[74] It was during the last years before the German invasion of the Netherlands in 1940 that photographers began to focus on electric illuminations during royal occasions. As in the Indies, such images symbolised not only the splendour of the House of Orange but also Wilhelmina's stewardship over a period of recent modernisation in the Netherlands, which included improvements to the electrical infrastructure of its major cities.[75] Such advances, as one contributor to an official commemorative volume declared in 1938, meant that '[t]he connection with the East Indies and other remote territories made things possible that one could not have dreamed of 40 years ago'.[76] In the particular context of the late 1930s, the increased uptake of modern conveniences such as electricity also signalled the technological preparedness (not-withstanding its reluctance) of the Netherlands for war, were an aggressor to violate the country's declared neutrality. That public rituals during celebrations for the House of Orange became explicitly militaristic during this period further demonstrates how authorities in both countries were using such events to show their own and perhaps also enemy populations – in the Indies' case, Japan – that they were capable of resisting invasion.[77] In both instances, this turned out to be bravado. The Netherlands fell to German invasion forces within a matter of days in May 1940, and the Indies was conquered by Japan a few weeks after its invasion in February 1942.

As shown by Cees Fasseur, Wilhelmina's most renowned biographer, the strength of the queen's moral leadership from London, where the royal court was exiled during the Second World War, made her the most popular Dutch monarch in history.[78] Her people were reluctant to see her go when she abdicated in 1948, shortly after the celebration of her golden jubilee, in favour of Juliana. As it transpired, the new queen was on the cusp of losing a large chunk of her overseas empire. Soekarno declared the independent Republic of Indonesia in August 1945, after the Japanese capitulated to Allied forces. Dutch attempts to recolonise the former Indies were met with fierce resistance, and a revolution began. Juliana's inauguration as queen in September 1948 happened only months before the second major Dutch military action in the Indonesian War of Independence was launched.[79]

In the Netherlands during this period, official attention shifted to the colonies that remained loyal to the House of Orange. For the first time in Wilhelmina's reign, a volume was published that was dedicated entirely to the 'six Caribbean pearls' in the Dutch crown (that is, the West Indies).[80] Of the five books that were published in 1948 to com-memorate Wilhelmina and Juliana's historic year, two were totally silent on the 'bonds' that such volumes normally celebrated between the Netherlands, the House of Orange and its largest and most lucrative colony, the East Indies.[81] The other three volumes contained images of light displays that emphasised unity between the Netherlands and its rogue colony. One included a photograph of the electrically illumi-nated governor-general's palace, with the caption eschewing the new Indonesian name for its address, 'Jakarta', in preference for the colonial 'Batavia'.[82] A second volume featured the same photograph beneath the heading '*Licht en sfeer in eigen land en overzee*' (Light and atmos-phere in our own country and overseas). The accompanying text held that the palace 'beamed like a fairy tale ending in the tropical night. Overseas the festivities of the jubilee and inauguration were also enthusiastically celebrated.'[83]

The third commemorative volume reflected more deeply on Wilhelmina's legacy. One of the authors was Jan Willem Rengelink, a socialist born in 1912 in Amsterdam to a working-class family. He spent the Second World War in a manner that Wilhelmina would have approved of (notwithstanding his left-wing politics): spreading anti-Nazi propaganda, for which he was temporarily imprisoned, and working for the Dutch resistance. Rengelink's commitment to social justice and flair for journalism were put to further use in 1945, when he became chief of the General Commission for Reconstruction and Public Housing, where he was still employed when Wilhelmina celebrated her golden jubilee.[84] Rengelink presented his overview of Wilhelmina's reign in the form of a story told to him by a grandfather who had lived through the same half-century as the queen. The metaphor of light occurred frequently in the narrative, in words as well as pictures. Housing conditions for Amsterdam's poor, for example, were described thus:

> The houses were sombre and dark and the light pushed its way through with difficulty. As dark as their houses were, so was the life of a great portion of the youth at that time. It is fortunate that during the reign of Queen Wilhelmina much changed for the better.[85]

Two photographs illustrated the contrast. The first depicted a gloomy, narrow lane somewhere in the back streets of Amsterdam. The second showed new apartment blocks bathed in daylight. A caption spanning both images read 'From dark slums to … modern housing'.[86] Elsewhere in the book, Rengelink listed electricity among the technologies that transformed the Netherlands under Wilhelmina's reign. Further, while he acknowledged that there had been some 'dark pages' in the history of the relations between the Netherlands and its 'overseas territories', he was sure that the 'Dutch pioneering spirit' had generally benefited the Indies and other colonies.[87] Even at the end of Wilhelmina's reign, then, in the midst of the Indonesian War of Independence, Dutch commentators were blinded by their own metaphors in seeking evidence of enlightened colonial rule overseen by the queen.

Conclusion

During the first half of the twentieth century, light generated by electricity and captured by cameras in the Netherlands and the Indies left its traces in photographs that linked spectators and participants in royal celebrations within a transnational community of subjects who shared the fruits of an enlightened monarchy. This triumphalist vision became salient at distinct historical moments and places according to its political utility as a symbol of progress: in the Indies, during the polarisation of conservative and radical opinion in the early 1920s, and in the Netherlands, in the context of looming war during the late 1930s. The idea at the core of such photographs – that electrification demonstrated the effectiveness of Ethical colonial rule, a principle that was championed by a well-intentioned queen – circulated in both visual and textual forms throughout Wilhelmina's reign, trafficking back and forth between the Netherlands and the Indies in a lively current of exchange.[88] Thus, studio and amateur photographs of electric illuminations in the Indies extended nineteenth-century Dutch written traditions for describing royal festivals. These were later taken up by official photographers in the Indies and then the Netherlands. They subsequently informed new textual metaphors in reflections on Wilhelmina's reign at her abdication.

The fact that images of electric illuminations at royal festivals emerged in the Indies first, and in vernacular sources (family photographs and studio presentation albums) before official publications (exemplified by the *gedenkboek* genre), reiterates the importance of restoring the spectator to studies of colonial spectacle. Witnesses to royal celebrations in the Indies actively participated in the shaping of colonial visual culture by producing their own images and commemorations of public festivals. In doing so, they expressed ways of seeing that sometimes deviated from official sources, as the selective omission of electric illuminations in the Netherlands from the 1937 *gedenkboek* made in the Indies for Juliana's wedding demonstrates.

Photographs produced by amateurs as well as studio photographers in the Indies also shed new light on the social, political and economic inequalities fostered by colonial regimes. Dutch authorities portrayed themselves as the sole bearers of modernity in the Indies, to the exclusion of Indonesian rulers, thus upholding the principle of dualism upon which official discrimination against 'natives' was based. Indies' photographs also exposed the self-interest that undermined the humanitarian rhetoric of electrification. During Wilhelmina's reign, electricity accompanied the vanguard of Dutch mercantile and military expansion and cleaved to the European enclaves spawned by these enterprises. The 'rest' of the archipelago – beyond the centres of colonial power on Java or the clusters of commercial activity in the Outer Provinces – remained under the pall of neglect. The legacies of this uneven development would be felt in the independent Republic of Indonesia long after formal decolonisation had taken place.[89]

Visual representations of electricity in the Dutch colonial world reveal the cultural associations between monarchy and empire that developed during the early twentieth century. Photographs of electric illuminations at celebrations for the royal House of Orange suggest that the iconography of modernity was not, contrary to David Cannadine's assertions, exclusively associated with fascist Europe between the 1920s and 1940s. Liberal imperialist nations such as the Netherlands also exploited the spectacularity of electricity, both to uphold their authoritarian colonial regimes abroad and to polemically resist the danger of encroaching enemies in Europe. Public celebrations for the Dutch monarchy, in the Netherlands as well as the Indies, promoted modernity as one of the central tenets of enlightened rule. The maintenance of tradition that European royalty was supposed to symbolise in the modern era of secular nation-states does not, therefore, necessarily equate with stasis, but rather, with maintenance of the *status quo*.

Notes

1 Queen Wilhelmina, 'Troonrede van 17 September 1901', in *Troonredes, Openingsredes, Inhuldingsredes 1814–1963*, introduced and annotated by E. van Raalte ('s-Gravenhage: Staatsuitgeverij, 1964), pp. 193–4, at p. 194.

2 P. Brooshooft, *De ethische koers in de koloniale politiek* (Amsterdam: J. H. de Bussy, 1901).

3 On Wilhelmina's limited claim to the status of *ethicus*, see M. Grever, 'Colonial queens: imperialism, gender and the body politic during the reign of Victoria and Wilhelmina', *Dutch Crossing: A Journal of Low Countries Studies*, 26.1 (2002): 99–114, at p. 108. On her contemporary association with the Ethical Policy, see H. te Velde, *Gemeenschapszin en plichtsbesef; Liberalisme en nationalisme in Nederland, 1870–1918* (The Hague: SDU, 1992), pp. 147, 151–2; B. Waaldijk and S. Legène, 'Ethische politiek in Nederland; cultureel burgerschap tussen overheersing, opvoeding an afscheid', in M. Bloembergen and R. Raben (eds), *Het koloniale beschavingsoffensief; Wegen naar het nieuwe Indië, 1890–1950* (Leiden: KITLV Press, 2009), pp. 187–216, at pp. 197–201.

4 S. Legène and B. Waaldijk, 'Mission interrupted: gender, history and the colonial canon', in S. Stuurman and M. Grever (eds), *Beyond the Canon: History for the Twenty-first Century* (Basingstoke: Palgrave Macmillan, 2007), pp. 188–204, at p. 199; S. Protschky, 'Camera ethica: photography, modernity and the governed in late-colonial Indonesia', in S. Protschky (ed.), *Photography, Modernity and the Governed in Late-Colonial Indonesia* (Amsterdam: Amsterdam University Press, 2015), pp. 11–40, at pp. 14–15.

5 E. Locher-Scholten, *Ethiek in fragmenten; vijf studies over koloniaal denken en doen van Nederlanders in de Indonesische Archipel 1877–1942* (Utrecht: HES, 1981), p. 176; M. Bloembergen and R. Raben, 'Wegen naar het nieuwe Indië, 1890–1950', in M. Bloembergen and R. Raben (eds), *Het koloniale beschavingsoffensief; Wegen naar het nieuwe Indië, 1890–1950* (Leiden: KITLV Press, 2009), pp. 7–24, at p. 9.

6 D. Cannadine, *Ornamentalism: How the British Saw Their Empire* (London: Allen Lane, 2001), p. 130. George V's silver jubilee was in 1935, and George VI was crowned in 1936.

7 Or rather, rule of the Indies from The Hague, which was the platform of Indies parties that wanted to guarantee 'the Indies for the Indies' (independence from the Netherlands), while remaining open to the idea of Europeans sharing power with Indonesians to govern the Indies: Locher-Scholten, *Ethiek in fragmenten*, pp. 181–2; Bloembergen and Raben, 'Wegen naar het nieuwe Indië', p. 21.

8 *De Locomotief*, October 1919: cited in P. Eckhardt, 'Wij zullen handhaven! De symbolische betekenis van de Nederlandse monarchie in Nederlands-Indië 1918–1940', MA dissertation, University of Amsterdam, 2002, p. 31.

9 Eckhardt, 'Wij zullen handhaven!', pp. 29, 40, 43–4. On photography at Boven Digoel and the implications for an 'ethical' colonial rule, see R. Mrázek, 'Say "cheese": images of captivity in Boven Digoel (1927–43)', in S. Protschky (ed.), *Photography, Modernity and the Governed in Late-Colonial Indonesia* (Amsterdam: Amsterdam University Press, 2015), pp. 255–80.

10 A. Zuiderweg, 'Vuurwerk, illuminaties en wijnspuitende fonteinen; VOC-feestvreugde in Batavia', *Indische Letteren; Feesten in Indië*, 21.1 (2006): 81–94, at p. 82.

11 J. J. F. Wap, *Gedenkboek der inhuldiging en feesttogten van Zijne Majesteit Willem II 1840–1842* ('s Hertogenbosch: J.F. Demelinne, 1842), pp. 39, 75, 77, 89, 122, 167, 181–2, 211, 276.

12 Wap, *Gedenkboek*, pp. 77, 182.

13 Wap, *Gedenkboek*, p. 373.

14 It would not be until the late nineteenth century, during the reign of King Willem III, that the Dutch secured a decisive military defeat over local opposition.

15 Wap, *Gedenkboek*, p. 375.

16 *Officieel programma van de feesten, die gevierd zullen worden te Batavia ter gelegenheid van de troonbestijging en inhuldiging van Hare Majesteit Wilhelmina Helena Paulina Maria, Koningin der Nederlanden* (Batavia: Het Centraal Comité, 1898).

17 I do not include Wilhelmina's mother, Emma of Waldeck and Pyrmont, because she ruled as regent and was never a sovereign monarch.

18 KHA Album FA/0786.

19 H. W. Dick, *Surabaya, City of Work: A Socioeconomic History, 1900–2000* (Athens, OH: Ohio University Centre for International Studies, 2002), p. 261.

20 Batavia's electricity network was operational in 1897, Medan's in 1899 and Surabaya's in 1900: Dick, *Surabaya*, pp. 28, 42, 262.

21 D. van Lente, *Techniek en ideologie; opvattingen over de maatschappelijke betekenis van technische vernieuwingen in Nederland, 1850–1920* (Groningen: Wolters-Noordhoff and Forsten, 1988), pp. 5, 7, 8; D. van Lente, 'Ideology and technology: reactions to modern technology in the Netherlands 1850–1920', *European History Quarterly*, 22 (1992): 383–414, at p. 383.

22 On Onnes Kurkdjian, see A. Groeneveld, 'Photography in aid of science', in *Toekang Potret: 100 Years of Photography in the Dutch Indies 1839–1939* (Amsterdam/ Rotterdam: Fragment Uitgeverij/Museum voor Volkenkunde, 1989), pp. 27, 122, 163, 184; H. Hinzler, 'Onnes Kurkdjian: viewmaker and entrepreneur', in J. L. Reed (ed.), *Toward Independence: A Century of Indonesia Photographed* (San Francisco: Friends of Photography, 1991), pp. 59–63.

23 *Aan Hare Majesteit Koningin Wilhelmina en Zijne Hoogheid Hertog Hendrik van Mecklenburg-Schwerin, ter gelegenheid van hoogst derzelver huwelijk op 7 Februari 1901; Namens Banda's ingezetenen eerbiedig aangeboden door hun afgevaardigde A.E. Brunier, Directeur van de Bandasche Perkeniers- en Handels Vereeniging te Banda Neira* (Banda Neira, 1901). It is unknown who took the photographs for this album.

24 S. Protschky, *Images of the Tropics: Environment and Visual Culture in Colonial Indonesia* (Leiden: Brill/KITLV Press, 2011), pp. 27–9, 40–3.

25 *Namens Banda's ingezetenen*, plates 1 and 2.

26 KHA FA/0768. Some of the images were listed in the typewritten captions as having been made by a Mr de Vletter, but most were by an anonymous photographer.

27 On growing Dutch interest in *batik* as a Javanese art form during the early twentieth century, see S. Legêne, 'Uitspaning en inkleuring; batik en koloniale beeldvorming in Nederland', in *Spiegelreflex; Culturele sporen van de koloniale ervaring* (Amsterdam: Bert Bakker, 2010), pp. 119–56.

28 KHA FA/0768-3 and 6.

29 KHA FA/0768-32.

30 K. Strassler, 'Cosmopolitan visions: ethnic Chinese and the photographic imagining of Indonesia in the late colonial and early postcolonial periods', *The Journal of Asian*

Studies, 67.2 (2008): 395–432; K. Strassler, *Refracted Visions: Popular Photography and National Modernity in Java* (Durham, NC: Duke University Press, 2010), pp. 6, 14–15; K. Strassler, 'Modelling modernity: ethnic Chinese photography in the Ethical era', in S. Protschky (ed.), *Photography, Modernity and the Governed in Late-Colonial Indonesia* (Amsterdam: Amsterdam University Press, 2015), pp. 195–222. On the role of the Chinese as pioneers of photography in South-east Asia generally, see R. C. Morris, 'Introduction. Photographies east: the camera and its histories in East and Southeast Asia', in R. C. Morris (ed.), *Photographies East: The Camera and its Histories in East and Southeast Asia* (Durham, NC: Duke University Press, 2009), pp. 1–28, at p. 20.

31   See, for example, the address from the 'Chinese citizens and subjects of Your Majesty' in Sukabumi, who wrote to Wilhelmina in 1940: KHA A50 VIIIc_21h. In the same year, the Chinese Trade Association (*Tiong Hoa Siang Hwee*) wrote to the governor of Surakarta (who must have forwarded the letter to Wilhelmina) as Wilhelmina's 'subjects': KHA A50 VIIIc 21p. In 1923 Wilhelmina also received a jubilee gift of embroidered silk from Lo Ek Tjong, the 'Captain Chinese' of Padang (KHA A50 XIVc 21); a handwritten card in Dutch and Chinese from the 'Chinese inhabitants of Surakarta' on her fiftieth birthday in 1930 (KHA A50 VIIIc 17); and an address in Indonesian and Chinese from the Chinese of Cirebon in 1940 (KHA A50 VIIIc 21j).

32   D. Kwartanada, 'The Tiong Hoa Hwee Koan School: a transborder project of modernity in Batavia, c. 1900s', in S. Sai and C. Hoon (eds), *Chinese Indonesians Reassessed: History, Religion and Belonging* (Abingdon: Routledge, 2013), pp. 27–44.

33   L. Suryadinata, *The Culture of the Chinese Minority in Indonesia* (Singapore: Times Books International, 1997), p. 81; M. T. N. Govaars-Tjia, 'Hollands onderwijs in een koloniale samenleving; de Chinese ervaring in Indonesië 1900–1942', PhD thesis, Leiden University, 1999, p. 67; F. Colombijn with M. Barwegen, *Under Construction: The Politics of Urban Space and Housing During the Decolonization of Indonesia, 1930–1960* (Leiden: KITLV Press, 2010), pp. 82, 85; Kwartanada, 'The Tiong Hoa Hwee Koan School', p. 30.

34   Kwartanada, 'The Tiong Hoa Hwee Koan School', p. 27.

35   C. V. Reed, *Royal Tourists, Colonial Subjects and the Making of a British World, 1860–1911* (Manchester: Manchester University Press, 2016), p. xxvi.

36   KHA FA/0768–37. There were also Javanese as well as 'native' children (pupils at the *Hollandsch-Inlandsche School*), plates 34 and 35.

37   See also KHA FA/0768–18 and 20, which show the Assistant Residency and council buildings.

38   F. A. W. van der Lip, *Nederlandsch-Indisch Herinnerings-Album aan de verloving en het huwelijk van H.K.H. Prinses Juliana [en] Z.K.H. Prins Bernhard* (Bandoeng: Alubu, 1937), n.p.

39   The two other commemorative works written about the Indies to mark a royal occasion were L. F. van Gent, W. A. Penard and D. A. Rinkes, *Gedenkboek voor Nederlandsch-Indië; Ter gelegenheid van het regeeringsjubileum van H.M. de Koningin, 1898–1923* (Batavia: G. Kolff & Co., 1923), and a locally produced volume, *Gedenkbladen 25-jarig regeerings-jubileum van H.M. onze geëerbiedigde Koningin Wilhelmina* (Soerabaya: Soerabaiasch Comité tot Herdenking van het Regeerings-Jubileum, 1923).

40   R. Mrázek, *Engineers of Happy Land: Technology and Nationalism in a Colony* (Princeton, NJ: Princeton University Press, 2002), p. 93.

41   Only a few locations in the 'Outer Provinces' beyond Java were depicted, all of them in Dutch Borneo.

42   H. Sutherland, *The Making of a Bureaucratic Elite: The Colonial Transformation of the Javanese* Priyayi (Kuala Lumpur and Hong Kong: Heinemann Educational Books (Asia), 1979), pp. 16–17, 33, 54, 69, 72, 79, 130.

43   The Dutch promoted a Western-style education for elite Javanese girls. Only in the late 1920s did the government also begin to encourage secondary education and professional training for a wider female demographic: E. Locher-Scholten, 'Colonial

ambivalencies: European attitudes towards the Javanese household (1900–1942)', in J. Koning et al. (eds), *Women and Households in Indonesia: Cultural Notions and Social Practices* (Richmond: Curzon Press, 2000), pp. 30, 38–9.

44 G. Oostindie, *De parels en de kroon; Het koningshuis en de koloniën* (Amsterdam: De Bezige Bij, 2006), pp. 58, 70.

45 L. Ouwehand, *Herinneringen in beeld; Fotoalbums uit Nederlands-Indië* (Leiden: KITLV Press, 2009), pp. 137–61.

46 KITLV Album 914, shelf marks 45755–45768.

47 H. Schulte Nordholt, 'Onafhankelijkheid of moderniteit? Een geïllustreerde hypothese', in M. Bloembergen and R. Raben (eds), *Het koloniale beschavingsoffensief; Wegen naar het nieuwe Indië, 1890–1950* (Leiden: KITLV Press, 2009), pp. 105–20, at pp. 106–8, 114; T. Hoogervorst and H. Schulte Nordholt, 'Urban middle classes in colonial Java (1900–1942): images and language', *Bijdragen tot de Taal-, Land- en Volkenkunde*, 173 (2017): 442–74.

48 See Raden Adjeng Kartini, *Door duisternis tot licht; Gedachten over en voor het Javaansche volk*, with an introduction by J. H. Abendanon ('s-Gravenhage: Luctor et Emergo, 1923). Benedict Anderson also notes that metaphors of light were common in publications by the proto-nationalist organisation Budi Utomo: B. Anderson, *Language and Power: Exploring Political Cultures in Indonesia* (Ithaca, NY: Cornell University Press, 1990), p. 243. On Philips advertising in the Indies, see H. Maier, 'Maelstrom and electricity: modernity in the Indies', in H. Schulte Nordholt (ed.), *Outward Appearances: Dressing State and Society in Indonesia* (Leiden: KITLV Press, 1997), pp. 181–99.

49 Only the buildings in the princely *kraton* of Mangkunegoro VII were photographed in an electrically illuminated state: see Van der Lip, *Nederlandsch-Indisch Herinnerings-Album*.

50 *Djåwå* was the official periodical of the Java Institute, established in Yogyakarta in 1919, an organisation whose European and Javanese members tended to be attached to the Central Javanese courts. The periodical was published from 1921 to 1941: S. Robson, 'Introduction', in S. Robson (ed.), *The Kraton: Selected Essays on Javanese Courts* (Leiden: KITLV Press, 2003), pp. ix–xxvi, at p. ix; J. Pemberton, *On the Subject of 'Java'* (Ithaca, NY: Cornell University Press, 1994), p. 103.

51 V. Zimmerman, 'The kraton of Surakarta in the year 1915', trans. R. Robson-McKillop, originally published in *Djåwå* in 1915, in S. Robson (ed.), *The Kraton: Selected Essays on Javanese Courts*, (Leiden: KITLV Press, 2003), pp. 41–64, at p. 58.

52 Robson, 'Introduction', p. 373.

53 Th. Pigeaud, 'The northern palace square in Yogyakarta', trans. R. Robson-McKillop, originally published in *Djåwå* in 1940, in S. Robson (ed.), *The Kraton: Selected Essays on Javanese Courts* (Leiden: KITLV Press, 2003), pp. 1–12, at p. 7.

54 See also KITLV Album 289, shelf marks 35206–35219.

55 Sutherland, *The Making of a Bureaucratic Elite*, pp. 13, 76, 154; Pemberton, *On the Subject of 'Java'*, pp. 121–2, 191.

56 W. M. F. Mansvelt, 'De economische ontwikkeling van Ned. Indië sedert 1898', in *Bij het regeerings jubileum 1898–1938 van Hare Majesteit Koningin Wilhelmina* (Batavia: Kantoor voor de Volkslectuur, 1938), pp. 51–63, at p. 57.

57 R. Raben, 'Hoe wordt men vrij? De lange dekolonisatie van Indonesië', in E. Bogaerts and R. Raben (eds), *Van Indië tot Indonesië* (Amsterdam: Boom, 2007), pp. 13–29, at p. 21. See more generally F. J. Lechner, who argues that globalisation has been 'irregular in strength, speed and impact. It varies over time: It is more intense in some periods than others': F. J. Lechner, *The Netherlands: Globalization and National Identity* (London: Routledge, 2008), p. 39.

58 Mrázek, *Engineers of Happy Land*, pp. 93, 95, 161; A. Vickers, *A History of Modern Indonesia* (Cambridge: Cambridge University Press, 2005), pp. 24–5.

59 Van Gent, Penard and Rinkes, *Gedenkboek voor Nederlandsch-Indië*, pp. 405–6, 407.

60 NL-HaNA, Tichelman 2.21.097.01, inv. nr. 13: *Bestuurs Memorie van Overgave der Onderafdeeling Tanah Boemboe dd. 10 Mei 1926*, pp. 1–2.

61 NL-HaNA, Tichelman 2.21.097.01, inv. nr. 20: 'Dagboek van de tijd: v[an] d[en]: Controleur der Onderafdeeling BARABAI over de maand Juni 1929', pp. 1–2.
62 See also photographs in NL-HaNA, Tichelman 2.21.097.01, inv. nr. 22.
63 NL-HaNA, Tichelman 2.21.097.01, inv. nr. 20: 'Dagboek van de tijd'. Problems with securing contractors and thus a regular supply continued right up until Tichelman's departure in 1929: NL-HaNA, Tichelman 2.21.097.01, inv. nr. 23, pp. 12–14.
64 KITLV Album 188, shelf mark 83653.
65 KITLV Album 189.
66 See also NL-HaNA, Tichelman 2.21.097.01, inv. nr. 23, p. 12.
67 J. G. Taylor, 'Ethical policies in moving pictures: the films of J. C. Lamster', in S. Protschky (ed.), *Photography, Modernity and the Governed in Late-Colonial Indonesia* (Amsterdam: Amsterdam University Press, 2015), pp. 41–70.
68 NL-HaNA, Tichelman 2.21.097.01, inv. nr. 21, p. 57; *Algemeene Memorie van Overgave der oderafdeeling Barabai*.
69 NL-HaNA, Tichelman 2.21.097.01, inv. nr. 23, pp. 12–14.
70 NL-HaNA, Tichelman 2.21.097.01, inv. nr. 22; KITLV Album 189.
71 See *Het Prinselijk Huwelijksfeest* (Haarlem: De Spaarnestad, 1937), pp. 22–3; *De veertigjarige regeering van H.M. Koningin Wilhelmina; 1898–6 September–1938. Oranje album* (Amsterdam: Holdert & Co., 1939); D. Kouwenaar, *Amsterdam tijdens het feestbetoon bij het 40-jarig regeeringsjubileum van H.M. Koningin Wilhelmina van 5 tot 12 September 1938* (Amsterdam: De Bussy, 1938).
72 J. W. Rengelink and I. Mug, *Koningin Wilhelmina 1898–1948* (Heemstede: Mubro, 1948), p. 8.
73 Juliana was not the first, nor would she be the last, Dutch monarch to marry German nobility. A German line runs at least as strongly as a Dutch one through the Oranje-Nassau dynasty: H. Dijkhuis, *Monarchia; Het fenomeen van het koningschap* (Amsterdam: Boom, 2010), p. 250; M. E. Hay, 'Russia, Britain and the House of Nassau: the re-establishment of the Orange dynasty in the Netherlands, March–November 1813', *BMGN/Low Countries Historical Review*, 133.1 (2018): 3–21.
74 Kouwenaar, *Amsterdam tijdens het feestbetoon*, p. 38.
75 An exhibition of advances in the residential and commercial uptake of electricity in Amsterdam was shown at the Colonial Institute in Amsterdam for Wilhelmina's silver jubilee in 1923: *Catalogus van de Jubileum-Tentoonstelling 1923 gehouden ter gelegenheid van het 25-jarig regeeringsjubileum van H.M. de koningin in het Koloniaal Instituut te Amsterdam 3–30 September* (Amsterdam: Van Holkema & Warendorf, 1923), p. 17. See also Van Lente, *Techniek en ideologie*, pp. 5, 7, 8.
76 J. Feith, *Wilhelmina Regina; Nederland gedurende veertig jaren* ('s-Gravenhage: Zuid-Hollandsche Uitgevers Maatschappij, 4th edn, 1938), p. 41.
77 There was a whole chapter on the colonial army in the 1923 commemorative book published in Amsterdam, but no photographs of militarised festivals: A. T. H. Winter, 'Het Nederlandsch-Indische Leger, 1898–1923', in W. G. de Bas, *25 jaar geschiedenis van Nederland 1898–1923* (Amsterdam: Dalmeijer's Volksuniversiteit, 1923), pp. 257–66. See photographs of military bands and pageants in *Herinnering aan den Oranje-Zaterdag 9 September 1933 ter gelegenheid van het 35-jarig Regeerings-Jubileum van H. M. Koningin Wilhelmina* (Amsterdam: N. V. Handelsdrukkerij Holdert & Co., 1933); *De veertigjarige regeering van H.M. Koningin Wilhelmina* (1939); *Oranje-album ter herinnering aan het 50-jarig regeringsjubileum en de abdicatie van H.M. Koningin Wilhelmina en de inhuldigingsfeesten van H.M. Koningin Juliana, September 1948* (Amsterdam: Holdert & Co., 1948).
78 C. Fasseur, *Wilhelmina; Krijgshaftig in een vormeloze jas* (Amsterdam: Balans, 2001), pp. 491–2, 570.
79 There were two so-called 'police actions' launched by the Dutch against Indonesian militias, the first from 21 July to 5 August 1947, and the second from 19 December 1948 to 5 January 1949. The campaigns' official names were 'Operation Product' and 'Operation Crow'.

80 *Oranje en de zes Caraïbische parelen; Officieel gedenkboek ter gelegenheid van het gouden regeringsjubileum van Hare Majesteit Koningin Wilhelmina, Helena, Pauline, Maria, 1898 – 31 augustus – 1948* (Amsterdam: De Bussy, 1948).

81 See *Wilhelmina-Juliana gedenkalbum 1948 uitgegeven ter gelegenheid van het gouden regeringsjubileum van H.M. Koningin Wilhelmina en de inhuldiging van H.M. Koningin Juliana, 31 Augustus–6 Sept. 1948* (Haarlem: Spaarnestad, 1948); and *De gouden kroon; Gedenkboek bij gelegenheid van het gouden regeringsjubileum van H.M. koningin Wilhelmina* (Haarlem: Spaarnestad, 1948).

82 *Oranje-Album ter herinnering aan het 50-jarig regeringsjubileum*, n.p.

83 *Wilhelmina-Juliana gedenkalbum 1948*, p. 9.

84 H. Wijfjes, 'Rengelink, Jan Willem (1912–1999)', in *Biografisch Woordenboek van Nederland*, www.inghist.nl/Onderzoek/Projecten/BWN/lemmata/bwn6/rengelink (last accessed 16 April 2018).

85 Rengelink and Mug, *Koningin Wilhelmina 1898–1948*, p. 18.

86 Rengelink and Mug, *Koningin Wilhelmina 1898–1948*, pp. 18–19.

87 Rengelink and Mug, *Koningin Wilhelmina 1898–1948*, pp. 24–6.

88 See also B. Waaldijk and S. Legêne, 'Ethische politiek in Nederland: cultureel burgerschap tussen overheersing, opvoeding en afscheid', in M. Bloembergen and R. Raben (eds), *Het koloniale beschavingsoffensief; Wegen naar het nieuwe Indië, 1890–1950* (Leiden: KITLV Press, 2009), pp. 187–216, at pp. 200–1, 205–10.

89 Raben, 'Hoe wordt men vrij?', pp. 18, 28.

CHAPTER FIVE

Snapshot diplomacy: photographic encounters between Dutch and Indonesian royals

In the 1990s, half a century after the King of Surakarta's death, the American anthropologist John Pemberton was in Central Java conducting fieldwork when he encountered a faintly salacious story about the erstwhile monarch that was still in circulation among Solonese:

> After hours and in the privacy of his inner Kraton quarters, Pakubuwana X was known to order palace servants carefully to pin great clusters of honorary medals to His Highness's behind. The king then sat quietly in state, smiling blissfully. Some courtiers argued that this was a gesture of protest against Dutch intrusion into Kraton affairs; others reasoned that although Pakubuwana X was endowed with a figure indeed grand, His Majesty had simply run out of space for all the honor bestowed on him.[1]

While there is (not surprisingly) no lasting visual evidence to support this legend of the Axis of the Cosmos sitting on his medals, Pemberton deemed the act 'quite plausible as an early twentieth century response to His Majesty's shrinking cosmos'.[2] He alludes here to the progressive Dutch incursion upon Central Javanese kings' powers in the Princely States (*vorstenlanden*), which I described in Chapter 2.

What we *do* know from photographs is that, throughout the 1920s and 1930s, Pakubuwono X sent many portraits of himself to Queen Wilhelmina and the Crown Princess Juliana that substantiate his proud possession of royal orders from the Dutch House of Orange (figure 5.1). Indeed, David Cannadine's satire of 'veritable walking Christmas trees of stars and collars, medals and sashes' would do for these portraits.[3] The enduring rumours around what Pakubuwono X did with these decorations in private illuminates how post-colonial Solonese remained divided over the ambiguous historical image of their former king's relationship with the Dutch. Was he, as Dutch officials of that period cynically held, a ruler whose compromised sovereignty was easily

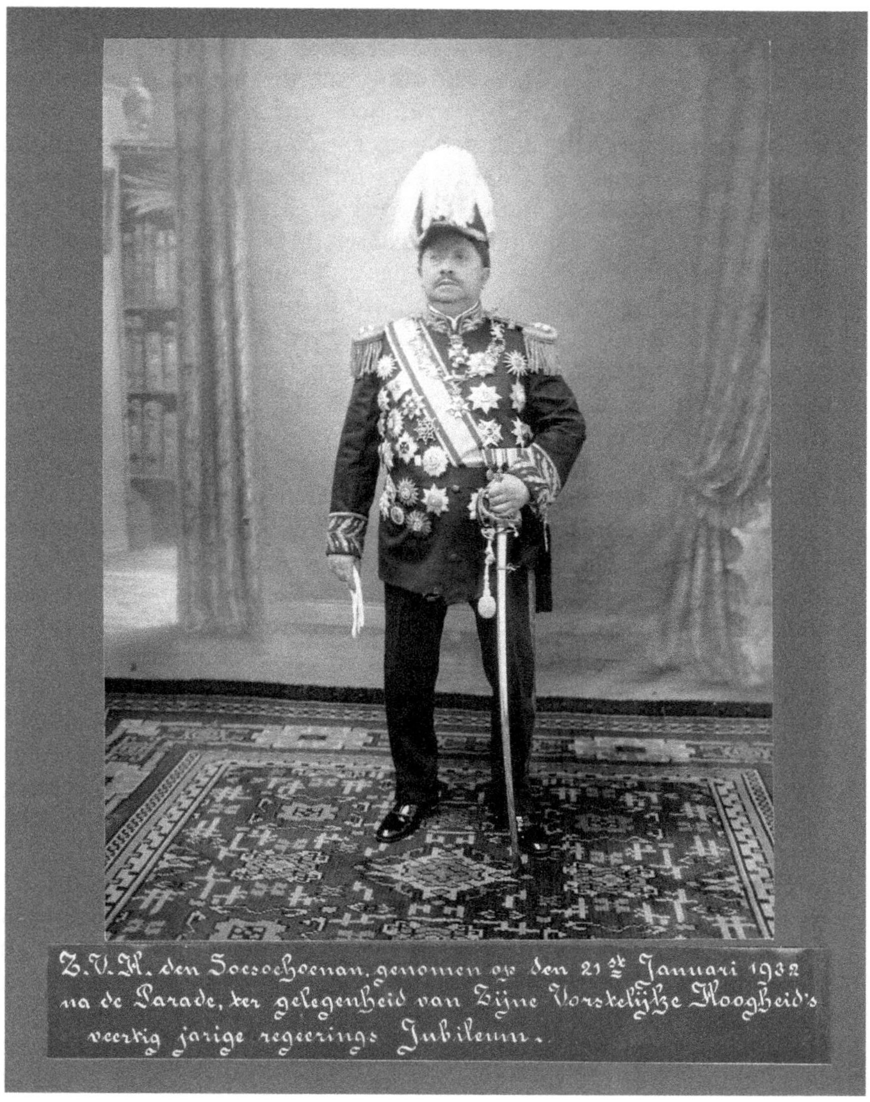

5.1 Album of Pakubuwono X, 'H[is] P[rincely] H[ighness], the *soesoehoenan*, taken on 21 January 1932 after the parade on the occasion of His Princely Highness's fortieth regnal jubilee'

placated by feeding his fetish for prestigious trinkets?[4] Or was he, as Pemberton and other scholars have characterised him, a seemingly compliant vassal to the Dutch monarch who found subtle and mischievous ways to rebel against his subordination?[5]

Throughout his long reign, from 1893 until his death in 1939, Pakubuwono X was an enthusiastic trader of gifts with Queen Wilhelmina's household.[6] At the same time, and despite his penchant for travel in the Indies, he staunchly abstained from ever visiting her court in the Netherlands. With the notable exception of the Mangkunegaran, the other royal houses of Central Java followed a similar pattern of preferring gift exchanges and delegations of their family members to personal audiences with the Dutch monarch. In fact, as I have discussed elsewhere, most of the Indigenous kings and princes of the Indies sent proxies from their households to honour the queen at her court rather than attend themselves.[7] Wilhelmina's famed disinclination to tour her colonies was thus reciprocated by the vast majority of Indonesian royals who refused to meet her on Dutch soil.[8]

Among the numerous truants at regnal milestones for Wilhelmina, the royals of Central Java were prominent in sending photographic portraits of themselves as diplomatic gifts. The absence of these royals from the queen's court in the Netherlands therefore needs to be understood as a political act in two parts: first, a refusal to simply present themselves as the vassals they were deemed to be, and second, a decision to engage in 'snapshot diplomacy', using photographs to negotiate a more nuanced recognition of their own sovereignty in dialogue with Dutch authority. The numerous portrait photographs that Indonesian royals sent of themselves instead of appearing in person at Wilhelmina's court might be interpreted as exercises of their right not to be present at all – just as the queen never deigned to visit the Indies in person, for reasons that included her reluctance to compromise her own singular authority as an imperial queen.

In this chapter I argue that, just as the proliferation of photography in the Netherlands Indies filled the void of Wilhelmina's absence with a visual and material culture rich in social and political functions, so photography enabled Central Javanese royals to pursue more complex relations with the Dutch monarchy than has previously been recognised. Indeed, the fact that Mangkunegoro VII (r. 1916–44), who was otherwise an avid sponsor of photography at his court, was the only Central Javanese royal both to meet the queen *and* not to send her an album as a gift reinforces the importance of photography as a proxy in snapshot diplomacy.[9]

Along with the photographic gifts of Pakubuwono X of Surakarta, this chapter examines two other Javanese royals who were contemporaries of Queen Wilhelmina: Sultan Hamengku Buwono VIII (r. 1921–39) and Prince Pakualam VII (r. 1906–37) of Yogyakarta. These three royals' photograph albums, which are now housed in the Dutch Royal

Collections, have rarely been examined as sources on diplomacy.[10] And yet the photographic exchanges between Central Javanese and Dutch royals were situated in an international context where a visual dialogue between Indigenous and European monarchs had been a standard component of imperial relations since the nineteenth century. Scholarship on this topic has revealed how visual encounters enabled Indigenous monarchs to exert agency over images of themselves and resist some colonial protocols of subordination. Sean Willcock has demonstrated how, by making uncooperative portrait-sitters, Indian rajas and maharajas thwarted British artists' attempts to celebrate Queen Victoria.[11] Maurizio Peleggi has shown how gifts of photographic portraits from Thai kings to European heads of state were material strategies in the Thai monarchy's attempts to iterate its modernity as an institution, preserve its sovereignty against European expansion, and assert its place among 'members of the world's royalty'.[12] Similarly, Anne Maxwell has argued that Hawai'ian monarchs issued portraits of themselves to an international public to promote their own modernity and dignity, and thereby refute the necessity of the annexation to America that finally came in 1898.[13]

In this chapter, I examine photographic gifts from Central Javanese royals to the Dutch monarchy both as Indonesian sources that provide an entry into Indigenous courts under colonial pressure, and as prisms into encounters with the House of Orange. Like their Asian and Pacific counterparts, Javanese royals – notably Pakubuwono X and Pakualam VII – exercised their prerogative to appear both in Western dress (and therefore, as moderns) *and* in Indigenous royal attire (ancient tradition being a hallmark of aristocracy). Hamengku Buwono VIII, by contrast, distinguished himself by refusing to appear even in portrait form before Queen Wilhelmina. In competition with Dutch pretensions of grandeur, the sultan and prince of Yogyakarta shared a flair for exploiting the material and visual potential of the album form to promote their court cultures: the sultan as an alternative to exhibiting himself, the prince in addition to showing his entire dynasty.

This chapter therefore extends a link with the House of Orange, and adds a photographic genealogy, to the historical reputation of the Yogyakarta aristocracy for resisting Dutch incursions on its sovereignty, made legendary by the formal assistance it extended to Indonesian nationalists during the late 1940s.[14] The necessary pragmatism of the Yogya royals in acquiescing to Dutch expectations remained, however, a component of their photographic diplomacy. Conversely, the *susuhunan* of Surakarta showed a penchant for subversion in his snapshot diplomacy that suggests he was rather less compliant with Dutch authority than is usually asserted. Acts of resistance as well as accommodation were mingled in both the form and content of all three royals' photographic gifts to the House of Orange.

Diplomatic gifts from Indonesian royals to the Dutch monarchy

Gifts and letters between Indonesian royals and members of the House of Orange had been changing hands since the advent of a Dutch maritime presence in the archipelago in the sixteenth century.[15] As Adam Clulow has shown, during the seventeenth and eighteenth centuries the House of Orange was often disadvantaged in its proxy encounters with monarchs in Asia, since the Princes of Orange were not kings in any sense, and it was a company, the Dutch East India Company, and its chief agent, the governor-general, that represented Dutch strategic interests in the region.[16] In 1800 the Dutch East India Company was dissolved. Meanwhile, the Napoleonic Wars in Europe left the stewardship of Dutch possessions in the Indies contested between France, the Netherlands and Britain. In 1816 Dutch authority on Java resumed, this time as a crown colony, for in 1814 the House of Orange had been installed as a monarchy, following the 'restoration' – or in the Dutch case, creation – of royal heads of state all over Europe in the wake of Napoleon's defeat. From then onwards, the fortunes of the Dutch monarchy in Asia ascended relative to Indonesian monarchies' decline, in tandem with the territorial and constitutional expansion of colonial authority across the archipelago. Treaties (*verklaringen*) of subjugation between colonial authorities and Indigenous royals were always made in the name of Dutch monarchs (even if, as the previous chapter explained, the nature of Indigenous sovereignty within the Dutch colonial state varied enormously from polity to polity).

Most of the royal gifts from Indonesia to the House of Orange during the colonial period comprised of costly objects in a distinctly Indonesian idiom: items considered *pusaka* (sacred heirlooms) in Indigenous courts throughout South-east Asia. These were precious objects of ivory, silver, gold and *suasa*, an alloy more prized in many parts of Indonesia than any single metal. *Sirih* (betel) sets and tea services were common gifts, as was the *kris*, a distinctive Javanese dagger with an undulating blade and jewelled hilt.[17] *Batik* cloth printed with patterns exclusive to royalty and textiles woven with gold and silver thread were also among the courtly gifts sent by sultans and rajas to celebrate the inaugurations and regnal milestones of Dutch royals.

From around the reign of Wilhelmina's father, King Willem III (r. 1849–90), the significance of these objects in Indonesian courts was often explictly conveyed not just in the letters of tribute that accompanied them from the royal senders, but also via explanatory missives passed on to the monarch, often through the Minister for the Colonies, which were written or translated by colonial officials trained in Indonesian languages, court arts and cultures, and ethnography.[18] By the time of Wilhelmina's reign, the established position of 'Indology' in Dutch academies and the colonial civil service, and the support of Javanese arts and crafts by the Dutch and colonial establishment – supported by Wilhelmina's patronage – made for a diplomatic environment in which such courtly gifts to the House of Orange were highly valued. The Indies Hall (*Indische Zaal*) in the Paleis Noordeinde, the gift to Queen Wilhelmina for her wedding that was funded by donations from the Netherlands Indies, represents the culmination of connoisseur and mainstream interest in courtly material cultures from Indonesia during her reign.[19]

Early modern princely collections represent the material roots of such modes of display, and their iconographic origins might be traced to seventeenth-century Dutch paintings of colonial trade commodities.[20] In the twentieth century, however, Dutch royal exhibitions of gifts from Indies kings and princes functioned as spectacular displays of *magisterial* authority, rather than princely power of the kind represented in curiosity cabinets or mercantile wealth flaunted in still life paintings. In the modern Netherlands, public showings of precious diplomatic gifts from its colonies gave novel form and meaning to older visual discourses of Dutch power.

An example of the Dutch monarchy's role in promoting these connections occurred in early 1937, soon after the wedding of Crown Princess Juliana. The *pusaka* items she received as gifts from Indonesian royals were displayed at an exhibition for the public at Kneuterdijk Palace in The Hague.[21] The exhibition reframed these gifts as ethnographic objects to encourage a peculiarly Western mode of seeing embedded in European histories of collecting and museums.[22] In doing so, these objects entered the Dutch public realm in ways that differed fundamentally from their customary uses in South-east Asian courts. Where *pusaka* in their local settings usually represented the supernatural or divine powers of Indigenous royals, in their Dutch palace and museums settings they were recast as tribute from overseas possessions commanded by the centripetal authority of a colonial monarchy.[23]

While scholarly interest in traditional, courtly gifts from Indonesian royals has been entirely proportionate to their number in Dutch royal collections, as well as their value to both the givers and the recipients both then and now, it to some extent also follows in the paths forged by colonial interests. These well-trodden trails have rarely digressed to the photographs that began to change hands between Dutch and Indonesian royals from the late nineteenth century onwards, and that proliferated during Wilhelmina's reign. The only scholar to have commenced work on these is Rita Wassing-Visser, who wrote the important but mostly descriptive catalogue of Indonesian gifts in the Dutch royal collections.[24] Perhaps this is because the receipt of photographic gifts by Dutch royalty was comparatively late by European standards. British monarchs had been receiving photographs of Asian kings since the nineteenth century. King Rama IV of Siam (r. 1855–68), for instance, was an avid sender of portraits to Queen Victoria.[25] In Central Java, some royals had already begun to embrace photography around the same time, notably Hamengku Buwono VI, who appointed Kassian Cephas (1845–1912) as his court photographer in 1871.[26] It was not until 1898, however, when Queen Wilhelmina was inaugurated, that a Dutch monarch received a photographic portrait from a Central Javanese king.

That portrait came from Pakubuwono X, the most enduring and prolific giver of photographs to the Dutch monarchy during Wilhelmina's reign. In 1898 the young king sent a pair of photographic portraits to Wilhelmina, one showing himself, and the other one of his wives, the Ratu Hemas. The next occasion was in 1923, to celebrate Wilhelmina's silver jubilee. This was the first time that he sent a whole photograph album, which showed the Surakarta *kraton* celebrations.[27] Two more followed: one in 1932, celebrating his own fortieth jubilee, and another in 1937, for Crown Princess Juliana's nuptials.[28] The latter showed the *susuhunan*'s participation in a gala dinner held on 7 January at the residence of Governor J. J. Treur. Juliana's wedding also prompted album gifts from Pakualam VII and Hamengku Buwono VIII, which I will also analyse in this chapter.

Evidence from the Dutch Royal Collections suggests that photographs were ranked quite low in Queen Wilhelmina's repertoire of gifts for and from Indies kings. In 1923, for example, Pakubuwono X, Pakualam VII and Hamengku Buwono VIII sent Wilhelmina gifts of framed photo-portraits of themselves and their chief spouses for her silver jubilee.[29] The queen's response reveals her sensitivity to the hierarchy of royals in Central Java, and her eagerness to exchange gifts with eminent rulers in a Javanese idiom.[30] She sent Pakualam VII a signed portrait of herself to thank him for his portrait gift, but the *susuhunan* of Surakarta and the Sultan of Yogyakarta each received a ceremonial sword (*prachtsabel*) inscribed with the words '[From] Queen Wilhelmina to [recipient] 1923'.[31] Wilhelmina thus appeared to deem modern gifts such as photographs appropriate for princes, but considered 'traditional' gifts such as bladed weapons a better offering for higher-ranking royals. At the public exhibition of Indonesian royal gifts for Juliana in 1937, the unprecedented array of Central Javanese photograph albums she received was notably absent.[32] This is perhaps surprising given that, of all the gifts sent by Indies royals, the albums were objects whose explicit and primary function was to be *looked at* rather than used in some other way. Further, the captions and dedications in all three albums were written in Dutch so that they could be read without the need for translation. The pages of black-and-white photographs that the albums contained were at once more ephemeral than the litany of glittering, solid objects that Juliana received and also more conspicuously modern, material representations of their senders than the ceremonial Indies gifts that her wedding occasioned. Perhaps it was for this reason that they were omitted from the exhibition. The photograph albums may not have appeared authentically exotic enough in the Dutch imagination to represent gifts from Indies sovereigns.

Yet the photograph albums given to Wilhelmina and Juliana in the 1920s and 1930s reveal how Pakubowono X, Hamengku Buwono VIII and Pakualam VII innovated on the art of diplomacy in their courts with these gifts. In this regard, I contest Wassing-Visser's otherwise important foundational work, which implicitly relies on notions of gift exchange that emphasise obligations of reciprocity and bonds of social solidarity.[33] Recent research reveals that 'gift practices tell conflicting narratives', and that the exchange of presents can productively be conceived as 'a form of social theatre in which shifting relationships are dramatised, created, dissolved'.[34] Interpreted in this way, the albums given by Javanese royals during Wilhelmina's reign were more than material tokens in a cross-cultural exchange intended to enhance good relations between noble families. Their content is frequently ambiguous, and the complex meanings that arise from their inconsistencies reveal how their Javanese senders used photography to negotiate their status and represent images of themselves as both modern and traditional rulers to their Dutch recipients.

Presenting as moderns: concessions and agency in photographic gifts from Central Java's kings

Even if by proxy rather than in person, Pakubuwono X and Pakualam VII conceded to presenting themselves to the Dutch monarchy in photographic form to mark royal occasions. The visual economy in which portraits of Central Javanese kings and princes circulated was fundamentally different from that of the Dutch royal family, and not for technological reasons. While the rulers of Central Java inhabited the same world of mass print media, visual representations of them continued to rest upon notions of kingship that emphasised the essential disparity between Asian monarchs and their subjects, concepts that focused on their divine status, dynastic dignity and public, ritual functions, rather than on their ordinariness, similitude to commoners and private pursuits. The preference for formal studio portraits among Javanese kings, rather than for the casual, candid photographs that middle-class Javanese were beginning to embrace in the early twentieth century, contributed to upholding these distinctions.[35]

That both Pakubuwono X and Pakualam VII wore honours bestowed by the House of Orange and elements of Western and Javanese dress signified complex negotiations of status with Dutch royal power. Further, Prince Pakualam VII's self-presentation as monogamous, despite the widespread practice of polygamy in his and other Central Javanese courts, was a straightforward concession to Dutch conventions that were formalised by protocols at Wilhelmina's court. In making these representations, however, the *susuhunan* of Surakarta and prince of Yogyakarta consistently positioned themselves as modern rulers, and thus as equals to leading members of the House of Orange.

Pakubuwono X proved to be Wilhelmina's most willing photographic subject. No other Indonesian monarch offered more photographs of himself to the House of Orange. Both he and Prince Pakualam VII gave portraits only partially showing themselves to Juliana.[36] The *susuhunan* 'presented' more of himself to the queen than to the princess: both the albums he sent Wilhelmina commenced with full-length portraits.[37] In 1932 he appeared as a learned, Westernised king, standing against a backdrop of bookshelves and clothed in the uniform of a major-general in the Netherlands Indies Army (KNIL) (figure 5.1). On gala occasions, Dutch military dress was imposed on all Javanese nobility.[38] In the 1937 album for Juliana, Prince Pakualam VII similarly had himself and all his ancestors represented in Dutch military jackets with gold epaulettes.[39] The prince is bare-headed and wears spectacles (figure 5.2). By contrast, colonial portrait and postcard archives from the nineteenth century onwards show that elite Javanese men more frequently had their portraits taken in hybrid costumes, with Dutch military-style jackets worn on their torso, Javanese *batik* as headgear, and *kain* (skirt-cloths) covering their lower bodies.[40] Pakualam VII's 1937 album, which contains portraits by Studio J. H. Zindler Jr in Yogyakarta, depicts only his two eldest sons in traditional dress. They wear head-cloths and body coverings of *batik* patterned with motifs that were restricted to the immediate members of the princely family, and pose so that their ceremonial krises are visible (figure 5.3).

Significantly, Pakualam VII's principal wife, who sits beside him in the portrait, also wears traditional costume (figure 5.2). The prince's spouse and sons thus visually preserve courtly customs even as the head of the dynasty leads the way into the future by sartorially

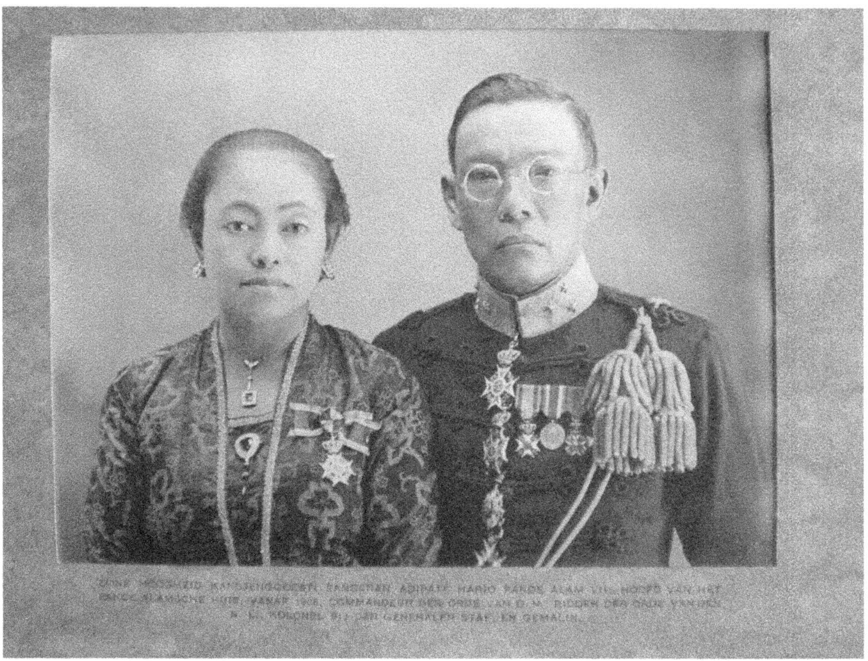

5.2   Atelier J. H. Zindler Jr, 'His Highness Kandjenggoesti Pangeran Adipati Hario Pakoe Alam VII, Head of the House of Pakoe Alam, from 1906, Commander in the Order of O[ranje-]N[assau], Knight in the Order of the D[utch] L[ion], Colonel in the General Staff, and consort'

demonstrating his facility with Western forms. Indeed, as Jean Gelman Taylor has shown, in the late colonial period it was chiefly elite Javanese men who were licensed to experiment with European influences through adopting the Western suit. Upper-class women, by contrast, were charged with bearing the standards of Javanese tradition.[41] Well into the twentieth century, women's adherence to *kain-kebaya* (*batik* skirt and blouse) in official photographs, as well as at public ceremonies, expressed gendered political spheres for Javanese elites.

At the same time, Pakualam VII's consort is the first and only woman in his dynasty to be depicted wearing the women's Order of the Dutch Lion (figure 5.2). All the princes of the line but one wear royal honours from the House of Orange.[42] Special distinction is reserved for Pakualam VII himself, who not only boasts the most medals but also has prestigious orders listed in the caption to his photograph: Knight in the Order of the Dutch Lion (worn on his breast) and Commander in the Order of Oranje-Nassau (the chain around his neck). Pakubuwono X's famous

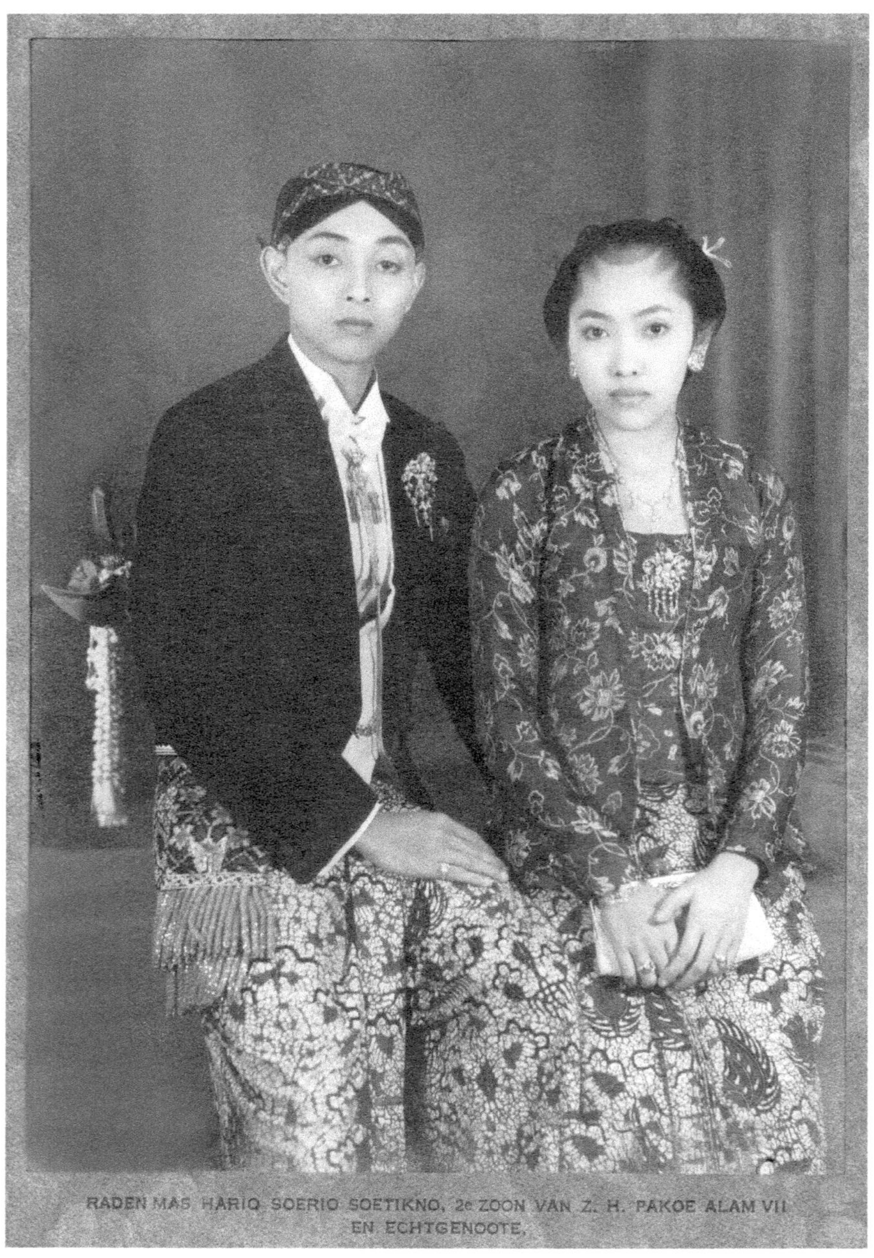

5.3   Atelier J. H. Zindler Jr, 'Raden Mas Hario Soerio Soetikno, second son
of H[is] H[ighness] Pakoe Alam VII and consort'

penchant for honours is evident in his photographs for Wilhelmina. In the 1932 portrait (figure 5.1), he stands in a virtual armour of more than twenty medals, including the prestigious Grand Cross of the Order of the Dutch Lion, which he received from Wilhelmina specifically to mark his forty years as king.[43] The *susuhunan* also wore civil orders of chivalry such as the Order of Oranje-Nassau, created in 1892 during the regency of Queen Emma. While the number of civil orders given out increased after around 1920, knighthoods and other high honours remained more or less reserved for nobility.[44]

For Javanese kings, much like their Indigenous counterparts in British colonies throughout Asia, royal distinctions from a foreign monarch were a double-edged sword. On the one hand, such awards brought Asian kings into an elite, international fellowship that augmented their prestige at home as well as abroad.[45] Certainly, in Javanese palaces Dutch royal honours were frequently transliterated into Javanese script and filled the first pages of palace documents that announced royal decrees. They were also read out among the king's titles at public ceremonies.[46] On the other hand, royal honours reinforced the subordination of Asian elites to the European monarchs who were, after all, sovereigns of these orders of chivalry.[47] In the Dutch empire such awards signalled recognition of service to the House of Orange.

Pakualam VII's and Pakubuwono X's posing for photographs in European clothes similarly suggests concession to colonial powers that had encroached on their very persons. Yet the Western suit also afforded elite Asian men 'an opportunity for sartorial play and for resembling the forms of European power'.[48] To wear a Western suit demonstrated an understanding of clothes as 'a powerful signifier of cultural and class identity in a society that was being increasingly mediated by visual apparatuses'.[49] Following Pemberton, the appropriation of European modes of dress can thus be interpreted as an act 'of cultural transvestitism that gave the Dutch an identifiable and implicitly subordinate place in Javanese court ceremony'.[50]

Importantly, it remained the unique prerogative of these Javanese royals to appear in their Indigenous regalia.[51] European authorities in the Indies did not have the same breadth of repertoire. Dutch officials wore European dress in public, and while many governors and governors-general were of noble birth, none could claim royal status and dress accordingly.[52] The capacity to combine Javanese and European elements of dress, as Pakubuwono X did, or to divide sartorial labours between members of the household, as did Pakualam VII, expressed the privilege of having it both ways: facility with Western culture, modern ways and deference to the House of Orange, as well as embodying local culture, traditional practices and pride in Central Javanese courts.

Where the *susuhunan* of Surakarta and the prince of Yogyakarta more clearly deferred to Dutch royal authority was in the photographic representation of their status as monogamous rulers. In all three of his album gifts, Pakubuwono X usually appeared with only his principal wife, mirroring the Dutch couple who were in attendance at all celebrations for the House of Orange, the Resident/governor and his wife.[53] The *susuhunan* broke from this convention in his visual diplomacy with the Dutch monarchy only once. Among the silver jubilee gifts he sent Wilhelmina in 1923 was a triptych of painted portraits, framed in elaborately carved teak, of himself, his queen (Ratu Pakubuwono) and his youngest wife (Ratu Mas).[54] However, the three portraits were separable, perhaps to give the queen the option of dismantling and rearranging the set. The representation of princely couples in Pakualam VII's 1937 album shows four of the six princes with a single wife (the others are represented alone).[55] All these portraits depart from more common Javanese photographic customs of rulers having themselves depicted with their multiple consorts and extended families.[56]

Given that all the kings and princes of Central Java were polygamous, the choice to have themselves depicted to the House of Orange with only one spouse signalled a nominal deference to European familial and sexual mores in general, and to Wilhelmina's preferences in particular. Similar concessions appear to have been made by Thai kings, who were polygamous until 1910, in the portraits they sent of themselves with their consorts to Western heads of state.[57] Wilhelmina was devoutly Christian, confessing in the autobiography published near the end of her life that, throughout her reign, she had often felt 'lonely but not alone', consoled by her faith in times of trial.[58] Some of her tribulations no doubt included her husband's infidelities, and later those of her son-in-law, Bernhard, a proclivity neither she nor Juliana shared.[59] Wilhelmina was devoted to Prince Hendrik while they were married and, like her cousin, Queen Victoria, remained a pious widow long after his death. Wilhelmina thus epitomised the feminine Christian virtues of religious faith and wifely fidelity.

As I have discussed elsewhere, from at least the mid-1920s, if not earlier, Wilhelmina's court enshrined these values in its protocol governing the reception of 'Native and Foreign Orientals' from the Indies. This document extended to regulating her encounters with the women of polygamous, mostly Muslim Indonesian dynasties.[60] It detailed the queen's preference for Indonesian royals not to bring their wives at all. If their presence could not be avoided, however, her audience with them occurred in private and 'in an entirely "European" fashion'.[61] Not just a polite Javanese regard for foreign customs, but also Dutch courtly instruments influenced how Indigenous kings and princes appeared to the Dutch monarchy, in person but perhaps also in photographs.

Powers of refusal: absence and (not) looking at the queen in snapshot diplomacy

Recent histories of settler colonialism have demonstrated the importance of refusal to engage as an important strategy of survival, maintaining sovereignty and preserving dignity for Indigenous people in their encounters with Europeans.[62] Fenneke Sysling has shown how Indonesians similarly used techniques of refusal – withholding access to their bodies, not allowing themselves to be photographed – in resisting the invasive and often degrading procedures that European physical anthropologists attempted in the course of their research.[63] Elites had even more recourse to such actions. With a few exceptions, the sultans and rajas of Indonesia declined to present themselves to Queen Wilhelmina at her court in the Netherlands, despite the fact that many were wealthy and well-travelled. The barb within the gifts of photograph albums that the royals of Central Java sent to Wilhelmina was their emphasis on images of people who refused to attend in person.

Sultan Hamengku Buwono VIII made perhaps the most emphatic point of his absence by declining to include a single portrait of himself in the album gifts he sent to Wilhelmina in 1923 and Juliana in 1937. Instead, his albums showed *wayang wong* (dance drama) performances held at the Yogyakarta *kraton* in their honour. In doing so, he complied with the necessity of celebrating the Dutch monarchy without having to negotiate the Dutch-inflected customs and rituals that Javanese royals were increasingly drawn into at celebrations for the House of Orange. This is not to say that Hamengku Buwono VIII was exempt from such duties. On the contrary, colonial photographic sources show the sultan taking his obligatory part in gala dinners for the Dutch monarchy, wearing his military uniform like the other Javanese kings (see figure 2.6).[64] By taking himself out of the picture in his albums for Wilhelmina and Juliana, however, the sultan refused to allow them even to set eyes on his portrait.

In his study of Javanese royals' interactions with Dutch colonial authorities at public festivals, John Pemberton focused on the residents and governors with whom ceremonial positions had to be negotiated *in situ*. He attends to the live audience of spectators and participants – Dutch officials, Javanese courtiers and masses of commoners – who were always present when court photographers recorded Central Javanese royals' roles in public festivals.[65] In the albums that Javanese royals sent to Dutch counterparts all these audiences were present, but the ultimate spectators were Wilhelmina or Juliana. Taking this combination of proximate and remote audiences into account is crucial for understanding the complex, triangular dialogue between Javanese royals as photographic subject-givers, their *in situ* audiences, and Dutch royal viewer-recipients. In Hamengku Buwono VIII's album, he virtually invites Wilhelmina and Juliana into the audience – perhaps as the guest of honour – to watch the performance that he commanded, but does not engage with them as a photographic subject. The albums of Pakubuwono X, which include numerous photographs of the *susuhunan*, invite the queen and crown princess to look at *him* as well as the proceedings.

The uses and directions of the king's gaze in this context are pertinent to understanding the encounters in this snapshot diplomacy. Scholars of colonial photography have had much to say about 'the gaze' as an element of relations between Indigenous photographic subjects and their Euro-American viewers, the power dynamics of which were often determined by the class of the sitter. Historical records are replete with photographs of impoverished, unfree or subjugated Indigenous people who were vulnerable to coercion from colonial authorities, including photographers whose ethnographic, medical, administrative and commercial projects impinged on the identity, agency and dignity of these sitters. The constructed 'otherness' of Indigenous people in such colonial encounters is often signalled by their averted gaze – their inability or disinclination to meet the eye of the photographer/viewer and submit to being looked at.[66] Indigenous elites throughout South and South-east Asia, by contrast, were avid patrons of photographic studios and, in many cases, their own court photographers. Their possession of wealth, prestige, power and even divinity in portrait photography is evident, among other features, in the direction of their gaze right back at the photographer.[67]

Importantly, however, the mark of power is not always that it looks into the camera. As Pemberton has explained in his examination of Pakubuwono X's court photographs, the king refused to meet the eye of the Dutch governor at *kraton* events even when Dutch convention demanded it, such as at the proposal of toasts.[68] It was the 'pronounced rivalry' between the king and the Dutch official that partly explains the former's asymmetric gaze.[69] However, it was also conventional for Javanese kings to appear thus before their subjects in public places outside the *kraton*, including at the governor's residence. When the king faced the people gathered on the northern square of his palace, he was meant to seem 'frozen in his capacity of portrayed perfection', like an icon or the statue of a god. Only in the inner parts of the *kraton*, where he received Javanese nobles and foreign dignitaries, was he to be seen in movement.[70]

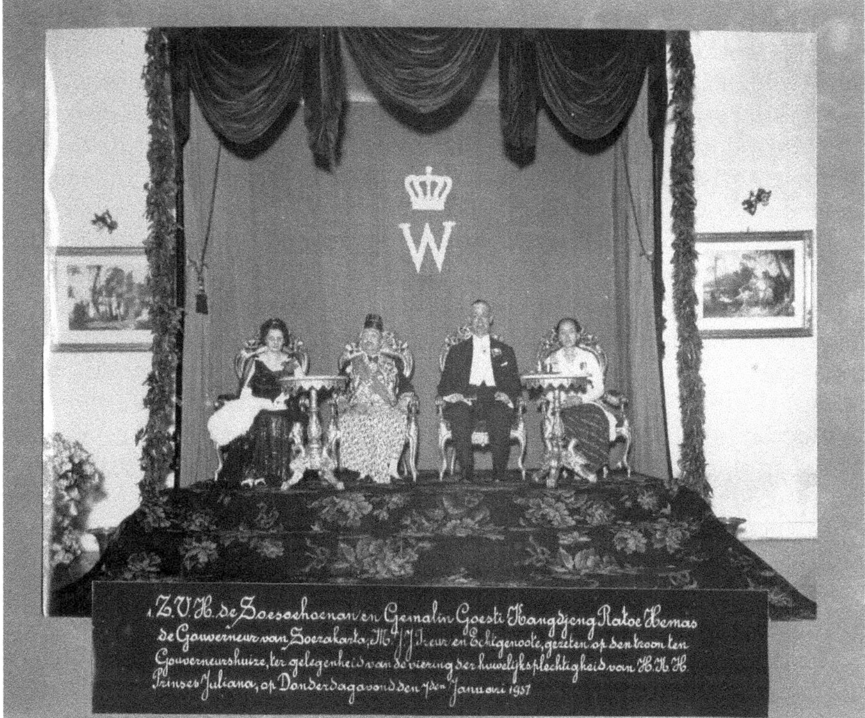

5.4 Album of Pakubuwono X, 'H[is] P[rincely] H[ighness] the *soesoehoenan* and consort Goesti Kandjeng Ratoe Hemas[,] the Governor of Surakarta, Mr J. J. Treur and wife, sitting on the throne at the Governor's House, on the occasion of the wedding celebration of HRH Princess Juliana, on Thursday evening of 7 January 1937'

Pakubuwono X's almost uniform decision to adopt a three-quarter profile in his album gifts for Wilhelmina takes on new implications when the queen is integrated into the picture as a spectator. Pakubuwono's refusal to look at – to recognise – Dutch authority extends to her. His disinclination to meet the viewer's eye is most pronounced in his album gift to Juliana in 1937, where the contrast between himself and the Dutch Governor Treur, who looks directly into the camera and smiles in every photograph, could not be more pronounced (figure 5.4). Photographs fix the iconic posture of the *susuhunan* perfectly and permanently, and extend it to *all* spectators, present and future, including the queen and her heir.

The 1932 album gift that Pakubuwono X sent to Wilhelmina to mark his own fortieth regnal jubilee departs somewhat from this mode.

Many of its photographs effectively place Wilhelmina in the audience among the king's subjects, as though looking at him: on his throne in the Golden Pavilion, on a balcony overlooking a parade of his troops, or passing street spectators in his royal coach. However, in every one of these photographs, Pakubuwono X shares the stage with the queen's representative, at that time Governor J. J. van Helsdingen. Indeed, the captions to the photographs taken in the pavilion mention a single throne (*troon*) rather than the seats that were allocated to each of the two men. As though to make the implications crystal clear, one set of photographs in the album actually reverses the conventional posture of these notional throne-sharers. In the first, Van Helsdingen mimics the regal, off-centre stare of the king. In the second, the governor and king sit side-by-side and Pakubuwono X finally looks into the camera.[71] Numerous photographs throughout the album evoke a shared perspective between the king and governor: for example, views of the distinguished guests taken from and looking back at the throne (figure 5.5), or perspectives on the triumphal arches raised throughout Solo's streets from the middle of the road rather than the sidelines, effectively replicating the view of the king and governor as they toured the city together in the royal carriage.

In the other albums, which celebrated Dutch royal milestones, it may have been permissible for Pakubuwono X to exercise his regal right to look away. But in the 1932 album, which celebrated his own prolonged kingship (and a milestone that Wilhelmina would not attain for another six years), Pakubuwono X had to diplomatically share his festival with the queen's representative. Here, the dialogue between the king's gaze, that of his colonial shadow and the spectating queen deferred to her privilege not only to look into but *with* the eyes of Pakubuwono X and the governor by his side.

Contests of tradition: asserting dynasty and celebrating court arts

Pakubuwono X's album celebrating a regnal jubilee of his own is one of two instances in the 1930s when Javanese royals asserted their dynasties in photographic gifts to the Dutch monarchy. His album signalled a relatively recent change in Javanese royal customs, namely, to adopt the Western practice of commemorating annual anniversaries.[72] It was a transformation that may have responded to the increasing energy that Dutch officials poured into organising annual celebrations for Queen's Day from the 1920s onwards. Then, in the 1930s, there seemed an endless string of new causes for celebrating the House of Orange, each of which prompted public pageantry and, for the royals

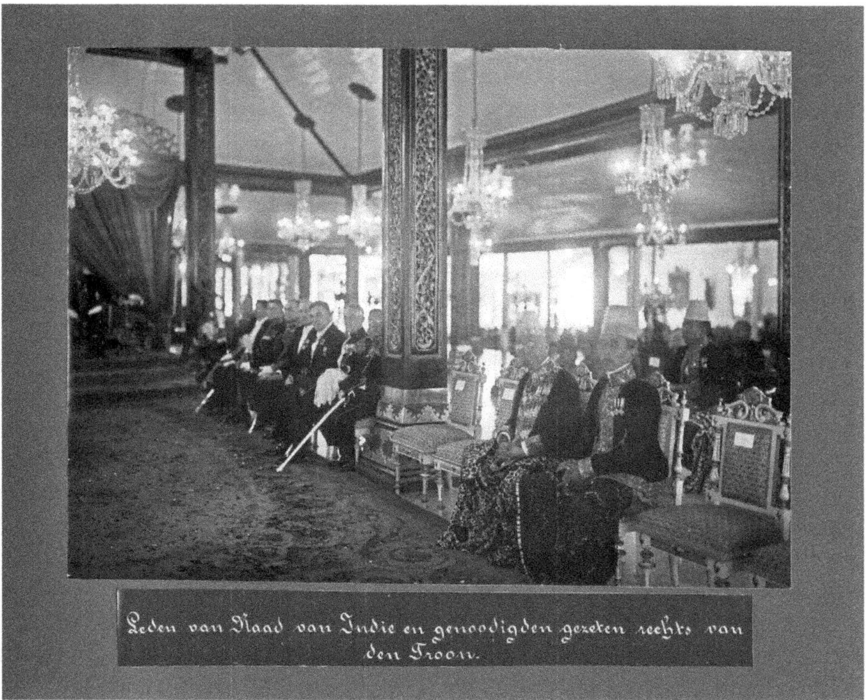

5.5 Album of Pakubuwono X, 'Members of the Council of the Indies and distinguished guests to the right of the throne'

of Central Java, required their participation in parties for the Dutch monarchy. Wilhelmina turned 50 in 1930. In 1933 there was the dynastic anniversary of the House of Orange, celebrating the birthday of the first Prince of Orange, Willem the Silent, four centuries earlier. The death in 1934 first of Wilhelmina's mother, Queen Emma, and then her husband, Prince Hendrik, cast somewhat of a pall in the middle of the decade. But this was followed by the crown princess's wedding in 1937, Wilhelmina's fortieth jubilee and the birth of Princess (later, Queen) Beatrix in 1938, and the birth of a second baby, Princess Irene, in 1939. For Pakubuwono X, the opportunity to celebrate his fortieth jubilee and mark the bicentenary of his dynasty in 1939 may have been too irresistible an opportunity to forgo in among all these festivals for the Dutch monarchy.[73]

Pakualam VII was evidently likewise inclined in 1937, when he sent an album as a wedding gift to Crown Princess Juliana. Within the flurry of royal celebrations around that time, her marriage was of great significance because, assuming Juliana was fertile (and she was), her wedding was the crucial first step in the production of legitimate heirs and the continuity of Wilhelmina's line. Pakualam VII chose this moment to send his first and only album, which came in the form of a visual genealogy of his heirs and forbears. The first five portraits in the album presented his predecessors, from Pakualam II to VI.[74] Although photography already existed during the reign of each of these princes (and photographic images of some survive); they were rendered in hand-drawn images by a Solo artist who appears to have made all the portraits during the 1930s.[75] Not until Pakualam VII and his wife were represented, half-way through the album, do the photographic portraits commence, and continue with images of the prince's heirs (figures 5.2 and 5.3).

Pakualam VII's decision to start the photographic part of the album with himself symbolised a claim of dynastic regeneration. A Javanese family's power was believed 'to grow diffuse over generations', following Benedict Anderson, and was in fact entirely diluted by the *seventh* generation so that, 'unless it was renewed and reintegrated by the personal efforts of a particular descendant, the dynasty would fall of its own enfeebled lack of weight'.[76] Further, the ability to reconcile opposites, including the skill of melding tradition with modernity, was held as the sign of a powerful ruler.[77] Being the seventh in the dynasty, the prince of Yogyakarta had a great responsibility to fulfil. Pakualam VII's use of photography – a modern technique for portraiture – to depict himself and his descendants visually asserted the rejuvenation of his dynasty at a crucial stage in its life cycle, as well as at an important moment in its relationship with the House of Orange.

Along with his appreciation for and patronage of modern arts such as photography, the prince of Yogyakarta was keen to promote the traditional arts of his court in his gift to the crown princess. As we shall see, he had much in common with the sultan in this regard. Both royals used their photograph albums for Juliana in 1937 to celebrate the cultures and luxuries produced in Yogya. Pakualam VII chose the material, decorative elements of his album to evoke court traditions. Its heavy, engraved silver binding, stamped with a crown and the prince's monogram, celebrated the distinctive silverwork of Yogyakarta for which the city remains famous today (figure 5.6).[78] The opening pages contain the Dutch-language dedication to Juliana and Bernard (and the only overt reference to the occasion for the gift), which is framed by a *wadana*, an ornamental frontispiece that functioned as a 'textual gateway' into Javanese palace manuscripts. The lavish frame was decorated with peacocks and the wings of the mythical *garuda* bird, Indic symbols of royalty and power (figure 5.7).[79]

The visual genealogy in Pakualam VII's gift to Juliana was therefore couched in an idiom that combined courtly Javanese material culture

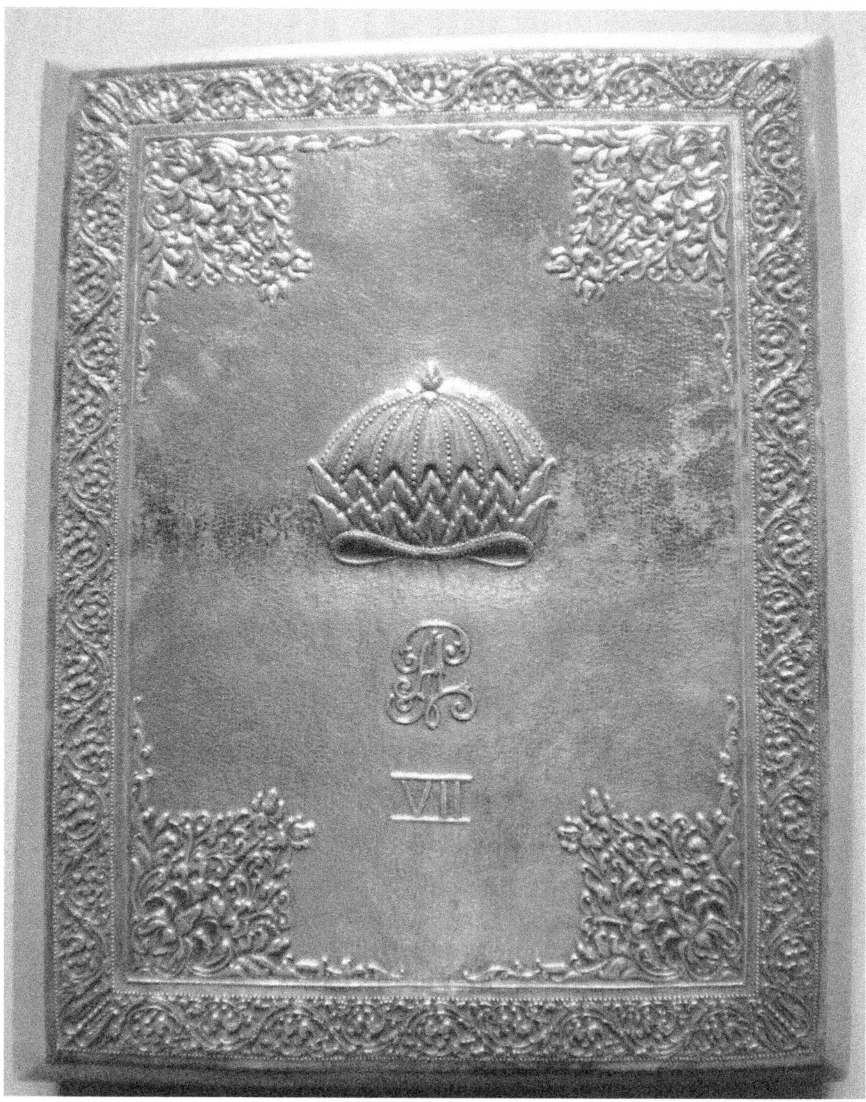

5.6   Cover of the album given as a wedding present by Pakualam VII to
Crown Princess Juliana, 1937

(silverwork, manuscript illumination and ceremonial costumes) with
elements that revealed his dynasty's partial incorporation into a colonial
order presided over by a rival monarchy (royal decorations, Dutch
military jackets and images of monogamous couples). These elements
can be interpreted as concessions to the celebration of Crown Princess

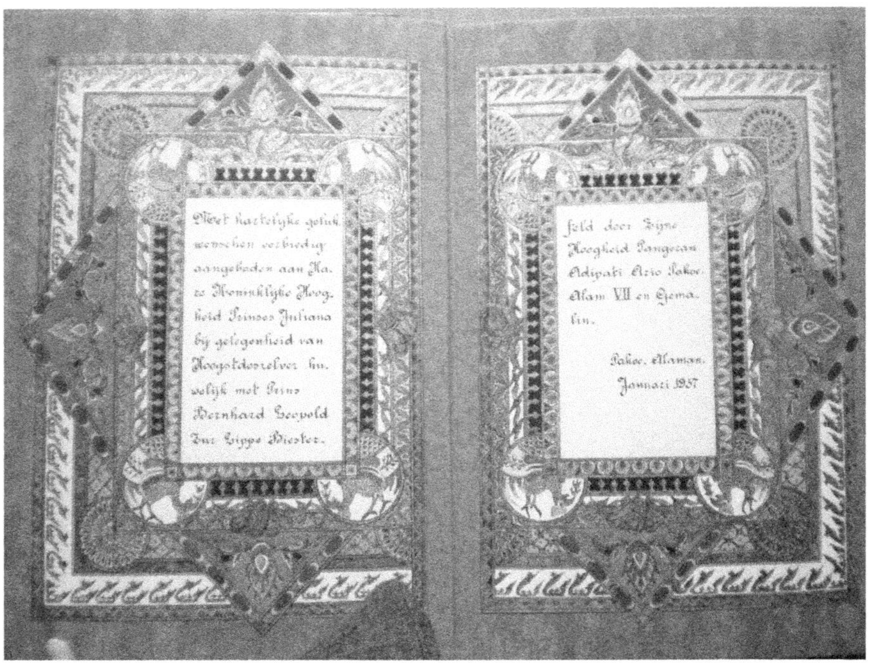

5.7 Album of Pakualam VII, illuminated dedication to Juliana
and Bernhard, 1937

Juliana's wedding that temper but do not essentially contradict the fundamental challenge posed by the gift. Indeed, the album entreats Juliana, on the cusp of reproducing her own dynasty, literally to look upon the Pakualaman as an aristocratic family in its own right, one with a lineage comparable to the Oranje-Nassau clan,[80] with its own dynastic renewal well under way and its courtly traditions thriving and, importantly, led by a man fluent in a modern visual language, photography, which – as we shall see in the next chapter – was perfectly suited for communicating both the peculiarity and the universality of the royal family in the early twentieth century.

Hamengku Buwono VIII similarly used albums combining Javanese court arts with photography to celebrate the achievements of his dynasty. Rather than show himself present at any celebrations for Dutch royals, either at the *kraton* or as the guest of the Dutch governor, the sultan had photographs taken of *wayang wong* (dance drama) performances held at his palace.[81] In its modern form, *wayang wong* was created at the inception of the Yogyakarta court in 1755. Some scholars say it emerged as an elaboration of state ritual that compensated for the loss of real power after the Dutch divided the kingdom of Mataram.[82] *Wayang wong* was thus from the outset a political performance of the sultan's rule as much as an artistic entertainment. If we extend this interpretation into the twentieth century, *wayang wong* performances in the Yogyakarta *kraton* reveal how Hamengku Buwono VIII, the most significant patron of the form, articulated his position as a Javanese sovereign within the late colonial order.

The *lakon Mintaraga*, or Mintaraga play, was his chosen gift to Juliana for her wedding. Otherwise known as the 'Asceticism of Arjuna', it is based on parts of the Indic *Arjunawiwaha* (Wedding of Arjuna) and was first written down in the eleventh century. Pakubuwono III composed the modern version of the play in 1778, and Sultan Hamengku Buwono VIII himself revised it in 1925. Before its 1937 iteration for Juliana and Bernhard, it was first performed in 1926 for the marriage of the sultan's daughters.[83] The play was summarised in the sultan's album gift in 53 large, glossy photographs, each with its own gilded caption in Dutch. These photographs distil moments in a long, complex drama about a princely hero and his wife. The play tells the story of Prince Arjuna's incarnation as the ascetic Suciptahening Mintaraga, his attainment of enlightenment, and the wife he gains as a reward for his efforts.[84] Arjuna encounters three trials along his journey: temptation by seven heavenly nymphs, challenges from a demon and confrontation with a god, Batara Guru (Siwa). The god encourages Arjuna to overcome the demon prince Winatakwaca. Aided by the nymph Dewi Supraba, Arjuna fulfils his destiny by piercing the demon's secret vulnerability, his palate. As a reward, Dewi Supraba becomes his wife.[85] With its emphasis on asceticism and meditation, the *lakon Mintaraga*'s perspective on royal marriage may have seemed an unusual theme for a wedding, but it was entirely in keeping with Javanese concepts of power and effective kingship.[86]

Accompanying the photograph album were two large volumes, the *serat kandha* or book(s) of narration, written in Javanese.[87] These texts record all the dialogue, the entrance and exit of characters, songs and music for a play. They also function as the basis for the spoken narration during the performance itself. The deluxe, hand-illuminated court copies of the *serat kandha* testify to the regard for such books as objects of art, not just as literary texts.[88] The language of the *serat kandha* made it incomprehensible to Juliana; indeed, to most Dutch people, save a small group of university-trained Indologists schooled in Javanese scripts. From a Dutch perspective, the more accessible part of the gift was the photograph album.

Hamengku Buwono VIII was not the first Sultan of Yogyakarta to choose a *wayang wong* performance as the theme of a photographic gift to a Dutch royal. In June 1899 his predecessor, Hamengku Buwono VII (r. 1877–1921), hosted a *wayang wong* performance to celebrate the naming of the crown prince, Gusti Raden Mas Putri (Hamenkunegoro III). Tens of thousands of spectators turned out to watch over the four days of the play.[89] Photographs of the performance were placed in a lavish presentation album, bound in purple velvet and adorned with diamond-studded gold filigree, and given to Queen Wilhelmina in 1901 for her wedding to Prince Hendrik of Mecklenburg-Schwerin.[90] Hamengku Buwono VIII sent an album of a *wayang wong* performance to Wilhelmina for her silver jubilee in 1923.[91] His later gift to Juliana in 1937 thus represented a recent tradition of Yogyakarta sultans bestowing photograph albums of courtly *wayang wong* performances upon women of the House of Orange. The histories of the House of Orange and the Yogyakarta sultanate in the twentieth century were thus intertwined, and photography provided a precious visual record of that connection.

The 1899 album given to Wilhelmina has no doubt received more attention than the 1937 gift for Juliana because the former contained images by Hamengku Buwono VII's renowned court photographer, Kassian Cephas, the first 'Javanese' commercial practitioner of the craft.[92] He had commenced producing collotypes of classical dances in the Yogyakarta *kraton* as early as 1888, and in 1901 received the gold medal of the Order of Oranje-Nassau for his achievements.[93] His palace photographs were published in collaboration with the sultan's personal physician, Isaac Groneman (1832–1912), whose works include an illustrated account of the *wayang wong* performance that was commemorated in the presentation album for Wilhelmina in 1899.[94] The 1923 photographs were taken by the renowned Tassilo Adam (1878–1955). The court photographer who made the images in the album from Hamengku Buwono VIII for Juliana in 1937 is not as well known to posterity as Cephas and Adam have become.[95] Nonetheless, this album deserves more attention than it has received because it demonstrates a renaissance in courtly arts under Hamengku Buwono VIII in dialogue with celebrations for the House of Orange.

Indeed, although *wayang wong* was also performed in the Surakarta Mangkunegaran,[96] the dance drama is most strongly associated with the sultanate of Yogyakarta, and it flourished during Hamengku Buwono VIII's reign as under no other king, before or since. In the first half of the twentieth century, it was part of a standard courtly education for *kraton* elites to learn *wayang wong*, and the sultan himself, together with many of his male relatives, sometimes took part in performances.[97] Hamengku Buwono VIII was the greatest patron of the form, sponsoring an unprecedented eleven performances during his reign, some of them entirely new plays, and many of them larger and more lavish than had ever been staged by his predecessors.[98] Of those held during Hamengku Buwono VIII's reign, most marked the weddings of his children, in keeping with their traditional purpose. However, the very first performance of his reign, staged in 1923, celebrated the silver jubilee of Queen Wilhelmina. Multiple copies of the photograph album recording the performance were made for Dutch officials in the Indies, not to mention the one for Wilhelmina herself.[99] It was later commemorated in a small book published by the Batavia firm, G. Kolff & Co.[100] At least one, and possibly three, further *wayang wong* performances were held to honour the House of Orange at the Yogyakarta *kraton* over the course of the 1930s, notwithstanding even the economic strain imposed by the Great Depression.[101] Hamengku Buwono VIII was also personally responsible for significant innovations to dance drama: he aided in the composition of new plays, introduced a wider range of stage props, devised novel costumes and choreography, and even supported the establishment of dance associations outside the *kraton*.[102]

In the album gift for Juliana, some of the photographs must have created a spectacle in their creation, particularly the battle scenes, as they required the pausing of action and the prolonging of difficult choreographical poses (figure 5.8). At first glance, such images appear to mimic classical forms for portraying Javanese *wayang* characters in profile, derived from shadow puppet plays (*wayang kulit*) and picture theatre (*wayang beber*).[103] It was precisely for their resonance with non-photographic visual forms, however, that these images were innovative. In preserving a sense of movement and action in the battle scenes of the play, Hamengku Buwono VIII's court photographer eschewed poses that might be described as 'consciously static, induced and controlled by the technical requirements' of the medium in favour of 'scenic action and human agency'.[104] Largely for technical reasons, such images were comparatively rare in earlier photographs of *wayang wong* performances at the Yogyakarta *kraton*. In the period when Cephas was active, for example, the size and weight of cameras, the brittleness of film and slower shutter speeds favoured the arrangement of groups in static poses, and fostered a longer focal distance between viewer and subject. Producing images of human figures that transferred the essence of classical *wayang* iconography into the new medium of photography was thus one of the modern developments, enabled by twentieth-century advances in photographic technologies, spawned by Hamengku Buwono VIII's preservation of courtly traditions.

The revival of *wayang wong* under Hamengku Buwono VIII and its close association with photography coincided with the boom in Dutch and Javanese royal celebrations of the 1920s and 1930s. At its apogee,

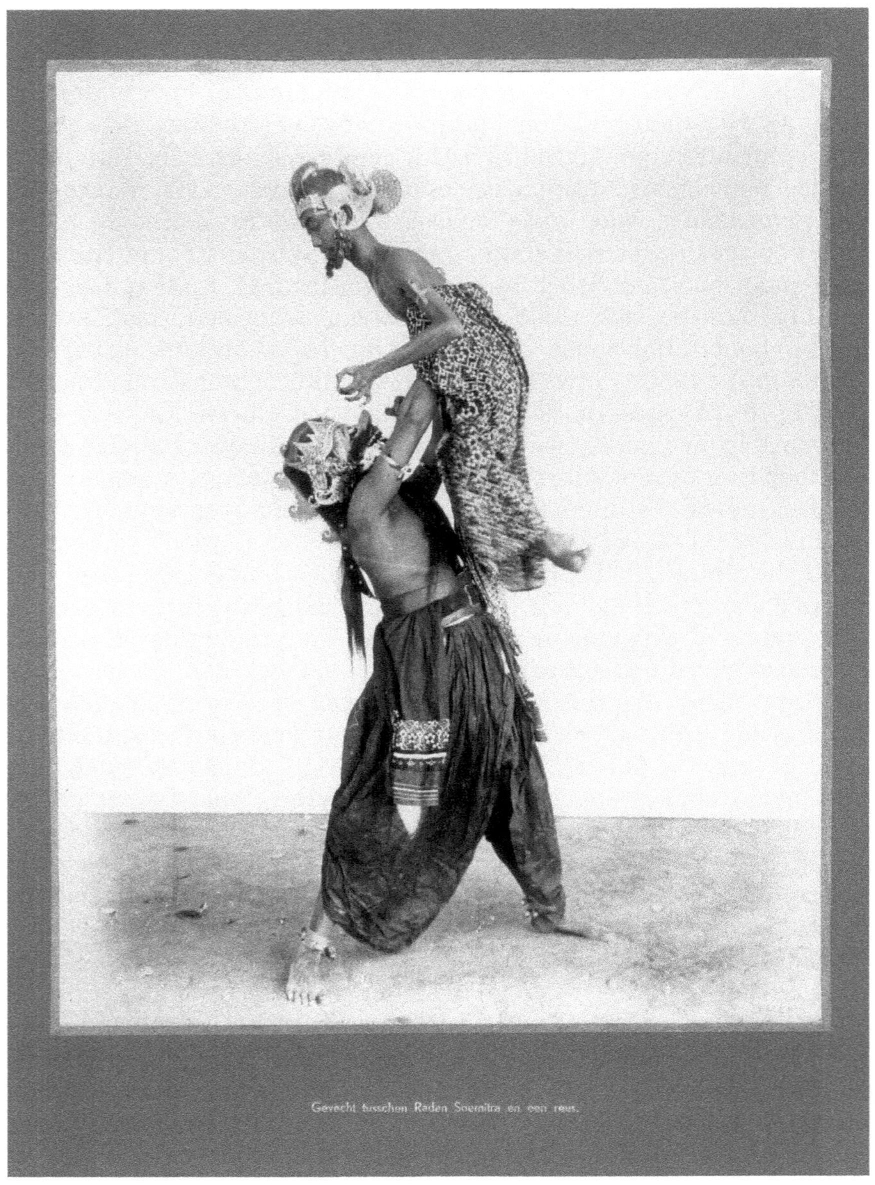

5.8 Album of Hamengku Buwono VIII, 'Fight between Raden Soemitra and a monster'

wayang wong was not just a rejuvenated and flourishing Javanese courtly art that celebrated the sultan, his dynasty and the kingdom. It was also a performance that incorporated the rites of passage of a foreign, colonial monarchy into Yogyakartan court life using a Javanese idiom. Hamengku Buwono VIII's encouragement of photography to record *wayang wong* performances constitutes a largely overlooked component of the form's revival. During his reign, photography was more extensively used than ever before; for example, to illustrate official programmes, printed in Dutch and Javanese, that advertised *wayang wong* performances, as well as for specialist publications on the subject.[105] While the sultan's portrait was absent from Wilhelmina's and Juliana's albums, then, the photographs therein nonetheless present a distinctive image of the sultan to the Dutch monarchy: as a conspicuously *Javanese* king and proud custodian of Yogyakarta's courtly arts, and as a contemporary ruler whose patronage of photography and willingness to engage creatively with a foreign sovereign signalled his worldliness.

Tradition and innovation in snapshot diplomacy

The photographic presentations of Central Javanese royals to the Dutch monarchy during Wilhelmina's reign represent not only a jostling for recognition in an international arena of royals, but also attempts to reposition monarchy within a novel cast of Indigenous political actors who were competing for power on Indies soil, often in opposition to colonial *and* aristocratic rule. There were rivalries between the royal families of Central Java, to be sure, but the bigger challenge to all these aristocrats in the 1920s and 1930s was their being deemed irrelevant to the needs of ordinary Indonesians. Nationalist, communist and Islamist visions for a future free from colonial rule and governed by and for ordinary Indonesians all vied for supremacy in the Indies in these decades. For aristocrats to be concerned with the welfare of their subjects was also demanded by the liberal reformist rhetoric of colonial rule during the Ethical Policy that spanned most of Wilhelmina's reign. The role of Indigenous elites in this period, according to some prominent Dutch and colonial thinkers, was to ensure progress and prosperity for the masses by gaining a Western education and leading by 'association' with Dutch partners, who would continue to steer the processes of development.[106]

Caught between Dutch expectations to collaborate as subordinates and Indigenous movements for democracy and self-determination, Pakubuwono X, Hamengku Buwono VIII and Pakualam VII in fact responded in similar ways throughout their reigns to the challenges of retaining power and relevance. Each sought to educate themselves and especially their children in Dutch to better promote the interests of their courts and dynasties, particularly when it was time to renegotiate the long and complex 'contracts' with the Dutch that marked each royal succession.[107] The Pakualaman produced the first Javanese lawyer, doctor, engineer and female teacher, as well as the only Indigenous member of the *Binnenlandsch Bestuur*, the executive arm of government that exclusively employed Europeans. A son of Pakualam V, Pangeran Adipati Ario Koesoemo Joedo, graduated from Leiden University in 1904 with a degree in Indology, was a member of the *Volksraad* from 1916 to 1927 and briefly served as an Aspirant Controleur at the behest of Governor-General van Heutsz. The appointment was short-lived. After seven months, under pressure from the *Binnenlandsch Bestuur*, Koesoemo Joedo was transferred laterally to a government department that allowed a 'mixed' office.[108] Hamengku Buwono VIII toured Europe as a crown prince and ensured that his sons, including his heir, were schooled in the Netherlands. The sons of Pakubuwono X were similarly Dutch-educated.[109]

Each royal also espoused 'Ethical' improvements in their kingdoms. Pakubuwono X implemented reforms that promoted health, welfare and education for the residents of his *kraton* and for the kingdom of Surakarta. These included opening a school (albeit only for the high-born children of his extended family), a hospital, and factories for processing sugar, tapioca and tobacco for the *kraton*. The king officiated at ceremonies for new bridges and other public utilities, sponsored credit programmes for Javanese of limited means and funded a home for the poor. He also built a zoological garden in the city of Surakarta, founded an archaeological museum, and modernised the *kraton* by having electric lighting installed.[110] Hamengku Buwono VIII restricted forced labour for peasants, undertook agrarian reforms and made himself available to launch various construction projects.[111]

To rule benevolently for the needs of the people, to embrace modernisation and Westernisation, and to retain the trappings of customary authority and Javanese courtly culture: these were the demands that Central Java's royals needed to balance in order to fulfil traditional notions of kingship, maintain their considerable privileges as hereditary elites, and satisfy the Dutch officials who determined their budgets and powers. It is this local, colonial context in which they were embedded that shaped the international, snapshot diplomacy of Central Java's royals with the Dutch monarchy. The albums that Pakubuwono X, Hamengku Buwono VIII and Pakualam VII gave to members of the House of Orange in the 1920s and 1930s departed significantly, both in style and substance, from the gifts that had traditionally been sent by Indigenous rulers to the Dutch monarchy. They were not replicas of objects extracted from Javanese courts, designed to foster conjugal conviviality or to enhance the power and status of the recipient. Rather, the albums were windows into the contemporary worlds of their senders. They reveal Javanese royals using gifts to position themselves as rivals to the pomp and tradition of the Dutch monarchy, *and* as equal to the task of enlightened rule in a colonial milieu that demanded cosmopolitan, modern Indigenous elites.

The combination of innovation and tradition in the content and formal qualities of Javanese royals' photographic gifts to the Dutch monarchy also took place in the context of a broader Indigenous preservationist movement in the Indies during Wilhelmina's reign. This movement was particularly pronounced on Java, and more prominently recruited photography to it than did other parts of the Indonesian archipelago.[112] However, the revival and recording of 'traditional' culture on Java in the early twentieth century, particularly in its courtly forms, was a distinctly modernist project in two regards: first, in utilising contemporary technologies and ways of seeing to represent antique arts and practices, and second, in responding to political and social developments that threatened the position of traditional Indigenous elites and the European colonial establishment that supported them. Among these were the rise of nationalist, communist and Islamist parties in the Netherlands during the 1910s and 1920s that were hostile to hereditary forms of authority. Javanese royals' adoption of photography to promote the traditional arts of their courts thus positioned them as rulers who were open to innovations not just in how the operations of their court were recorded, but also in how their relations with a foreign, colonial monarchy might be conducted.

Conclusion

In embracing the genre of the photographic album and packaging it as a royal gift, the royals of Central Java combined modern ways of *seeing* power with customary modes of *thinking* about it in novel ways that articulated a complex, ambiguous relationship with the House of Orange. On the one hand, the album gifts communicated a certain unity between Javanese rulers and their Dutch counterparts, one founded on shared reverence for the elite fellowship of aristocracy. For the kings and princes of Central Java, as much as for the queen and crown princess of the Netherlands, their individual eminence was best demonstrated through communing with other royals. Photographic exchanges between Dutch and Javanese royal houses in this context thus fostered an 'ironic solidarity between the upper classes of Europe and Asia', one that 'laced together the monarchs and statesmen of far-flung worlds in deferred but reciprocal gazes'.[113] On the other hand, the gifts articulated hierarchies; relations of vassalage and suzerainty. Rather than consistently subordinate their Javanese senders to the royal Dutch recipients, the photograph albums registered distinctions that oscillated within their covers, tilting towards tribute from the Javanese rulers in some instances and sliding towards assertion of their own sovereignty in others.

Pakubuwono X presented as an ambiguous subject to the Queen of the Netherlands and her heir, willing for his person to be photographed at all manner of royal celebrations (theirs as well as his own), but resistant to signalling subject status to his viewers. Pakubuwono X's comportment, gaze and position relative to his constant shadow, the Dutch governor, drew Wilhelmina and Juliana into a terse and unstable contest between these two men, one played out far from their court on Indies soil, and one that alternately forced both men into ceremonial equality before the two women's royal eyes, or else suggested that it was in fact they who were the subjects of the *susuhunan*.

Hamengku Buwono VIII circumvented this ambivalent encounter in his album gift for Juliana by removing himself from the picture and focusing instead on the thriving dramatic arts of his court. His album was not, however, devoid of self-representation, nor of a tributary message – indeed, the *wayang wong* performance that the album recorded was specifically held to commemorate Juliana's wedding. But in choosing a traditional performance for his theme, and in sponsoring innovative photographic techniques to represent it, the sultan was also foregrounding an image of himself as a ruler whose power rested in his ability to reconcile modernity with tradition, and thus to elegantly concentrate the opposing forces of his era within himself as well as his realm. The signal to Juliana in the sultan's gift was about his own sovereignty, even while it tendered congratulations to her.

Pakualam VII achieved the same end by the opposite means. He personally featured in his album gift for the crown princess, but in the curiously neutral space forged by formal portraiture rather than in the situated context of a celebration for the House of Orange. His sartorial concessions to Dutch customs in the portraits – Western suits for the leading men and the wearing of Dutch royal orders – were countered by the visual exposition of his entire genealogy, an assertion of his own dynasty and its renewal at the very moment when the House of Orange was poised to reproduce itself. Like Hamengku Buwono VIII, the prince combined a command of modern visual genres – in this case, the family album – with mastery of courtly arts that demonstrated his support of Javanese tradition.

Notes

1 J. Pemberton, *On the Subject of 'Java'* (Ithaca, NY: Cornell University Press, 1994), p. 121.
2 Pemberton, *On the Subject of 'Java'*, p. 122. 'Pakubuwono' means 'Axis of the Cosmos'. 'Hamengku Buwono' means 'Authority of the Cosmos'.
3 Although Cannadine was in fact describing British viceroys at the height of the Raj: D. Cannadine, *Ornamentalism: How the British Saw Their Empire* (London: Allen Lane, 2001), p. 95.
4 R. Wassing-Visser, *Koninklijke geschenken uit Indonesië; Historische banden met het huis Oranje-Nassau (1600–1938)* (Den Haag/Zwolle: Stichting Historische Verzamelingen van het Huis Oranje-Nassau/Waanders, 1995), p. 109.
5 Pemberton, *On the Subject of 'Java'*, pp. 37, 59, 93–4. A recent publication sponsored by Pakubuwono XII (r. 1944–2004) remembers his predecessor thus: 'Facing political pressure from the Dutch colonial government, he [Pakubuwono X] succeeded, very cunningly, in reinvigorating the court's power through a cultural approach': J. Miksic and M. Heins, *Karaton Surakarta: A Look into the Court of Surakarta Hadiningrat, Central Java* (Singapore: Marshall Cavendish, 2006), p. 372.
6 Wassing-Visser, *Koninklijke geschenken uit Indonesië*, pp. 15, 113, 150, 155, 178, 203, 212, 236.
7 S. Protschky, 'Strained encounters: royal Indonesian visits to the Dutch court in the early twentieth century', in R. Aldrich and C. McCreery (eds), *Royals on Tour: Politics, Pageantry and Colonialism* (Manchester: Manchester University Press, 2018), pp. 233–49.
8 The largest number ever in attendance at her court were the eight who went to her fortieth jubilee celebrations in 1938: Wassing-Visser, *Koninklijke geschenken uit Indonesië*, pp. 234–5.
9 J. Pemberton, 'The ghost in the machine', in R. C. Morris (ed.), *Photographies East: The Camera and its Histories in East and Southeast Asia* (Durham, NC: Duke University Press, 2009), pp. 29–56
10 Important details about the commissioning, provenance and materials of these photographs are given in Wassing-Visser, *Koninklijke geschenken uit Indonesië*.
11 S. Willcock, 'Composing the spectacle: colonial portraiture and the coronation durbars of British India, 1877–1911', *Art History*, 40.1 (2017): 132–55.
12 M. Peleggi, *Lords of Things: The Fashioning of the Siamese Monarchy's Modern Image* (Honolulu, HI: University of Hawai'i Press, 2002), pp. 85, 93, quote at p. 89.
13 A. Maxwell, 'Colonial photography and indigenous resistance in Hawai'i: the case of the last royal family', in *Colonial Photography and Exhibitions: Representations of the 'Native' and the Making of European Identities* (London: Leicester University Press, 1999), pp. 192–223.
14 B. D. Kurniadi, 'Yogyakarta in decentralised Indonesia: integrating traditional institution in democratic transitions', *Jurnal Ilmu Sosial dan Ilmu Politik*, 13.2 (2009): 190–203; J. Monfries, 'The sultan and the revolution', *Bijdragen tot de Taal-, Land- en Volkenkunde*, 164.2–3 (2008): 269–97; J. Monfries, *A Prince in a Republic: The Life of Sultan Hamengku Buwono IX of Yogyakarta* (Singapore: ISEAS Publishing, 2015).
15 G. Oostindie, *De parels en de kroon; Het koningshuis en de koloniën* (Amsterdam: De Bezige Bij, 2006); Wassing-Visser, *Koninklijke geschenken uit Indonesië*.
16 A. Clulow, *The Company and the Shogun: The Dutch Encounter with Tokugawa Japan* (New York: Columbia University Press).

17 I. Marwoto-Johan, 'Ritual heirlooms in the Islamic kingdoms of Indonesia', in J. Bennet (ed.), *Crescent Moon: Islamic Art and Civilisation in Southeast Asia* (Adelaide/Canberra: Art Gallery of South Australia/National Gallery of Australia, 2005), pp. 144–58; D. van Duuren, *De kris; Een aardse benadering van een kosmisch symbool* (Amsterdam: Koninklijk Instituut voor de Tropen, 1996).

18 KHA A50 XIVc 2.

19 The Indies Hall took five years to build: it was finally opened on 18 December 1906. The room was designed by Ir. L. J. C. van Es, who was inspired by Javanese antiquities and modelled the hall on houses on the north coast of Java. The extensive wood carving was done on commission by Javanese craftsmen. Wassing-Visser, *Koninklijke geschenken uit Indonesië*, pp. 14, 124–46, 141, 146–7. See also Oostindie, *De parels en de kroon*, pp. 85–6.

20 S. Protschky, 'Dutch still lifes and colonial visual culture in the Netherlands Indies, 1800–1949', *Art History*, 34.3 (2011): 510–35.

21 Wassing-Visser, *Koninklijke geschenken uit Indonesië*, p. 228.

22 S. Alpers, 'The museum as a way of seeing', in I. Karp and S. D. Lavine (eds), *Exhibiting Cultures: The Poetics and Politics of Museum Display* (Washington, DC: Smithsonian Institution Press, 1991), pp. 25–32.

23 On centripetal symbolism in Dutch still lifes, see N. Bryson, *Looking at the Overlooked: Four Essays on Still Life Painting* (Cambridge, MA: Harvard University Press, 1990), p. 105.

24 Wassing-Visser, *Koninklijke geschenken uit Indonesië*.

25 R. C. Morris, 'Photography and the power of images in the history of power: notes from Thailand', in R. C. Morris (ed.), *Photographies East: The Camera and its Histories in East and Southeast Asia* (Durham, NC: Duke University Press, 2009), pp. 121–60, at pp. 125–6.

26 G. Knaap, with a contribution by Y. Soerjoatmodjo, *Cephas, Yogyakarta: Photography in the Service of the Sultan* (Leiden: KITLV Press, 1999).

27 For the 1898 portrait, see Wassing-Visser, *Koninklijke geschenken uit Indonesië*, p. 106. For the 1923 album, see KHA FA/0772.

28 KHA FA/0695 (1932), KHA FA/0777A (1937).

29 Inventory of gifts received by Wilhelmina in 1923: KHA A50 XIVc 2. Mangkunegoro VII once again, and inexplicably (given his inclination for photography), abstained from sending a similar gift: see Pemberton, 'The ghost in the machine'.

30 These gifts consisted largely of the *pusaka* described: Wassing-Visser, *Koninklijke Geschenken uit Indonesië*, pp. 106–7, 150–4, 196–9, 210, 212.

31 The queen received a *batik dodot* (man's ceremonial skirt cloth) from Mangkunegoro VII, which was 'to be used as a door-curtain' (*als portière te gebruiken*). He received a signed portrait from the queen in return. The other gifts sent by Pakubuwono X included a writing desk, a gong and four pieces of *batik*. Hamengku Buwono VIII sent Wilhelmina a *kris* and a pike: KHA A50 XIVc 2.

32 A photograph of the vitrine was published in F. A. W. van der Lip, *Nederlandsch-Indisch Herinnerings-Album aan de verloving en het huwelijk van H.K.H. Prinses Juliana [en] Z.K.H. Prins Bernhard* (Bandoeng: Alubu, 1937).

33 Wassing-Visser, *Koninklijke Geschenken uit Indonesië*, pp. 216–33. See also the work of the anthropologist Marcel Mauss on 'primitive' societies in the 1920s: M. Mauss, *The Gift: The Form and Reason for Exchange in Archaic Societies*, trans. W. D. Halls (London: Routledge, 1990 [1950]); and more recently, A. E. Komter, *Social Solidarity and the Gift* (Cambridge: Cambridge University Press, 2005).

34 M. Osteen, 'Introduction: questions of the gift', in M. Osteen (ed.), *The Question of the Gift: Essays across Disciplines* (London: Routledge, 2002), pp. 1–42, quotes at pp. 9 and 25.

35 On amateur photographs of middle-class Javanese families, see S. Protschky, 'Tea cups, cameras and family life: picturing domesticity in elite European and Javanese family photographs from the Netherlands Indies, c. 1900–1942', *History of Photography*, 36.1 (2012): 44–65. On the formality of photographs of Javanese kings, see J. G. Taylor, 'Costume and gender in colonial Java, 1800–1942', in H. Schulte

Nordholt (ed.), *Outward Appearances: Dressing State and Society in Indonesia* (Leiden: KITLV Press, 1997), pp. 85–116, at p. 101.

36 KHA MU/5449 (Album of Pakualam VII, 1937); KHA FA/0777A (Album of Hamengku Buwono VIII).

37 KHA FA/0772 (Album of Pakubuwono X, 1923); KHA FA/0695 (Album of Pakubuwono X, 1932).

38 Military dress for Javanese aristocrats became convention during the rule of Governor-General (Marshal) Herman Willem Daendels (served 1808–11): H. Sutherland, *The Making of a Bureaucratic Elite: The Colonial Transformation of the Javanese* Priyayi (Kuala Lumpur and Hong Kong: Heinemann Educational Books (Asia), 1979), p. 7. Pakubuwono X was promoted from major-general to lieutenant-general of the Netherlands Indies Army in 1924: Miksic and Heins, *Karaton Surakarta*, pp. 82, 372.

39 Only Pakualam II is shown wearing a jacket without epaulettes: see KHA MU/5449.

40 Taylor, 'Costume and gender in colonial Java', pp. 90, 97.

41 Taylor, 'Costume and gender in colonial Java', pp. 105, 107, 112.

42 The exception is Pakualam III. Pakualam II, IV, V and VI all had the Order of the Dutch Lion, established in 1815 by King Willem I. In addition, Pakualam IV and V wore an Officer's Cross for Long Service, an order that was introduced in 1844 for people who gave fifteen years' service or more to the Dutch crown. It was handed out annually on 6 December, King Willem II's birthday: C. G. Evers, *Onderscheidingen; Leidraad voor de decoraties van het Koninkrijk der Nederlanden* (Amsterdam: De Bataafsche Leeuw, 2001), pp. 30, 66.

43 Wassing-Visser, *Koninklijke Geschenken uit Indonesië*, p. 215.

44 K. Bruin, 'Distinction and democratization: royal decorations in the Netherlands', *The Netherlands' Journal of Sociology*, 23.1 (1987): 17–30, at pp. 17, 19–20.

45 Cannadine, *Ornamentalism*, p. 21.

46 Pemberton, *On the Subject of 'Java'*, p. 94. Pemberton points out that, in Javanese documents, royal orders were written out in full, whereas they were abbreviated in Dutch documents from the Indies. However, his conclusion that 'through Dutch administrative lenses the Pakubuwana was, in the end, a great ceremonial "en zo voort," a royal "Etc"', is unfounded, for official documents from the *Koninklijk Huisarchief* (Royal Collections) in The Hague frequently show that, in the Netherlands, the titles of members of the Dutch royal family were also abbreviated. The Dutch did not, therefore, discriminate between their own and Javanese royalty in how their titles were textually recorded. There were, however, differences in how the Dutch and Javanese courts recorded the titles of their respective monarchs.

47 Cannadine, *Ornamentalism*, p. 100.

48 Morris, 'Photography and the power of images in the history of power', pp. 126–9. Similarly, Pemberton has argued that, for Javanese kings, 'To dress Dutch ... was, somehow, to share in the strange power that the persistent presence of the Dutch must have represented to Javanese rulers by the late eighteenth century': Pemberton, *On the Subject of 'Java'*, p. 58.

49 Maxwell, 'Colonial photography and indigenous resistance in Hawai'i', p. 198.

50 Pemberton, *On the Subject of 'Java'*, p. 59.

51 See also Morris, 'Photography and the power of images in the history of power', pp. 126–9.

52 In this regard, Dutch governors differed from their British counterparts. Some viceroys of India, notably Louis Mountbatten, were in fact royalty themselves.

53 There is one photograph that seems to show another wife standing next to Gusti Kanjeng Ratu Hemas in KHA FA/0772 (1923 album), on the grandstand overlooking a parade of the Legion of the Mangkunegaran.

54 Wassing-Visser, *Koninklijke Geschenken uit Indonesië*, pp. 195, 203.

55 The monogamous princes were Pakualam III, V, VI and VII: KHA MU/5449.

56 Taylor, 'Costume and gender in colonial Java', p. 378.

57 Peleggi, *Lords of Things*, p. 85.

58 Queen Wilhelmina, *Eenzaam maar niet alleen* (Amsterdam: Ten Have, 1959).
59 J. Withuis, *Juliana; Vorstin in een mannenwereld* (Amsterdam: De Bezige Bij, 2016).
60 Protschky, 'Strained encounters'.
61 KHA A50 Xxa 355.
62 See, for example, S. B. Ortner, 'Resistance and the problem of ethnographic refusal', *Comparative Studies in Society and History*, 37.1 (1995): 173–93; A. Simpson, 'The ruse of consent and the anatomy of "refusal": cases from indigenous North America and Australia', *Postcolonial Studies*, 20.1 (2017): 18–33. These works have informed my thinking on refusal here, but I do not consider my case studies to be equivalent to the subaltern examples Ortner and Simpson developed. I am not dealing here, as Simpson does, with forms of Indigenous refusal that are 'deep instantiations of life in the face of death' (Simpson, 'Ruse of consent', p. 25). Elite, aristocratic Javanese men were rather at the *top* of Indigenous social hierarchies in the Indies, even if they were often subordinated by Dutch authorities. Thanks to Kat Ellinghaus for bringing this field to my attention.
63 F. Sysling, 'Geographies of difference: Dutch physical anthropology in the colonies and the Netherlands, ca. 1900–1940', *BMGN/Low Countries Historical Review*, 128.1 (2013): 105–26, at p. 123; F. Sysling, *Racial Science and Human Diversity in Colonial Indonesia* (Singapore: NUS Press, 2016), pp. 48, 59, 80, 129.
64 This photograph comes from an album of R. H. W. H. Bijleveld-Visser, wife of J. W. Bijleveld, Health Officer of Yogyakarta; see the figure caption for archive reference.
65 Pemberton, *On the Subject of 'Java'*.
66 E. Edwards, *Anthropology and Photography, 1860–1920* (New Haven, CT: Yale University Press, 1992); E. M. Hight and G. D. Sampson, 'Introduction: photography, "race", and post-colonial theory', in E. M. Hight and G. D. Sampson (eds), *Colonialist Photography: Imag(in)ing Race and Place* (London: Routledge, 2002), pp. 1–19; C. Pinney, *Camera Indica: The Social Life of Indian Photographs* (Chicago: University of Chicago Press, 1997), p. 70; C. Pinney, *Photography and Anthropology* (London: Reaktion, 2011), pp. 17–29.
67 J. Coté, 'Reversing the lens: Kartini's image of a modernised Java', in S. Protschky (ed.), *Photography, Modernity and the Governed in Late-Colonial Indonesia* (Amsterdam: Amsterdam University Press, 2015), pp. 176–84; Taylor, 'Costume and gender in colonial Java'. As Christopher Pinney points out for colonial India, photography in the hands of Indigenous photographers producing for elite Indian sitters emerged as 'a creative space in which new aspirant identities and personae can be conjured' (Pinney, *Camera Indica*, p. 85).
68 Pemberton, *On the Subject of 'Java'*, p. 95. For a similar example, see Maxwell, 'Colonial photography and indigenous resistance in Hawai'i', p. 198.
69 Pemberton, *On the Subject of 'Java'*, p. 94.
70 R. Wessing, 'The kraton-city and the realm: sources and movement of power in Java', in P. J. M. Nas, G. A. Persoon and R. Jaffe (eds), *Framing Indonesian Realities: Essays in Symbolic Anthropology in Honour of Reimar Schefold* (Leiden: KITLV Press, 2003), pp. 199–250, at pp. 224, 237.
71 KHA FA/0695.
72 Javanese rulers traditionally celebrated their name days, on which their subjects and subordinates would come and pay tribute to them, every 35 days: Sutherland, *The Making of a Bureaucratic Elite*, p. 23. Jubilees became more popular among Javanese kings in the twentieth century: L. Adam, 'The courtyards, gates and buildings of the Kraton of Yogyakarta', trans. R. Robson-McKillop, first published 1940, in S. Robson (ed.), *The Kraton: Selected Essays on Javanese Courts* (Leiden: KITLV Press, 2003), pp. 13–40, at p. 36.
73 23 April 1933 was the 400th anniversary of the birth of Willem I (1533–84), founder of the House of Oranje-Nassau: P. Eckhardt, 'Wij zullen handhaven! De symbolische betekenis van de Nederlandse monarchie in Nederlands-Indië 1918–1940', MA dissertation, University of Amsterdam, 2002, p. 61. In Javanese years, the

Pakubuwonan bicentenary marked the period 1670–1870. This was the longest that any Javanese royal house had managed to rule in the one location. Pakubuwono X did not live quite long enough to see this celebration; it was left instead to his successor, Pakubuwono XI: Pemberton, *On the Subject of 'Java'*, p. 28.

74 Why Pakualam I was omitted is unclear. Pakualam I (born Pangeran Natakusuma) was a brother of Hamengku Buwono II, and was involved in the tensions within the sultanate of Yogyakarta that ultimately led to its subdivision in 1812. Having been exiled by Governer-General Daendels in 1811 for his suspected involvement in a rebellion, Pangeran Natakusuma was later recalled by the British in 1812 to assist with conquering the kingdom of Yogyakarta. He was rewarded for his efforts by being given independent heritable lands within that kingdom, and was named Pangeran (Prince) Pakualam I: M. C. Ricklefs, *A History of Modern Indonesia since c. 1200* (Stanford, CA: Stanford University Press, 4th edn, 2008), pp. 134, 137–8.

75 Three of the five drawings are signed 'E. Su-Josif, Solo', and the other two appear to have been made by the same artist. The last image, of Paku Alam VI and his wife, is dated 1932. KITLV Special Collections has photographs of Pakualam II (shelf mark 116385), Pakualam III (4721) and Pakualam V (857161).

76 B. Anderson, *Language and Power: Exploring Political Cultures in Indonesia* (Ithaca, NY: Cornell University Press, 1990), p. 41.

77 Anderson, *Language and Power*, p. 30.

78 P. W. H. Kal, *Yogya Silver: Renewal of a Javanese Handicraft* (Amsterdam: KIT Publishers, 2005).

79 T. E. Behrend, 'Textual gateways: the Javanese manuscript tradition', in A. Kumar and J. H. McGlynn (eds), *Illuminations: The Writing Traditions of Indonesia* (Jakarta, New York and Toronto: The Lontar Foundation, Weatherill, 1996), pp. 161–200, at pp. 191–2. A similar frontispiece from the Pakualaman, dated 1841 and showing *garuda* wings framed in a *wadana*, is reproduced in Behrend's study (p. 196). The album dedication reads: 'With heartfelt good wishes, respectfully offered to Her Royal Highness Princess Juliana on the occasion of her marriage to Prince Bernhard Leopold zur [*sic*] Lippe Biesterfeld from His Highness Pangeran Adipati Ario Paku Alam VII and his wife. Pakualaman. January 1937.'

80 The House of Orange was constituted as a monarchy in 1813. The Pakualaman was founded in 1812.

81 KHA FA/0702. *Wayang wong* is also known by its high Javanese variant as *ringgit tiyang*.

82 G. Kam, '*Wayang wong* in the court of Yogyakarta: the enduring significance of Javanese dance drama', *Asian Theatre Journal*, 4.1 (1987): 29–51, at p. 30. Others have argued that the dance drama represents an assertion of the authority of the sultan as the true heir of Majapahit: Soedarsono, *Wayang Wong: The State Ritual Dance Drama in the Court of Yogyakarta* (Yogyakarta: Gadja Mada University Press, 1984), pp. 17, 40, 54, 107.

83 Soedarsono, *Wayang Wong*, pp. 117, 121.

84 Soedarsono translates Suciptahening Mintaraga as 'one who has a very clear mind, the sage who has succeeded in throwing away his human passions' (Soedarsono, *Wayang Wong*, p. 122).

85 Soedarsono, *Wayang Wong*, pp. 122–32. In the Arjunawiwaha, from which the Mintaraga is derived, Arjuna marries the seven heavenly nymphs as his reward. The *lakon* developed by Hamengku Buwono VIII is therefore, whether by design or not, more in keeping with European concepts of marriage and propriety.

86 Anderson, *Language and Power*, p. 24.

87 KHA MU/5449.

88 Soedarsono, *Wayang Wong*, pp. 142, 149.

89 A. Vickers, *A History of Modern Indonesia* (Cambridge: Cambridge University Press, 2005), p. 36.

90 Wassing-Visser, *Koninklijke Geschenken uit Indonesië*, p. 155.

91 KIT TM-ALB-1462.

92 Knaap, *Cephas, Yogyakarta*. I have placed 'Javanese' in inverted commas because Cephas was in fact Indo-European, and while he began life as Javanese, he was baptised a Christian in 1860, took the Christian surname of 'Cephas' in 1889 and, together with his two eldest sons, was granted European-equivalent status in 1891: Knaap, *Cephas, Yogyakarta*, pp. 16–17. Knaap insists that he nonetheless 'remained Indigenous' and assumes that Cephas acquired European status simply for business reasons (Knaap, *Cephas, Yogyakarta*, p. 17). I would contend that, in the absence of autobiographical sources, we cannot know whether Cephas considered himself to be ethnically Javanese, European or both, depending on circumstances.

93 Knaap, *Cephas, Yogyakarta*, pp. 15, 20. The 1888 collotypes appeared in I. Groneman, *In den kedáton te Jogjåkártå; Oepåtjårå, ampilan en toneeldansen* (Leiden: Brill, 1888).

94 I. Groneman, *De wajang orang Pregiwa in den kraton te Jogjakarta, in Juni 1899* (Semarang: Van Dorp & Co., 1899). A text-only version was republished later that year by Van der Hucht of Yogyakarta. See also Knaap, *Cephas, Yogyakarta*, p. 20.

95 The photographer is not identified in the album or in the archival documents accompanying it, but we can safely assume that it was the work of Hamengku Buwono VIII's court photographer.

96 Soedarsono, *Wayang Wong*, p. 15.

97 *Wayang wong* was performed only by men in the Yogyakarta *kraton*, even the female roles (Soedarsono, *Wayang Wong*, pp. 25–6, 31–2, 100).

98 Soedarsono, *Wayang Wong*, p. 33; Kam, 'Wayang wong in the court of Yogyakarta', p. 29.

99 KIT TM-ALB-1470 and TM-ALB-1471.

100 J. Kats and R. Sastrawidjana, *Wajang-wong-spelen, gehouden op 3, 4, 5 en 6 September 1923 in de Kraton te Jogjakarta; In opdracht van Z.H. den Sultan Hamengkoe Boewana VIII* (Weltevreden: G. Kolff and Co., 1924).

101 The first performance was in September 1923, for Wilhelmina's silver jubilee, as already mentioned. Then there was the performance held for Juliana in 1937. The performances held in August 1934 and August 1939 very likely celebrated *koninginnedag* (Queen's Day). The other seven performances were held for weddings of the sultan's children (in 1926, 1928, 1929 and 1939), for the visit of Governor-General Tjarda van Starkenborgh in 1938, and for *kraton* occasions in 1932 and 1933 (Soedarsono, *Wayang Wong*, pp. 29–31, 97–8).

102 The *Kridha Beksa Wirama*, although founded outside the *kraton* in 1918, was nonetheless directed by Hamengku Buwono VIII's sons (Soedarsono, *Wayang Wong*, pp. 30, 101).

103 On the aesthetic, structural and plot similarities between *wayang kulit* and *wayang wong*, see H. Susilo, 'Wayang wong panggung: its social context, technique and music', in S. Morgan and L. J. Sears (eds), *Aesthetic Tradition and Cultural Transition in Java and Bali* (Madison, WI: Centre for Southeast Asian Studies, University of Wisconsin, 1984), pp. 117–62, at p. 117.

104 A. Appadurai, 'The colonial backdrop', *Afterimage* (1997): 4–7, at p. 5. Appadurai makes this distinction in a brief comparison between painted eighteenth-century Mughal portraits and nineteenth-century studio photography, but it effectively evokes *wayang* imagery from Java for my purposes.

105 Kam, 'Wayang wong in the court of Yogyakarta', p. 33; Soedarsono, *Wayang Wong*, illustrations between pp. 144 and 145.

106 E. Locher-Scholten, *Ethiek in fragmenten; Vijf studies over koloniaal denken en doen van Nederlanders in de Indonesische Archipel 1877–1942* (Utrecht: HES, 1981), pp. 2, 184–5; Sutherland, *The Making of a Bureaucratic Elite*, pp. 113–14; H. van Miert, *Bevlogenheid en onvermogen; Mr. J.H. Abendanon (1852–1925) en de Ethische richting in het Nederlandse kolonialisme* (Leiden: KITLV Press, 1991), pp. 16, 135, 137, 146–7; R. Cribb, 'Introduction: the late colonial state in Indonesia', in R. Cribb (ed.), *The Late Colonial State in Indonesia: Political and Economic Foundations of the Netherlands Indies 1880–1942* (Leiden: KITLV Press, 1994), pp. 1–10, at pp. 5, 7–8.

107 Monfries, *A Prince in a Republic*, p. 51.
108 M. Djajadiningrat-Nieuwenhuys, 'Noto Soeroto: his ideas and the late colonial intellectual climate', *Indonesia*, 55 (1993): 41–72. As Heather Sutherland has observed, 'the [colonial administrative] system could not absorb such highly trained natives' (Sutherland, *The Making of a Bureaucratic Elite*, pp. 47, 50–2).
109 Monfries, *A Prince in a Republic*, pp. 29, 36–7, 70.
110 Pemberton, *On the Subject of 'Java'*, p. 116; V. Zimmerman, 'The *kraton* of Surakarta in the year 1915', trans. R. Robson-McKillop, first published 1915, in S. Robson (ed.), *The Kraton: Selected Essays on Javanese Courts* (Leiden: KITLV Press, 2003), pp. 41–64, at p. 51.
111 Monfries, *A Prince in a Republic*, pp. 30, 33.
112 J. T. Siegel, 'The curse of the photograph: Atjeh 1901', in R. C. Morris (ed.), *Photographies East: The Camera and its Histories in East and Southeast Asia* (Durham, NC: Duke University Press, 2009), pp. 57–78, at pp. 59–60.
113 Morris, 'Introduction', p. 21.

CHAPTER SIX

Governing difference: unity in diversity at royal celebrations

We first encountered the photograph album of E. P. L. de Hoog, a Dutch engineer who worked in New Guinea in the late 1930s, in Chapter 3. De Hoog's images revealed how, even in communities far from the centres of Dutch colonial power, Queen Wilhelmina's fortieth jubilee in 1938 prompted a major public festival, with crowds of participants drawn from the large Javanese and Papuan workforce at Babo. During the day, men congregated at the town's airfield to watch and participate in contests of speed, strength and endurance that were simple to organise: mast- and rope-climbing races, timed obstacle courses and other feats of skill (see figure 3.5). In the evenings an aircraft hangar served as the festival hall where men took their meals and watched performances, including a *komedi bangsawan* (Malay opera).[1] De Hoog's camera also recorded the performance of various dances associated with particular ethnic groups that were increasingly appropriated for *koninginnedag* celebrations: for instance, the *kuda kepang*, or 'bamboo horse' dance, the hallmark of immigrant Javanese communities throughout the archipelago; and a Chinese dragon dance, traditionally reserved for New Year celebrations, but now a staple at Queen's Day festivals (figure 6.1).[2]

Photographs of games and competitions, traditional dances adapted to new purposes and the distinctive costumes of folk and ethnic 'types' at royal celebrations appeared frequently in the photographs of European elites throughout the Dutch colonial world.[3] In the Netherlands East Indies, such photographs attest to the labour migrations encouraged or coerced by Dutch colonial agriculture and industry. They depict the mixed and mobile Indonesian communities whose cultural forms were given a space for display at festivals for the Dutch monarchy. Photographs also reveal the increasingly popularised ethnographic gaze that informed Dutch authorities' interest in local participants at royal celebrations.

In this chapter, I present the first analysis to bring together photographs of Wilhelmina's subjects participating in *koninginnedag*

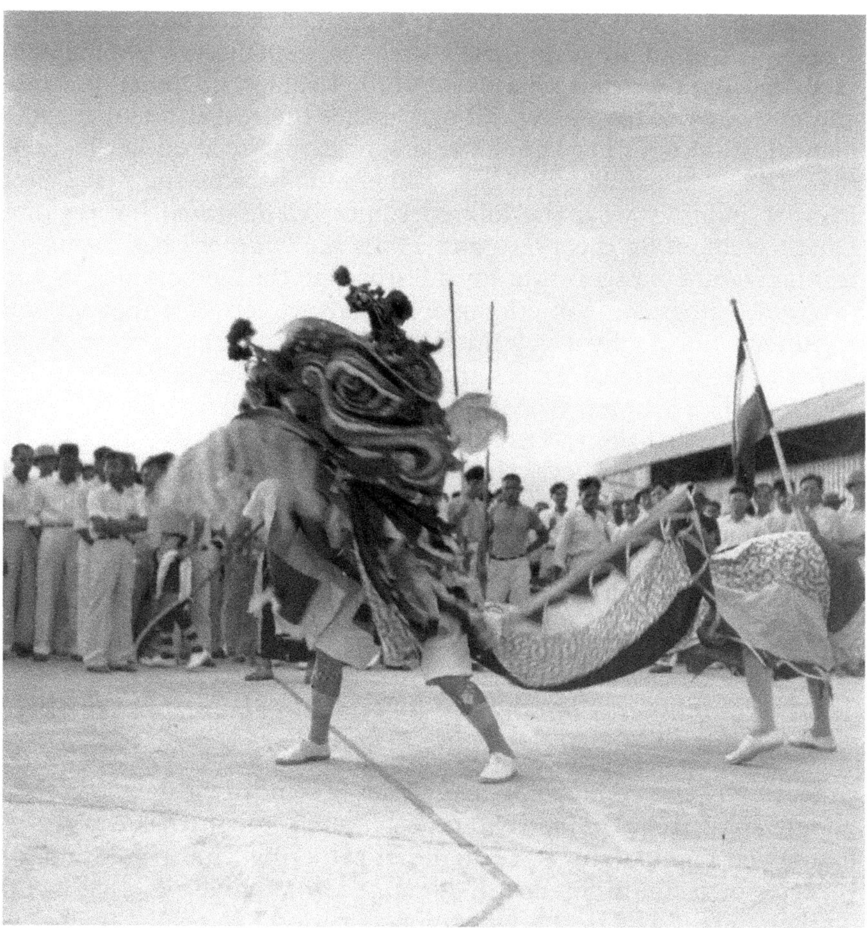

6.1 E. P. L. de Hoog, 'The flight service's dragon', Babo (New Guinea), 1938

festivals from both the East Indies and the Netherlands. I argue that the monarch who emerged as the tributary figure of such displays was an inherently imperial one. In photographs taken by colonial elites, the queen's look of recognition was invoked to harmonise spectacles of ethnic and folk diversity among both her Dutch and colonial subjects across the realm. In the early twentieth century, photography therefore legitimised in novel ways the historic precedents in Europe as well as Asia for royal dynasties to reign over discontiguous territories and populations differentiated by language, religion, customs or material culture.[4]

This chapter also attends to representations of the monarch's body – here, that of a European, female king – to explain how photography mediated Wilhelmina's relationship to her subjects. Official portraits and postcards of the queen throughout her life reveal how her racial identification with her Dutch subjects was inscribed on her body. In the 1890s, while still a princess, Wilhelmina became the first Dutch royal to publicly wear the folk costumes (*klederdracht*) of regional Dutch women. By the 1920s and 1930s *klederdracht* had become a regular feature of pageants at royal festivals in the Netherlands, as part of a wider programme of ethnographic 'salvage' projects that actively recruited photography to capture folk practices thought to be vanishing in the wake of national 'modernity'.[5] In also having herself photographed wearing folk costumes, Wilhelmina bodily identified with and mirrored the diversity that she was expected to recognise in her Dutch subjects. By contrast, the queen never physically embodied the ethnic and religious diversity of her colonial subjects. She received ethnographic dolls as gifts, and was a patron of colonial exhibitions. But to *only* gaze upon her colonial subjects' differences upheld the boundary separating her visual recognition of them from the bodily identification she reserved for Dutch women.

Ethnography and photography at royal celebrations in the Netherlands East Indies

Colonial physical anthropology has produced some of the most notorious photographic tropes of Indigenous people subject to intrusive measurements and manipulations, all in aid of gathering data to substantiate theories of racial difference. It remained a marginal practice in the Netherlands Indies in the late colonial period.[6] Here, the dominant fields of inquiry were in fact cultural anthropology and ethnography (*volkenkunde*), which examine humans as bearers of culture, particularly material culture.[7] Colonial ethnographers too produced photographs that scholars and present-day Indigenous communities now believe differed radically from how Indigenous subjects would have represented themselves. Since ethnographers thought individuals signified the general characteristics of the whole group, colonial photographs of ethnic 'types' fetishised Indigenous bodies, faces and adornments, and routinely left their unnamed subjects socially and environmentally decontextualised.[8]

In the Netherlands and its colonies, it was not until the mid-twentieth century that anthropology and ethnography became professionalised disciplines whose practitioners were concentrated in universities. Before then, ethnographers in the Indies worked in diverse, frequently opportunistic situations of encounter between Europeans and Indigenous people, which included everyday governing, military expeditions, missionary work, trade and scientific exploration.[9] It was in these contexts, as well as in photographic studios, that the best-known examples of ethnographic photography were produced.

Of those photographs made in the course of scientific and geographical expeditions in the East Indies, some became renowned through published albums, like those of the Danish photographer Kristen Feilberg (1839–1919) in Sumatra, Penang and Singapore, and Jean Demmeni (1866–1939) in Borneo.[10] Military conquests of new territory similarly recruited army doctors and other personnel to take photographs of local populations, partly with the aim of distinguishing between vanquished foes and friends of the colonial state.[11] Throughout colonised Asia, governing imperatives remained in the minds of scholar-administrators long after conquest. As Christopher Pinney demonstrated in his work on British India, the categorisation of populations into loyal and potentially rebellious groups was an enduring concern for officials, who recruited ethnography for governing purposes.[12]

Indies studio photographers – the other major source of ethnographic photographs in the late nineteenth and early twentieth centuries – carefully staged portraits to suit an indoor environment, with props and backdrops that enhanced the exotic appearance of their human subjects (figure 6.2). Such photographs had a wide public reach and remained in circulation long after they were made, enabling the practice of ethnography as an armchair pursuit for international enthusiasts.[13] The global circulation of ethnographic portraits increased as print and photographic technologies advanced, with images appearing in newspapers, at public lectures and exhibitions, as well as in the collections of scholars and institutions of learning.[14] With the rise of snapshot photography after 1900, amateurs were limited only by their means and opportunities to take ethnographic photographs through their own encounters in the Indies.[15] By the twentieth century, then, a wide range of people with varying skills and interests were taking, circulating and viewing ethnographic portraits of Indigenous peoples, in specialist as well as generalist venues: in scholarly books and journals, memoirs and travelogues, postcards, official reports, commercial albums, and at art and trade exhibitions.[16]

Historians of ethnographic photography in the Indies have focused on the works of studio photographers and the personnel accompanying scientific and military expeditions.[17] However, there were many other situations of encounter between Europeans and Indigenous people in which amateur photographers could 'do' ethnography, if so inclined. One of those circumstances was at royal celebrations for the Dutch monarchy, particularly at the annual Queen's Day festivals. These were

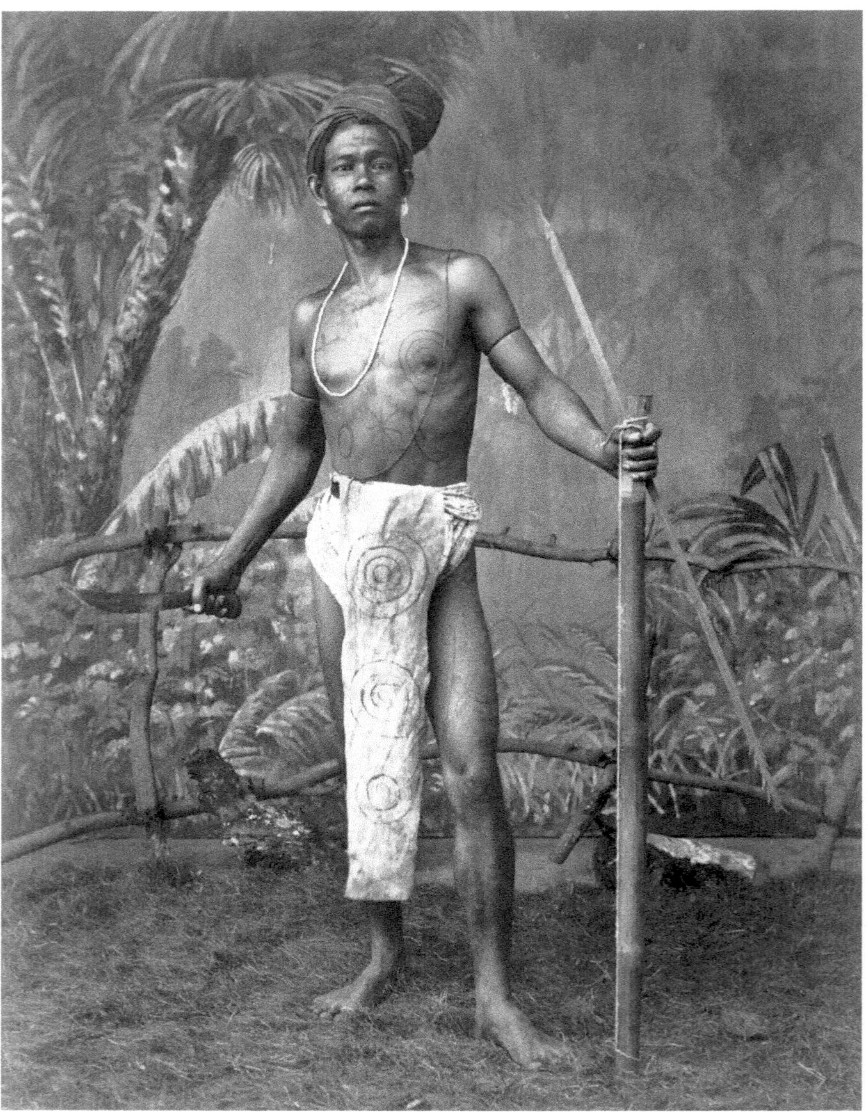

6.2 Unknown photographer, studio portrait of an 'Alfuru' from Ceram

foreseeable, organised occasions when Dutch authorities encouraged the participation of local populations as part of the pageantry, often in ways that gave distinctive groups a chance to display themselves and their customs. For camera-holding spectators, Queen's Day festivals provided unique opportunities to observe and record the bodies, costumes

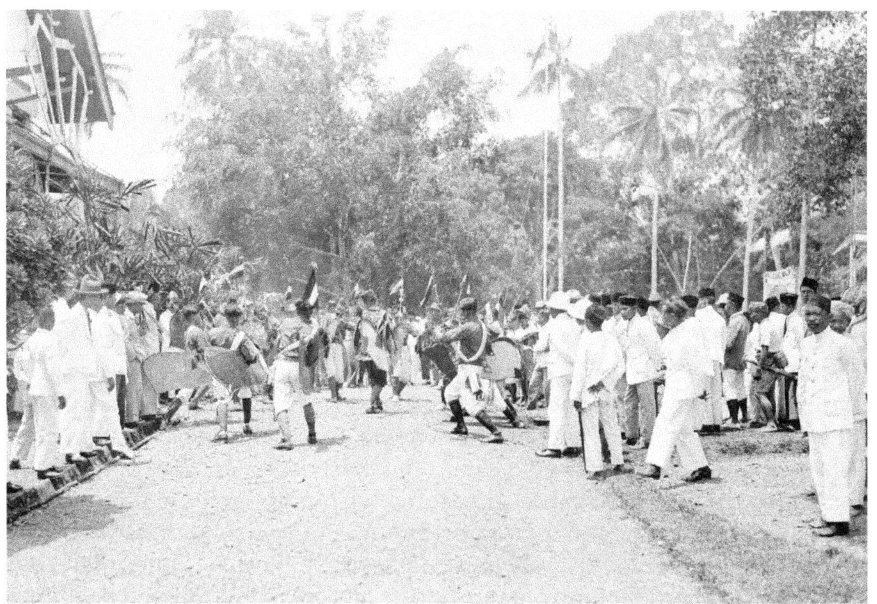

6.3   G. L. Tichelman, *Kuda kepang* on Queen's Day, Barabai
(Dutch Borneo), 1926

and performative rituals of different Indies ethnic groups. Indeed, an ethnographic way of seeing – an eye for collective 'types', for ornamentation and costume, and for exotic displays – permeates the private, amateur photograph collections of Dutch colonial elites to an extent that suggests that the ruling classes of the Indies were not just consumers but also producers of ethnographic photography in the Indies.

The profuse photographs and written works of the civil servant G. L. Tichelman are exemplary for revealing how educated Europeans who had regular access to ethnographic 'subjects' made photography integral to their practices. Tichelman's photographs from the 1920s, when he governed as a lower official in the Outer Provinces, have been discussed twice in this book already: in Chapter 2, which featured the portraits of Queen Wilhelmina that he used as effigies during royal celebrations, and in Chapter 4, which examined how Tichelman's photographs recorded the infrastructure projects in his jurisdiction and thus positioned himself as an 'Ethical' governor. He also, like De Hoog, photographed *kuda kepang* performances by Javanese migrants in the Outer Islands (figure 6.3).

Tichelman belonged to the last generation of amateur ethnographers before the practice became the domain of university academics. This transformation was already well under way in other parts of the colonial world, particularly in Britain and its empire;[18] but in the Netherlands East Indies, colonial civil servants produced a significant amount of ethnographic scholarship through opportunities afforded them in the course of their work, at frontier postings and on tour. This was certainly true for Tichelman, whose encounters with the so-called 'Alfuru' of Ceram, Batak tribes of Sumatra and people of Aceh yielded extensive material for studies that appeared in a wide range of newspapers, specialist periodicals and museum literature.[19] In fact, Tichelman's ethnographic experience gained while on the job as a civil servant supported his second career when he retired from the civil service and returned to the Netherlands in 1937. Thereafter, he worked at the Colonial Institute (later the Royal Institute for the Tropics) in Amsterdam in a number of roles, including as conservator in the Ethnographic Department.[20] At the institute he produced educational materials for children, including an Indies-themed card game illustrated with ethnographic photographs of his own making, and a book on ethnography for young adults.[21]

As I have detailed elsewhere, the photographs that Tichelman took at Queen's Day celebrations and then placed in his personal albums and official reports reveal the imbrication of his intellectual pursuits in ethnography with his career interests as a governing official.[22] The ethnic diversity of south-eastern Borneo in particular, where he served from 1923 to 1929, both fascinated and concerned Tichelman. His jurisdiction contained Dayak, Bugis, Malays, Javanese, Madurese and Bajau (all classed as *Inlander* or 'Native' in his logbooks), as well as a growing number of 'Foreign Orientals', consisting of several hundred Chinese, Hadrami Arabs and 'Hindus' from British India who formed important trade and business enclaves.[23]

Tichelman's service files and photographs disclose his conviction that it was the role of the colonial government to shield the 'Natives' of the Indies from the shocks of modern Ethical reform with sensitivity towards the cultural limits of diverse ethnic groups under colonial guidance. He deemed the Dayak, for instance, too primitive to join the modern future that the Dutch envisioned, paternalistically, for their Indies possessions. Dayak were worthy of ethnographic scrutiny, but such a gaze was purely academic: it had no administrative urgency. By contrast, an eye had to be kept on those groups that had responded well to reformist programmes *and* managed to maintain their ethnic distinctiveness: the flourishing Malay majority of farmers and traders, Javanese who had taken up the challenge of resettlement, and the commercially successful communities of Foreign Orientals. The latter two minorities were particularly concerning for colonial authorities because of the local resentment they often attracted. Thriving minorities were a cause for both celebration and vigilance, their robustness singling them out as potential threats to *rust en orde* (peace and order) as much as worthy recipients of Ethical welfare.[24] It was for similar reasons that, in the 1890s, the colonial government sent ethnographic photographers – Jean Demmeni and A. W. Nieuwenhuys (1864–1953) – to investigate political relations in Pontianak and Samarinda before establishing colonial offices there.[25]

As we will see, the photographs taken at Queen's Day celebrations by Tichelman and other Dutch elites in government, business and industry did more than provide an 'exhibition space' for Indies ethnic groups to perform their unity in diversity under the Dutch crown.[26] Their cameras brought these groups into a visual sphere that 'marked the emergence of the modern world as spectacle',[27] where subjects were on display and sovereigns appealed to, but where different fields of power determined the visibility of participants.

Importantly, the work of these mostly male photographers emerges from an era when masculine work and leisure were not rigidly separated in spatial, temporal or intellectual terms. Their personal albums do not follow the pattern of visible homes and invisible workplaces that several scholars have identified as typical to white, female, middle-class family photography later in the twentieth century.[28] Instead, a common feature of Dutch male elites' personal albums is their combination of images of private life (family dinners, afternoon teas, galas and tennis parties) with snapshots of activities 'on the job', both in the narrow sense (as an official or engineer, for instance, interacting with Indonesians) and as connoisseurs of ethnography.

Traditional dances in photographs of royal celebrations from the Indies

E. P. L. de Hoog was by no means the only Dutch observer to photograph 'traditional' dances at Queen's Day festivals in the Indies. The Resident of Borneo's Western District, K. A. James, was given a presentation album by the Sultan of Sambas to mark the visit of Governor-General Van Limburg Stirum for Queen's Day in 1920. Among the images the album contained was a performance of a dragon dance outside the Assistant Resident's house.[29] The fact that an Indies sultan had commissioned this album is significant, for it is further evidence of Indonesian elites engaging in photographic dialogues with their European counterparts.[30] War dances, often performed by men in distinctive costumes brandishing weapons, were even more popular themes in photographs of royal celebrations.[31] Scholars of worlds' fairs and popular ethnography have argued that European interest in Indigenous war

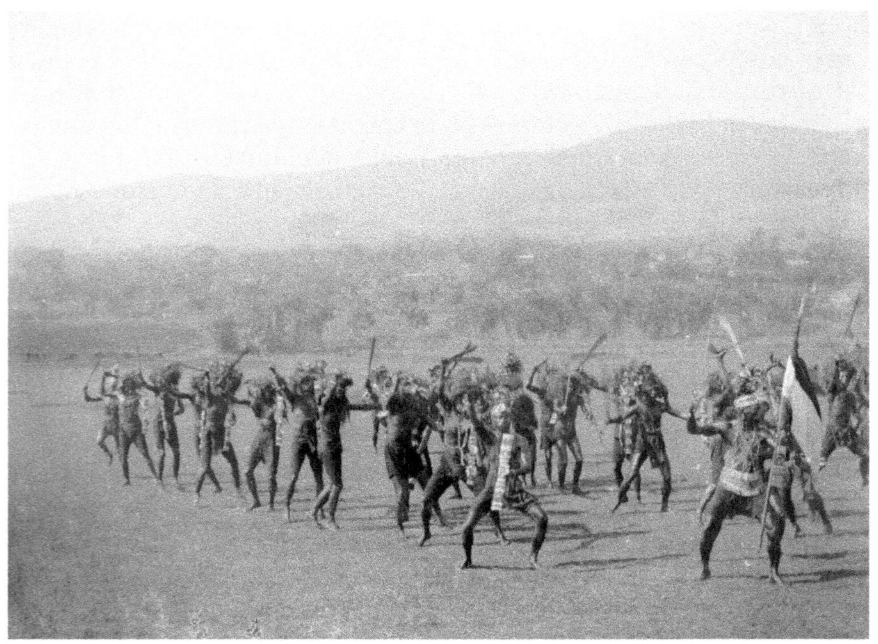

6.4 Unknown photographer, war dance, Lesser Sunda Islands, Queen's Day c. 1920

dances was enabled by the political success of colonial conquest, the attenuation of violent resistance into performance and the aesthetic triumph of a colonial picturesque that relied on retaining elements of the savage.[32] The element of spectacle that a live war dance entailed in the East Indies is evident in photographs that show the crowds of people drawn to watch them at royal celebrations.[33] Tribes with distinctive head-dresses, tattoos and weapons were a special part of royal celebrations in Maluku.[34] The adaptation of traditional war dances to contemporary, post-conquest conditions on such occasions is evident in the Dutch flags that the warriors brandished in place of spears (figure 6.4). In some cases, performers even adopted Western costumes, as in the example of the Papuan dancers that Jan van Baal photographed in Merauke in 1937.[35] The future governor of Dutch New Guinea and eminent anthropologist at Leiden University had only just begun his Indies career at that time, and the marriage of Crown Princess Juliana was one of the first major festivals he witnessed in the colony. Dutch government photographers in New Guinea captured similar scenes for Juliana at Queen's Day celebrations in 1955, when Van Baal was governor (figure 6.5).

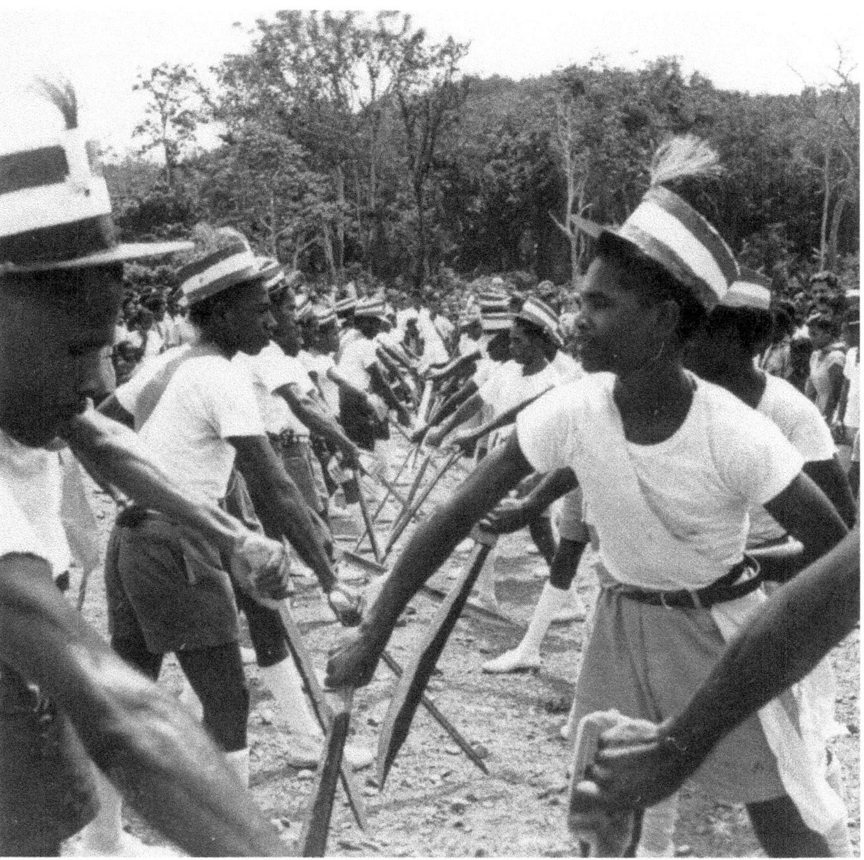

6.5   Netherlands New Guinea Government, dancers from Tabati (New Guinea), 31 April 1955

The photographs of *kuda kepang* dances that De Hoog and Tichelman took in New Guinea and Borneo reveal how the dance intrigued Dutch observers throughout the 1920s and 1930s.[36] A. J. Resink-Wilkens (1880–1945), mother of the eminent Indonesianist G. J. Resink (1911–97), was renowned in Yogyakarta as an expert on *kraton* culture and a collector of Javanese antiquities.[37] She noted in the early 1930s that Javanese dances such as the *kuda kepang* were traditional at Garebeg Mulud, during which the Sultan of Yogyakarta led celebrations for the Prophet Muhammad's birthday.[38] An ancient dance with its origins in combat rituals, *kuda kepang* has been associated with eroticism, fertility rites, trance and animism. Variations in the name of the dance, the number of 'riders' and the materials that the horses are made from

[163]

occur not just throughout Java but in other islands of the Indonesian archipelago and throughout the Malay world.[39] The American art historian Claire Holt observed during her fieldwork in Yogyakarta during the mid-1950s that 'entrancement' for the performers was the principal aim of the dance.[40] Even so, Holt assumed that its 'original meaning and function' had been lost over time. Apart from its performance at the odd wedding or circumcision, *kuda kepang* had declined to 'a diverting spectacle' by the mid-twentieth century.[41] Working in the same region a few decades later, the anthropologist John Pemberton bemoaned how, under President Suharto's New Order regime, the dance was 'routinely trotted out for bank dedication ceremonies and similarly auspicious occasions'.[42]

Notable in all these accounts by European and American observers is the tendency to uphold discourses of primitivism and salvage first developed by colonial ethnographers: the notion that Indigenous cultures were degraded by encounters with the 'modern' and always already on the brink of extinction. It may well be that the performance of *kuda kepang* at Queen's Day celebrations in the 1920s and 1930s represented this dance's ritual death knell, even as photographers flocked to capture its distinctive authenticity. Alternately, these *koninginnedag* performances may also contain the earliest indications of how the dance has evolved across the twentieth century in ways that were not properly grasped by ethnographers, past and present: by adapting to the demand for spectacles of inclusion and diversity by various regimes that sought to unite disparate populations under a central authority. Long before Suharto, that figure was the Dutch queen Wilhelmina.

The performance of such dances at royal festivals was meant to display the persistence of tradition among Wilhelmina's ethnically diverse subjects in the Indies. What they arguably demonstrate, however, is the Dutch appropriation *and* local adaptation of customs in flux to colonial conditions. While European photographs taken at royal celebrations give little indication of the dance's significance to the Javanese who performed and observed it, such images do commemorate a new public use for the dance. In Tichelman's photographs, for instance, the Dutch flags festooning the horses and the location of the performance under the watchful eyes of white-clad officials – indeed, under the very eaves of the Assistant Residency, which Tichelman himself occupied – represent the orchestrated participation of Javanese emigrants to Borneo in a festival meant to celebrate the longevity of a Dutch queen and her authority over a diverse but well-managed population of colonial subjects. Tichelman's and De Hoog's photographs of *kuda kepang* performances on Queen's Day also illustrate the rapid, recent changes to the social fabric of these 'Outer Provinces' that followed colonial intervention in the region. The fact that Javanese men were present to dance at *koninginnedag* at all reflects migration programmes intended to alleviate over-population on Java by relocating whole communities to labour-deficit sites of economic activity. The Javanese in Tichelman's district emigrated to Borneo on the promise of becoming agricultural colonists on land set aside by government decree in 1923. As Tichelman recorded in his logbook with some dismay, many Javanese sold their allotments and rapidly emerged as a landholding class, causing tensions within the local community and a subsequent headache for officials on the ground.[43] Late colonial iterations of *kuda kepang* therefore signified the most recent in a series of changes to the social and cultural functions of the dance in a long line of alterations that have continued to recent times.

The politics of popular monarchism in the Netherlands coincided with colonial authorities' concerns for orchestrating local participation, particularly for promoting spectacles of ethnic diversity. It was necessary for Dutch elites in the Indies to do so, given the wide variety of ethnic, language and religious groups in Indonesia, and the fact that colonial agriculture and industry continued to stimulate significant labour migrations across the archipelago during Wilhelmina's reign. It was in the interests of colonial authorities to promote harmony and inclusion at royal festivals, and these governing priorities intersected with what I have characterised as an ethnographic way of seeing at such occasions. Colonial photographers used royal celebrations as opportunities to record the costumes, customs and material cultures of the diverse communities among whom they lived and worked, even as they ensured smooth proceedings and broad participation. These mostly European photographers (although an Indonesian sultan was also among the examples in the previous section) were thus *producing* popular ethnography in a situation that was ostensibly incidental to anthropological fieldwork, but in fact instrumental for asserting colonial authority and the symbolism of governance.

Colonial elites were also *consuming* visual forms of ethnography in modes that involved casting a gaze from the colonies towards Europe. Just as *cartes-de-visites* of East Indies ethnic 'types' circulated in an international sphere, so too did postcards of Dutch folk types have an audience in the colonies. G. M. G. Douwes Dekker (1883–1959), a senior Indies technocrat and descendant of the famed 'Multatuli' (aka Edouard Douwes Dekker, author of the 1860 novel *Max Havelaar*), was a keen, life-long amateur photographer.[44] On holiday in Europe with his family in 1929, he undertook an extended *fietstocht* (bike tour) through the islands of the southern Netherlands. The photograph album he compiled of his adventures combined photographs of his own making with postcards purchased on the trip. One page included a group portrait of children in local *klederdracht* whom he found so 'sweet and picturesque' that he could not resist asking them to pose for him.[45] Two whole pages were devoted to postcards of people in *'Zeeuwsche volksklederdrachten'* (the folk costume of Zeeland).[46]

What were the circumstances that led to a Dutchman in the Indies collecting ethnographic postcards of his own compatriots? The answer requires an examination of Queen's Day celebrations in the Netherlands in the 1920s and 1930s, where Dutch participants were being integrated and photographed in novel ways.

'Folklore' studies and diversity at royal celebrations and in the Netherlands

As discussed in Chapter 1, from a young age Wilhelmina was given to understand how important her dynasty's popularity was for the continuing legitimacy of the Dutch monarchy. It was during her lifetime that royal birthdays went from being irregular festivals, reserved only for major milestones, to becoming annual carnivals with a strong *volks karakter* reflecting the diversity of the Netherlands' population, organised by local subcommittees and encouraging mass participation.[47] By the 1920s and 1930s new technologies, urban developments and affordable, illustrated commemorative materials combined to produce royal festivals as mass events. Nowhere was this more evident than in Amsterdam, the Dutch capital and site of the royal palace used for state occasions. In 1928 a new stadium was opened in the south of the city for the summer Olympics. Initially it held more than 30,000 spectators, but its capacity was doubled in 1937 with the completion of an extension. Commemorative books for major royal festivals in this period show how the Olympic stadium was used to host large celebrations that brought Queen Wilhelmina in contact with her subjects.[48] She presided over festivities in modes meant for the masses, addressing the crowd via a microphone from the royal podium, and receiving distinguished visitors in the centre of the amphitheatre before an audience of tens of thousands. From the royal box, the queen also joined her subjects watching the pageant in her honour.[49] The display included processions of floats attended by marchers in folk costume, each representing communities from the Dutch provinces beyond the urbanised west coast. Commentary in the text of one *gendenkboek* for Wilhelmina's fortieth jubilee in 1938 described 'a procession full of colour and joy [...] [E]ach province gives an idea of the folkloric, but also, of the modern,

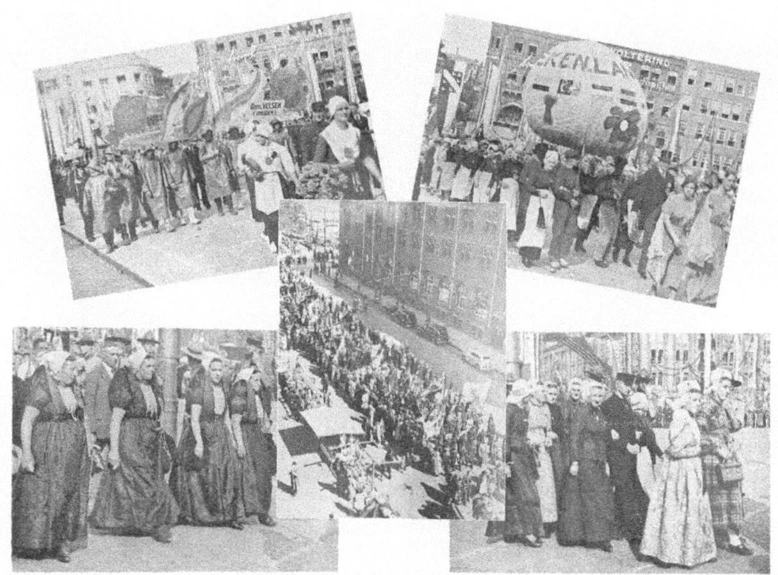

6.6 Unknown photographer, folk groups from Ijmuiden, the Langendijken and Goes parading on Queen's Day, Amsterdam (Netherlands), 1938

industrious life within [the Netherlands'] borders.'[50] Another book from 1938 pictured groups of women from various villages, each in distinctive head-dresses and costumes that evoked images of the seventeenth century more typically seen in Golden Age paintings than twentieth-century photographs (figure 6.6).

The same book, which sold for only *f1. 25* (the price of a few tram rides), contained photographs of the processions representing the East and West Indies (figure 6.7). The 'Bali-float', as it became known, was pictured on one page together with 'the people from Scheveningen and the district of Princevlag' in the Netherlands. The Amsterdam Olympic stadium thus brought together all the queen's subjects across the empire in a spectacle of unity in diversity. In selecting Bali to represent the Indies display, the Amsterdam organisers continued a tradition, established at the 1900 Paris Exposition Universelle (and making a resurgence at the 1931 Paris Colonial Exposition), of favouring Hindu-Balinese material culture as the emblem of an archipelago where Islam was in

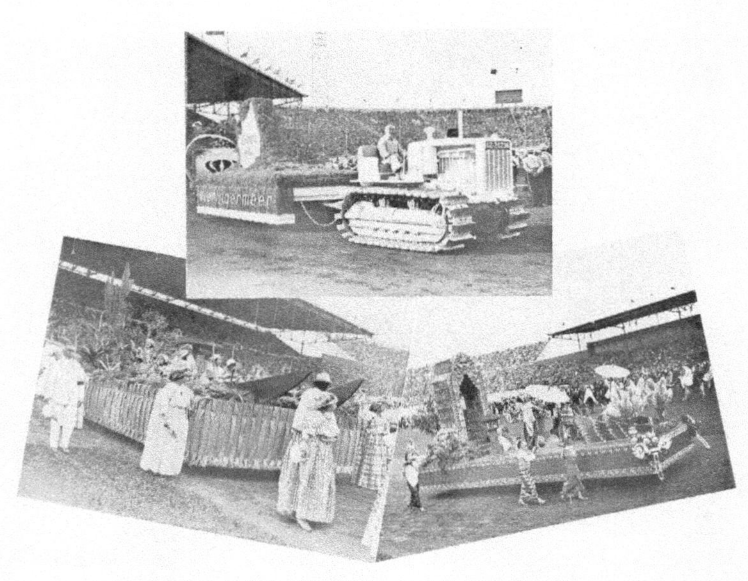

6.7   Unknown photographer, the West and East Indies (bottom row) represented for Wilhelmina's fortieth jubilee at the Amsterdam Olympic Stadium, 1938

fact the dominant religion.[51] In a separate *gendenkboek*, which likewise printed a photograph of the Bali float, the legacy of Dutch imperial exhibitions was explicit in the description, which combined a celebration of the tropical products of the Indies with fascination for Javanese, Balinese and Chinese cultural forms. A 'beautifully decorated "Gunungan" [mountain]' served to

> symbolically offer the products of Insulinde to the celebrating Sovereign. Accompanied by the sound of 'Angkloengs' [bamboo percussion instruments], 'Kembang Manggar' [coconut flower stems] and other figures symbolising Fertility walk past Her Majesty. Before a temple gate in the Hindu-Javanese style the priestess stands stiffly before the sacrificial altar, muttering prayers, while graceful 'Lègongs' perform ritual dances. Young women bring fragrant offerings to the temple by way of thanks to the gods for the rich harvest. And after them comes, with infernal music, the high note of the procession, a Chinese 'Tjap-go-meh' dragon, which is meant to ensure that no calamity will befall the land.[52]

[168]

The procession of costumed dancers, music and performative rituals divorced from their original contexts, all in tribute to Queen Wilhelmina, would have looked very familiar to spectators at royal celebrations in the East Indies. The only element absent from photographs of such occasions in the Indies was the participation of Dutch folk groups in the procession. Yet in amateur photography from the Indies and official photography from the Netherlands, performances of ethnic diversity at Queen's Day celebrations reveal a common tendency: for cameras to be used to produce popular ethnography and an image of Wilhelmina's diverse subjects brought together harmoniously in her honour. The transnational expansion of mass photography in tandem with the increased pomp and organisation of royal festivals across the Dutch colonial world help account for the context of these coincidences in the 1920s and 1930s. The rise of *volkskunde* ('folklore studies') in the Netherlands, alongside and intersecting with *volkenkunde* ('ethnography') in the Indies, is the final, decisive factor in explaining the emergence of Queen's Day as a celebration of Wilhelmina's symbolic role in governing ethnic diversity across her realm.

During the 1930s the Netherlands was in the grip of a boom in folklore studies, a field to which photography was recruited as a documentary tool for recording folk 'types' and their traditional costumes.[53] The Dutch were not alone in this regard. In Germany, the scholarly preoccupation with national *volksgruppen*, and particularly their Aryan lineages, was well under way. (Indeed, Dutch forays into this German-dominated, eugenically inflected field during the 1930s were directly related to its academic decline in the Netherlands after the Second World War.)[54] In England, an ethnographic turn similarly informed amateur 'survey' photography. Until the end of the First World War, as Elizabeth Edwards has shown, English survey photographers were driven by salvage impulses that resonated with colonial ethnographic projects: an 'entropic anxiety' that 'modernity' would obscure the English past unless its traces were preserved in objective 'records' (photographs).[55] People and places that bore the marks of the 'primitive rural' were deemed to be the most direct, authentic and fragile bearers of the English past.[56] Remco Ensel has demonstrated a similar discourse in the Netherlands, where photographers were especially fascinated with the people of the Zuiderzee ('South Sea') fishing villages. These communities, flood-prone for centuries, were relocated between 1920 and 1932 in a major project to dam the ocean inlet (now the Ijsselmeer) with the Afsluitdijk. As Ensel shows, at the very moment of the coast's enclosure, its population became the iconic image of an 'authentic Netherlander ... who embodied the real Netherlands that the modern Dutch citizen had left behind'.[57]

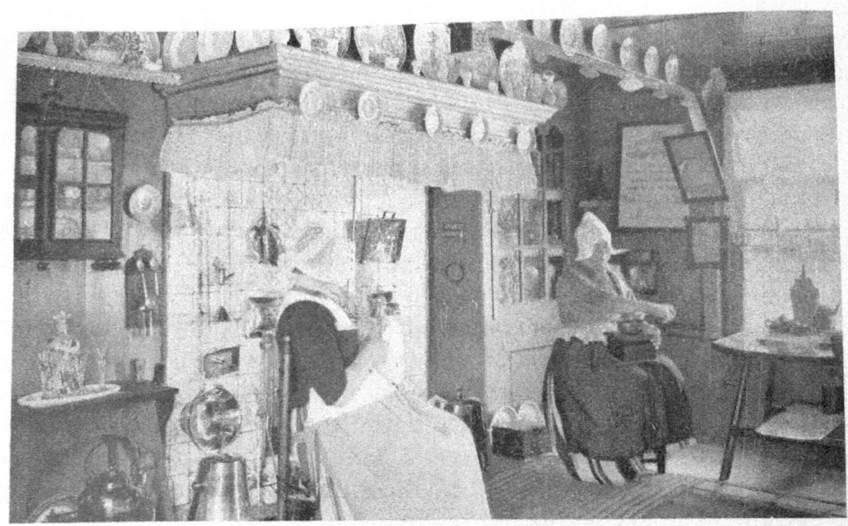

6.8   Unknown photographer, 'Volendammer interior'

The dresses, headgear, hairstyles and jewellery distinctive to Volen-dammer fishermen, or the women and children of Marken, cast such groups both as exotic others within the national body politic and as relics of an essential *oer-Nederland* (primeval Netherlands). They were well represented in D. J. van der Ven's book, *Neerlands Volksleven* (*Dutch Folkways*), published in 1920 and richly illustrated with pho-tographs of peasant dwellings, men's and women's trades and handicrafts, marriage and funerary rites, and folk costumes (figure 6.8). The book was issued two years after the inauguration of the Open-Air Museum in Arnhem, where rural traditions and industries were preserved and are still displayed to this day.[58] It was these and other folk groups, visually defined by their costume, that were paraded at celebrations before Wilhelmina in the 1930s in popular displays of *volkskunde*. In the process, the queen was called upon to perform an ancient, funda-mental duty of the monarch: to present herself to and look upon the people of her realm.

In the period from 1923 until 1938, when Wilhelmina's reign seemed consolidated and public festivals in her honour became more orchestrated and important, folklorists and anthropologists in the Netherlands and the East Indies were also sharing their work and ideas. There was some circulation of personnel between the Indies and the Netherlands, as Fenneke Sysling and Remco Ensel have demonstrated, most notably among physical anthropologists (many of whom nurtured a closet interest in ethnography) who moved between the two places throughout their careers.[59] Sysling found that two anthropologists with experience in the Indies were advisors on the project to photograph and study Zuiderzee communities. These specialists made explicit comparisons between the 'natives' of Dutch villages such as Marken and the so-called primitive peoples of central New Guinea, both of whom were seen as 'older strata' of their respective populations.[60] The search for the 'noble peasant' and the 'primitive within' in the Netherlands was thus related, through intellectual networks and ideas, to the pursuit of the 'noble savage' and the 'exotic other' in the Indies. As Rob van Ginkel and Barbara Henkes explain, the development of anthropology has usually been understood as being linked to colonial expansion, while the rise of folklore studies is typically connected to nationalism.[61] However, if we examine Queen's Day celebrations in the Indies and the Netherlands at the height of Wilhelmina's reign, and attend to how Dutch authorities photographed displays of ethnic unity in diversity in each location, it is clear that national and imperial concerns for governing difference were clearly interlinked at royal festivals.

The female queen and her body politic(s) in the Netherlands and the East Indies

Costumed folk pageants at Queen's Day celebrations also gave Wilhelmina, a female king, a unique opportunity to perform 'incorporation rituals' that bound her to her Dutch subjects. This concept borrows from scholarship on royal gift exchanges in a very different context – from the British Raj in Mughal India[62] – but the historical analysis of modern European kingship rituals is so underdeveloped that there are few other examples to draw upon. In Wilhelmina's lifetime, the invention of a tradition of women in the Dutch royal family wearing – and importantly, being photographed wearing – the folk costumes of their subjects arguably became significant because of their unprecedented visibility as female kings.

When Wilhelmina's mother, Queen Regent Emma, ushered in what became more than a century of female kingship in the Netherlands and its colonies, from 1890 to 2013, a 'Mother of the [Father]land' was celebrated for the first time since the Dutch monarchy's constitution in 1814.[63] Emma and her long line of sovereign female heirs were heads of state as well as being tasked with the fundamental role of monarchy to biologically reproduce itself. Male kings, by contrast, need to contract the latter task out, through marriage and (legal) paternity. In further distinction to Kings Willem I (r. 1815–40), II (1840–49) and III (1849–90), whose constitutional powers much exceeded her own, the popular foundations for Wilhelmina's legitimacy reformulated the monarch's symbolic association, from 'father-government-state' to 'mother-monarchy-nation'.[64] Scholars have often turned to ancient metaphors of the ruler's relation to the 'body politic' to represent this transition. Remco Ensel, for instance, has noted how '[t]he royal family, which came from the people and stood for the ultimate family, returned in "the body of the people"' in Wilhelmina's reign.[65] Henk te Velde notes that Wilhelmina embraced the embodied connection to her subjects, describing herself as *'het vleeschgeworden Nederlandsche volkskarakter'* ('the fleshly embodiment of the Dutch national character').[66]

The clothes that Wilhelmina wore visually expressed this embodied connection to her people. Like other monarchs, at state events and in official portraits Wilhelmina bore the vestments of royalty, such as crown jewels, ermine and a sceptre, all of which marked her out as distinct from her subjects. But from an early age, as part of her mother's plan to present her as a people's princess, Wilhelmina was also obliged to show herself, through dress, as one with her subjects. She did this most powerfully by adopting *klederdracht* on certain occasions. Although she was neither the first nor the last woman in the House of Orange to do so,[67] it was during Wilhelmina's youth that a tradition of Dutch queens in folk costume became established.

Wilhelmina was an 11-year-old princess when she received her first gift of a regional costume. It was 1892 and she was touring the provinces of the Netherlands with her mother. She appeared in public in Frisian *klederdracht* to great acclaim from a people whose dialect and customs are, to this day, perceived as distinct from the rest of the Netherlands.[68] In 1905 Wilhelmina returned to Friesland, this time as a married woman and a queen. In a classic example of traditions invented, a gala costume was made for the occasion, similar to what might have been worn by elite Frisian women. However, since few such costumes actually existed to refer to, and Wilhelmina did not favour the dark colours of the local nobility's clothing, the queen had hers made in a light palette.[69]

Importantly, both of the queen's appearances in Frisian costume were photographed and published, making them visible to a larger public.[70] Wilhelmina herself encountered the folkways of the Netherlands' regions through photography, both in the form of works presented to her and through her own camera lens. As a girl, she visited Walcheren in 1894, then still an island in the Scheldt estuary. A local association presented her with a monumental book of hand-coloured photographs showing girls her own age wearing traditional costumes.[71] In later life, as a keen photographer herself, Wilhelmina often took pictures of villagers she encountered while horse-riding in the countryside, and sometimes sent servants to deliver the prints to the subjects.[72]

Wilhelmina's heir, the Crown Princess Juliana, bore the full extent of the monarch's embrace of folk costume. Juliana received her first costume as a teenager, in 1922, and was photographed wearing it in the same year. It was an Axels gown and, unlike the dresses made for her mother, it was an authentic version of what commoner women wore (although, in the photograph, she and the other girls she posed with wore princely jewels, given as gifts to the participants) (figure 6.9).[73] Placing the princess among other girls in the same outfit, made by their hands, enhanced her appearance as one of her people. It happened again later, when she was photographed in *klederdracht* with girls from Zuid (South) Beverland.[74] Over time, the photo opportunity became the moment when Juliana's costumes were at their most replete. The dress she received in 1929 from the people of Land van Hulst was only ever worn in its complete iteration in the portrait taken of Juliana.

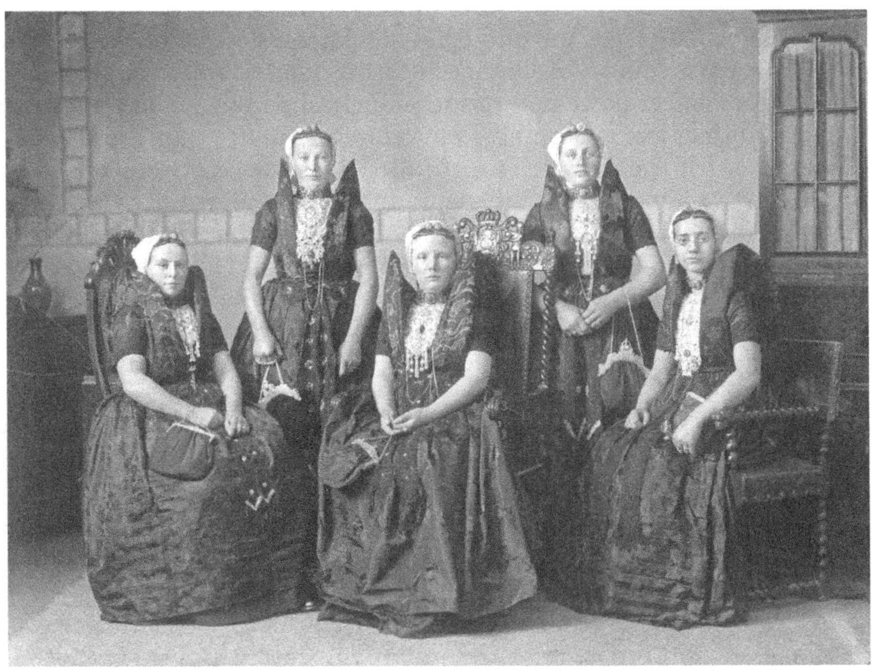

6.9 Herman Deutmann, Princess Juliana in Axels costume among girls from Zaamslag, Zeeland, 1922

Afterwards, parts of the costume were lost and she never publicly appeared in it again.[75] Similarly, Juliana was photographed in, but never wore in public, the Frisian costume she received as a wedding gift from a women's committee in 1937. Unlike her mother's gowns, Juliana's dress had no regal embellishments, but was decorated with authentic Frisian motifs. Her purse was embroidered with a key, the symbol of the housewife.[76]

Where Wilhelmina embodied 'the people' without compromising her aristocracy, for Juliana the folk authenticity of her costumes eclipsed sartorial proof of her nobility. As I described in Chapter 3, this shift was in keeping with the more democratised, 'ordinary' model of monarchy that Juliana's coming of age signalled in the late 1930s. For Juliana's firstborn, the future Queen Beatrix (b. 1938, r. 1980–2013), the imperative to appear in regional costume began very early. In 1944, while in wartime exile with Juliana's family in Ottawa, Beatrix was photographed with a friend in *'Volendamse muts en klompen'* (Volendammer cap and clogs).[77]

Within three generations and in Wilhelmina's own lifetime, it had therefore become a tradition for female kings in the House of Orange to perform incorporation rituals, whereby photographs captured how the clothing of their people, worn on their own bodies, bound them to their subjects. Indeed, the photographic portraits made of the leading women in the House of Orange wearing *klederdracht* appeared in newspapers and as postcards during Wilhelmina's reign, and were more important than live appearances for the larger publics they could reach. Together with the exhibitions of folk costumes that were staged in Wilhelmina's honour, at her inauguration in 1898 and at her abdication half a century later,[78] these photographs forged an identification between the body of the monarch and the diversity of the Dutch subjects she represented, not just in the cosmopolitan cities of the western seaboard, but also in the rural Netherlands.

The explicit message of these visual associations, as museum conservator Henneke van Suthem argues, was that the queen reigned over 'unity in diversity' (*eenheid in verscheidenheid*).[79] That her subjects understood the political claims of these royal gestures is evident in the modes of resistance occasionally mounted against them. In 1898 the largely socialist-voting and anti-monarchist province of Giethoorn declined to contribute a regional costume to the *klederdracht* exhibition for Wilhelmina's inauguration.[80]

As Alexander Maxwell has argued in his history of clothing and nationalism in Europe, after the mid-nineteenth-century revolutions it became politically expedient for female kings not to appear too luxuriously clothed. The 'cult of folk costume completed the social democratization of the nation', and it became more common for elites to 'adopt the costume of subalterns[;] thus the national costume would spread from the bottom up, at least symbolically'.[81] Indeed, folk costume developed in many European countries as a feminine sphere for expressing patriotism in ways that did not challenge national sovereignty as a masculine prerogative.[82] Gender also figures strongly in Remco Ensel's analysis of photography's role in furthering folklore studies and nationalism in the Netherlands in the interwar period. Dutch women, especially mothers, were cast as the bearers of a particular kind of national character: as natural, mysterious figures who bound the people to the past, different from the rational, future-oriented father-figure who represented culture and the state.[83] Most evocatively, Ensel argues that '[m]otherhood is the memory of the everyday, fatherhood is that of great events'.[84]

What might be the implications for female kingship in such a schema? Arguably, a queen traverses both spheres. She is the link to a primeval past, the embodiment of the nation and its memory, and the sign of a 'natural' order (so long as it persists uncontested). At the same time, she generates great events through coronations, births, deaths, marriages and anniversaries. Female kings, as Wilhelmina and especially Juliana demonstrated in the first half of the twentieth century, were icons both of the quotidian *and* the extraordinary to their subjects.

However, the incorporation rituals that these queens were increasingly expected to perform for their Dutch subjects did not extend to their subjects in the colonies. As I discussed in Chapter 5, official photographs from the mid-nineteenth century onwards reveal that ethnic cross-dressing was a privilege of male, Indigenous monarchs. The kings and princes of Central Java were among peers in their prerogative to wear either Western suits or, as protocol might demand, traditional sumptuary attire. Modern European monarchs did not, as a rule, have portraits made of themselves in the costumes of Asian sovereigns; this was true even of those with renowned Orientalist inclinations, such as Queen Victoria.[85] The same went for Wilhelmina and her heirs during her reign. The queen did, however, receive costume gifts from the East Indies in other forms, and her public relation to these gifts provides important insights into how the colonial body politic was integrated into the symbolism of monarchy.

Queen Emma was interested in the Netherlands' colonies, and saw to it that Wilhelmina was taught the human geography of her empire. Her lessons incorporated dolls wearing costumes from throughout Java, which were meant to signify different classes as well as ethnicities. Among them were miniatures of the Crown Prince of Yogyakarta, his spouse and a retainer; court dancers; villagers; and a lower official and his family.[86] The Java dolls were part of a set of 350 wax dolls, all in folk costume, sent as a gift in 1893 from the 'Ladies of the Netherlands East Indies'. The gift was organised by the wife of Governor-General C. Pijnacker Hordijk (served 1888–93), formally supported by all the royals of the East Indies, and involved the contribution of European and Indigenous officials from across the archipelago. The costumes were all accurate, and the dolls were carved from wood by two Javanese craftsmen, Kerto and Werioningrat, with a few made by unknown carvers. Contact between elite Javanese women and Dutch women in the Indies was the original impetus behind the gift. Indeed, women were frequently 'the initiators of such domesticated images of the empire' with the queen at its centre, particularly at milestones such as births and marriages.[87] Among the many hands that made the gift, the most famous was arguably Raden Ajeng Kartini (1879–1904), a present-day Indonesian national hero for her advocacy of women's and children's rights. She was only a year older than Wilhelmina, and reputedly contributed to the crafting of some dolls. She also posed for a photograph with her sisters in a *batik* demonstration that was meant to show the queen how costumes were made for real people.[88]

Rather than wear full-size costumes, then, the queen was given miniature representations to look at and manipulate in order to learn about, but not embody, the ethnic diversity of her overseas possessions. Models and miniatures were a common form of condensing and visually representing complex information, particularly to young audiences, for colonial exhibitions in the late nineteenth and early twentieth centuries.[89] Indeed, the whole collection was displayed in Batavia before being shipped to the princess in the Netherlands. Once there, it was displayed for a further two weeks at the Kneuterdijk Palace in The Hague, where the explicit instructional aims were anthropological. The dolls were surrounded by landscape paintings by Antoine Payen (1792–1853), the first artist to receive an official commission to paint in the East Indies.[90] To reinforce that the collection was a gift to Wilhelmina, a bust of the princess was installed at the exhibition, and Queen Emma herself endorsed it with a visit. The show was popular, drawing a thousand visitors per day who helped to finance, with their entry fees, the first scientific expedition to the interior of Dutch Borneo. In 1938, at Wilhelmina's fortieth jubilee, the dolls were brought out for a repeat exhibition at the Colonial Museum in Amsterdam.[91]

In the intervening years, Wilhelmina was called upon to patronise numerous exhibitions in the Netherlands, including at the Colonial Institute in Amsterdam in her silver jubilee year of 1923. The institute staged a retrospective in her honour of how Dutch knowledge of lands and people in the 'overseas regions' (*overzeesche gewesten*) had progressed.[92] It included ethnographic displays from New Guinea, the Minangkabau and Batak lands of Sumatra, South Sumatra and Aceh, Maluku and the Lesser Sunda islands, the interior of Borneo, Bali, Hindu-Buddhist antiquities and the court arts of Java. The West Indies were also represented, and there were photographs of ethnic types.[93] The impact of a quarter-century of Ethical policies in the East Indies was exhibited in the section on 'tropical hygiene', which showed photographs and wax models of people suffering endemic diseases such as *'framboesia'* (yaws), leprosy, malaria, smallpox and cholera; arguably, diseases of poverty rather than a specific geographical region. There was also a 'trade museum' which showed plants, animals and other natural resources that had been integrated into the Dutch colonial economy.[94]

As Susan Legêne and Berteke Waaldijk have argued, exhibitions in the Netherlands for milestones in Wilhelmina's reign 'created and canonized a multi-ethnic transnational unity' between her subjects across the Dutch colonial world.[95] This was nowhere more evident than at the fortieth jubilee celebrations in 1938, which once again prompted an exhibition at the Colonial Institute. Its centre-piece, according to one contemporary observer, was a 'symbolic representation' of '"imperial unity in trade [*ambacht*]": a Dutch person busy making cheese, a Javanese making *batik*, an Indian woman from Suriname spinning cotton, and a girl from Curaçao weaving a hat'. The writer continued:

> The central idea expressed in this exposition was the crowning moment of the [queen's] forty-year reign: the securing of Dutch authority over the whole area of the Outer Provinces, which brought with it: entry into the Pax Neerlandica, the precondition for peaceful development, and the opening of the Indies.[96]

Significantly, among the portraits hung to illustrate key figures in the consolidation of colonial power in the Indies were not just Dutch conquerors (notably Minister Cremer, a 'pioneer' of the Deli region, and Governor-General van Heutsz, vanquisher of the Acehnese) but also Sajjid Oethman bin Jahja and Tjong Ah Fie, representing Arab and Chinese groups 'in the new development of the Netherlands Indies'.[97] Finally, upon entering the central room of the exhibition, 'one saw opposite the Throne, around which were grouped different representatives of peoples [*volken*] who bore their dedication to the Kingdom'. Surrounding these statues in turn were portraits of Indigenous and European governing elites, including doctors and missionaries, as well as portrayals of military expeditions and the 'opening of an old forest'.[98] A whole, progressive, inclusive East Indies world was constructed around the throne symbolising the queen, who reigned *in absentia* over her distant subjects even as they were given form for a Dutch audience through a variety of visual representations.[99] The queen was called upon to recognise and oversee the diverse people of her East Indies realm, who were represented to her photographically, in clothed wax and wood models, and by name. But she was never obliged to embody this polity of subjects by placing herself in their clothes in the same way that she was expected to for her Dutch subjects.

Conclusion

In her book *Global Indonesia*, Jean Gelman Taylor observes that '[ne]ither rule by sultans, governors-general, Japanese military nor by Soekarno conditioned Indonesians for compromise and protecting difference in the public arena, for rubbing along together in the one polity'.[100] There is no evidence to suggest that the Dutch monarchy did anything practical to foster social and political cohesion in colonial Indonesia under Wilhelmina's reign. Yet the spectacle of royal festivals – the image of unity in ethnic diversity that captured the interest of colonial elites – certainly provided colonial elites with opportunities for reflecting on how to govern difference. Photographs show how royal festivals involved identifying and categorising groups, giving them an 'exhibition space', reflecting on the modes and meanings of difference in intellectual (ethnographic) as well as instrumental (governmental) terms, and orchestrating a public performance of harmonious 'rubbing along'. They also developed techniques of spectacle that post-colonial authorities (especially during the New Order) may well have perfected, but that had their modern origins in royal festivals for a Dutch imperial monarchy.

Dutch authorities were clearly informed by a curiosity for the materiality of difference, an interest that was intellectually disciplined by ethnographic ways of seeing. Ethnographic images were widely circulating in late colonial visual culture, and amateur photographers – many of whom had governing interests – in the Indies not only consumed but also contributed to that culture through the images they made at royal celebrations. These festivals were among the many situations that civil servants in particular took advantage of in the course of their life and work, to practise ethnography as well as think about the tasks involved in governing a diverse population.

The queen was central to these spectacles, even if she was never present in the Indies. She was the benevolent figure in whose honour the diverse communities across her kingdom were brought together. When we look at participants in photographs of royal celebrations in the Netherlands and the East Indies, remarkable similarities arise in how public rituals involved – indeed, starred – commoners, and constructed a notion of the queen's subjects, 'the people'. In this regard, photographs of royal celebrations for Wilhelmina bound the Dutch nation and its colonies together in an empire through performative practices and visual culture.

However, photographic sources also reveal important differences between colony and metropole, not least in how the queen herself was constructed as symbolic overseer of events. In the Netherlands, through explicitly feminised representations and practices, Dutch female kings were figured as *volksmoeder* ('mother of the people'). Here, Wilhelmina and her heirs embodied the diversity of their people by being photographed wearing a variety of women's folk costumes. In the Indies, by contrast, the queen's body was not identified with her racially Other subjects. Instead, as the recipient of ethnographic gifts and patron of colonial exhibitions in which Indies people were visually represented to a Dutch public, Wilhelmina was figured as supreme collector of the colony's ethnic diversity and as commander of exhibitionary spaces. As Susan Broomhall and Jacqueline van Gent have shown, the women of the House of Oranje-Nassau had for centuries been exercising and conveying their power by collecting objects amassed from across the Dutch empire.[101] Wilhelmina was unprecedented in her dynasty's history for continuing these practices in the role of an imperial, female king.

This was a symbolic role that dynastic monarchies have practised for centuries, and continue to perform (constitutionally, in many cases) today, even in the age of 'commonwealths', 'overseas territories' and other post-colonial euphemisms for the remnants of empire. It is a role that sits in tension and competition with the self-determinative aspirations of the nation-state – and also with the nation's idealisation of settled borders and homogeneous populations. Indeed, at precisely the time when Wilhelmina's reign was at its height and Indonesian nationalists were gathering force in the 1920s and 1930s, Dutch elites used discourses of understanding and promoting cultural diversity to argue that only the Netherlands could govern the Indies.[102] As we shall see in the final chapter, even as an independent, republican Indonesia firmly took shape in the 1940s, Dutch defenders of the empire clung to the 'East Indies' by continuing to evoke the monarchy.

Notes

1 KITLV Album 1042, shelf marks 140554, the unnumbered photograph beside it, and 140566.
2 See KITLV Album 1042, shelf marks 140555, 140556. Other names for the horse dance include *jaran képang* and *kuda lumping*.
3 S. Legêne, *Spiegelreflex; Culturele sporen van de koloniale ervaring* (Amsterdam: Bert Bakker, 2010), p. 95.

4 H. Dijkhuis, *Monarchia; Het fenomeen van het koningschap* (Amsterdam: Boom, 2010), p. 250; R. Aldrich and C. McCreery, 'European sovereigns and their empires "beyond the seas"', in R. Aldrich and C. McCreery (eds), *Crowns and Colonies: European Monarchies and Overseas Empires* (Manchester: Manchester University Press, 2016), pp. 1–26, at p. 6.

5 R. Ensel, *De Nederlander in beeld; Fotografie en nationalisme tussen 1920 en 1945* (Amsterdam: Amsterdam University Press, 2014), pp. 10, 51, 58–9, 74, 109, 205.

6 For an examination of the discipline of physical anthropology as it *did* exist in the East Indies, see F. Sysling, *Racial Science and Human Diversity in Colonial Indonesia* (Singapore: National University of Singapore Press, 2016). See also D. van Duuren, 'Expeditions, collection, science: the Dutch fascination for the Papuans of New Guinea', in S. Legêne and J. van Dijk (eds), *The Netherlands East Indies at the Tropenmuseum: A Colonial History* (Amsterdam: KIT Publishers, 2011), pp. 97–112, at p. 102; S. Vink, 'Photography and science', in J. van Dijk et al., *Photographs of the Netherlands East Indies at the Tropenmuseum* (Amsterdam: KIT Publishers, 2012), pp. 91–106, at p. 85; Legêne, *Spiegelreflex*, p. 174; E. Edwards, *Raw Histories: Photographs, Anthropology and Museums* (Oxford: Berg, 2001), pp. 90–3; C. Pinney, *Camera Indica: The Social Life of Indian Photographs* (Chicago: University of Chicago Press, 1997), pp. 20–4, 33–5, 44–5, 52–3, 57; C. Pinney, *Photography and Anthropology* (London: Reaktion, 2011), pp. 18–41; A. Maxwell, *Colonial Photography and Exhibitions: Representations of the 'Native' and the Making of European Identities* (London: Leicester University Press, 1999), pp. 38–59; J. Lydon, *Photography, Humanitarianism, Empire* (London: Bloomsbury, 2016), pp. 47–55.

7 A. Groeneveld, 'Photography in aid of science', in *Toekang Potret: 100 Years of Photography in the Dutch Indies 1839–1939* (Amsterdam/Rotterdam: Fragment/ Museum voor Volkenkunde, 1989), pp. 15–48, at p. 36; L. Roodenburg, *Anceaux's Glasses: Anthropological Photography Since 1860* (Leiden: National Museum of Ethnology, 2002), p. 30; Sysling, *Racial Science and Human Diversity*, p. 16.

8 E. Edwards, 'Photographic "types": the pursuit of method', *Visual Anthropology*, 3.2–3 (1990): 235–58, at pp. 241, 253; L. Conor, *Skin Deep: Settler Impressions of Aboriginal Women* (Crawley: UWA Publishing, 2016), p. 89.

9 Edwards, 'Photographic "types"', pp. 241, 253; Roodenburg, *Anceaux's Glasses*, p. 34; F. Sysling, 'Geographies of difference: Dutch physical anthropology in the colonies and the Netherlands, ca. 1900–1940', *BMGN/Low Countries Historical Review*, 128.1 (2013): 105–26, at p. 111; L. Ouwehand, *Herinneringen in beeld; Fotoalbums uit Nederlands-Indië* (Leiden: KITLV Press, 2009), pp. 90–1; Vink, 'Photography and science', p. 95.

10 Groeneveld, 'Photography in aid of science', pp. 23, 37, 39; Roodenburg, *Anceaux's Glasses*, p. 7.

11 Ouwehand, *Herinneringen in beeld*, pp. 88–9; see also P. Bijl, *Emerging Memory: Photographs of Colonial Atrocity in Dutch Cultural Remembrance* (Amsterdam: Amsterdam University Press, 2015), pp. 73–5.

12 Pinney, *Camera Indica*, pp. 34, 35, 44–6.

13 Groeneveld, 'Photography in aid of science', p. 36; I. Zweers, 'Commercial photography', in *Toekang potret: 100 Years of Photography in the Dutch Indies 1839–1939* (Amsterdam/ Rotterdam: Fragment/Museum voor Volkenkunde, 1989), pp. 53–120, at pp. 75, 82; Ouwehand, *Herinneringen in beeld*, pp. 38, 166–7; R. Jongmans and J. van Dijk, 'Photographs from the Netherlands East Indies: changing perspectives, different views', in J. van Dijk et al., *Photographs of the Netherlands East Indies at the Tropenmuseum* (Amsterdam: KIT, 2012), pp. 15–39, at pp. 32–3.

14 Edwards, 'Photographic "types"', pp. 238, 241; D. Poole, *Vision, Race, and Modernity: A Visual Economy of the Andean Image World* (Princeton, NJ: Princeton University Press, 1997), p. 15.

15 Roodenburg, *Anceaux's Glasses*, p. 31; Ouwehand, *Herinneringen in beeld*, pp. 60–3.

16 Poole, *Vision, Race, and Modernity*; Maxwell, *Colonial Photography and Exhibitions*; M. Bloembergen, *Colonial Spectacles: The Netherlands and the Netherlands-Indies at the World Exhibitions, 1880–1931* (Singapore: NUS Press, 2006).

17 See notes 6 and 13, above.

18 Edwards, *Raw Histories*, pp. 37, 46–7.

19 For a comprehensive list of Tichelman's published and unpublished works, see the meticulous inventory compiled by G. J. Knaap, *Inventaris Collectie G.L. Tichelman H814* (Leiden: KITLV Press, 1995). Tichelman also published on people and places in the Indies where he had not served as an official, especially New Guinea, which he wrote about with growing frequency from the late 1940s onwards to promote it as a Dutch colony rather than a province of the Republic of Indonesia.

20 In 1945 Tichelman was transferred to Central Information at what was then the Indies Institute. In 1951, when the Institute acquired its current name (*Koninklijk Instituut voor de Tropen*, Royal Tropical Institute), Tichelman was moved to Tropical Products, where he remained until his retirement in 1958 (Knaap, *Inventaris Collectie G.L. Tichelman*, pp. 11–13).

21 G. L. Tichelman, *Indonesische Bevolkingstypen* (Rotterdam and 's-Gravenhage: Nijgh and Van Ditmar N.V., 1948). On the card game, see Legêne, *Spiegelreflex*, pp. 162, 168.

22 S. Protschky, 'Ethical projects, ethnographic orders and colonial notions of modernity in Dutch Borneo: G. L. Tichelman's Queen's Birthday photographs from the late 1920s', in S. Protschky (ed.), *Photography, Modernity and the Governed in Late-Colonial Indonesia* (Amsterdam: Amsterdam University Press, 2015), pp. 71–102.

23 On the category of 'Foreign Oriental' in the Indies, see C. A. Coppel, 'The Indonesian Chinese as "Foreign Orientals" in the Netherlands Indies', in T. Lindsey (ed.), *Indonesian Law and Society* (Sydney: The Federation Press, 1999), pp. 33–41. Europeans such as Tichelman and those with 'equivalent' status, including a small community of Japanese entrepreneurs (among them studio photographers), made up a tiny proportion of the population, some 30 people in 1928: NL-HaNA, Tichelman 2.21.097.01, inv. nr. 21: *Memorie van Overgave*, Barabai (1926–29), p. 57. Tichelman's 1927 family album included photographs of stalls run by Japanese studio photographers at the annual fair that was introduced to coincide with Queen's Day in Barabai during his tenure: KITLV Album 187, shelf marks 83597, 83600.

24 Protschky, 'Ethical projects, ethnographic orders and colonial notions of modernity'.

25 Groeneveld, 'Photography in aid of science', p. 38.

26 On 'exhibition space', see Edwards, *Raw Histories*, p. 184. Roslyn Poignant uses a cognate concept, 'show space', in R. Poignant, 'The making of professional "savages": from P.T. Barnum (1883) to the *Sunday Times* (1998)', in C. Pinney and N. Peterson (eds), *Photography's Other Histories* (Durham, NC: Duke University Press, 2003), pp. 55–84, at p. 56.

27 Poignant, 'The making of professional "savages"', p. 56.

28 D. Chambers, 'Family as place: family photograph albums and the domestication of public and private space', in J. M. Schwartz and J. R. Ryan (eds), *Picturing Place: Photography and the Geographical Imagination* (London: I.B. Tauris, 2003), pp. 96–114, at pp. 97–8; G. Rose, 'Photographs and domestic spacings: a case study', *Transactions of the Institute of British Geographers*, 28.1 (2003): 5–18, at pp. 6, 8.

29 KITLV Album 44, shelf mark 12395.

30 See also S. Protschky, 'Tea cups, cameras and family life: picturing domesticity in elite European and Javanese family photographs from the Netherlands Indies, c. 1900–1942', *History of Photography*, 36.1 (2012): 44–65.

31 See, for example, KIT TM-60042741, by an unknown photographer, showing a shield dance of Muslim Sasak warriors in Mataram, Lombok, in 1922; KIT TM-30011061, TM-30011062, by an unknown photographer, showing Javanese men performing a dance with krises around 1910.

32 Zweers, 'Commercial photography', p. 87; Maxwell, *Colonial Photography and Exhibitions*, pp. 18–20.

33 Unknown photographer, war dance at Queen's Day, Maluku, 1920: KITLV Album 199, shelf mark 84314.

34 See also KITLV Album 577, shelf marks 519180, 51915, 51916, 51932; and the album of W. G. N. van der Sleen, KIT TM-10028203, TM-10028204, TM-60024922.

35 KITLV Album 266, shelf mark 14140.

36 See W. Staugaard, 'Koeda-K'pang', *Handelingen van het eerste congres voor de Taal-, Land- en Volkenkunde van Java* (Weltevreden: Albrecht, 1921); A. J. Resink-Wilkens, 'The Yogya festival calendar', trans. R. Robson-McKillop, first published 1932, in S. Robson (ed.), *The Kraton: Selected Essays on Javanese Courts* (Leiden: KITLV Press, 2003), pp. 83–90, at p. 87. See also images by the photographer and ethnographer W. G. N. van der Sleen (1886–1967), KIT TM-10028196, TM-10028197, TM-10028198, TM-10028199, TM-10028200, TM-10028201.

37 S. Robson (ed.), *The Kraton: Selected Essays on Javanese Courts* (Leiden: KITLV Press, 2003), p. 373.

38 Resink-Wilkens, 'The Yogya festival calendar', p. 87.

39 M. J. Kartomi, 'Music and meaning of *réyog ponorogo*', *Indonesia*, 22 (1976): 84–130, at pp. 88, 105; C. Holt, *Art in Indonesia: Continuities and Change* (Ithaca, NY: Cornell University Press, 1967), pp. 105–6; Resink-Wilkens, 'The Yogya festival calendar', p. 87.

40 Holt, *Art in Indonesia*, pp. 104–5.

41 Holt, *Art in Indonesia*, p. 106.

42 J. Pemberton, *On the Subject of 'Java'* (Ithaca, NY: Cornell University Press, 1994), p. 256.

43 NL-HaNA, Tichelman 2.21.097.01, inv. nr. 21: *Memorie van Overgave*, Barabai (1926–1929), pp. 96–7.

44 See KITLV Album 169 and KITLV H923, 34, 35, 37, 39. At the peak of his career, before he retired in the late 1930s, G. M. G. Douwes Dekker was Director of Finance in the state railway on Java.

45 KITLV Album 169, p. 39.

46 KITLV Album 169, pp. 45–6.

47 J. van Osta, *Het theater van de Staat; Oranje, Windsor en de moderne monarchie* (Amsterdam: Wereldbibliotheek, 1998), pp. 90–1, 135.

48 See *Herinnering aan den Oranje-Zaterdag 9 September 1933 ter gelegenheid van het 35-jarig regeerings-jubileum van HM Koningin Wilhelmina* (Amterdam: Holdert & Co., 1933); *Nationaal huldigingsdéfilé voor H.M. de Koningin op zaterdag 9 september 1933 in het Olympisch Stadion te Amsterdam* (Amsterdam: L. F. J. Thoolen, 1933); *Oranje Album 1898–September–1938 veertig jaren koningin* (Amsterdam: Holdert & Co., 1938); *Oranje-album ter herinnering aan het 50-jarig regeringsjubileum en de abdicatie van HM Koninging Wilhelmina en de inhuldigingsfeesten van HM Koningin Juliana* (Amsterdam: Holdert & Co. NV, 1948); Th. C. M. Visser, *Jubileum Manifestatie ter gelegenheid van het 50-jaring regeringsjubileum van H.M. Koningin Wilhelmina; 31 augustus 1948, Olympisch Stadion te Amsterdam* (1948).

49 *Herinnering aan den Oranje-Zaterdag 9 September 1933; Oranje Album 1898–September–1938*.

50 D. Kouwenaar, *Amsterdam tijdens het feestbetoon bij het 40-jarige regeeringsjubileum van HM Koningin Wilhelmina* (Amsterdam: De Bussy, 1938), p. 219.

51 Bloembergen, *Colonial Spectacles*, pp. 166, 195–7, 202, 208–13, 270–1, 296–8; S. Protschky, *Images of the Tropics: Environment and Visual Culture in Colonial Indonesia* (Leiden: KITLV Press/Brill, 2011), pp. 103–26.

52 Kouwenaar, *Amsterdam tijdens het feestbetoon*, pp. 219–20.

53 F. Bool, 'Between modernisation and tradition, 1925–1945', in F. Bool et al. (eds), *Dutch Eyes: A Critical History of Photography in the Netherlands* (Zwolle: Waanders, 2007), p. 165; Ensel, *De Nederlander in beeld*, pp. 13, 109, 113, 191.

54 Ensel, *De Nederlander in beeld*, pp. 155–78.

55 E. Edwards, *The Camera as Historian: Amateur Photographers and Historical Imagination, 1885–1918* (Durham, NC: Duke University Press, 2012), pp. 81, 96–7, 163–4, 167.

56 Edwards, *The Camera as Historian*, p. 175.

57 Ensel, *De Nederlander in beeld*, pp. 42–3, 58–9, 65, 70, 132, quote at p. 59. See also Sysling, 'Geographies of difference', pp. 114, 116.

58 D. J. van der Ven, *Neerlands Volksleven* (Zaltbommel: P.M. Wink, 1920). On the museum and the costumes exhibition, see P. de Rooy, 'In oude en nieuwe vormen verpakte illusies: naar aanleiding van enkele recente studies over de geschiedenis van de volkskunde in Nederland', *BMGN/Low Countries Historical Review*, 118 (2003): 193–205, at p. 202. See also http://www.openairmuseum.nl/about-us/who-are-we/ (last accessed 23 October 2018).

59 Ensel, *De Nederlander in beeld*, p. 122, mentions the Dutch physical anthropologist J. P. Kleiweg de Zwaan, who had photographed in Sumatra.

60 Sysling, 'Geographies of difference', pp. 105, 113–14.

61 R. van Ginkel and B. Henkes, 'On peasants and "primitive peoples": moments of rapprochement and distance between folklore studies and anthropology in the Netherlands', *Ethnos: Journal of Anthropology*, 68.1 (2003): 112–34, at pp. 121, 129.

62 B. S. Cohn, 'Representing authority in Victorian India', in E. Hobsbawm and T. Ranger (eds), *The Invention of Tradition* (Cambridge: Cambridge University Press, 1983), pp. 165–209, at p. 168. Cohn describes how Mughal rulers presented *khelat* (items of clothing and body ornaments) to subjects in exchange for tribute from them, and, of course, this reverses the order of the transaction I describe, where Wilhelmina received the dress from her subjects. The key point about this transaction, however, is Cohn's reference to the importance of gifts that emphasise bodily contact through the medium of clothing, or ritual incorporation.

63 The language of motherhood occurs in *gedenkboeken*, for example, T. Tal, *Oranjebloesems uit de gedenkbladen van Nederlands Israel* (Amsterdam: Van Creveld & Co., 1898), p. 134; J. W. Rengelink and I. Mug, *Koningin Wilhelmina 1898–1948* (Heemstede: Mubro, 1948), pp. 5, 7.

64 Ensel, *De Nederlander in beeld*, p. 186.

65 Ensel, *De Nederlander in beeld*, p. 186.

66 H. te Velde, 'De koning is onschendbaar: de permanente spanning tussen Oranje en de grondwet', in R. Meijer and H. J. Schoo (eds), *De monarchie; Staatsrecht, volksgunst en het huis van Oranje* (Amsterdam: Prometheus, 2002), pp. 49–72, at p. 60.

67 For example, Princess Sophie (Willem III's first wife) had a lithographic portrait of herself made in Frisian costume in 1841: M. Jansen, 'De nationale gedaante', in *Oranje en de Nationale Streeckdrachten* (Apeldoorn: Nationaal Museum, Paleis Het Loo, 2012), pp. 8–17, at pp. 8–9.

68 T. R. de Carvalho, 'De koninklijke streekdrachtkostuums nader bekeken', in *Oranje en de Nationale Streeckdrachten* (Apeldoorn: Nationaal Museum, Paleis Het Loo, 2012), pp. 3–7, at p. 3.

69 De Carvalho, 'De koninklijke streekdrachtkostuums', p. 4.

70 Jansen, 'De nationale gedaante', pp. 4, 8–9.

71 Ensel, *De Nederlander in beeld*, p. 74.

72 M. Jansen, 'Koningin Wilhelmina en de fotografie', in M. E. Spliethoff et al., *Koningin Wilhelmina; Schilderijen en tekeningen* (Zwolle: Waanders and Stichting Paleis Het Loo, 2006), pp. 57–68, at p. 62.

73 De Carvalho, 'De koninklijke streekdrachtkostuums', p. 6. The dress was made by the girls pictured with Juliana and given to her in a large painted box. Both were exhibited in 1936 when the princess got engaged: Jansen, 'De nationale gedaante', pp. 4–6.

74 Jansen, 'De nationale gedaante', p. 7.

75 De Carvalho, 'De koninklijke streekdrachtkostuums', pp. 6–7.

76 De Carvalho, 'De koninklijke streekdrachtkostuums', p. 5; Jansen, 'De nationale gedaante', pp. 8–9.
77 Jansen, 'De nationale gedaante', p. 12.
78 H. van Zuthem, 'Nationale kleederdrachten van Harer Majesteits onderdanen bekeken', in *Oranje en de Nationale Streeckdrachten* (Apeldoorn: Nationaal Museum, Paleis Het Loo, 2012), pp. 14–19. The exhibition planned for Wilhelmina's abdication in 1948 did not, for planning reasons, come to fruition until October 1949.
79 Van Zuthem, 'Nationale kleederdrachten van Harer Majesteits', p. 14.
80 Van Zuthem, 'Nationale kleederdrachten van Harer Majesteits', p. 17.
81 A. Maxwell, *Patriots against Fashion: Clothing and Nationalism in Europe's Age of Revolutions* (Basingstoke: Palgrave Macmillan, 2014), p. 160.
82 Maxwell, *Patriots against Fashion*, pp. 161, 168–9.
83 Ensel, *De Nederlander in beeld*, pp. 183, 185, 189.
84 Ensel, *De Nederlander in beeld*, p. 190.
85 A. M. Lyden, *A Royal Passion: Queen Victoria and Photography* (Los Angeles: Getty Publications, 2014).
86 R. Wassing-Visser, *Koninklijke geschenken uit Indonesië; Historische banden met het huis Oranje-Nassau (1600–1938)* (Den Haag/Zwolle: Stichting Historische Verzamelingen van het Huis Oranje-Nassau/Waanders, 1995), pp. 94–5.
87 S. Legêne and B. Waaldijk, 'Mission interrupted: gender, history and the colonial canon', in S. Stuurman and M. Grever (eds), *Beyond the Canon: History for the Twenty-first Century* (Basingstoke: Palgrave Macmillan, 2007), pp. 188–204, at p. 194; S. Protschky, 'Orangists in a red empire: salutations from a Dutch queen's supporters in a British South Africa', in R. Aldrich and C. McCreery (eds), *Crowns and Colonies: Monarchies and Empires* (Manchester: Manchester University Press, 2016), pp. 97–118.
88 Legêne, *Spiegelreflex*, p. 138; Wassing-Visser, *Koninklijke geschenken uit Indonesië*, pp. 97–8.
89 S. Legêne and J. van Dijk, 'Colonial collections at the Tropenmuseum', in S. Legêne and J. van Dijk (eds), *The Netherlands East Indies at the Tropenmuseum: A Colonial History* (Amsterdam: KIT Publishers, 2011), pp. 113–60, at p. 155.
90 M. Scalliet, *Antoine Payen, peintre des Indes orientales vie et écrits d'un artiste du XIXe siècle (1792–1853)* (Leiden: Research School CNWS, 1995); M. Scalliet, '"Back to nature" in the East Indies: European painters in the nineteenth-century East Indies', in M. Scalliet et al., *Pictures from the Tropics: Paintings by Western Artists during the Dutch Colonial Period in Indonesia* (Amsterdam: Pictures Publications/ KIT Publishers, 1999), pp. 39–89, at pp. 47–57.
91 Wassing-Visser, *Koninklijke geschenken uit Indonesië*, pp. 96–7, 99, 100–2.
92 *Catalogus van de Jubileum-Tentoonstelling 1923 gehouden ter gelegenheid van het 25-jarig regeringsjubileum van HM de Koningin in het Koloniaal Instituut te Amsterdam* (Amsterdam: Holkema & Warendorf, 1923), p. 7.
93 Jongmans and Van Dijk, 'Photographs from the Netherlands East Indies', p. 47.
94 *Catalogus van de Jubileum-Tentoonstelling 1923*, pp. 32–59.
95 Legêne and Waaldijk, 'Mission interrupted', pp. 190–1.
96 Kouwenaar, *Amsterdam tijdens het feestbetoon*, p. 246.
97 Kouwenaar, *Amsterdam tijdens het feestbetoon*, pp. 246–7.
98 Kouwenaar, *Amsterdam tijdens het feestbetoon*, p. 247.
99 Legêne and Waaldijk, 'Mission interrupted', p. 195; S. Legêne, 'Dwinegeri: multi-culturalism and the colonial past (or: the culture borders of being Dutch)', in B. Kaplan, M. Carlson and L. Cruz (eds), *Boundaries and their Meanings in the History of the Netherlands* (Leiden: Brill, 2009), pp. 223–42, at p. 240.
100 J. G. Taylor, *Global Indonesia* (London: Routledge, 2013), p. 133.
101 S. Broomhall and J. van Gent, *Dynastic Colonialism: Gender, Materiality and the Early Modern House of Orange-Nassau* (London: Routledge, 2016), pp. 223–30, 247–79.
102 Sysling, 'Geographies of difference', p. 115.

CHAPTER SEVEN

The empire is dead, long live the queen!

It was 1955 and Jan van Baal was now governor of Dutch New Guinea. His private albums from this period of his career were like those of countless other Dutch officials who had served before him, in that they featured photographs of *koninginnedag* celebrations.[1] There were images of local children participating in a torchlight procession (figure 7.1). There was a men's choir and a marching band, Dutch flags were brandished and hand-made banners with crowns and monarchist slogans were carried about. There was even a photograph showing the use of a montage of royal portraits in a procession.[2] It could have been thirty years earlier, anywhere in the archipelago – on the Tanimbar Islands in 1923, for example (see figure 2.1). Other photographs taken by Dutch settlers in New Guinea during the 1950s show similar rituals – discussed throughout this book – involving Indigenous participation in festivals for the Dutch monarchy.[3] Everything appeared to be business as usual.

In fact, much had changed. In August 1948, after celebrating her golden jubilee, Wilhelmina abdicated in favour of her heir. In doing so, she initiated an unbroken chain of Dutch monarchs, continuing to the present day, who have chosen their moment for the *troonwisseling* ('throne change') rather than vacating the throne by leaving the land of the living. After half a century, then, Wilhelmina's reign had finally come to an end – and Juliana was now Queen of the Netherlands.

Van Baal's albums record the new date of Queen's Day: 30 April, Juliana's birthday. We know from Chapter 3 that he had been following her fortunes since his Indies career began in the late 1930s. Now he was Juliana's representative. His photograph albums show that it was her image on the banners and effigies carried by Papuan participants in *koninginnedag* parades, and her portrait that hung on the wall of his Residency building.[4] Curiously, it showed neither a state portrait of Juliana nor her persona as an 'ordinary' royal, surrounded by her husband and children.[5] Instead, it was the glamour portrait made in

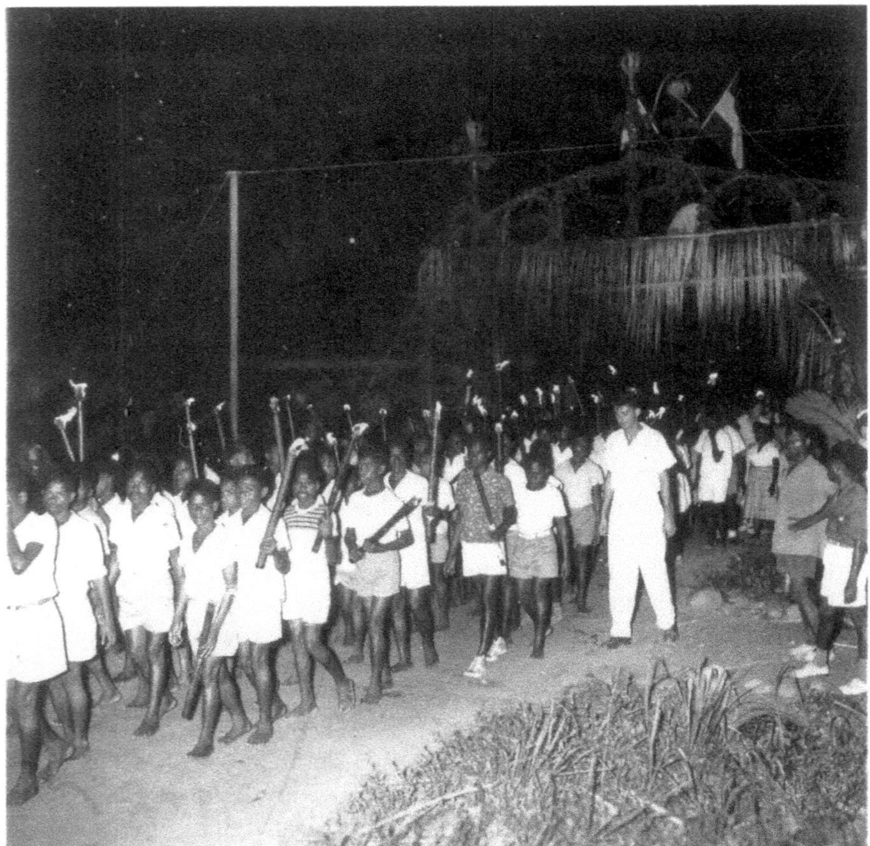

7.1 Netherlands New Guinea Government, torchlight procession, 30 April 1955, New Guinea

1937 by Franz Ziegler, figuring Juliana in an uncharacteristically provocative pose, a fashionable evening gown, and wearing the wedding gift she had received from the people of the Netherlands East Indies: a costly bracelet made from South African diamonds set in the pattern of a crown flanked by two *garuda* birds.[6]

Perhaps the bracelet and the jaunty young queen reminded Van Baal of better times. For in 1955 Dutch New Guinea was the last remaining outpost of the Netherlands' former empire in Asia, which had reached its modern zenith during Wilhelmina's reign, but was formally dissolved within a year of her heir becoming queen. Van Baal was now Juliana's *only* representative, a lone governor on half an island. Further, 'Dutch' New Guinea was a disputed territory, the cause of diplomatic and even military tensions between the Netherlands and Indonesia over who should control the western part of the island.[7]

Migration lobbyists were influential among the voices pressuring the Dutch parliament to insist on control of New Guinea in order to secure a 'homeland' for Indo-Europeans. This notion had been circulating in Indo-European political circles since the 1920s, when Indonesian nationalism first raised the spectre of discrimination against people of mixed ethnicity. The issue became more urgent in 1946 when anti-colonial militias murdered thousands of Eurasians during the so-called *bersiap* emergency, and nationalist forces concentrated tens of thousands more in 'protection' camps.[8] Even so, the impact of the migration lobby on Dutch foreign policy in the late 1940s was ironic, given that most of the Indo-Europeans who emigrated from the Indonesian archipelago from this time onwards preferred the Netherlands, Australia, New Zealand or California to New Guinea.[9] Indeed, by the end of 1950 there were only 8,516 (Indo-)Europeans in New Guinea, most of them *not* farmers (as migration lobbyists had long envisioned), but rather working in government and private firms.[10] Many greeted the resumption of Queen's Day celebrations in the 1950s with pleasure and patriotism, and observed with dismay President Soekarno's order to seize Dutch assets and enterprises in Indonesia in 1957, a response to the stand-off with the Netherlands over sovereignty in New Guinea. The dispute also triggered turmoil within the Indonesian government and the cessation of diplomatic relations with the Netherlands in 1960. In 1962, under international pressure, the Netherlands agreed to transfer what is currently known as the province of West Papua to Indonesia, with the United Nations to oversee a referendum on whether the territory would remain part of Indonesia or become independent. By that time 22,000 Dutch and Indo-European residents had fled New Guinea, and the dream of an 'Indo' colony was over.[11]

The roots of these and other disputes over sovereignty in different parts of Indonesia were in the early years of Wilhelmina's reign: in the rise of movements to promote Indies self-rule and in the emergence of Indigenous nationalist, communist and Islamist parties. Indeed, by the 1920s the queen was imbricated in the world of the colonial state's enemies. The political dissidents exiled to New Guinea by the Dutch colonial government from the mid-1920s onwards were surrounded by reminders of Wilhelmina. The site of their prison camp at Tanah Merah may well have been 455 kilometres up the Digoel River – three and a half days' travel – in the middle of a sparsely populated, malaria-infested wilderness. But even here, none of the inmates could escape the Dutch monarchy: the hospital for internees was named after Wilhelmina. There was an 'Oranje Park' near the main residences of the civilian and military authorities. Wilhelmina's portrait hung in official buildings, and all internees were expected to participate in *koninginnedag* festivities.[12]

We know that Wilhelmina was aware of the camp because her subjects there appealed to her directly for mercy. In August 1930 a group of prisoners who had been arrested after a communist uprising in Sumatra in November 1926 petitioned Wilhelmina with a birthday gift. It was a photograph of her in a carved wooden frame; evidence, perhaps, that she was revered even in this remote corner of her empire. They also sent a letter declaring their remorse for participating in the uprising, pledging their loyalty to the queen and asking for clemency.[13] By the 1930s Queen's Day had become quite the institution for pardoning political dissidents. The future president of the Republic, Soekarno, had his prison sentence for nationalist agitation commuted following a Queen's Day decision.[14] In December 1930 Governor-General A. C. D. de Graeff (served 1926–31) released 219 internees from Tanah Merah.[15] Neither he nor Wilhelmina and Juliana could have guessed that New Guinea would be all that was left of the Netherlands East Indies two decades later.

The end of Dutch rule began in March 1942, when Japan invaded the East Indies as part of its war in the Pacific. During the occupation, internment camps were established for European civilians and prisoners of war. Photography was not allowed in the camps, and celebrations for the Dutch monarchy were explicitly banned as a relic of the former colonial power's glory. Japanese authorities encouraged Indonesian nationalism and anti-colonialism, but also caused much suffering for Indonesians – food shortages and famines, forced migrations and coerced labour – by diverting resources to the Japanese war effort. Two days after Japan capitulated to Allied forces, on 17 August 1945, nationalist leaders Soekarno and Muhammad Hatta issued what has become known simply as the *proklomasi*, the Proclamation of Indonesian Independence. In response, the Dutch government neither acquiesced nor declared war. Instead, it sent troops and eventually launched two so-called 'police actions' (*politionele acties*) to restore 'peace and order' to a colony that it refused to relinquish. A long conflict ensued, known in Indonesian histories as the National Revolution. The Netherlands committed its largest ever contingent of troops – 220,000 in total – against Indonesian guerrillas and conventional forces that were united in opposition to colonial rule, but divided among themselves over the form of post-colonial nation they envisaged. Indeed, what followed was a civil war *between* Indonesian militias and political factions, and *against* a colonial counter-insurgency.[16] It took several rounds of negotiations between Dutch and Indonesian authorities, and considerable international pressure, before the Netherlands finally conceded to a transfer of sovereignty and withdrew its troops in December 1949. In the interim, more than 6,000 Dutch soldiers and an estimated 100,000 Indonesian combatants and civilians were killed or died.[17]

This chapter reviews the major themes of this book by analysing the continuity and change in colonial photographs of royal celebrations made by Dutch soldiers during the military actions in Indonesia. After the Japanese occupation – less than a five-year hiatus in the thinking of colonists who attempted to pick up where they had left off in the 'Indies' – festivals for the Dutch monarchy resumed, and continued right up until 1949 wherever the Netherlands held power in the archipelago. Yet the late 1940s have been brushed over in histories of the Dutch monarchy in Indonesia, except to say that Indonesia's independence prompted an awkward period of post-colonial diplomatic relations between the Dutch monarchy and the Republic.[18] There are a number of reasons why this might be the case. The war itself has long been steeped in public silence and denials over atrocities committed on both sides, which have only recently been acknowledged by the Dutch government.[19] During the 'throne change' of 1948, in the thick of the conflict, and after years of representing the Netherlands' largest and most lucrative colony as a major achievement of Wilhelmina's, commemorative books made for her golden jubilee prudently turned away from the mutinous East Indies and instead concentrated on the Netherlands' compliant colonies, the West Indies (or Antilles) and Suriname.[20] Constitutionally, of course, the House of Orange had no role in either the decision to commence military actions (which was taken by the prime minister and cabinet), or in the political resolution to the conflict – except to ratify the transfer of sovereignty.[21] Indeed, this was to be Juliana's last act as head of state in Indonesia, a moment that generated some famous photographs and film clips which invariably focus on the political ceremonial of terminating an empire (figure 7.2).

In this book, an examination of the rise of mass photography during Wilhelmina's reign and in the last half-century of Dutch rule in Indonesia has revealed how different modes of photography interacted to produce a participatory visual culture around celebrations of the monarchy. The queen's subjects in the Netherlands and its overseas possessions – European commoners and Indigenous royals, commercial and amateur photographers, Dutch and Indonesian spectators and participants at royal festivals – were all figured in relation to the monarchy whenever they looked at, collected, made or exchanged photographs of their observance of royal milestones. In the process, they articulated what it meant to be a subject of an imperial, European, female king who presided over discontiguous territories and diverse peoples with differing political rights.

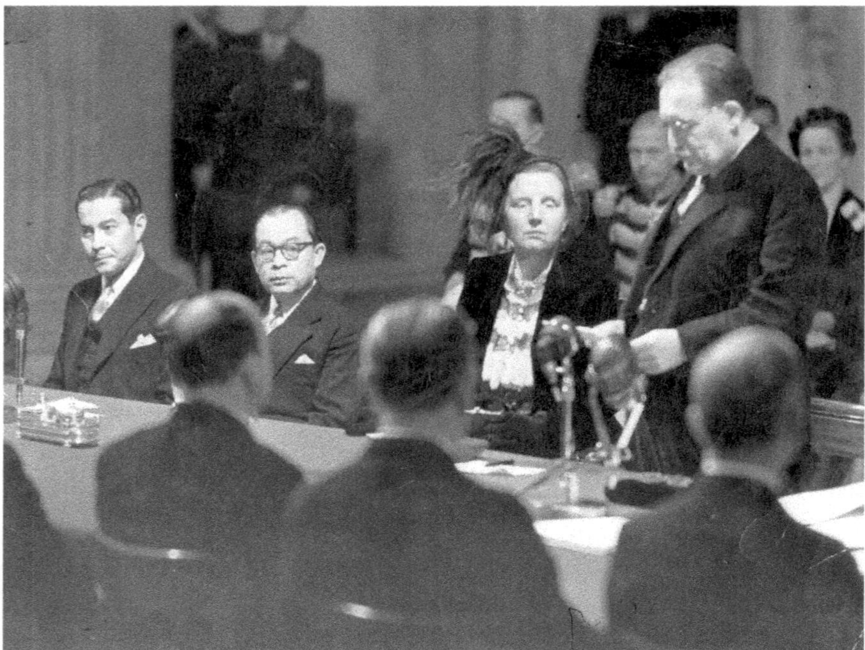

7.2 Joop van Bilsen (from left): Sultan Hamid, Indonesian Prime Minister Mohammed Hatta, Queen Juliana and Dutch Prime Minister Willem Drees during the transfer of sovereignty to Indonesia, Royal Palace on the Dam, Amsterdam, 27 December 1949

By the late 1940s, decades of innovation in hand-held camera and fast-developing film technologies had created a situation where ordinary soldiers were able to generate a record of their experiences and aspirations during wartime. Dutch soldiers took thousands of amateur photographs during their service in the conflict, including at royal celebrations, which show how these men saw themselves and the Indonesian combatants and civilians they encountered as the new Queen Juliana's subjects. In doing so, their photographs throw into sharp relief the rhetorical value that Queen's Day celebrations had always held for Dutch authorities claiming sovereignty in Indonesia. We know in hindsight that, in the late 1940s, the Dutch monopoly on power in the East Indies, and a general world order in which monarchies supported empires, were on the brink of collapse. However, if we examine the photographs of the Dutch soldiers who were sent to defend this schema in Indonesia, it becomes evident that royal celebrations played two important roles in the colonial counter-insurgency.

First, soldiers' photographs celebrated royal festivals as Dutch victories in (re-)claiming territory from Indonesian forces. Second, combatants' photographs reveal the propaganda function of royal celebrations in battles for civilian hearts and minds. Queen's Day and other royal festivals became an opportunity to extend the benevolent 'Ethical' policies that had once been associated with Wilhelmina to Juliana's reign. Soldiers' photographs of their encounters with Indonesians at royal festivals served to legitimise the restoration of colonial rule by positioning Dutch soldiers as humanitarians who were saving civilians from 'terrorists', rather than prosecuting a counter-insurgency against an organised and broad-based Indonesian resistance.

The soldiers' queen

Wilhelmina had been a soldiers' queen from early on in her life. After the Dutch subjugation of Lombok in 1894, she was invoked as a virginal princess in whose honour colonists had chivalrously defended the empire.[22] Queen Emma even had her 14-year-old daughter decorate soldiers returned from Lombok, and Wilhelmina attended veterans' commemorations from this campaign into the 1930s.[23] Van Heutsz's military exploits in 'pacifying' Aceh in the early 1900s evidently left a life-long impression on her, if her memoir is anything to go by.[24] It was the Second World War, however, that arguably fixed her reputation. The eminent Dutch historian Cees Fasseur subtitled the second volume in his monumental biography of Wilhelmina 'warlike in a formless jacket' (*krijgshaftig in een voormeloze jas*), in reference to the enduring visual image of Wilhelmina as a patriotic queen who dispensed with sartorial formalities in empathy with her soldiers and the Dutch home front.[25] Her wartime broadcasts to the Nazi-occupied Netherlands through the Radio Oranje programme contributed to her immense, enduring popularity for decades afterwards, despite the fact that she had reigned in exile from London and, at times, in conflict with the Dutch government.[26]

In Indonesia during the Dutch military actions of the late 1940s, in the final years of her reign, Wilhelmina was still revered as a soldiers' queen. Celebrations in her honour resumed here in 1946, amid an Indonesian resistance that was not abating as expected. By that time the Dutch government had taken the decision to supplement existing troops – comprising around 40,000 Dutch volunteers and 80,000 local *Koninklijk Nederlandsch-Indisch Leger* (Royal Netherlands-Indies Army, KNIL) soldiers – with another 100,000 conscripts direct from the Netherlands, many of whom were young men who had grown up during the Nazi occupation, and with no prior experience of the East Indies.[27]

It was in this context that the Dutch military Welfare Service (*Dienst Welzijnsverzorging*) issued blank albums to soldiers to encourage correspondence with the home front in the Netherlands.[28] The offer was taken up by many with enthusiasm. In the words of one soldier, Cees Taillie (1920–2005), whose natural skill with a camera saw him hired for his work by the army, he took photographs 'to let [the people] at home see what I went through and for the boys who had no camera'.[29] Dutch archives hold a large (and growing) number of such albums, as well as unbound photograph collections and related biographical documents, that view the Indonesian Revolution from behind the barrel of Dutch soldiers' guns.[30]

Combatants used 'family album' techniques, which have been discussed throughout this book, to organise a photographic collection that, superficially, looked rather different to most personal albums from the colonial period,[31] *except* that they diligently recorded the participation of Dutch authorities and local Indonesian populations in royal celebrations. At first glance, photographs of these festivals look like victory parades and seem unrelated to the House of Orange. But Dutch soldiers upheld the colonial practice of annotating the photographs taken for royal celebrations with titles and dates, singling out these rituals with captions for posterity. This mode of marking time, of observing the fortunes of the royal dynasty and linking it with their own lives, carried on in wartime as it had done for decades beforehand.

During the military actions in Indonesia, royal milestones included Queen's Day, Prince Bernhard's birthday, the birth of Princess Marijke in 1947 and Wilhelmina's golden jubilee and *troonwisseling* in 1948. Juliana's family was important for this period. That Bernhard was given senior titles in the Dutch and colonial defence forces elicited the loyalty of soldiers in Indonesia, who were encouraged to celebrate him as one of their leaders. The birth of a child to Bernhard and Juliana during the conflict resonated for Dutch soldiers with news from home of newborn nieces and nephews or, for slightly older soldiers, of children born *in absentia*. For men separated from wives and sweethearts, children signalled the deferred duties and pleasures of marriage. Soldiers used photographs of celebrations for the birth of the princess and other royal milestones to stay connected to family and friends, sending snapshots from the front with their (often daily) letters to prove how they maintained Dutch traditions such as Sinterklaas (St Nicholas's Day) and Queen's Day in the tropics, and to reassure correspondents with images of the more palatable aspects of daily life about the billet, the barracks or the local *kampung*.[32] The photographs taken by Dutch soldiers among and for themselves thus reveal the urgent emotional significance of the monarchy – not just the queen, but the whole royal family – at a time when they were far from home.

Soldiers' photographs also show how some of the social functions of images made and used at royal celebrations remained the same as they were before 1942. Portraits of the monarch continued to be used as portable objects in the spectacle of royal ceremonies. One soldier commemorated his participation in a festival for Wilhelmina by photographing a comrade standing before a provisional shrine of hubcaps, which were arranged in the shape of a large 'W' and supported a tyre framing a recent portrait of Wilhelmina (figure 7.3). This rough and rudimentary memorial to the queen by no means suggests irreverence. On the contrary, it shows how soldiers devoted creative time and scarce resources to honouring a queen who was 65 years old, almost half a century on the throne and a veteran of several wars. The photograph shows how a new generation of colonists treated Wilhelmina as a soldiers' queen.

This and other photographs also reveal how military equipment was appropriated for celebrations. Army and ambulance trucks made for odd-looking 'floats' in jungle-combat drag (figure 7.4). White stones were arranged on the lawn of one residential house, which happened to be a soldiers' garrison, to spell the dates 1898 and 1948. Palm fronds were formed into a triumphal arch at the garden gate and topped with a paper lantern crown.[33] Buildings were illuminated at night.[34] Parades carried on wherever possible, always with a focus on gathering local spectators.[35] Hurdles, sack and boat races (figure 7.5), tug-of-war and mast-climbing competitions were organised for Indonesian children.[36] That there were striking continuities between how things had been done in the past, as I have detailed throughout this book, and how Dutch soldiers in the late 1940s orchestrated and observed festivals demonstrates how readily the pre-war rituals and symbols of colonial authority were revived.

Sovereignty: royal celebrations and Dutch military victories

Certainly, as the creative redeployment of military equipment indicates, the restoration of royal celebrations in the late 1940s was often a provisional affair. Photographs of such adaptations recall the many absences in soldiers' photographs – of uniformed Indonesian schoolchildren performing songs, costumed pageants and richly decorated triumphal arches: the relative luxuries of peacetime, not least for an Indonesian population still suffering from the deprivations of the Japanese occupation. Soldiers' albums also reveal a strategic function to the staging of these pageants. Tanks and trucks, uniformed marches, mortars

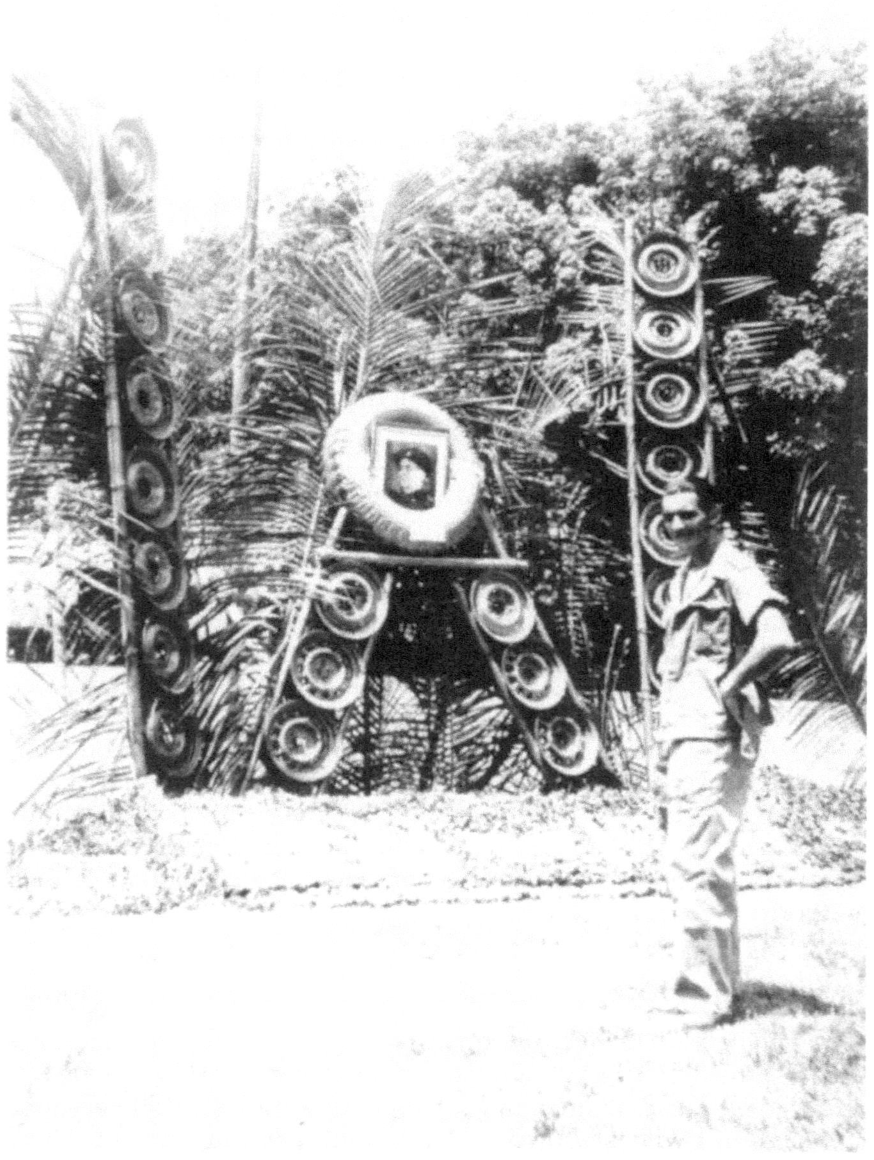

7.3 Collection J. J. Abbo, a Dutch soldier poses before a hub-cap shrine in the shape of a 'W' supporting a portrait of Wilhelmina

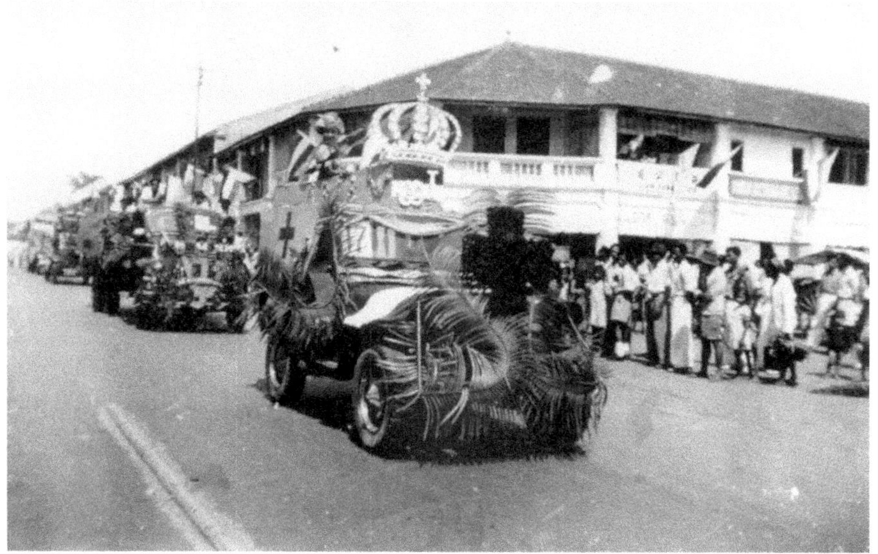

7.4 Collection J. C. Hunselaar, a motor parade, 1948

and aeroplanes, palm fronds evoking camouflage (as well as tropical décor): these were precisely the kinds of displays that made tactical sense for a regime seeking to convey success to populations in doubt about who was the sovereign power in a contested Indonesia.[37] In soldiers' albums, more so than in loose photograph collections, the narrative structure their makers imposed through the ordering of images and the use of captions reveals how royal parades were often only days apart from military actions, and were in fact conflated with other acts of counter-insurgency.

G. M. Nafzger was stationed with a storm trooper battalion in Palembang (Sumatra) in February 1947, when Juliana and Bernhard's youngest child, Marijke, was born. His photograph album shows the military parades through the streets of the city that were held in celebration of the Dutch monarchy's dynastic success, with local residents corralled on to the streets to watch (figure 7.6).[38] Just a few weeks earlier there had been an 'action'. The photographs Nafzger kept of burned-out Indonesian army barracks, and killed and wounded Indonesian soldiers – some of them just 'children', according to his own dismayed annotations on the reverse side of one photograph (figure 7.7) – fill the pages surrounding the princess's birthday parades.[39] They attest to the militarised context in which a display of Dutch manpower determined the nature of public celebrations for the birth of a royal baby.

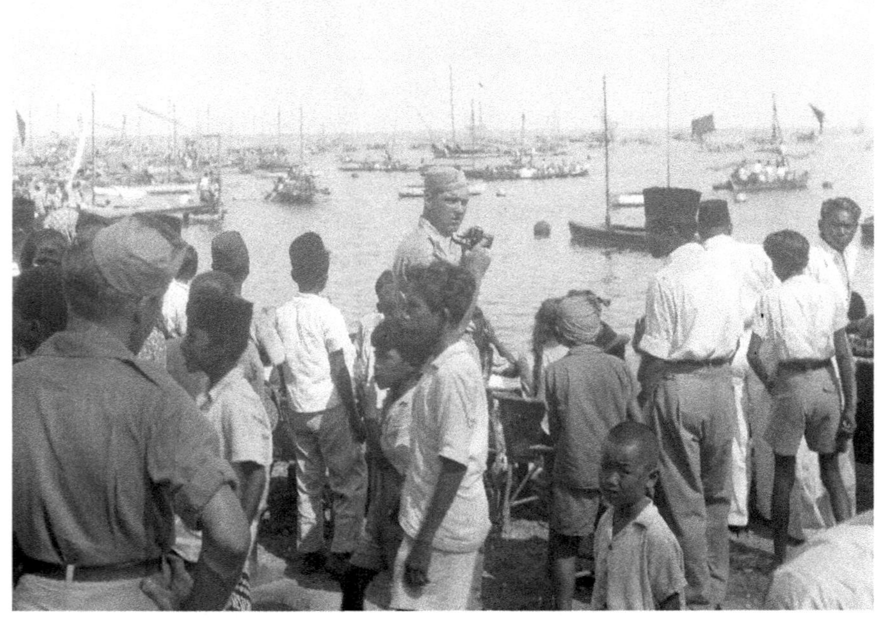

7.5 Cees Taillie, preparing to photograph a rowing race, Queen's Day, Makassar, 1948/9

Similarly, Piet Kossen was stationed in Yogyakarta in April 1949 for the first and last ever Queen's Day celebrated for Juliana in Java (figure 7.8). He had been conscripted in 1947 to the 'Tiger Brigade' of the Fifth Infantry Regiment, in which he served until his repatriation in 1949. His albums showed his involvement in patrols, 'cleansing actions' (*zuiveringsacties*), the taking of enemy prisoners and the funerals of fellow soldiers.[40] One of his own photographs, of prisoners taken during a cleansing action only four days before Queen's Day in 1949, was reproduced fifty years later in a commemorative book for veterans of his battalion (figure 7.9).[41] These were photographs that illustrated

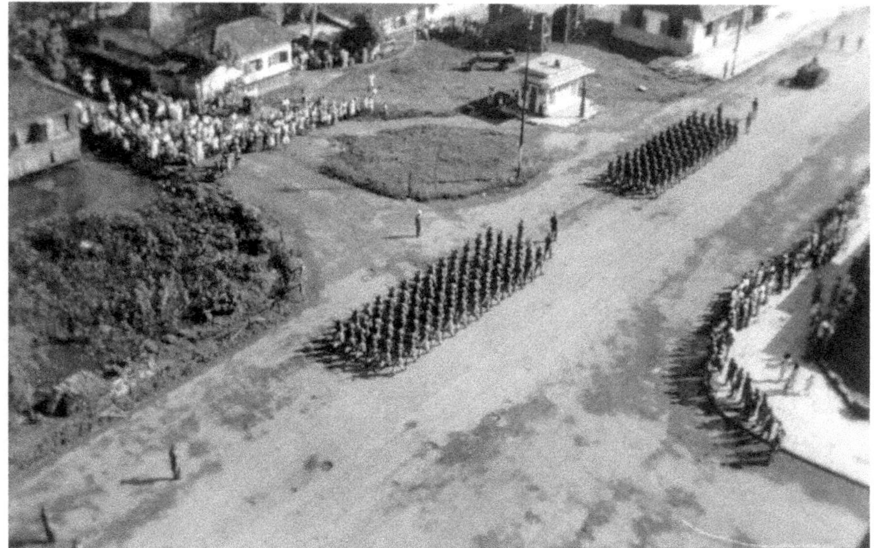

7.6 Collection G. M. Nafzger, 'Parade for Princess Marijke, Palembang 18.2.47'

communal memories of the Dutch version of decolonisation many decades after the war had been 'lost'.

Neither of these examples from Nafzger and Kossen coincided with the two major Dutch campaigns of the war: Operation Product (21 July–5 August 1947) and Operation Crow (19 December 1948–45 January 1949), more commonly known as the First and Second 'Police Actions'. The Dutch excelled in these conventional military engagements, which made use of their superior weapons and resources. But the gains made here were undermined in the guerrilla war that prevailed in between, during which most of the Dutch casualties were sustained and morale declined. As recent studies have demonstrated, it was during the routine 'cleansing actions' in the guerrilla fighting between major campaigns that Dutch combatants also perpetrated the greatest number of atrocities against Indonesians, especially when villages were 'swept' and prisoners were taken for questioning. During such actions, civilians were terrorised, prisoners were tortured and extra-judicial killings were carried out.[42]

From soldiers' own photographs of royal festivals, which are often jarringly close – temporally and spatially – to images of military actions, celebrations for the monarchy can be interpreted as choreographed displays of Dutch dominance, intended to congratulate and celebrate the exploits of the Dutch military, warn the civilian population to

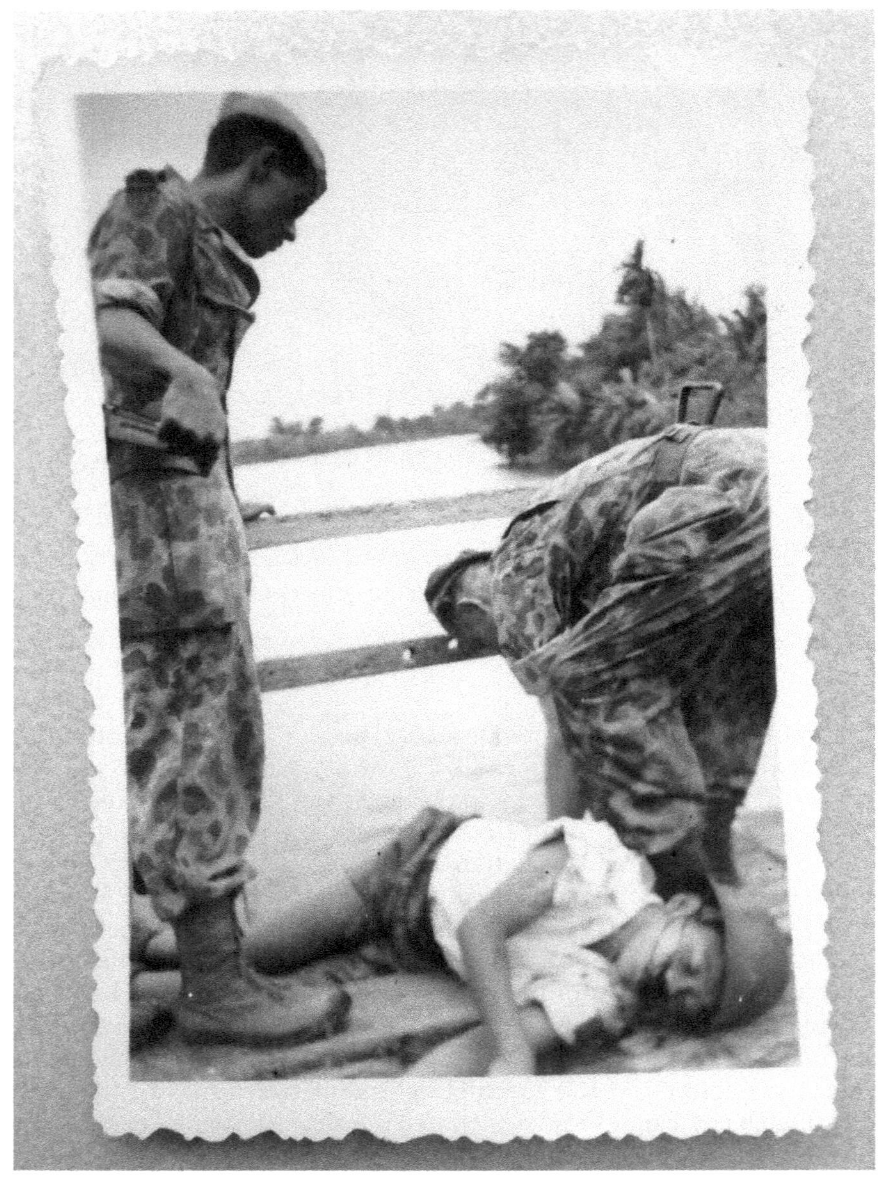

7.7 Collection G. M. Nafzger, 'Action Jan. [19]47', Palembang (Sumatra)

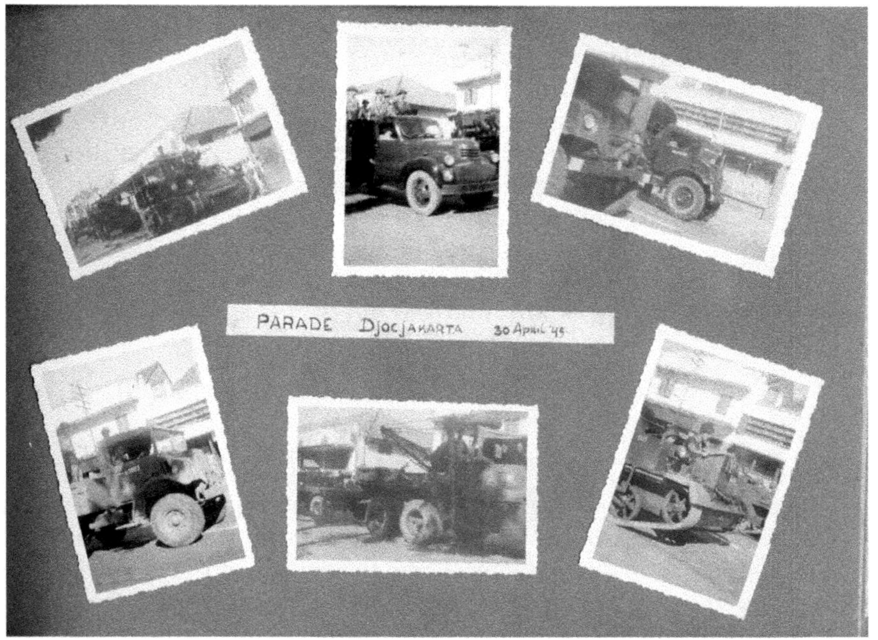

7.8 Collection Piet Kossen, 'Parade Yogyakarta 30 April [19]49'

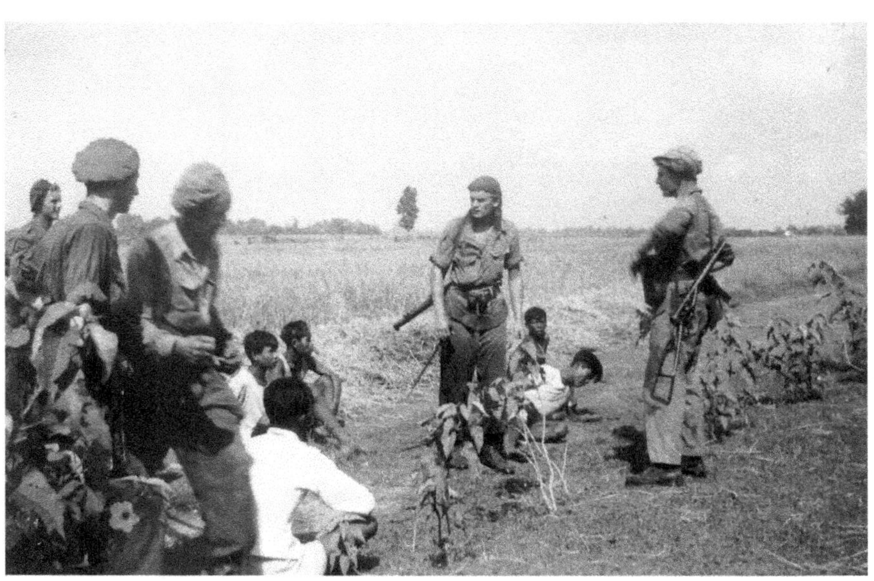

7.9 Collection Piet Kossen, 'Cleansing action' on the way to Piyungan (Central Java), 26 April 1949

choose their loyalties wisely, and intimidate Indonesian rebels into retreat and capitulation. However, in some photographs, the close confinement of royal festivals to areas adjacent to Dutch army barracks tells a more ambivalent story.[43] The spaces that Dutch authorities were able to claim in wartime were increasingly constrained, militarised and official, unlike the expansive, civic places that royal festivals had occupied during peacetime. Indeed, as was more generally true for the Dutch experience of the war, royal celebrations staged between major campaigns were sometimes held in places where it was difficult to distinguish between civilians and 'enemies'.[44]

Hearts and minds: the battle over civilians at royal celebrations

Chapters 4, 5 and 6 of this book demonstrated how royal celebrations often became opportunities for subjects of the queen in colonial Indonesia to articulate their claims for rights and recognition by 'presenting' themselves to her in photographs. These tendencies appeared to continue during the military actions of the late 1940s. J. C. Hunselaar, the soldier whose photographs show the versatility of army trucks (figure 7.4), pictured Chinese youths from Pematang Siantar in Sumatra marching for Queen's Day in 1948 (figure 7.10). At the same time, elsewhere in

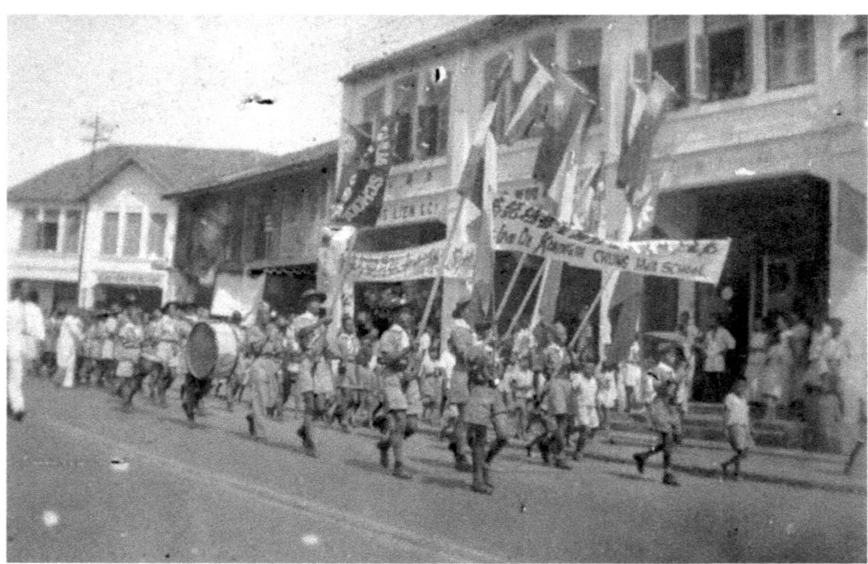

7.10 Collection J. C. Hunselaar, a Chinese youth association and Chung Hwa school marching in 1948, Pematang Siantar (Sumatra)

the archipelago, another combatant photographed the festive gateway over the entrance to a Chinese quarter.[45] Chinese communities in Indonesia were evidently still celebrating Wilhelmina as they had been before the war. This time, however, their appeals for recognition were more urgent and specific. As Dutch soldiers participated in actions that involved the reconquest of territory abandoned by Indonesian forces, they diligently documented the massacre of Chinese Indonesians who were the subject of reprisals and pogroms.[46] Extreme violence against Chinese communities in revolutionary Indonesia was indeed endemic, but Dutch authorities used photographs of atrocities to formulate a narrative about the presence of their soldiers on humanitarian grounds: to protect civilians against the barbarities of Republican rule and promote harmonious coexistence in a land where ethnic tensions between diverse populations seemed inevitable.[47] In a context where civilians were both targets of and audiences for contests over legitimacy between colonial and Indonesian forces, soldiers' photographic interest in Chinese communities' fortunes at royal celebrations were in fact part of the Dutch battle for hearts and minds.

This image of the Dutch counter-revolt as a humanitarian action emerged at the outset of the conflict, in photographs of royal celebrations on Bali in 1946. P. L. Dronkers (1917–93) had qualified in Leiden for a position in the *Binnenlandsch Bestuur* (Interior Administration) in 1941, and was among the first contingent of Dutch government officials sent to the Indies after the Japanese occupation. At this time, the *Binnenlandsch Bestuur* was under the command of the Civil Affairs Branch of the Allied Military Administration. Dronkers commenced his work in Bali with the rank of Aspirant Controleur in 1946, then moved up the ranks quickly before his 'repatriation' to the Netherlands in April 1950.[48] As an official, he also reported to the Netherlands Indies Government Information Service, a civilian arm of the various Dutch intelligence organisations that operated during the military actions. Among Dronkers's files were a number of small albums made from pieces of blue card, pasted with his own photographs and extensively annotated with typed and handwritten notes organised according to his own series numbers. They showed the celebration of Prince Bernhard's birthday in Jembrana in June 1946, and the celebration of Queen's Day for Wilhelmina in Penebel and Negara later that same year.

In the album that Dronkers entitled 'Queen's Day … in a liberated land', he showed *koninginnedag* as an affair of mast-climbing competitions, music performances and a feast for two thousand children.[49] His notes also detailed the spontaneous local establishment of a night guard (*desapolitiecorps*, or village police corps) to protect the community from revolutionary 'terrorists'. He described an atmosphere 'that is free from the deep influence of the terror, in the midst of strong, self-sufficient people who have overcome years of fear and insecurity [under Japanese occupation] and do not need to be encouraged to celebrate Queen's Day with a thankful and happy heart'.[50]

In an essay that Dronkers entitled 'Festivals on Bali', he revived venerable colonial discourses about the creative spirit and peaceful proclivities of the Balinese that had been popular since the 'discovery' of the island by Western artists and tourists in the 1920s.[51] He contended that the Balinese resented the Japanese for banning religious festivals and *wayang* performances, whereas the Dutch took care to restore those aspects of Balinese life that had always been nurtured under colonial rule. Traditional Balinese modes of celebration were encouraged on Queen's Day in 1946, for instance: 'The festival went for two days, with dance, music and games interrupted only by great feasts.'[52] One of Dronkers's albums includes photographs of a play in which Balinese, to the great delight of spectators, enacted the defeat of armed *pemuda* ('youths': more specifically in this context, resistance fighters) by Gajah Merah, the 'red elephant' that was the symbol of the KNIL Y-Brigade.[53] A new form of colonial triumphalism, stemming from a belief that the Dutch would prevail in reconquering the Indies, combined in Dronkers's official notes with an anthropological fascination with Balinese arts that administrators had for decades pursued in the course of their postings.

Importantly, in the oration for Queen's Day that Dronkers delivered as the presiding official in Jembrana, he portrayed the Dutch and the Balinese as equal subjects under Wilhelmina, in that both had been prevented from celebrating royal festivals for five years by their German and Japanese oppressors. 'While we suffered', he told his listeners in *bahasa Indonesia*,

> she [the queen] worked for our freedom. May H.M. therefore be named the Queen who brought freedom. She was thus in the Netherlands, she is also thus in Indonesia ... Her troops have defeated the rebels [*kaoem kaoem peroesoeh*] on Bali and restored freedom ... May we bestow thanks and honour on Her Majesty, who is the protector of us all.[54]

The visual emphasis on children's participation at Balinese festivals for the Dutch monarchy in Dronkers's photographs is striking. Certainly, celebrations for Wilhelmina in the late nineteenth-century Netherlands had their origins in summertime *kinderfeesten* (children's festivals).[55] In colonial photographs from before the war, however, attention was generally on how adult Indonesians participated in celebrations for the Dutch monarchy. By contrast, in photographs from revolution-era Bali, the restoration of schooling and the provision of food and clothing to children at the hands of Dutch authorities were the major focus (figure 7.11).

For Prince Bernhard's birthday in June 1946, Dronkers photographed schoolchildren singing, hoisting the Dutch flag, playing games and receiving prizes. For entertainment, they watched a clown perform and burned Japanese money. They received a lunch, handouts of clothing and portraits of the Queen.[56] Dronkers explained in an address to the Balinese schoolchildren that their counterparts in 'America' had sent the gift of clothing, and that the sweet porridge and royal portraits came from the Netherlands. He also explained that Bernhard was a man who had helped defeat the German foe, was the husband of Crown Princess Juliana, and the father of three little girls.[57] Balinese children – and by extension, their families – were clearly the target of Dutch propaganda at royal celebrations early on in the counter-insurgency.

The provision of food and clothing at royal celebrations in 1946 was also the theme of soldiers' amateur photographs (figure 7.12). As usual, albums combined photographs of recent military actions (figure 7.13) with activities for Queen's Day: in this case, Dutch 'humanitarian' campaigns targeting children on Bali. As I have argued elsewhere, throughout the Indonesian archipelago wherever Dutch soldiers went they selectively photographed both the war they prosecuted *and* how they assisted civilians caught in the cross-fire.[58] The modes through which Dutch forces themselves contributed to the suffering of civilians were rarely a feature of their camera work. At royal celebrations, therefore, the imbrication of counter-insurgency with campaigns for the hearts and minds of civilians drew on photographic practices developed during Wilhelmina's reign. Soldiers' photographs were the latest (and last) iteration of images that positioned Dutch monarchs as benevolent guarantors of Ethical rule and overseers of unity in diversity among Indonesians.

Photographic subjects

In 1971 Juliana was also a soldiers' queen: or rather, perhaps, one for veterans. That year she became the first Dutch monarch ever to visit Indonesia. In doing so, she reciprocated President Suharto's visit to the Netherlands the previous year. This diplomatic exchange between the two countries signalled a period of 'normalisation' following the tensions that had reigned since 1950.[59] Juliana and Bernhard's tour was captured in a short, Dutch-language commemorative book titled *Oranje & Indonesië*. It mentioned the war that had severed the colonial ties between their nations only obliquely, but included photographs of the royal couple visiting and laying wreaths at military cemeteries of Dutch

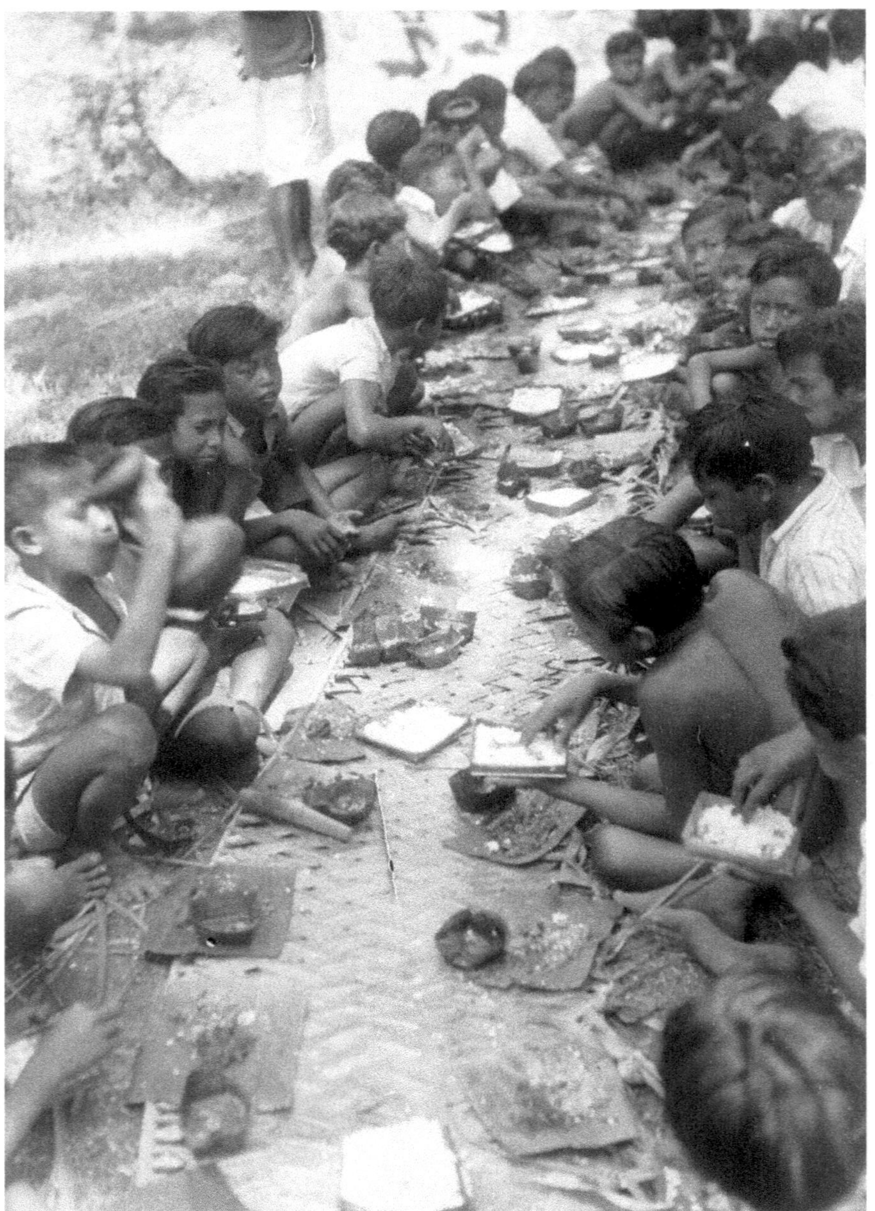

7.11 P. L. Dronkers, a feast for children on Queen's Day, August 1946, Negara (Bali)

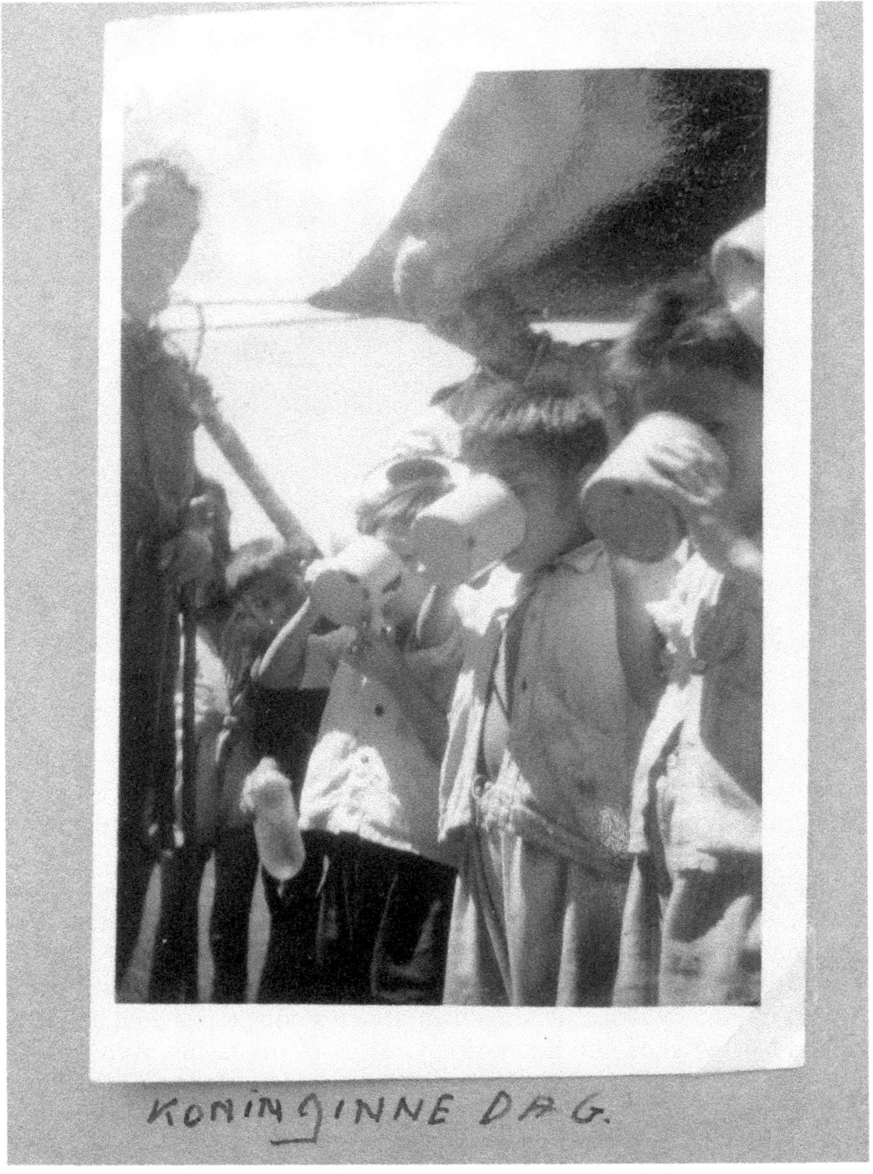

7.12 Collection G. H. van Broeckhuijsen, Dutch soldiers watch over Balinese children being fed on Queen's Day, 1946

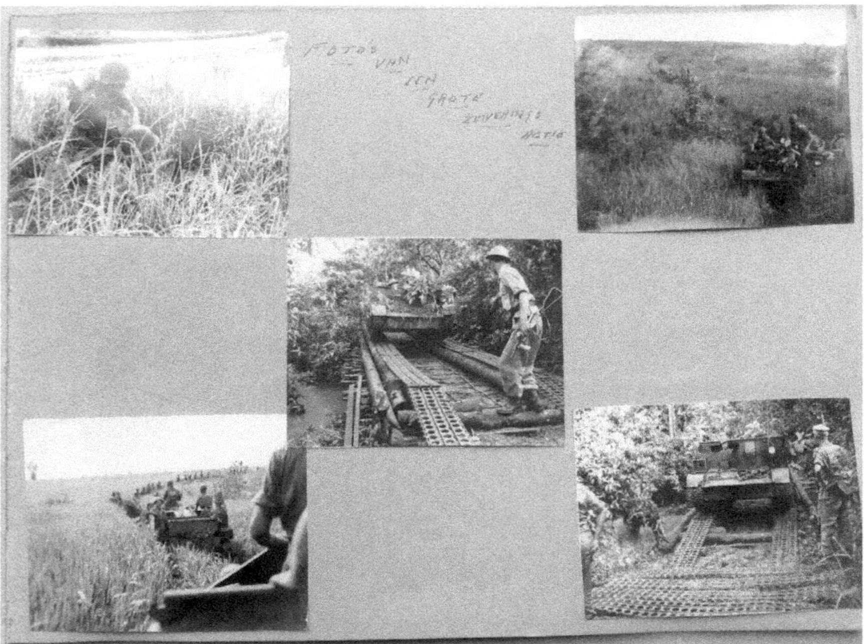

7.13   Collection G. H. van Broeckhuijsen, 'Photos of a big cleansing action'

soldiers killed in the actions of the late 1940s.[60] The remains of others (including Indonesian soldiers who had fought in the KNIL) had already been deposited at the Dam Square war memorial in Amsterdam in 1956.[61]

Remarkably, despite the post-colonial, post-conflict circumstances of the queen's tour to Indonesia, the text and photographs selected for the commemorative book invoked established traditions for representing the Dutch monarchy as a crucial institution entwining the shared histories of the Netherlands and Indonesia. Crowds of thousands were shown greeting the royals at the airport, in the streets of Jakarta, Jogjakarta and Bandung, and in Sumatra and Bali.[62] Many of the photographs were now in colour, but otherwise they might have been taken half a century earlier. They showed familiar rites, such as painted portraits of Juliana being used in public pageants, Indonesian schoolchildren waving Dutch flags and singing Dutch songs, costumed dancers performing, and women from different ethnic groups in traditional dress lining the streets.[63] Indeed, in the official address given at her reception with President Suharto, Juliana approvingly mentioned the Indonesian national motto, 'Unity in Diversity' (*Bhinneka Tunggal*

Ika).[64] This book has argued that it was her mother, Queen Wilhelmina, who was the first to be invoked, through photography, by authorities in Indonesia for the purposes of uniting the archipelago and its people.

However, photographs in the 1971 commemorative book also captured some remarkable departures from colonial tradition. Juliana's portrait appeared not alone, but alongside that of President Suharto, under whose New Order regime public pageantry in Indonesia was being significantly reinvented. Bernhard, for the first time in Dutch royal history, received and was photographed wearing Indigenous *klederdracht* (traditional costume) on Indonesian soil.[65] Another significant first was signalled in the many photographs showing Juliana and Bernhard meeting the only Indonesian royal who had survived the revolution with some of his hereditary status intact. Sultan Hamengku Buwono IX (1912–88) was photographed greeting the couple as they arrived at the airport, and escorting them back to his *kraton* to exchange gifts, extend them a reception and show off the arts and cultures of his court, where they also met Pakualam VIII.[66] Did Juliana mention, in her chats with these royals, that she had known their forefathers through photographs given to her as wedding presents in 1937, while Wilhelmina still reigned over an empire? Did they discuss family resemblances, and continuity and change? We cannot know.

Wilhelmina's half-century on the throne remains the longest of any Dutch monarch to date. She had been the first sovereign female king to lead the House of Orange. She was the last monarch to reign over the modern Dutch empire in its most complete form. The greater Kingdom of the Netherlands that Queen Juliana inherited in 1948 was mired in conflict and dwindled rapidly during her reign. First the empire in the 'East' ended with Indonesia's independence in 1949; then came Suriname's independence in 1975, leaving only the six islands of the former West Indies, or 'Netherlands Antilles', as Juliana's overseas realm. As we saw at the beginning of this chapter, Juliana was celebrated (at the orchestration of colonial authorities) in New Guinea until the cession of Dutch authority to Indonesia in 1962. However, it was still the case that no part of the East Indies/Indonesia was visited by any Dutch monarch while it was a colony of the Netherlands.

Wilhelmina's reign in the first half of the twentieth century had coincided both with the last decades of Dutch rule in Indonesia and with the rise of photography not only as a mass print medium, but also as an amateur pursuit that enabled a larger number of people than ever before in history to create autobiographical archives, replete with interpretations of how ordinary lives intersected with major historical events. Mass and popular photography coexisted for the first time in this period with older forms such as studio photography, and with increasingly specialist modes of photography for academic and scientific purposes. The profuse functional differentiation of photography in this period enabled vast numbers of Indonesians and Europeans, in the East Indies and the Netherlands, to consume photographic images and, importantly, allowed growing numbers to collect and produce photographs of their own.

In this book, looking at photographs of Wilhelmina and her household, and of royal celebrations in the Indies and the Netherlands, has functioned as a prism for looking into the Dutch empire, particularly late colonial Indonesia and the Netherlands. Indeed, Wilhelmina and Juliana have been the frame rather than the focus of *Photographic subjects*, which has not been concerned with what the Dutch monarchy did in or with Indonesia. Rather, this book has examined what a range of people in the East Indies/Indonesia and the Netherlands did with the monarchy through photographs taken at royal celebrations. Particularly, I have shown how positions of agency and subjecthood were articulated on these occasions through photography.

Methodologically, this book has attended closely to the functions and 'social lives' of photographs to reconstruct both fine-grained narratives and larger historical patterns that reveal the important role of the Dutch monarchy in the articulation of social and political relations in the East Indies during Wilhelmina's reign. The iconography of Wilhelmina and Juliana at royal celebrations, the materiality of their portraits on these occasions, the ways in which photographs made at royal spectacles were made and exchanged to commemorate, communicate and articulate relations between royal subjects and with their monarchs across the Dutch colonial world: these elements constitute a historically specific visual economy (comprising makers, collectors, viewers, correspondents and consumers) and visual culture (comprising certain aesthetic norms, practices and shared meanings) that revolved and evolved around the Dutch monarchy in a colonial context. Photographs of and for Wilhelmina and her family illustrate the importance of monarchies as a focus for transnational loyalties, forging and maintaining imperial networks and nurturing colonial forms of citizenship in a globalised world.

One of the central arguments of this book has been that the rise of mass photography in the early twentieth century not only negated the absence of the Dutch monarch as a corporeal presence in her colonies; it created unique opportunities for her subjects to relate to a key imperial institution. Photography was an increasingly accessible technology for inserting the queen (as an image and an object) into daily lives, and for commemorating ordinary people's participation in historic, international events. Photographic sources from Wilhelmina's reign show how the camera made subjects, not just in the passive sense of East Indies people receiving the queen's image and being pictured at her festivals, but also in the way her subjects actively created their positions relative to the monarchy and each other. Indeed, through photography, Wilhelmina's subjects in the Indies made her an imperial queen in ways that she never achieved through the Dutch constitution and political practice.

Photographic sources provide unique insights into the gendered and racialised construction of imperial kingship in the era of mass photography. For royals in Indonesia, snapshot diplomacy was preferable to in-person encounters with Dutch monarchs, because photographic gifts could more fully represent the status of Indigenous kings than the restrictive protocols allowed at a foreign court. Indeed, this book confirms the privileges of male Indigenous kings in switching sartorial registers and experimenting with photographic forms in diplomatic encounters with European monarchs. This book has also shown how photography empowered female kings such as Wilhelmina and, particularly, Juliana to claim popular legitimacy as wives and mothers, and thereby identify with female subjects across the Dutch colonial world. Further, the nationalist expectation that female kings should embody their European subjects augmented rather than undermined more traditionally masculine imperial governing traits, such as overseeing unity and classifying diversity among their subjects. Female kingship worked for empire, in that reigning queens' reproductive roles extended the relevance of monarchy to territories where subjects differed between themselves as to political rights, but belonged equally to a body politic where the sovereign superseded yet did not threaten the 'real' powers that were still enacted by governing men.

In all these regards, this book has demonstrated that Wilhelmina was significant to Indonesians as an imperial monarch. Photographs were prominent among the gifts that Indies commoners sent the queen and her family, the purposes of which were often political. Dissidents appealed to her for clemency with photographs sent from prison. Chinese fraternities lobbied to be recognised, through photographs, as her subjects, and thus to be seen as equal to other civilised peoples in the queen's transnational realm, regardless of how they were differentiated by juridical rights. Indigenous elites traded photographs and even albums of royal celebrations with their Dutch counterparts in the civil administration. Indigenous royals sent photographic portraits and gifts to the House of Orange to negotiate their complex status as both vassals within a Dutch colonial hierarchy *and* as traditional authorities on their home soil.

[209]

We can rarely know what Wilhelmina and her household saw and thought when they received and perused these photographic gifts from Indonesians. Certainly, the acknowledgements and counter-gifts sent by her aides in the royal household, often via governors-general and colonial officials, were as courteous as the rank of her correspondents demanded, generally increasing in pomp and detail according to the sender's status. Arguably, however, what the queen saw matters less than what photographic gifts reveal from East Indies perspectives: these were articulations of agency and negotiated subject positions, made and exchanged in a late colonial culture that was at once internationalist and parochial, cosmopolitan and repressive. Photography gave the Dutch queen's subjects in the Indies novel opportunities to situate themselves within this colonial world and engage with the supreme figure of imperial rule in comparable ways to those of citizen-voters in the Netherlands. For in both places, Wilhelmina was equally (ir)relevant to her subjects' political rights (which were determined by governments), yet frequently invoked by Dutch governing authorities as legitimising their power. Her dynasty persisted while governments came and went, and this was her rhetorical value to her subjects in the Netherlands and the East Indies alike.

Indonesians have also been central to this book because they were the starring subjects in the vast majority of the photographs taken at royal festivals during Wilhelmina's reign. After all, Indonesians almost always comprised the majority of the population in the streets and at the fairgrounds. At celebrations, we see East Indies people largely through the camera lenses of European observers and Dutch authorities. Indonesian participants were instrumental to the colonial visualision of benevolent reign that Wilhelmina symbolised for Dutch authorities, particularly in the era of the Ethical Policy. It did not matter that the queen was absent. Local participation at royal festivals in the Indies gave Dutch authorities material for visual narratives of *rust en orde*, prosperity and modernity, unity in diversity and legitimate rule, all addressed to the monarch in whose honour spectators and participants were joined through photography. Significantly, the tiny, distant Netherlands was all but elided in photographic narratives linking Wilhelmina with her empire. Instead, the East Indies emerged at the centre of contemporary understandings of the Dutch colonial world. The script to the photographic storyboards that European observers in the Indies made was framed by colonial social and political contexts. Nonetheless, their photographs of Indonesians at royal celebrations provincialised Europe by placing East Indies people, practices and subjects at the hub of an empire with a queen who existed, for them, mostly through photographs.

Notes

1 See KITLV Albums 267 (1955) and 270 (1956). Jan van Baal was governor of New Guinea from 1952 to 1958.

2 KITLV Album 267, unnumbered photograph.

3 See KITLV Album 1094, collection of E. Dubois-Stumpf, early 1950s; KIT IWI Collection, TM-30028944, 1954; KIT TM-30005620, showing schoolchildren in a procession between 1959 and 1962; KIT IWI Collection TM-3005623, mast-climbing, 1961.

4 KITLV Album 270: in the series of photographs with the caption 'Ladies Night "Rotary" 1956'.

5 The photograph can be viewed at https://commons.wikimedia.org/wiki/File:Prinses_Juliana_1937.jpg (last accessed 23 October 2018).

6 P. Eckhardt, 'Wij zullen handhaven! De symbolische betekenis van de Nederlandse monarchie in Nederlands-Indië 1918–1940', MA thesis, University of Amsterdam, 2002, p. 76; R. Wassing-Visser, *Koninklijke geschenken uit Indonesië; Historische banden met het huis Oranje-Nassau (1600–1938)* (Den Haag/Zwolle: Stichting Historische Verzamelingen van het Huis Oranje-Nassau/Waanders, 1995), pp. 216–19.

7 Albums compiled by government photographers during Van Baal's tenure show the extent of the Dutch military forces gathered in New Guinea: KITLV Albums 974 and 981.

8 U. Bosma, *Indiëgangers; Verhalen van Nederlanders die naar Indië trokken* (Amsterdam: Bert Bakker, 2010), pp. 234–9, 246; W. H. Frederick, 'The killing of Dutch and Eurasians in Indonesia's national revolution (1945–49): a "brief genocide" reconsidered', in B. Luttikhuis and D. Moses (eds), *Colonial Counterinsurgency and Mass Violence: The Dutch Empire in Indonesia* (London: Routledge, 2014), pp. 133–54.

9 Bosma, *Indiëgangers*, p. 253.

10 C. L. M. Penders, *The West New Guinea Debacle: Dutch Decolonisation and Indonesia 1945–1962* (Leiden: KITLV Press, 2002), pp. 85–6.

11 Bosma, *Indiëgangers*, p. 255.

12 T. Shiraishi, 'The phantom world of Digoel', *Indonesia*, 61 (1996): 93–118, at pp. 96–8, 101–9; H. A. Poeze, 'From foe to partner to foe again: the strange alliance of the Dutch authorities and Digoel exiles in Australia, 1943–1945', *Indonesia*, 94 (2012): 57–84, at p. 58.

13 See KHA A50 VIIIc 19. The prisoners were Dasri, Wiromartono, Hadji Alirosid, N. Soemantri, Kartajaman, Prawirohardjo, Oeton and Prawirosimoen. Also discussed in Eckhardt, 'Wij zullen handhaven!', pp. 44–9.

14 Eckhardt, 'Wij zullen handhaven!', p. 18.

15 Shiraishi, 'The phantom world of Digoel', p. 100.

16 H. A. Poeze, 'Walking the tightrope: internal Indonesian conflict, 1945–49', in B. Luttikhuis and D. Moses (eds), *Colonial Counterinsurgency and Mass Violence: The Dutch Empire in Indonesia* (London: Routledge, 2014), pp. 176–97; G. Oostindie, in cooperation with I. Hoogenboom and J. Verwey, *Soldaat in Indonesië 1945–1950; Getuigenis van een oorlog aan de verkeerde kant van de geschiedenis* (Amsterdam: Prometheus, 2015), pp. 19, 22–3.

17 Oostindie, *Soldaat in Indonesië*, p. 26.

18 G. Oostindie, *De parels en de kroon; Het koningshuis en de koloniën* (Amsterdam: De Bezige Bij, 2006), pp. 100–1, 115–18, 130.

19 S. Scagliola, 'Cleo's "unfinished business": coming to terms with Dutch war crimes in Indonesia's war of independence', in B. Luttikhuis and D. Moses (eds), *Colonial Counterinsurgency and Mass Violence: The Dutch Empire in Indonesia* (London: Routledge, 2014), pp. 240–60; I. van Ooijen and I. Raaijmakers, 'Competitive or multidirectional memory? The interaction between postwar and postcolonial memory in the Netherlands', in B. Luttikhuis and D. Moses (eds), *Colonial Counterinsurgency and Mass Violence: The Dutch Empire in Indonesia* (London: Routledge, 2014), pp. 308–28; P. Bijl, 'Colonial memory and forgetting in the Netherlands and Indonesia', in B. Luttikhuis and D. Moses (eds), *Colonial Counterinsurgency and Mass Violence: The Dutch Empire in Indonesia* (London: Routledge, 2014), pp. 261–81.

20   J. R. H. van Schaik, *Koningin Juliana; Officieel gedenkboek ter gelegenheid van de troonsbestijging van Hare Majesteit Koningin Juliana* (Amsterdam: Scheltens & Giltay, 1948); P. A. Kasteel (ed.), *Oranje en de zes Caraïbische parelen; Officieel gedenkboek ter gelegenheid van het gouden regeringsjubileum van Hare Majesteit Koningin Wilhelmina* (Amsterdam: De Bussy, 1948).

21   Wilhelmina was in favour of regaining Indonesia in 1945, but her influence was restricted to the endorsement of Van Mook as governor-general during the war: C. Fasseur, *Wilhelmina; Krijgshaftig in een vormeloze jas* (Amsterdam: Balans, 2001), pp. 528, 534.

22   H. te Velde, *Gemeenschapszin en plichtsbesef; Liberalisme en nationalisme in Nederland, 1870–1918* (The Hague: SDU, 1992), p. 153; M. Bossenbroek, *Holland op zijn breedst; Indië en Zuid-Afrika in de Nederlandse cultuur omstreeks 1900* (Amsterdam: Bert Bakker, 1996), p. 235.

23   M. Grever, 'Colonial queens: imperialism, gender and the body politic during the reign of Victoria and Wilhelmina', *Dutch Crossing: A Journal of Low Countries Studies*, 26.1 (2002): 99–114, at pp. 106–7; Fasseur, *Wilhelmina; Krijgshaftig in een vormeloze jas*, p. 225.

24   Queen Wilhelmina, *Eenzaam maar niet alleen* (Amsterdam: Uitgeverij W. ten Have, 1959), pp. 112–13, 142.

25   Grever, 'Colonial queens', p. 108. Fasseur, *Wilhelmina; Krijgshaftig in een vormeloze jas*.

26   H. J. van den Broek, *Hier Radio-Oranje; Vijf jaar radio in oorlogstijd* (Amsterdam: Vrij Nederland, 1947); J. Schaap, *Het recht om te waarschuwen; Jodenvervolging en vernieuwing in de Radio Oranje-toespraken van Wilhelmina* (Groningen: Wolters-Noordhoff, 2005); M. G. Schenk and J. B. Th. Spaan, *De koningin spraak; Proclomaties en radio-toespraken van HM Koningin Wilhelmina gedurende de oorlogsjaren 1940–1945* (Driebergen: Christelijk Lektuurkontakt, 1985). Wilhelmina also mentioned the East Indies under Japanese occupation in one Radio Oranje broadcast in 1942, and she and Juliana discussed Indonesia during the revolution on Radio Hilversum in 1948 and 1949: *Koninklijke woorden over Nederland-Indonesië van Hare Majesteiten Koningin Wilhelmina en Juliana* (Amsterdam and Antwerp: Wereldbibliotheek Vereeniging, 1950).

27   The Dutch armed forces were the Royal Army and Royal Marines (*Koninklijke Landmach* and *Koninklijke Marine*). Oostindie, *Soldaat in Indonesië*, pp. 19, 22–3.

28   R. Kok, E. Somers and L. Zweers, *Koloniale oorlog 1945–1949; Van Indië naar Indonesië* (Amsterdam: Carrera, 2015), p. 144.

29   J. van Dijk, 'C.J. (Cees) Taillie' (1920–2005), http://collectie.tropenmuseum.nl/Default.aspx?ccid=P7972 (last accessed 23 October 2018). The Tropenmuseum in Amsterdam also held an exhibition on Taillie, *Van Kolonie tot Republiek, Indonesie in foto's van Cees Taillie 1946–1949, KIT Tropenmuseum, 21 oktober 2004–30 januari 2005*.

30   This chapter draws on thousands of amateur Dutch soldiers' photographs across more than fifty individual albums and collections in the KITLV Special Collections, Leiden University Library, and the Dutch Military Actions (1945–50) collections at the Institute for War, Holocaust and Genocide Studies (*Nederlands Instituut voor Oorlogs-, Holocaust- en Genocide Studies*, henceforth NIOD), Amsterdam. There are further archives at the Netherlands Institute for Military History (NIMH) in The Hague and the Museum Bronbeek. The 'behind the barrel of a gun' perspective paraphrases B. Luttikhuis and C. Harink, 'Voorbij het koloniale perspectief; Indonesische bronnen en het onderzoek naar de oorlog in Indonesië, 1945–49', *BMGN/Low Countries Historical Review*, 132.2 (2017): 51–76, at p. 53.

31   I have argued elsewhere for other important similarities and differences between Dutch soldiers' albums and 'family' albums made in the East Indies during the first half of the twentieth century: S. Protschky, 'Soldiers as humanitarians: photographing war in Indonesia (1945–49)', in J. Lydon (ed.), *Visualising Human Rights* (Perth: UWA Publishing, 2018), pp. 39–62; S. Protschky, 'Burdens of proof: photography

and evidence of atrocity during the Dutch military actions in Indonesia (1945–50)', *Journal of Southeast Asian Studies*, forthcoming 2020.

32 Kok, Somers and Zweers, *Koloniale oorlog*; Kossen Collection, Letters, Box 1 (of 3), A5683, NIOD, Amsterdam; Protschky, 'Burdens of proof'.

33 Unknown soldier, NIOD, Amsterdam, BC224.

34 Unknown soldier, NIOD, Amsterdam, BC530.

35 Unknown soldier, NIOD, Amsterdam, BC224.

36 Cees van Drongelen (1927–2009), NIOD, Amsterdam, BC458; see also KIT Collection Cees Taillie, TM-10029804, TM-10029787.

37 J. Kropf (1908–89), NIOD, Amsterdam, BC542.

38 G. M. Nafzger, NIOD, Amsterdam, BC265.

39 G. M. Nafzger, NIOD, Amsterdam, BC265 (folder B): 'Are these soldiers? Here, children! But they have a gun in their hands, so for our own safety we have to deal with them.' The youthfulness of Indonesian soldiers was also remarked upon in the soldiers' testimonies reproduced in Oostindie, *Soldaat in Indonesië*, p. 99.

40 Piet Kossen (1926–2014), NIOD, Amsterdam, BC594.

41 J. Schouten, T. J. Jansen Venneboer and H. A. Bijker (eds), *1947–1997 5–5-R.I.* (Doetinchem: WEDEO, 1997), p. 160, in Kossen Collection, A5683, Box 2 (of 3), NIOD, Amsterdam.

42 R. Limpach, *De brandende kampongs van Generaal Spoor* (Amsterdam: Boom, 2016); Kok, Somers and Zweers, *Koloniale oorlog*, p. 5.

43 See the album of J. Kropf, major of the infantry at Braga near Bandung, 1948: NIOD, Amsterdam, BC542.

44 Luttikhuis and Harink, 'Voorbij het koloniale perspectief'.

45 F. de Jong, 'Triumphal arch over entrance to Chinese quarter', NIOD, Amsterdam, BC224.

46 M. S. Heidhues, 'Anti-Chinese violence in Java during the Indonesian Revolution, 1945–49', in B. Luttikhuis and D. Moses (eds), *Colonial Counterinsurgency and Mass Violence: The Dutch Empire in Indonesia* (London: Routledge, 2014), pp. 155–75; Kok, Somers and Zweers, *Koloniale oorlog*, p. 34.

47 See, for example, P. L. Dronkers, NL-HaNA, Collectie 577 P. L. Dronkers, 1946–1949, number 2.21.281.25, inv. nr. 3, 'Pemoedas op Bali; Bali bevrijd. Fotoserie No 3', in which he discusses photographs of murdered Chinese; and for the same, KITLV Album 216 (Nieuwenhuyzen).

48 A. M. Tempelaars, *Inventaris van het archief van P.L. Dronkers*, NL-HaNA, Collectie 577 P. L. Dronkers, 1946–1949, number 2.21.281.25, Collection 577, p. 7.

49 NL-HaNA, Collectie 577 P. L. Dronkers, 1946–1949, number 2.21.281.25, inv. nr. 3, 'Queen's Day … in a liberated land: Negara, Bali, August 1946'.

50 NL-HaNA, Collectie 577 P. L. Dronkers, 1946–1949, number 2.21.281.25, inv. nr. 3, 'Queen's Day … in a liberated land: Negara, Bali, August 1946'.

51 A. Vickers, *Bali: A Paradise Created* (Ringwood, Vic.: Penguin, 1989).

52 NL-HaNA, Collectie 577 P. L. Dronkers, 1946–1949, number 2.21.281.25, inv. nr. 3, 'Fotoserie Bali XV, Koninginnefeest in Penebel (Bali), No. 14'.

53 NL-HaNA, Collectie 577 P. L. Dronkers, 1946–1949, number 2.21.281.25, inv. nr. 3, 'Feesten op Bali: Bali bevrijd Fotoserie No 5'.

54 Collectie 577 P .L. Dronkers, 1946–1949, number 2.21.281.25, inv. nr. 3, inv. nr. 4, 'Toespraak ter gelegenheid van de opening van de feestelijkheden op 31 Augustus ter eere van H. M. de Koningin Wilhelmina en de vrede in het landschap Djembrana'. Interestingly, in the Dutch-language version of this speech, Dronkers used a combination of Dutch and Indonesian phrases to describe the rebels: 'kaoem pemberontak, de terroristen' or 'belligerents, the terrorists'.

55 J. van Osta, *Het theater van de Staat; Oranje, Windsor en de moderne monarchie* (Amsterdam: Wereldbibliotheek, 1998), p. 144.

56 NL-HaNA, Collectie 577 P. L. Dronkers, 1946–1949, number 2.21.281.25, inv. nr. 3, 'Feesten op Bali'.

57 NL-HaNA, Collectie 577 P. L. Dronkers, 1946–1949, number 2.21.281.25, inv. nr. 4, 'Een brief van den Adspirant-Controleur [*sic*] van Djembrana aan alle leerlingen

van de scholen in het landschap Djembrana, ter gelegenheid van de geboortedag van Z.K.H. Prins Bernhard op 29 Juni 1946'.
58 Protschky, 'Soldiers as humanitarians'.
59 Oostindie, *De parels en de kroon*, pp. 116–17.
60 R. F. Kaan, *Oranje & Indonesië; Officieel herdenkingsalbum van het staatsbezoek van H.M. Koningin Juliana en Z.K.H. Prins Bernard aan Indonesië, in de zomer van 1971* (Den Haag: Zuid-Hollandsche Uitgeversmaatschappij, 1971), p. 18.
61 E. Locher-Scholten, 'From urn to monument: Dutch memories of World War II in the Pacific, 1945–1995', in A. L. Smith (ed.), *Europe's Invisible Migrants* (Amsterdam: Amsterdam University Press, 2003), pp. 105–28, at p. 113.
62 Kaan, *Oranje & Indonesië*, pp. 8, 16, 22, 27.
63 Kaan, *Oranje & Indonesië*, pp. 16, 29, 30–4, 39.
64 Kaan, *Oranje & Indonesië*, p. 15.
65 Kaan, *Oranje & Indonesië*, pp. 5, 39.
66 Kaan, *Oranje & Indonesië*, pp. 8, 11, 27–9.

BIBLIOGRAPHY

Archives

Koninklijk Instituut voor Taal-, Land-, en Volkenkunde/Royal Netherlands Institute of South-east Asian and Caribbean Studies (KITLV), Leiden University Library Special Collections, Leiden.

Koninklijk Bibliotheek/Royal Library (KB), The Hague.

Koninklijk Huisarchief/Royal Collections (KHA), The Hague.

Nederlands Instituut voor Oorlogs Documentatie/Institute for War, Holocaust and Genocide Studies (NIOD), Amsterdam.

Koninklijk Instituut voor de Tropen/Royal Tropical Institute (KIT), Amsterdam.

Nationaal Archief/National Archive (NL-HaNA), The Hague.

Published primary sources

Aan Hare Majesteit Koningin Wilhelmina en Zijne Hoogheid Hertog Hendrik van Mecklenburg-Schwerin, ter gelegenheid van hoogst derzelver huwelijk op 7 Februari 1901; Namens Banda's ingezetenen eerbiedig aangeboden door hun afgevaardigde A.E. Brunier, Directeur van de Bandasche Perkeniers- en Handels Vereeniging te Banda Neira (Banda Neira, 1901).

Adam, L., 'The courtyards, gates and buildings of the Kraton of Yogyakarta', trans. Rosemary Robson-McKillop, first published 1940, in S. Robson (ed.), *The Kraton: Selected Essays on Javanese Courts* (Leiden: KITLV Press, 2003), pp. 13–40.

Bas, W. G. de (ed.), *25 jaar geschiedenis van Nederland 1898–1923* (Amsterdam: Dalmeijer's Volksuniversiteit, 1923).

Broek, H. J. van den, *Hier Radio-Oranje; Vijf jaar radio in oorlogstijd* (Amsterdam: Vrij Nederland, 1947).

Brooshooft, P., *De ethische koers in de koloniale politiek* (Amsterdam: J. H. de Bussy, 1901).

Catalogus van de Jubileum-Tentoonstelling 1923 gehouden ter gelegenheid van het 25-jarig regeeringsjubileum van H.M. de koningin in het Koloniaal Instituut te Amsterdam 3–30 September (Amsterdam: Van Holkema & Warendorf, 1923).

De gouden kroon; Gedenkboek bij gelegenheid van het gouden regeringsjubileum van H.M. koningin Wilhelmina (Haarlem: Spaarnestad, 1948).

De veertigjarige regeering van H.M. Koningin Wilhelmina; 1898–6 September–1938. Oranje album (Amsterdam: Holdert & Co., 1939).

Djajadiningrat, A., *Herinneringen van Pangeran Aria Achmad Djajadiningrat* (Amsterdam and Batavia: G. Kolff & Co., 1936).

Gedenkbladen 25-jarig regeerings-jubileum van H.M. onze geëerbiedigde Koningin Wilhelmina (Soerabaya: Soerabaiasch Comité tot Herdenking van het Regeerings-Jubileum, 1923).

Gent, L. F. W. A. van Penard, and D. A. Rinkes, *Gedenkboek voor Nederlandsch-Indië; Ter gelegenheid van het regeeringsjubileum van H.M. de Koningin, 1898–1923* (Batavia: G. Kolff & Co., 1923).

Groneman, I., *In den kedáton te Jogjåkártå; Oepåtjårå, ampilan en toneeldansen* (Leiden: Brill, 1888).

Groneman, I., *De wajang orang Pregiwa in den kraton te Jogjakarta, in Juni 1899* (Semarang: Van Dorp & Co., 1899).

Herinnering aan den Oranje-Zaterdag 9 September 1933 ter gelegenheid van het 35-jarig regeerings-jubileum van HM Koningin Wilhelmina (Amterdam: Holdert & Co., 1933).

Het Prinselijk Huwelijksfeest (Haarlem: De Spaarnestad, 1937).

Hoofdbestuur, Studeerenden Vereeniging Jong-Java, *Jong-Java's Jaarboekje* (Weltevreden: Kolff, 1923).

Jagt, M. B. van der, *Mollukkenreis 10 September–3 November 1923* (Den Haag: 1935).

Kaan, R. F., *Oranje & Indonesië; Officieel herdenkingsalbum van het staatsbezoek van H.M. Koningin Juliana en Z.K.H. Prins Bernard aan Indonesië, in de zomer van 1971* (Den Haag: Zuid-Hollandsche Uitgeversmaatschappij, 1971).

Kalff, S., 'Indië en het Oranjehuis', *Het Koloniaal Tijdschrift*, 8 (1919): 1351–71.

Kartini, Raden Adjeng, *Door duisternis tot licht; Gedachten over en voor het Javaansche volk*, with an introduction by J. H. Abendanon ('s-Gravenhage: Luctor et Emergo, 1923).

Kasteel, P. A. (ed.), *Oranje en de zes Caraïbische parelen; Officieel gedenkboek ter gelegenheid van het gouden regeringsjubileum van Hare Majesteit Koningin Wilhelmina* (Amsterdam: De Bussy, 1948).

Kats, J., and R. Sastrawidjana, *Wajang-wong-spelen, gehouden op 3, 4, 5 en 6 September 1923 in de Kraton te Jogjakarta; In opdracht van Z.H. den Sultan Hamengkoe Boewana VIII* (Weltevreden: G. Kolff and Co., 1924).

Kielstra, J. C., *Gedenkboek van het Algemeen Nederlandsch Verbond* (Dordrecht and Amsterdam: Wereldbibliotheek, 1923).

Koninklijke woorden over Nederland-Indonesië van Hare Majesteiten Koningin Wilhelmina en Juliana (Amsterdam and Antwerp: Wereldbibliotheek Vereeniging, 1950).

Kouwenaar, D., *Amsterdam tijdens het feestbetoon bij het 40-jarig regeerings-jubileum van H.M. Koningin Wilhelmina van 5 tot 12 September 1938* (Amsterdam: De Bussy, 1938).

Lip, F. A. W. van der, *Nederlandsch-Indisch Herinnerings-Album aan de verloving en het huwelijk van H.K.H. Prinses Juliana [en] Z.K.H. Prins Bernhard* (Bandoeng: Alubu, 1937).

Mansvelt, W. M. F., 'De economische ontwikkeling van Ned. Indië sedert 1898', in *Bij het regeerings jubileum 1898–1938 van Hare Majesteit Koningin Wilhelmina* (Batavia: Kantoor voor de Volkslectuur, 1938), pp. 51–63.

Nationaal huldigingsdéfilé voor H.M. de Koningin op zaterdag 9 september 1933 in het Olympisch Stadion te Amsterdam (Amsterdam: L. F. J. Thoolen, 1933).

NNGPM, *Oil Facilities: Nederlandsche Nieuw Guinee Petroleum Maatschappij* (The Hague: Nederlandsche Nieuw Guinee Petroleum Maatschappij, 1957).

Officieel programma van de feesten, die gevierd zullen worden te Batavia ter gelegenheid van de troonbestijging en inhuldiging van Hare Majesteit Wilhelmina Helena Paulina Maria, Koningin der Nederlanden (Batavia: Het Centraal Comité, 1898).

Oranje Album 1898–September–1938 veertig jaren koningin (Amsterdam: Holdert & Co, 1938).

Oranje en de zes Caraïbische parelen; Officieel gedenkboek ter gelegenheid van het gouden regeringsjubileum van Hare Majesteit Koningin Wilhelmina, Helena, Pauline, Maria, 1898–31 augustus–1948 (Amsterdam: De Bussy, 1948).

Oranje-album ter herinnering aan het 50-jarig regeringsjubileum en de abdicatie van H.M. Koningin Wilhelmina en de inhuldigingsfeesten van H.M. Koningin Juliana, September 1948 (Amsterdam: Holdert & Co., 1948).

Pigeaud, Th., 'The northern palace square in Yogyakarta', trans. R. Robson-McKillop, originally published in *Djåwå* in 1940, in S. Robson (ed.), *The Kraton: Selected Essays on Javanese Courts* (Leiden: KITLV Press, 2003), pp. 1–12.

Queen Wilhelmina, 'Troonrede van 17 September 1901', in *Troonredes, Openingsredes, Inhuldingsredes 1814–1963*, introduced and annotated by E. van Raalte ('s-Gravenhage: Staatsuitgeverij, 1964), pp. 193–4.

Queen Wilhelmina, *Eenzaam maar niet alleen* (Amsterdam: Uitgeverij W. ten Have, 1959).

Rengelink, J. W., and I. Mug, *Koningin Wilhelmina 1898–1948* (Heemstede: Mubro, 1948).

Resink-Wilkens, A. J.,'The Yogya festival calendar', trans. R. Robson-McKillop, first published 1932, in S. Robson (ed.), *The Kraton: Selected Essays on Javanese Courts* (Leiden: KITLV Press, 2003), pp. 83–90.

Schaik, J. R. H. van, *Koningin Juliana; Officieel gedenkboek ter gelegenheid van de troonsbestijging van Hare Majesteit Koningin Juliana* (Amsterdam: Scheltens & Giltay, 1948).

Schouten, J., T. J. Jansen Venneboer and H. A. Bijker (eds), *1947–1997 5–5-R.I.* (Doetinchem: WEDEO, 1997).

Sjahrir, S., *Indonesische overpeinzingen* (Amsterdam: De Bezige Bij, 1945).

Stratenus, L., *Oranje-album, uitgegeven ter gelegenheid van het huwelijk van H.M. Koniningin Wilhelmina der Nederlanden en Z.H. Hertog Hendrik van Mecklenburg-Schwerin* (Amsterdam: Boon, 1901).

Tal, T., *Oranjebloesems uit de gedenkbladen van Nederlands Israel* (Amsterdam: Van Creveld & Co., 1898).

Tichelman, G. L., *Indonesische Bevolkingstypen* (Rotterdam and 's-Gravenhage: Nijgh and Van Ditmar N.V., 1948).

Ven, D. J. van der, *Neerlands Volksleven* (Zaltbommel: P.M. Wink, 1920).

Visser, Th. C. M., *Jubileum Manifestatie ter gelegenheid van het 50-jaring regeringsjubileum van H.M. Koningin Wilhelmina; 31 augustus 1948, Olympisch Stadion te Amsterdam* (1948).

Wap, J. J. F., *Gedenkboek der inhuldiging en feesttogten van Zijne Majesteit Willem II 1840–1842* ('s Hertogenbosch: J.F. Demelinne, 1842).

Wilhelmina-Juliana gedenkalbum 1948 uitgegeven ter gelegenheid van het gouden regeringsjubileum van H.M. Koningin Wilhelmina en de inhuldiging van H.M. Koningin Juliana, 31 Augustus–6 Sept. 1948 (Haarlem: De Spaarnestad, 1948).

Winter, A. T. H., 'Het Nederlandsch-Indische Leger, 1898–1923', in W. G. de Bas, *25 jaar geschiedenis van Nederland 1898–1923* (Amsterdam: Dalmeijer's Volksuniversiteit, 1923), pp. 257–66.

Zeeuw, P. de (ed.), *Vorstin en Volk; Woorden van H.M. Koningin Wilhelmina* (Baarn: Hollandia, 1945).

Zimmerman, V., 'The *kraton* of Surakarta in the year 1915', trans. Rosemary Robson-McKillop, originally published in *Djåwå* in 1915, in S. Robson (ed.), *The Kraton: Selected Essays on Javanese Courts* (Leiden: KITLV Press, 2003), pp. 41–64.

Secondary sources

Aldrich, R., *Vestiges of Colonial Empire in France* (New York: Palgrave Macmillan, 2005).

Aldrich, R., and C. McCreery, 'Empire tours: royal travel between colonies and metropoles', in R. Aldrich and C. McCreery (eds), *Royals on Tour: Politics, Pageantry and Colonialism* (Manchester: Manchester University Press, 2018), pp. 1–22.

Aldrich, R., and C. McCreery, 'European sovereigns and their empires "beyond the seas"', in R. Aldrich and C. McCreery (eds), *Crowns and Colonies: European Monarchies and Overseas Empires* (Manchester: Manchester University Press, 2016), pp. 1–26.

Alpers, S. 'The museum as a way of seeing', in I. Karp and S. D. Lavine (eds), *Exhibiting Cultures: The Poetics and Politics of Museum Display* (Washington, DC: Smithsonian Institution Press, 1991).

Anderson, B., *Language and Power: Exploring Political Cultures in Indonesia* (Ithaca, NY: Cornell University Press, 1990).

Anrooij, F. van, *De koloniale staat 1854–1942; Gids voor het archief van het ministerie van Koloniën De Indische archipel* (Den Haag: Nationaal Archief, 2009).

Appadurai, A., 'The colonial backdrop', *Afterimage* (1997): 4–7.

Baggerman, A., 'Autobiography and family memory in the nineteenth century', in R. Dekker (ed.), *Egodocuments and History: Autobiographical Writing and its Social Context since the Middle Ages* (Hilversum: Verloren, 2002), pp. 161–74.

Batchen, G., *Each Wild Idea: Writing, Photography, History* (Cambridge, MA: MIT Press, 2001).

Batchen, G., *Forget Me Not: Photography and Remembrance* (Amsterdam/New York: Van Gogh Museum/Princeton Architectural Press, 2004).

Behrend, T. E., 'Textual gateways: the Javanese manuscript tradition', in A. Kumar and J. H. McGlynn (eds), *Illuminations: The Writing Traditions of Indonesia* (Jakarta, New York and Toronto: The Lontar Foundation, Weatherill, 1996), pp. 161–200.

Bennett, J. (ed.), *Crescent Moon: Islamic Art and Civilisation in Southeast Asia* (Adelaide/Canberra: Art Gallery of South Australia/National Gallery of Australia, 2006).

Berge, T. van den, *H.J. van Mook; Een vrij en gelukkig Indonesië* (Bussum: Thoth, 2014).

Beunders, H., 'Regina vivat! Regie vivat? In de publicitaire monarchy is de liefde tussen volk en vorst als het leven zelf', in R. Meijer and H. J. Schoo (eds), *De monarchie; Staatsrecht, volksgunst en het huis van Oranje* (Amsterdam: Prometheus, 2002), pp. 101–36.

Bijl, P., 'Colonial memory and forgetting in the Netherlands and Indonesia', in B. Luttikhuis and D. Moses (eds), *Colonial Counterinsurgency and Mass Violence: The Dutch Empire in Indonesia* (London: Routledge, 2014), pp. 261–81.

Bijl, P., *Emerging Memory: Photographs of Colonial Atrocity in Dutch Cultural Remembrance* (Amsterdam: Amsterdam University Press, 2015).

Billig, M., *Talking of the Royal Family* (London: Routledge, 1992).

Bloembergen, M., *Colonial Spectacles: The Netherlands and the Netherlands-Indies at the World Exhibitions, 1880–1931* (Singapore: NUS Press, 2006).

Bloembergen, M., and R. Raben, 'Wegen naar het nieuwe Indië, 1890–1950', in M. Bloembergen and R. Raben (eds), *Het koloniale beschavingsoffensief; Wegen naar het niewe Indië, 1890–1950* (Leiden: KITLV Press, 2009), pp. 7–24.

Boerdam, J., and W. O. Martinius, 'Family photographs: a sociological approach', *The Netherlands' Journal of Sociology*, 16.2 (1980): 95–120.

Bool, F., 'Between modernisation and tradition, 1925–1945', in F. Bool, M. Boom and F. Gierstberg (eds), *Dutch Eyes: A Critical History of Photography in the Netherlands* (Zwolle: Waanders, 2007), pp. 147–90.

Boom, B. van der, 'Orangisme en de bezetting', in H. te Velde and D. Haks (eds), *Oranje onder; Populair Orangisme van Willem van Oranje tot nu* (Amsterdam: Prometheus/Bert Bakker, 2014), pp. 221–42.

Bosma, U., *Indiëgangers; Verhalen van Nederlanders die naar Indië trokken* (Amsterdam: Bert Bakker, 2010).

Bosma, U., and R. Raben, *Being 'Dutch' in the Indies: A History of Creolisation and Empire, 1500–1920*, trans. W. Shaffer (Athens, OH: Ohio University Press, 2008).

Bossenbroek, M., *Holland op zijn breedst; Indië en Zuid-Afrika in de Nederlandse cultuur omstreeks 1900* (Amsterdam: Bert Bakker, 1996).

Braam, E. van, and E. Elzinga, *Wilhelmina; Koninklijk gekleed 1880–1962* (Zwolle: Waanders Uitgevers, 1998).

Bree, H. van, *Het aanzien van Juliana* (Utrecht: Het Spectrum, 2004).

Broomhall, S., 'Emotions in the household', in S. Broomhall (ed.), *Emotions in the Household, 1200–1900* (Basingstoke: Palgrave Macmillan, 2008), pp. 1–37.

Broomhall, S., and J. van Gent, *Dynastic Colonialism: Gender, Materiality and the Early Modern House of Orange-Nassau* (London: Routledge, 2016).

Broomhall, S., and J. van Gent, *Gender, Power and Identity in the Early Modern House of Orange-Nassau* (London: Routledge, 2016).

Bruin, K., 'Distinction and democratization: royal decorations in the Netherlands', *The Netherlands' Journal of Sociology*, 23.1 (1987): 17–30.

Bryson, N., *Looking at the Overlooked: Four Essays on Still Life Painting* (Cambridge, MA: Harvard University Press, 1990).

Cannadine, D., 'The context, performance and meaning of ritual: the British monarchy and the "invention of tradition", ca. 1820–1977', in E. Hobsbawm and T. Ranger (eds), *The Invention of Tradition* (Cambridge: Cambridge University Press, 1983), pp. 101–64.

Cannadine, D., *Ornamentalism: How the British Saw Their Empire* (London: Allen Lane, 2001).

Captain, E., M. de Haan, F. Steijlen and P. Westerkamp (eds), *De Indische zomer in Den Haag: Het cultureel erfgoed van de Indische hoofdstad* (Leiden: KITLV Press, 2005).

Carpenter, B., *Willem Hofker 1902–1981: Painter of Bali* (Wijk en Aalburg: Pictures Publishers, 1993).

Carvalho, T. R. de, 'De konkinklijke streekdrachtkostuums nader bekeken', in *Oranje en de Nationale Streeckdrachten* (Apeldoorn: Nationaal Museum, Paleis Het Loo, 2012), pp. 3–7.

Chambers, D., 'Family as place: family photograph albums and the domestication of public and private space', in J. M. Schwartz and J. R. Ryan (eds), *Picturing Place: Photography and the Geographical Imagination* (London: I.B. Tauris, 2003), pp. 96–114.

Clulow, A., *The Company and the Shogun: The Dutch Encounter with Tokugawa Japan* (New York: Columbia University Press, 2013).

Cohn, B. S., 'Representing authority in Victorian India', in E. Hobsbawm and T. Ranger (eds), *The Invention of Tradition* (Cambridge: Cambridge University Press, 1983), pp. 165–209.

Colenbrander, Th., 'De Koningin naar Indië', *De Gids*, 83 (1919): 162–3.

Colombijn, F., with M. Barwegen, *Under Construction: The Politics of Urban Space and Housing During the Decolonization of Indonesia, 1930–1960* (Leiden: KITLV Press, 2010).

Conor, L., *Skin Deep: Settler Impressions of Aboriginal Women* (Crawley: UWA Publishing, 2016).

Coppel, C. A., 'The Indonesian Chinese as "Foreign Orientals" in the Netherlands Indies', in T. Lindsey (ed.), *Indonesian Law and Society* (Sydney: The Federation Press, 1999), pp. 33–41.

Coté, J., 'Reversing the lens: Kartini's image of a modernised Java', in S. Protschky (ed.), *Photography, Modernity and the Governed in Late-Colonial Indonesia* (Amsterdam: Amsterdam University Press, 2015), pp. 176–84.

Cribb, R., 'Introduction: the late colonial state in Indonesia', in R. Cribb (ed.), *The Late Colonial State in Indonesia: Political and Economic Foundations of the Netherlands Indies 1880–1942* (Leiden: KITLV Press, 1994), pp. 1–10.

Dick, H. W., *Surabaya, City of Work: A Socioeconomic History, 1900–2000* (Athens, OH: Ohio University Centre for International Studies, 2002).

Dijk, J. van, R. Jongmans, A. Mansfeld, S. Vink and P. Westerkamp, *Photographs of the Netherlands East Indies at the Tropenmuseum* (Amsterdam: KIT Publishers, 2012).

Dijkhuis, H., *Monarchia; Het fenomeen van het koningschap* (Amsterdam: Boom, 2010).

Djajadiningrat-Nieuwenhuys, M., 'Noto Soeroto: his ideas and the late colonial intellectual climate', *Indonesia*, 55 (1993): 41–72.

Doel, H. W. van den, 'Military rule in the Netherlands Indies', in R. Cribb (ed.), *The Late Colonial State in Indonesia: Political and Economic Foundations of the Netherlands Indies 1880–1942* (Leiden: KITLV Press, 1994), pp. 57–78.

Drieënhuizen, C., 'Objects, nostalgia and the Dutch colonial elite in times of transition, ca. 1900–1970', *Bijdragen tot de Taal-, Land- en Volkenkunde*, 170 (2014): 504–29.

Drieënhuizen, C., 'Social careers across imperial spaces: an empire family in the Dutch-British world, 1811–1933', *Journal of Imperial and Commonwealth History*, 44.3 (2016): 397–422.

Drooglever, P., 'De monarchie in Indië', *Ex Tempore*, 17 (1998): 221–36.

Duuren, D. van, *De kris; Een aardse benadering van een kosmisch symbool* (Amsterdam: Koninklijk Instituut voor de Tropen, 1996).

Duuren, D. van, 'Expeditions, collection, science: the Dutch fascination for the Papuans of New Guinea', in S. Legêne and J. van Dijk (eds), *The Netherlands East Indies at the Tropenmuseum: A Colonial History* (Amsterdam: KIT Publishers, 2011), pp. 97–112.

Duuren, D. van, 'Governors-general and civilians', in M. Scalliet, K. van Brakel, D. van Duuren and J. ten Kate, *Pictures from the Tropics: Paintings by Western Artists during the Dutch Colonial Period in Indonesia* (Amsterdam: KIT Publishers, 1999), pp. 90–102.

Eckhardt, P., 'Wij zullen handhaven! De symbolische betekenis van de Nederlandse monarchie in Nederlands-Indië 1918–1940', MA dissertation, University of Amsterdam, 2002.

Eckhardt, P., '"Wij zullen handhaven!" Oranje feesten in Indië (1918–1940)', *Indische Letteren; Feesten in Indië*, 21.1 (2006): 31–44.

Edwards, E., *Anthropology and Photography, 1860–1920* (New Haven, CT: Yale University Press, 1992).

Edwards, E., *The Camera as Historian: Amateur Photographers and Historical Imagination, 1885–1918* (Durham, NC: Duke University Press, 2012).

Edwards, E., 'Photographic "types": the pursuit of method', *Visual Anthropology*, 3:2–3 (1990): 235–58.

Edwards, E., *Raw Histories: Photographs, Anthropology and Museums* (Oxford: Berg, 2001).

Edwards, E., and J. Hart, 'Introduction: photographs as objects', in E. Edwards and J. Hart (eds), *Photographs, Objects, Histories: On the Materiality of Images* (London: Routledge, 2004), pp. 1–15.

Ensel, R., *De Nederlander in beeld; Fotografie en nationisme tussen 1920 en 1945* (Amsterdam: Amsterdam University Press, 2014).

Eustace, N., E. Lean, J. Livingstone, J. Plamper, W. M. Reddy and B. H. Rosenwein, 'AHR conversation: the historical study of emotions', *American Historical Review*, 117.5 (2012): 1487–1531.

Evers, C. G., *Onderscheidingen; Leidraad voor de decoraties van het Koninkrijk der Nederlanden* (Amsterdam: De Bataafsche Leeuw, 2001).

Fasseur, C., *Wilhelmina; Krijgshaftig in een vormeloze jas* (Amsterdam: Balans, 2001).

Fasseur, C., and D. H. A. Kolff, 'Some remarks on the development of colonial bureaucracies in India and Indonesia', *Itinerario*, 10.1 (1986): 31–56.

Feith, J., *Wilhelmina Regina; Nederland gedurende veertig jaren* ('s-Gravenhage: Zuid-Hollandsche Uitgevers Maatschappij, 4th edn, 1938).

Frederick, W. H., 'The killing of Dutch and Eurasians in Indonesia's national revolution (1945–49): a "brief genocide" reconsidered', in B. Luttikhuis and D. Moses (eds), *Colonial Counterinsurgency and Mass Violence: The Dutch Empire in Indonesia* (London: Routledge, 2014), pp. 133–54.

Ginkel, R. van, and B. Henkes, 'On peasants and "primitive peoples": moments of rapprochement and distance between folklore studies and anthropology in the Netherlands', *Ethnos: Journal of Anthropology*, 68.1 (2003): 112–34.

Gorman, D., *Imperial Citizenship: Empire and the Question of Belonging* (Manchester: Manchester University Press, 2006).

Govaars-Tjia, M. T. N., 'Hollands onderwijs in een koloniale samenleving; de Chinese ervaring in Indonesië 1900–1942', PhD thesis, Leiden University, 1999.

Graaff, B. de, and E. Locher-Scholten, *J.P. Graaf van Limburg Stirum; Tegendraads landvoogd en diplomaat* (Zwolle: Waanders, 2007).

Grever, M., 'Colonial queens: imperialism, gender and the body politic during the reign of Victoria and Wilhelmina', *Dutch Crossing: A Journal of Low Countries Studies*, 26.1 (2002): 99–114.

Grever, M., 'Koningin Wilhelmina en het feminisme of de ogenschijnlijke onverenigbaarheid van karakters', *Tijdschrift voor Genderstudies*, 2.3 (1999): 4–19.

Grever, M., 'Staging modern monarchs: royalty at the World Exhibitions of 1851 and 1867', in H. te Velde (ed.), *Mystifying the Monarch: Studies on Discourse, Power, and History* (Amsterdam: Amsterdam University Press, 2006), pp. 161–79.

Grever, M., 'Vorstin voor heel het vaderland? Orangisme en feminisme in het laatste kwaart van de negentiende eeuw', *De Negentiende Eeuw*, 23.1 (1999): 76–88.

Grever, M., and B. Waaldijk (eds), *Transforming the Public Sphere: The Dutch National Exhibition of Women's Labor in 1898* (Durham, NC: Duke University Press, 2004).

Grever, M., and B. Waaldijk, 'Women's labor at display: feminist claims to Dutch citizenship and colonial politics around 1901', *Journal of Women's History*, 15.4 (2004): 11–18.

Groeneveld, A., 'Photography in aid of science', in *Toekang potret: 100 Years of Photography in the Dutch Indies 1839–1939* (Amsterdam/Rotterdam: Fragment/Museum voor Volkenkunde, 1989), pp. 15–48.

Hay, M. E., 'Russia, Britain and the House of Nassau: the re-establishment of the Orange dynasty in the Netherlands, March–November 1813', *BMGN/Low Countries Historical Review*, 133.1 (2018): 3–21.

Heidhues, M. S., 'Anti-Chinese violence in Java during the Indonesian Revolution, 1945–49', in B. Luttikhuis and D. Moses (eds), *Colonial Counterinsurgency* and *Mass Violence: The Dutch Empire in Indonesia* (London: Routledge, 2014), pp. 155–75.

Heuven-van Nes, E. van, '"Een aandachtige bezichting ten volle waard": De tentoonstelling van het werk van koningin Wilhelmina', in M. E. Spliethoff, E. van Heuven-van Nes, M. Jansen and P. Rem, *Koningin Wilhelmina; Schilderijen en tekeningen* (Zwolle: Waanders and Stichting Paleis Het Loo, 2006), pp. 37–56.

Hight, E. M., and G. D. Sampson, 'Introduction: photography, "race", and post-colonial theory', in E. M. Hight and G. D. Sampson (eds), *Colonialist Photography: Imag(in)ing Race and Place* (London: Routledge, 2002), pp. 1–19.

Hinzler, H., 'Onnes Kurkdjian: viewmaker and entrepreneur', in J. L. Reed (ed.), *Toward Independence: A Century of Indonesia Photographed* (San Francisco: Friends of Photography, 1991), pp. 59–63.

Hirsch, J., *Family Photographs: Content, Meaning and Effect* (Oxford: Oxford University Press, 1981).

Hirsch, M., *Family Frames: Photography, Narratives and Postmemory* (Cambridge, MA: Harvard University Press, 1997).

Hirsch, M., 'Introduction: familial looking', in M. Hirsch (ed.), *The Familial Gaze* (Hanover, NH: University Press of New England, 1999), xi–xxv.

Holt, C., *Art in Indonesia: Continuities and Change* (Ithaca, NY: Cornell University Press, 1967).

Hoogervorst, T., and H. Schulte Nordholt, 'Urban middle classes in colonial Java (1900–1942): images and language', *Bijdragen tot de Taal-, Land- en Volkenkunde*, 173 (2017): 442–74.

Houben, V. J. H., *Kraton and Kumpeni: Surakarta and Yogyakarta, 1830–1870* (Leiden: KITLV Press, 1994).

Jansen, M., 'Koningin Wilhelmina en de fotografie', in M. E. Spliethoff, E. van Heuven-van Nes, M. Jansen and P. Rem, *Koningin Wilhelmina; Schilderijen en tekeningen* (Zwolle: Waanders and Stichting Paleis Het Loo, 2006), pp. 57–68.

Jansen, M., 'Moeder en dochter in het Koninklijk Huisarchief', *Fotografisch Geheugen*, 79 (2013): 7–9.

Jansen, M., 'De nationale gedaante', in *Oranje en de Nationale Streeckdrachten* (Apeldoorn: Nationaal Museum, Paleis Het Loo, 2012), pp. 8–17.

Jansen, M., 'Uit de praktijk van hoffotograaf Franz Ziegler', in N. Coppes, M. van Heteren and M. Jansen, *Franz Ziegler, Virtuoso Fotograaf (1893–1939)* (Zutphen: Walburg Pers, 2009), pp. 33–50.

Jongmans, R., and J. van Dijk, 'Photographs from the Netherlands East Indies: changing perspectives, different views', in J. van Dijk, R. Jongmans, A. Mansfeld, S. Vink and P. Westerkamp, *Photographs of the Netherlands East Indies at the Tropenmuseum* (Amsterdam: KIT Publishers, 2012), pp. 15–39.

Kal, P. W. H., *Yogya Silver: Renewal of a Javanese Handicraft* (Amsterdam: KIT Publishers, 2005).

Kam, G., '*Wayang wong* in the court of Yogyakarta: the enduring significance of Javanese dance drama', *Asian Theatre Journal*, 4.1 (1987): 29–51.

Kartomi, M. J., 'Music and meaning of *réyog ponorogo*', *Indonesia*, 22 (1976): 84–130.

Knaap, G. J., *Inventaris Collectie G.L. Tichelman H814* (Leiden: KITLV Press, 1995).

Knapp, G. J., with a contribution by Y. Soerjoatmodjo, *Cephas, Yogyakarta: Photography in the Service of the Sultan* (Leiden: KITLV Press, 1999).

Koch, J., *Koning Willem I 1772–1843* (Amsterdam: Boom, 2013).

Kok, R., E. Somers and L. Zweers, *Koloniale oorlog 1945–1949; Van Indië naar Indonesië* (Amsterdam: Carrera, 2015).

Komter, A. E., *Social Solidarity and the Gift* (Cambridge: Cambridge University Press, 2005).

Kuhn, A., 'A meeting of two queens: an exercise in memory work', in M. Hirsch (ed.), *The Familial Gaze* (Hanover, NH: University Press of New England, 1999), pp. 196–207.

Kuitenbrouwer, V., 'Songs of an imperial underdog: imperialism and popular culture in the Netherlands, 1870–1960', in J. M. MacKenzie (ed.), *European Empires and the People: Popular Responses to Imperialism in France, Britain, the Netherlands, Belgium, Germany and Italy* (Manchester: Manchester University Press, 2011), pp. 90–123.

Kurniadi, B. D., 'Yogyakarta in decentralised Indonesia: integrating traditional institution in democratic transitions', *Jurnal Ilmu Sosial dan Ilmu Politik*, 13.2 (2009): 190–203.

Kwartanada, D., 'The Tiong Hoa Hwee Koan School: a transborder project of modernity in Batavia, c. 1900s', in S. Sai and C. Hoon (eds), *Chinese Indonesians Reassessed: History, Religion and Belonging* (Abingdon: Routledge, 2013), pp. 27–44.

Langford, M., 'Speaking the album: an application of the oral-photographic framework', in A. Kuhn and K. E. McAllister (eds), *Locating Memory: Photographic Acts* (New York: Berghahn, 2006), pp. 223–45.

Langford, M., *Suspended Conversations: The Afterlife of Memory in Photographic Albums* (Montreal: McGill-Queen's University Press, 2001).

Lechner, F. J., *The Netherlands: Globalization and National Identity* (London: Routledge, 2008).

Legêne, S., *De bagage van Blomhoff en Van Breugel; Japan, Java, Tripoli en Suriname in de negentiende-eeuwse Nederlandse cultuur van het imperialisme* (Amsterdam: KIT Publishers, 1998).

Legêne, S., 'Dwinegeri: multiculturalism and the colonial past (or: the culture borders of being Dutch)', in B. Kaplan, M. Carlson and L. Cruz (eds), *Boundaries and their Meanings in the History of the Netherlands* (Leiden: Brill, 2009), pp. 223–42.

Legêne, S., 'Enlightenment, empathy, retreat: the cultural heritage of the *Ethische Politiek*', in P. ter Keurs (ed.), *Colonial Collections Revisited* (Leiden: CNWS, 2007), pp. 220–45.

Legêne, S., 'Flatirons and the folds of history: on archives, cultural heritage and colonial legacies', in S. W. Wieringa (ed.), *Traveling Heritages: New Perspective on Collecting, Preserving and Sharing Women's History* (Amsterdam: Aksant, 2008), pp. 47–64.

Legêne, S., *Spiegelreflex; Culturele sporen van de koloniale ervaring* (Amsterdam: Bert Bakker, 2010).

Legêne, S., 'Uitspaning en inkleuring; batik en koloniale beeldvorming in Nederland', in *Spiegelreflex; Culturele sporen van de koloniale ervaring* (Amsterdam: Bert Bakker, 2010), pp. 119–56.

Legêne, S., and J. van Dijk, 'Colonial collections at the Tropenmuseum', in S. Legêne and J. van Dijk (eds), *The Netherlands East Indies at the Tropenmuseum: A Colonial History* (Amsterdam: KIT Publishers, 2011), pp. 113–60.

Legêne, S., and B. Waaldijk, 'Mission interrupted: gender, history and the colonial canon', in S. Stuurman and M. Grever (eds), *Beyond the Canon: History for the Twenty-first Century* (Basingstoke: Palgrave Macmillan, 2007), pp. 188–204.

Legge, J. D., *Sukarno: A Political Biography* (Singapore: Archipelago Press, 2003).

Lente, D. van, 'Ideology and technology: reactions to modern technology in the Netherlands 1850–1920', *European History Quarterly*, 22 (1992): 383–414.

Lente, D. van, *Techniek en ideologie; opvattingen over de maatschappelijke betekenis van technische vernieuwingen in Nederland, 1850–1920* (Groningen: Wolters-Noordhoff and Forsten, 1988).

Lewis, S. L., *Cities in Motion: Urban Life and Cosmopolitanism in Southeast Asia, 1920–1940* (Cambridge: Cambridge University Press, 2016).

Limpach, R., *De brandende kampongs van Generaal Spoor* (Amsterdam: Boom, 2016).

Locher-Scholten, E., 'Colonial ambivalencies: European attitudes towards the Javanese household (1900–1942)', in J. Koning, M. Nolten, J. Rodenburg and R. Saptari (eds), *Women and Households in Indonesia: Cultural Notions and Social Practices* (Richmond: Curzon Press, 2000), pp. 28–44.

Locher-Scholten, E., *Ethiek in fragmenten; Vijf studies over koloniaal denken en doen van Nederlanders in de Indonesische Archipel 1877–1942* (Utrecht: HES, 1981).

Locher-Scholten, E., 'From urn to monument: Dutch memories of World War II in the Pacific, 1945–1995', in A. L. Smith (ed.), *Europe's Invisible Migrants* (Amsterdam: Amsterdam University Press, 2003), pp. 105–28.

Luttikhuis, B., 'Beyond race: constructions of "Europeanness" in late-colonial legal practice in the Dutch East Indies', *European Review of History*, 20.6 (2013): 539–58.

Luttikhuis, B., and C. Harink, 'Voorbij het koloniale perspectief; Indonesische bronnen en het onderzoek naar de oorlog in Indonesië, 1945–49', *BMGN/ Low Countries Historical Review*, 132.2 (2017): 51–76.

Luttikhuis, B., and D. Moses (eds), *Colonial Counterinsurgency and Mass Violence: The Dutch Empire in Indonesia* (London: Routledge, 2014).

Lyden, A. M., *A Royal Passion: Queen Victoria and Photography* (Los Angeles: Getty Publications, 2014).

Lydon, J., *Photography, Humanitarianism, Empire* (London: Bloomsbury, 2016).

Maier, H., 'Maelstrom and electricity: modernity in the Indies', in H. Schulte Nordholt (ed.), *Outward Appearances: Dressing State and Society in Indonesia* (Leiden: KITLV Press, 1997), pp. 181–99.

Margry, P. J., 'Het "oranjegevoel" van koninginnedag; een ritualistische ver-zoening met de anachronie van de monarchie', in H. te Velde and D. Haks (eds), *Oranje onder; Populair Orangisme van Willem van Oranje tot nu* (Amsterdam: Prometheus/Bert Bakker, 2014), pp. 243–66.

Marwoto-Johan, I., 'Ritual heirlooms in the Islamic kingdoms of Indonesia', in J. Bennet (ed.), *Crescent Moon: Islamic Art and Civilisation in Southeast Asia* (Adelaide/Canberra: Art Gallery of South Australia/National Gallery of Australia, 2005), pp. 144–58.

Mauss, M., *The Gift: The Form and Reason for Exchange in Archaic Societies*, trans. W. D. Halls (London: Routledge, 1990 [1950]).

Maxwell, A., *Colonial Photography and Exhibitions: Representations of the 'Native' and the Making of European Identities* (London: Leicester University Press, 1999).

Maxwell, A., *Patriots against Fashion: Clothing and Nationalism in Europe's Age of Revolutions* (Basingstoke: Palgrave Macmillan, 2014).

Meulen, D. van der, *Koning Willem III 1817–1890* (Amsterdam: Boom, 2013).

Miert, H. van, *Bevlogenheid en onvermogen; Mr. J.H. Abendanon (1852–1925) en de Ethische richting in het Nederlandse kolonialisme* (Leiden: KITLV Press, 1991).

Miksic, J., and M. Heins, *Karaton Surakarta: A Look into the Court of Surakarta Hadiningrat, Central Java* (Singapore: Marshall Cavendish, 2006).

Monfries, J., *A Prince in a Republic: The Life of Sultan Hamengku Buwono IX of Yogyakarta* (Singapore: ISEAS Publishing, 2015).

Monfries, J., 'The sultan and the revolution', *Bijdragen tot de Taal-, Land- en Volkenkunde*, 164.2–3 (2008): 269–97.

Monter, W., *The Rise of Female Kings in Europe, 1300–1800* (New Haven, CT: Yale University Press, 2012).

Montijn, I., *Hoog geboren; 250 jaar adelijk leven in Nederland* (Amsterdam/Antwerp: Uitgeverij Contact, 2012).

Morris, R. C., 'Introduction. Photographies east: the camera and its histories in East and Southeast Asia', in R. C. Morris (ed.), *Photographies East: The Camera and its Histories in East and Southeast Asia* (Durham, NC: Duke University Press, 2009), pp. 1–28.

Morris, R. C., 'Photography and the power of images in the history of power: notes from Thailand', in R. C. Morris (ed.), *Photographies East: The Camera and its Histories in East and Southeast Asia* (Durham, NC: Duke University Press, 2009), pp. 121–60.

Mrázek, R., *Engineers of Happy Land: Technology and Nationalism in a Colony* (Princeton, NJ: Princeton University Press, 2002).

Mrázek, R., 'Say "cheese": images of captivity in Boven Digoel (1927–43)', in S. Protschky (ed.), *Photography, Modernity and the Governed in Late-Colonial Indonesia* (Amsterdam: Amsterdam University Press, 2015), pp. 255–80.

Nugent, M., and S. Carter, 'Introduction: Indigenous histories, settler colonies and Queen Victoria', in M. Nugent and S. Carter (eds), *Mistress of Everything: Queen Victoria in Indigenous Worlds* (Manchester: Manchester University Press, 2016), pp. 1–24.

Ooijen, I. van, and I. Raaijmakers, 'Competitive or multidirectional memory? The interaction between postwar and postcolonial memory in the Netherlands', in B. Luttikhuis and D. Moses (eds), *Colonial Counterinsurgency and Mass Violence: The Dutch Empire in Indonesia* (London: Routledge, 2014), pp. 308–28

Oostindie, G., *De parels en de kroon; Het koningshuis en de koloniën* (Amsterdam: De Bezige Bij, 2006).

Oostindie, G., in cooperation with I. Hoogenboom and J. Verwey, *Soldaat in Indonesië 1945–1950; Getuigenis van een oorlog aan de verkeerde kant van de geschiedenis* (Amsterdam: Prometheus, 2015).

Ortner, S. B., 'Resistance and the problem of ethnographic refusal', *Comparative Studies in Society and History*, 37.1 (1995): 173–93.

Osta, J. van, 'The emperor's new clothes: the reappearance of the performing monarchy in Europe, c. 1870–1914', in H. te Velde (ed.), *Mystifying the Monarch: Studies on Discourse, Power, and History* (Amsterdam: Amsterdam University Press, 2006), pp. 181–92.

Osta, J. van, *Het theater van de staat; Oranje, Windsor en de moderne monarchie* (Amsterdam: Wereldbibliotheek, 1998).

Osteen, M., 'Introduction: questions of the gift', in M. Osteen (ed.), *The Question of the Gift: Essays Across Disciplines* (London: Routledge, 2002), pp. 1–42.

Ouwehand, L., *Herinneringen in beeld; Fotoalbums uit Nederlands-Indië* (Leiden: KITLV Press, 2009).

Pattynama, P., 'Interracial unions and the Ethical Policy: the representation of the everyday in Indo-European family albums', in S. Protschky (ed.), *Photography, Modernity and the Governed in Late-Colonial Indonesia* (Amsterdam: Amsterdam University Press, 2015), pp. 133–62.

Peleggi, M., *Lords of Things: The Fashioning of the Siamese Monarchy's Modern Image* (Honolulu, HI: University of Hawai'i Press, 2002).

Pemberton, J., 'The ghost in the machine', in R. C. Morris (ed.), *Photographies East: The Camera and its Histories in East and Southeast Asia* (Durham, NC: Duke University Press, 2009).

Pemberton, J., *On the Subject of 'Java'* (Ithaca, NY: Cornell University Press, 1994).

Penders, C. L. M., *The West New Guinea Debacle: Dutch Decolonisation and Indonesia 1945–1962* (Leiden: KITLV Press, 2002), pp. 85–6.

Phillips, L., 'Media discourse and the Danish monarchy: reconciling egalitarianism and royalism', *Media, Culture & Society*, 21 (1999): 221–45.

Pijper, G., 'Professor Dr. Pangeran Ario Hoesein Djajadiningrat. 8 December 1886–12 November 1960', *Bijdragen tot de Taal-, Land- en Volkenkunde*, 117.4 (1961): 401–9.

Pinney, C., *Camera Indica: The Social Life of Indian Photographs* (Chicago: University of Chicago Press, 1997).

Pinney, C., *Photography and Anthropology* (London: Reaktion, 2011).

Poeze, H. A., 'From foe to partner to foe again: the strange alliance of the Dutch authorities and Digoel exiles in Australia, 1943–1945', *Indonesia*, 94 (2012): 57–84.

Poeze, H. A., 'Walking the tightrope: internal Indonesian conflict, 1945–49', in B. Luttikhuis and D. Moses (eds), *Colonial Counterinsurgency and Mass Violence: The Dutch Empire in Indonesia* (London: Routledge, 2014), pp. 176–97.

Poignant, R., 'The making of professional "savages": from P.T. Barnum (1883) to the *Sunday Times* (1998)', in C. Pinney and N. Peterson (eds), *Photography's Other Histories* (Durham, NC: Duke University Press, 2003), pp. 55–84.

Poole, D., *Vision, Race, and Modernity: A Visual Economy of the Andean Image World* (Princeton, NJ: Princeton University Press, 1997).

Protschky, S., 'Burdens of proof: photography and evidence of atrocity during the Dutch military actions in Indonesia (1945–50)', *Journal of Southeast Asian Studies*, forthcoming 2020.

Protschky, S., 'Camera ethica: photography, modernity and the governed in late-colonial Indonesia', in S. Protschky (ed.), *Photography, Modernity and the Governed in Late-Colonial Indonesia* (Amsterdam: Amsterdam University Press, 2015), pp. 11–40.

Protschky, S., 'Dutch still lifes and colonial visual culture in the Netherlands Indies, 1800–1949', *Art History*, 34.3 (2011): 510–35.

Protschky, S., 'Ethical projects, ethnographic orders and colonial notions of modernity in Dutch Borneo: G. L. Tichelman's Queen's Birthday photographs from the late 1920s', in S. Protschky (ed.), *Photography, Modernity and the Governed in Late-Colonial Indonesia* (Amsterdam: Amsterdam University Press, 2015), pp. 71–102.

Protschky, S., 'The flavour of history: food, family and subjectivity in two Indo-European women's memoirs', *Journal of the History of the Family*, 14 (2009): 369–85.

Protschky, S., 'Herman Salzwedel, antiquity and the camera', in G. Newton (ed.), *Garden of the East: Photography in Indonesia 1850s–1940s* (Canberra: National Gallery of Australia, 2014), pp. 68–70.

Protschky, S., *Images of the Tropics: Environment and Visual Culture in Colonial Indonesia* (Leiden: KITLV Press/Brill, 2011).

Protschky, S., 'Modern times in Southeast Asia, 1920s–1970s', in S. Protschky and T. van den Berge (eds), *Modern Times in Southeast Asia, 1920s–1970s* (Leiden: Brill, 2018), pp. 1–14.

Protschky, S., 'Orangists in a red empire: salutations from a Dutch queen's supporters in a British South Africa', in R. Aldrich and C. McCreery (eds), *Crowns and Colonies: Monarchies and Empires* (Manchester: Manchester University Press, 2016), pp. 97–118.

Protschky, S., 'Personal albums from early twentieth-century Indonesia', in G. Newton (ed.), *Garden of the East: Photography in Indonesia 1850s–1940s* (Canberra: National Gallery of Australia, 2014), pp. 48–55.

Protschky, S., 'Race, class and gender: debates over the character of social hierarchies in the Netherlands Indies, circa 1600–1942', *Bijdragen tot de Taal-, Land- en Volkenkunde*, 167.4 (2011): 543–56.

Protschky, S., 'Soldiers as humanitarians: photographing war in Indonesia (1945–49)', in J. Lydon (ed.), *Visualising Human Rights* (Perth: UWA Publishing, 2018), pp. 39–62.

Protschky, S., 'Strained encounters: royal Indonesian visits to the Dutch court in the early twentieth century', in R. Aldrich and C. McCreery (eds), *Royals on Tour: Politics, Pageantry and Colonialism* (Manchester: Manchester University Press, 2018), pp. 233–49.

Protschky, S., 'Tea cups, cameras and family life: picturing domesticity in elite European and Javanese family photographs from the Netherlands Indies, c. 1900–1942', *History of Photography*, 36.1 (2012): 44–65.

Raben, R., 'Hoe wordt men vrij? De lange dekolonisatie van Indonesië', in E. Bogaerts and R. Raben (eds), *Van Indië tot Indonesië* (Amsterdam: Boom, 2007), pp. 13–29.

Ravesloot, M., 'Jonkheer A.W.L. Tjarda van Starkenborgh Stachouwer 1888–1978: Landvoogt in tijden van crisis', MA dissertation, Universiteit Utrecht, 2010.

Reed, C. V., *Royal Tourists, Colonial Subjects and the Making of a British World, 1860–1911* (Manchester: Manchester University Press, 2016).

Rehwinkel, P., 'Royalty is not essential … zoolang politici hun verantwoordelijkheid nemen', in R. Meijer and H. J. Schoo (eds), *De monarchie; Staatsrecht, volksgunst en het huis van Oranje* (Amsterdam: Prometheus, 2002), pp. 73–100.

Reid, A., *An Indonesian Frontier: Acehnese and Other Histories of Sumatra* (Singapore: Singapore University Press, 2005).

Ricklefs, M. C., *A History of Modern Indonesia since c. 1200* (Stanford, CA: Stanford University Press, 4th edn, 2008).

Robson, S., 'Introduction', in S. Robson (ed.), *The Kraton: Selected Essays on Javanese Courts* (Leiden: KITLV Press, 2003), pp. ix–xxvi.

Roodenburg, L., *Anceaux's Glasses: Anthropological Photography Since 1860* (Leiden: National Museum of Ethnology, 2002).

Rooy, P. de, 'In oude en nieuwe vormen verpakte illusies: naar aanleiding van enkele recente studies over de geschiedenis van de volkskunde in Nederland', *BMGN/Low Countries Historical Review*, 118 (2003): 193–205.

Rose, G., *Doing Family Photography: The Domestic, the Public and the Politics of Sentiment* (Farnham: Ashgate, 2010).

Rose, G., 'Photographs and domestic spacings: a case study', *Transactions of the Institute of British Geographers*, 28.1 (2003): 5–18.

Rosenwein, B. H., *Emotional Communities in the Early Middle Ages* (Ithaca, NY: Cornell University Press, 2006).

Rosenwein, B. H., 'Worrying about emotions in history', *American Historical Review*, 107.3 (2002): 821–45.

Said, E. W., *Culture and Imperialism* (London: Random House, 1993).

Said, E. W., *Orientalism: Western Conceptions of the Orient* (New York: Pantheon, 1978).

Scagliola, S., 'Cleo's "unfinished business": coming to terms with Dutch war crimes in Indonesia's war of independence', in B. Luttikhuis and D. Moses (eds), *Colonial Counterinsurgency and Mass Violence: The Dutch Empire in Indonesia* (London: Routledge, 2014), pp. 240–60.

Scalliet, M., *Antoine Payen, peintre des Indes orientales vie et écrits d'un artiste du XIXe siècle (1792–1853)* (Leiden: Research School CNWS, 1995).

Scalliet, M., '"Back to nature" in the East Indies: European painters in the nineteenth-century East Indies', in M. Scalliet, K. van Brakel, D. van Duuren and J. ten Kate, *Pictures from the Tropics: Paintings by Western Artists during the Dutch Colonial Period in Indonesia* (Amsterdam: Pictures Publications/ KIT Publishers, 1999), pp. 39–89.

Schaap, J., *Het recht om te waarschuwen; Over de Radio Oranje-toespraken van koningin Wilhelmina* (Amsterdam: Anthos, 2007).

Schenk, M. G., and J. B. Th. Spaan, *De koniningin spraak; Proclomaties en radio-toespraken van HM Koningin Wilhelmina gedurende de oorlogsjaren 1940–1945* (Driebergen: Christelijk Lektuurkontakt, 1985).

Schoonhoven, G. van, '"Houd Oranje boven in de troep eronder"; de geschiedenis van de nationale feestdag Koninginnedag', in R. Meijer and H. J. Schoo (eds), *De monarchie; Staatsrecht, volksgunst en het huis van Oranje* (Amsterdam: Prometheus, 2002), pp. 137–68.

Schoorl, J., 'In memoriam J. van Baal, 25-11-1909–9-8-1993', *Bijdragen tot de Taal-, Land- en Volkenkunde*, 150.1 (1994): 3–12.

Schulte Nordholt, H., 'Modernity and middle classes in the Netherlands Indies: cultivating cultural citizenship', in S. Protschky (ed.), *Photography, Modernity and the Governed in Late-Colonial Indonesia* (Amsterdam: Amsterdam University Press, 2015), pp. 223–54.

Schulte Nordholt, H., 'Onafhankelijkheid of moderniteit? Een geïllustreerde hypothese', in M. Bloembergen and R. Raben (eds), *Het koloniale beschavingsoffensief; Wegen naar het nieuwe Indië, 1890–1950* (Leiden: KITLV Press, 2009), pp. 105–20.

Schwarzenbach, A., *Königliche Träume: Eine Kultuurgeschichte der Monarchie von 1789 bis 1997* (Munich: Collection Rolf Heyne, 2012).

Schwarzenbach, A., 'Royal photographs: emotions for the people', *Contemporary European History*, 13.3 (2004): 255–80.

Shiraishi, T., 'The phantom world of Digoel', *Indonesia*, 61 (1996): 93–118.

Siegel, J. T., 'The curse of the photograph: Atjeh 1901', in R. C. Morris (ed.), *Photographies East: The Camera and its Histories in East and Southeast Asia* (Durham, NC: Duke University Press, 2009), pp. 57–78.

Simpson, A., 'The ruse of consent and the anatomy of "refusal": cases from indigenous North America and Australia', *Postcolonial Studies*, 20.1 (2017): 18–33.

Soedarsono, *Wayang Wong: The State Ritual Dance Drama in the Court of Yogyakarta* (Yogyakarta: Gadja Mada University Press, 1984).

Spence, J., and P. Holland (eds), *Family Snaps: The Meanings of Domestic Photography* (London: Virago Press, 1991).

Staugaard, W., 'Koeda-K'pang', *Handelingen van het eerste congres voor de Taal-, Land- en Volkenkunde van Java* (Weltevreden: Albrecht, 1921).

Stoler, A. L., *Along the Archival Grain: Epistemic Anxieties and Colonial Common Sense* (Princeton, NJ: Princeton University Press, 2009).

Stoler, A. L., *Carnal Knowledge and Imperial Power* (Berkeley, CA: University of California Press, 2002).

Stolwijk, A., *Atjeh; Het verhaal van de bloedigste strijd uit de Nederlandse koloniale geschiedenis* (Amsterdam: Prometheus, 2016).

BIBLIOGRAPHY

Strassler, K., 'Cosmopolitan visions: ethnic Chinese and the photographic imagining of Indonesia in the late colonial and early postcolonial periods', *The Journal of Asian Studies*, 67.2 (2008): 395–432.

Strassler, K., 'Modelling modernity: ethnic Chinese photography in the Ethical era', in S. Protschky (ed.), *Photography, Modernity and the Governed in Late-Colonial Indonesia* (Amsterdam: Amsterdam University Press, 2015), pp. 195–222.

Strassler, K., *Refracted Visions: Popular Photography and National Modernity in Java* (Durham, NC: Duke University Press, 2010).

Stuurman, S., *Wacht op onze daden; Het liberalisme en de vernieuwing van de Nederlandse staat* (Amsterdam: Bert Bakker, 1992).

Suryadinata, L., *The Culture of the Chinese Minority in Indonesia* (Singapore: Times Books International, 1997).

Susilo, H., '*Wayang wong panggung*: its social context, technique and music', in S. Morgan and L. J. Sears (eds), *Aesthetic Tradition and Cultural Transition in Java and Bali* (Madison, WI: Centre for Southeast Asian Studies, University of Wisconsin, 1984), pp. 117–62.

Sutherland, H., *The Making of a Bureaucratic Elite: The Colonial Transformation of the Javanese* Priyayi (Kuala Lumpur and Hong Kong: Heinemann Educational Books (Asia), 1979).

Sutherland, H., 'Notes on Java's regent families: Part I', *Indonesia*, 16 (October 1973): 112–47.

Sutherland, H., 'Notes on Java's regent families: Part II', *Indonesia*, 17 (April 1974): 1–42.

Sysling, F., 'Geographies of difference: Dutch physical anthropology in the colonies and the Netherlands, ca. 1900–1940', *BMGN/Low Countries Historical Review*, 128.1 (2013): 105–26.

Sysling, F., *Racial Science and Human Diversity in Colonial Indonesia* (Singapore: National University of Singapore Press, 2016).

Taylor, J. G., 'Costume and gender in colonial Java, 1800–1942', in H. Schulte Nordholt (ed.), *Outward Appearances: Dressing State and Society in Indonesia* (Leiden: KITLV Press, 1997), pp. 85–116.

Taylor, J. G. 'Ethical policies in moving pictures: the films of J. C. Lamster', in S. Protschky (ed.), *Photography, Modernity and the Governed in Late-Colonial Indonesia* (Amsterdam: Amsterdam University Press, 2015), pp. 41–70.

Taylor, J. G., *Global Indonesia* (London: Routledge, 2013).

Taylor, J. G., *Indonesia: Peoples and Histories* (New Haven, CT: Yale University Press, 2003).

Theuns-de Boer, G., and S. Assa (with contributions by S. Wachlin), *Isidore van Kinsbergen (1821–1905): Photo Pioneer and Theatre Maker in the Dutch East Indies* (Zaltbommel, Leiden and Amsterdam: Aprilis/KITLV Press, 2005).

Toekang Potret: 100 Years of Photography in the Dutch East Indies 1839–1939, trans. M. Gibbs (Rotterdam/Leiden: Fragment/Museum voor Volkenkunde, 1989).

Toer, P. A. *This Earth of Mankind*, trans. M. Lane (Ringwood, Vic.: Penguin, 1982). First published as *Bumi Manusia* (Jakarta: Hasta Mitra, 1980).

Velde, H. te, 'Cannadine, twenty years on: monarchy and political culture in nineteenth-century Britain and the Netherlands', in H. te Velde (ed.), *Mystifying the Monarch: Studies on Discourse, Power, and History* (Amsterdam: Amsterdam University Press, 2006), pp. 193–203.

Velde, H. te, *Gemeenschapszin en plichtsbesef; Liberalisme en nationalisme in Nederland, 1870–1918* (The Hague: SDU, 1992).

Velde, H. te, 'De koning is onschendbaar: de permanente spanning tussen Oranje en de grondwet', in R. Meijer and H. J. Schoo (eds), *De monarchie; Staatsrecht, volksgunst en het huis van Oranje* (Amsterdam: Prometheus, 2002), pp. 49–72.

Vickers, A., *Bali: A Paradise Created* (Ringwood, Vic.: Penguin, 1989).

Vickers, A., *A History of Modern Indonesia* (Cambridge: Cambridge University Press, 2005).

Vink, S., 'Photography and science', in J. van Dijk, R. Jongmans, A. Mansfeld, S. Vink and P. Westerkamp, *Photographs of the Netherlands East Indies at the Tropenmuseum* (Amsterdam: KIT Publishers, 2012), pp. 91–106.

Waaldijk, B., and S. Legêne, 'Ethische politiek in Nederland; cultureel burgerschap tussen overheersing, opvoeding an afscheid', in Marieke Bloembergen and Remco Raben (eds), *Het koloniale beschavingsoffensief; Wegen naar het niewe Indië, 1890–1950* (Leiden: KITLV Press, 2009), pp. 187–216.

Wachlin, S., *Woodbury & Page: Photographers Java* (Leiden: KITLV Press, 1994).

Wassing-Visser, R., *Koninklijke geschenken uit Indonesië; Historische banden met het huis Oranje-Nassau (1600–1938)* (Den Haag/Zwolle: Stichting Historische Verzamelingen van het Huis Oranje-Nassau/Waanders, 1995).

Wassing-Visser, R., *Royal Gifts from Indonesia: Historical Bonds with the House of Orange-Nassau (1600–1938)* (The Hague/Zwolle: House of Orange-Nassau Historic Collections Trust/Waanders, 1995).

Wessing, R., 'The kraton-city and the realm: sources and movement of power in Java', in P. J. M. Nas, G. A. Persoon and R. Jaffe (eds), *Framing Indonesian Realities: Essays in Symbolic Anthropology in Honour of Reimar Schefold* (Leiden: KITLV Press, 2003), pp. 199–250.

Wijfjes, H., 'Rengelink, Jan Willem (1912–1999)', in *Biografisch Woordenboek van Nederland*, http://inghist.nl/Onderzoek/Projecten/BWN/lemmata/bwn6/rengelink (last accessed 16 April 2018).

Willcock, S., 'Composing the spectacle: colonial portraiture and the coronation durbars of British India, 1877–1911', *Art History*, 40.1 (2017): 132–55.

Wilterdink, N., 'The monarchy contested: anti-monarchism in the Netherlands', *The Netherlands' Journal of Social Sciences*, 26.2 (1990): 3–16.

Withuis, J., *Juliana; Vorstin in een mannenwereld* (Amsterdam: De Bezige Bij, 2016).

Woodall, J., 'Introduction', in J. Woodall (ed.), *Portraiture: Facing the Subject* (Manchester: Manchester University Press, 1997), pp. 1–28.

Zanten, J. van, *Koning Willem II 1792–1849* (Amsterdam: Boom, 2013).

Zuiderweg, A., 'Vuurwerk, illuminaties en wijnspuitende fonteinen; VOC-feestvreugde in Batavia', *Indische Letteren; Feesten in Indië*, 21.1 (2006): 81–94.

BIBLIOGRAPHY

Zuthem, H. van, 'Nationale kleederdrachten van Harer Majesteits onderdanen bekeken', in *Oranje en de Nationale Streeckdrachten* (Apeldoorn: Nationaal Museum, Paleis Het Loo, 2012), pp. 14–19.

Zweers, I., 'Commercial photography', in *Toekang potret: 100 Years of Photography in the Dutch Indies 1839–1939* (Amsterdam/Rotterdam: Fragment/ Museum voor Volkenkunde, 1989), pp. 53–120.

Zweers, L., *De gecensureerde oorlog; Militairen versus media in Nederlands-Indië 1945–1949* (Zutphen: Walburg Pers, 2013).